PAINT, PATTERN & PEOPLE

aint,

Pattern & People

FURNITURE OF

SOUTHEASTERN PENNSYLVANIA

1725 – 1850

Wendy A. Cooper
and
Lisa Minardi

A WINTERTHUR BOOK

Distributed by
The University of Pennsylvania Press

Winterthur Museum acknowledges The Richard C. von Hess Foundation for its generous support of this publication and the following for additional support of the publication and accompanying exhibition.

The Americana Foundation
DuPont Company
Elizabeth B. McGraw Foundation
H. B. Ebert Foundation
Henry Luce Foundation
Kaufman Americana Foundation and Linda H. Kaufman
Marian S. Ware 2003 Charitable Lead Annuity Trust
National Endowment for the Arts
National Endowment for the Humanities
Wyeth Foundation for American Art

PAINT, PATTERN & PEOPLE:
FURNITURE OF SOUTHEASTERN PENNSYLVANIA, 1725–1850
HAS BEEN SELECTED BY THE PENNSYLVANIA GERMAN SOCIETY
AS VOLUME 45 IN ITS ANNUAL VOLUME SERIES

Library of Congress Cataloging-in-Publication Data

Cooper, Wendy A.
   Paint, pattern & people : furniture of southeastern Pennsylvania, 1725-1850 / Wendy A. Cooper and Lisa Minardi. — 1st ed.
      p. cm.
   Issued in connection with an exhibition held in 2011 at the Henry Francis du Pont Winterthur Museum, Winterthur, Delaware.
   Includes bibliographical references and index.
   ISBN 978-0-912724-69-0 (alk. paper)
   1. Furniture—Pennsylvania—History—18th century—Exhibitions. 2. Furniture—Pennsylvania—History—19th century—Exhibitions. I. Minardi, Lisa, 1983- II. Henry Francis du Pont Winterthur Museum. III. Title. IV. Title: Paint, pattern and people : furniture of southeastern Pennsylvania, 1725-1850.
   NK2435.P42S683 2011
   749.09748'1—dc22
                        2010037384
   ISBN 978-0-912724-69-0

Editor: Onie Rollins
Photographer: Laszlo Bodo
Designed by Peter M. Blaiwas, Vern Associates, Inc., Newburyport, Massachusetts
   www.vernassoc.com
Printed and bound by Capital Offset Company, Inc., Concord, New Hampshire, U.S.A.
Distributed by The University of Pennsylvania Press

Jacket front (*details, clockwise from top left*):
Chest (fig. 2.45), Collection of Dr. and Mrs. Donald M. Herr
Small chest-over-drawers (fig. 2.71), Private collection
Stone house of the Berks County almshouse (fig. 2.64), Historical Society of Berks County Museum & Library
Portrait of Samuel Ensminger, Jr. (fig. 2.72), Collection of Stephen and Dolores Smith
Spice box (fig. 2.18), Chester County Historical Society, gift of Bart Anderson
Chest-over-drawers (fig. 3.48), Collection of Carl and Julie Lindberg

Jacket back: Desk (fig. 2.55), Winterthur Museum

Half-title page: Pennsylvania coat of arms, York County Heritage Trust

CONTENTS

FOREWORD

Winterthur is situated in Delaware's Brandy-wine Valley just a few miles from the southeastern border of Pennsylvania and Chester County, one of the three original counties laid out by William Penn. This alone accounts for an interest in the exploration of the material heritage of that region by Winterthur scholars. But the fact that Winterthur's founder, Henry Francis du Pont, was an active collector of the arts of Pennsylvania from the 1920s onward presents an even stronger rationale for this scholarly publication and its accompanying exhibition.

Thanks to H. F. du Pont's interest in the nearby counties of southeastern Pennsylvania, the Winterthur collections are rich in all manner of Pennsylvania arts, including furniture, earthenware, fraktur, and ironwork. Since 1952 and the founding of the Winterthur Program in American Material Culture with the University of Delaware, many students and scholars have studied these objects and produced a wide variety of publications on the subject. Winterthur curators in particular have made notable contributions. Charles F. Hummel, curator emeritus, collaborated with Beatrice B. Garvan of the Philadelphia Museum of Art in producing a groundbreaking exhibition and publication in 1982, *The Pennsylvania Germans: A Celebration of Their Arts*. Scott T. Swank co-authored a seminal volume entitled *Arts of the Pennsylvania Germans*, which was published by Winterthur in 1983 and remains a standard reference.

Building on the museum's leadership in the field, in 2004 Wendy A. Cooper, the Lois F. and Henry S. McNeil senior curator of furniture, initiated the Southeastern Pennsylvania Furniture Project—an exploration of the fascinating and diverse furniture of the region through the people who made, owned, inherited, and collected it. Over the past six years, she and Lisa Minardi, assistant curator of furniture for the project, have surveyed some 250 public and private collections, attended auctions, and visited numerous dealers in their search for documented objects that can be directly tied to their makers, original owners, and places of origin. Their study looks at the furniture of both English- and German-speaking settlers, offering a thorough understanding of the localisms and regionalisms of form, ornament, and construction that developed throughout southeastern Pennsylvania in the 1700s and early 1800s.

Paint, Pattern & People is truly a collaborative work, involving museum colleagues as well as benefactors, collectors, and dealers. We thank you all for your outstanding support of this important project and are pleased to present this publication as the latest in Winterthur's ongoing commitment to research on American decorative arts.

David P. Roselle
Director
Winterthur Museum, Garden & Library

ACKNOWLEDGMENTS

Since its inception in 2004, the Southeastern Pennsylvania Furniture Project has enjoyed the encouragement and assistance of numerous individuals, institutions, and foundations. We are exceedingly grateful to all who have helped make our vision a reality.

A project of this magnitude cannot possibly be undertaken without strong financial support, and we are thankful for the generosity of many. An initial consultation grant from the National Endowment for the Humanities enabled a group of scholars to convene at Winterthur in 2006 to discuss the project and the path it might take. For their creative suggestions we thank Cindy Falk, Bernie Herman, Charlie Hummel, David Jaffee, Gabrielle Lanier, Sally McMurry, and Judy Ridner. With a good plan in hand for the exhibition and publication, Thomas Hills Cook of the Richard C. von Hess Foundation stepped forward with the first major grant, followed shortly by generous commitments from John and Marjorie McGraw through the Elizabeth B. McGraw Foundation and Linda H. Kaufman and the Kaufman Americana Foundation. Additional funding then came from the Americana Foundation, American Folk Art Society, Barr Foundation, DuPont Company, H.B. Ebert Foundation, Henry Clay Frick Foundation, Henry Luce Foundation, National Endowment for the Arts, National Endowment for the Humanities, Pook & Pook Inc., Potter Anderson & Corroon LLP, Saul Foundation, Shelley Pennsylvania German Heritage Fund, Marian S. Ware 2003 Charitable Lead Annuity Trust, the Wood Foundation of Chambersburg, Pa., and the Wyeth Foundation for American Art.

We also thank the many individuals who provided financial support and shared their knowledge and collections with us. To the following we are greatly indebted: Jim and Pam Alexander, Syed Ali and Susan Doherty, Steve and Susan Babinsky, Mr. and Mrs. Chester T. Bartoli, Max and Heidi Berry, Mrs. George P. Bissell, Jr., Katharine and Robert Booth, Paul T. Clark, Thomas Hills Cook, Chloe Darling, Richard and Ginger Dietrich, Dean and Marie Failey, Robert and Bobbie Falk, Susan Fetterolf and Jeffrey Gorrin, Victor and Joan Johnson, Thomas Johnson, Tom and Karen Helm, Mr. and Mrs. Joseph C. Hoopes, Jr., Dr. and Mrs. Henry A. Jordan, Jane and Gerald Katcher, George M. and Linda H. Kaufman, Kelly Kinzle, Carl and Julie Lindberg, Forbes and Sara Maner, Anne McPherson, Richard and Pamela Mones, Bess Naylor, Dr. and Mrs. J. Brien Murphy, John Nackley, Burn and Susan Oberwager, Nancy Kollisch and Jeff Pressman, Harriet Robbins, Gene and Lynn Roberts, Arthur D. Robson, Dr. Margaret Ruttenberg, David A. Schorsch and Eileen M. Smiles, Irvin and Anita Schorsch, Jr., Katharine Draper Schutt, Stephen and Dolores Smith, John J. Snyder, Jr., Charles and Brenda Thurlow, Matt Thurlow, William W. Upton, Stanley and Beth Weiss, and Kem and Betsy Widmer.

We are also indebted to those who were helpful during the documentation, research, and writing phases of this study, including William K. du Pont, who shared his extensive knowledge of the field as well as his superb collection, and Charles F. Hummel, whose experience as co-curator of the Pennsylvania German arts exhibition in 1982 was of enormous help. Alan Keyser assisted with German translations and, with John J. Snyder, Jr., recalled countless details about objects and craftsmen that greatly enriched the study. Alan Andersen, Patrick Bell, Philip Bradley, Skip Chalfant, Vernon Gunnion, Harry Hartman, Don and Trish Herr, Ed Hild, Greg Kramer, Ron and James Pook, Jamie Price, Todd Prickett, David Schorsch, and Richard Worth offered assistance in locating objects, and Elaine Rice Bachmann, Johanna Brown, Mike Emery, Ellen Endslow, Lanie Graf, Jim Guthrie, Clarke Hess, Sasha Laurie, June Lucas, Barry Rauhauser, Becky Roberts, and Merri Lou Schaumann helped with various research inquiries.

Other individuals who shared knowledge, allowed us to study their collections, and provided valuable leads include Bailey Adams, Steve and Denise Adams, Harry Alden, Ted and Barbara Alfond, George Allen, Lydia Bartholomew, Louisa Bartlett, Charles and Martha Bartlett,

Luke Beckerdite, Paul and Caroline Edge Beideman, Dianna Bittel, Eleanor Bittle, John Boger, Philip and Judy Bohne, Ronald Bourgeault, Geoff Boyer, Troy Boyer, Derin Bray, Lester and Barbara Breininger, David Brocklebank, David Bronstein, Jay and Ellen Brooks, Francis Brown, Andrew Brunk, Ray Brunner, Jack and Ruth Bryson, Nicholas Buonato, Jim and Pat Burnett, Jim Buttrick, Lynda Cain, Jim Cawley, Tara Cederholm, Eugene and Vera Charles, John Chaski, Rick and Terry Ciccotelli, Joyce Collis, Bill Coon, Frank and Sarah Coulson, Jack Dau, Mike D'Ambra, Peter Deen, Carrie de Clerque, Jeffrey DeHart, Carl and Yvonne De Paulis, James Ditmar, Mike Dudrear, Mark and Joanne Eaby, Russell and Corinne Earnest, Byron and Margaret Ebersole, Donald Eby, Isobel Ellis, Carolyn Faris, Beulah Fehr, Curtis Fenstermacher, Nancy Fenstermacher, Mitch and Janet Fetterolf, Fred and Thère Fiechter, Gordon Fine, Larry and Lori Fink, Paul and Rita Flack, Ed and Helen Flanagan, Rick and Helen Marie McFalls Flanders, Laurel Fletcher, Sam Forsythe, Jim Gergat and Kathy Lesieur, Nancy Gingrich, Jim and Nancy Glazer, Ivan Glick, Peter and Bonnie Goetz, David Good, Barbara Gordon, Tom Gray, Lindsay Grigsby, Cornelia Gromadzki, Erik Gronning, Wallace Gusler, Alan Gutchess, Dave Hansen, Ron, Nancy, and Doug Harper, H.G. Haskell, James and Linda Hastrich, Jim and MaryLou Hawkes, Bill and Connie Hayes, Steve and Marcy Hench, Chip and Vonnie Henderson, Margaret Hensler, Jeff Herb, John and Judy Herdeg, Don and Trish Herr, Mary Jane Hershey, Betty Hess, Dave Hoffman, Frank L. Hohmann III, John Holden, Carroll and Claudia Hopf, Dale Hunt, Char-Ann Ireland, Bill Ivey, Pepi and Vera Jelinek, Harwood Johnson, Christopher Jones, Trip Kahn, Neil Kamil, Jane and Gerald Katcher, Allan and Penny Katz, James Keener, Pat Keller, Leigh Keno, Leslie Keno, Jim Kilvington, Joe and Jennifer Kindig, Steve Kindig, Mary Kirk, Robert and Anne Kline, John Kolar, John Kraft, Greg Kramer and Nancy Pennypacker, Eric Kramer, Ralph and Glee Krueger, Mary Louise Krumrine, Edward Lacy, Ed LaFond, Margaret Landis, Chris and Lynne Lang, Conrad and Sabrina du Pont Langenegger, Marge and David Lee, Richard Levengood, Pat Levin, Darlene Lowe, Eric Maffei, Deirdre Pook Magarelli, Andy and June Maier, Jerry Martin, Johanna McBrien, Sam and Patty McCullough, Joseph and Jean McFalls, Jay and Marguerite McFalls, DeeDee and Scott Mayer, Milly McGehee, David Miller, Bill Miller, Leslie Miller and Richard Worley, Kendl Monn, Doug Mooberry, Roddy and Sally Moore, John McDowell Morris, Dennis and Linda Moyer, Mark and Anna Myers, Larry Neff, Thurston Nichols, E. J. Nusrala, Bill Ostman, Kerry Pae, Karl Pass, Duncan Patterson, Clark Pearce, Lyman and Kate Perry, Peter Pfaffenroth, Jim Plumer, Deb Pook, Kyle Pook, Robert Pyle, Chris Rebollo, Jim Reis, John Renshaw, Warren and Christine Reynolds, Irwin Richman, Andrew Richmond, Al and Bridget Ritter, Park Ritter, Salvatore Rizzuto, Brett Robbins, Charles and Maureen Rogers, Marshall Rumbaugh, John Ruth, Oveda Rutledge, Tom Ryan, Albert Sack, Bill Samaha, Mary Schantz, Margaret Schiffer, Peggy Schumo, Tom and Sara Sears, Peter Seibert, Pen and Kellie Seltzer, Wesley Sessa, Brooke Sivo, Lawrence and Margaret Skromme, Joane Smith, Newbold and Peggy Smith, Walter and Jeanette Smith, Roy Smith, Al Snyder, Lita Solis-Cohen, Brent Souder, Clarence Spohn, Bill and Maureen McFalls Starr, Susan Stautberg, Maureen Stewart, Jay Stiefel, Steve Still, Penny Stillinger, Grace Stirba, Marie Louise Stokes, Susan Stoudt, Meredith Strutt, Ted and Betty Stvan, Gary Sullivan, Scott Swank, Mike and Marijean McFalls Szep, Nancy Taylor, Don Tharpe, Cathi Thompson, Peter and Jeffrey Tillou, Barry Torrente, Mark Turdo, Charlie and Liz Umstott, Fred Vogel, William Muhlenberg Wagner, Ron Walter, Peter and Leslie Warwick, Sue Watkins, William Woys Weaver, Dawson Weigley, Mary Weigley, Frederick S. Weiser, Hermann Wellenreuther, Carolyn Wenger, David Wheatcroft, Rob Wood, Doug Wyant, Gordon Wyckoff, Don Yoder, Renn Zimmerman, and Philip Zimmerman.

Colleagues and friends at numerous churches, meetinghouses, historical societies, museums, and libraries were also essential to the success of this undertaking, and we thank the following institutions and staff: American Folk Art Museum, Stacy Hollander, Ann-Marie Reilly, Lee Kogan; American Revolution Center, Scott

Stephenson; Augustus Lutheran Church, Dick Buckmaster; Baltimore Museum of Art; Barnes Foundation, Barbara Buckley; Bartram's Garden, Joel Fry; Berman Museum of Art at Ursinus College, Lisa Hanover, Sue Calvin, Julie Choma; Biggs Museum of American Art, Ryan Grover; Blue Ridge Institute, Roddy Moore; Carnegie Museum of Art, Jason Busch, Rachel Delphia; Center for Scotch-Irish Studies, Richard Mac-Master; Central Moravian Church, Carol Reifinger, Rev. Janel Rice, Diane Shaw, Pat Smith; Chester County Historical Society, Ellen Endslow, Andrea Cakars, Pamela Powell; Chipstone Foundation, Luke Beckerdite; Cleveland Institute of Art, Charlie Bergengren; Colonial Williamsburg Foundation, Ron Hurst, Tara Chicirda, Barbara Luck; Columbia County Historical Society, Bill Baillie; Cumberland County Historical Society, Merri Lou Schaumann, Richard Tritt, Rachael Zuch; Daniel Boone Homestead: A Property of the Pennsylvania Historical and Museum Commission, James Lewars; Dietrich American Foundation, Debbie Rebuck; Donegal Presbyterian Church, Rev. Thomas McKinnon, Mary Karnes; Ephrata Cloister: A Property of the Pennsylvania Historical and Museum Commission, Beth Rump, Kerry Mohn, Michael Showalter; Free Library of Philadelphia, Janine Pollock; Frontier Culture Museum of Virginia, David Puckett, Ray Wright; Germantown Historical Society, Laura Beardsley, Betsy Solomon; Graeme Park: A Property of the Pennsylvania Historical and Museum Commission, John Brunner; 1719 Hans Herr House, Becky Gochnauer; Harriton House, Bruce Gill; Henry Ford Museum, Charles Sable, Leslie Mio; Heritage Center of Lancaster County, Wendy Nagle, Wendell Zercher; Hershey Museum, Valerie Seiber; Historic Bethlehem, Bonnie Stacy; Historic Odessa Foundation, Debbie Buckson; Historic Preservation Trust of Berks County, Larry Ward, Jon Hartman, Rob Reynolds; Historic Schaefferstown, Inc., Diane Wenger; Historical Society of Berks County, Sime Bertolet, Joshua Blay, George Meiser IX; Historical Society of Carroll County, Cathy Baty; Historical Society of the Cocalico Valley, Cynthia Marquet, Jim Tshudy, Dave Willett; Historical Society of Dauphin County, Ken Frew; Historical Society of Lebanon County;

Historical Society of Trappe, Collegeville, and the Perkiomen Valley, Dona McDermott, Rev. Bob Meschke, Linda Wiernusz; Historical Society of Frederick County, Heidi Campbell-Shoaf; Historical Society of Montgomery County, Jeff McGranahan; Independence National Historical Park, Karie Diethorn; LancasterHistory.org, Thomas Ryan, Barry Rauhauser, Robin Sarratt; Lancaster Mennonite Historical Society, Carolyn Wenger; Landis Valley Museum: A Property of the Pennsylvania Historical and Museum Commission, James Lewars, Russell Swody, Bruce Bomberger, Mike Emery, Nicole Wagner; Lehigh County Historical Society, Jill Youngken; Lititz Moravian Church, Tom Wentzel; Lower Merion Historical Society, Max Buten, Jerry Francis, Ted Goldsborough; Lutheran Theological Seminary at Philadelphia, Natalie Hand, Karl Krueger, John Peterson, Mary Redline; Maryland State Archives, Elaine Rice Bachmann, Sasha Laurie; Mennonite Heritage Center, Sarah Heffner, Joel Alderfer; Mercer Museum of the Bucks County Historical Society, Cory Amsler, Sara Good; Metropolitan Museum of Art, Morrie Heckscher, Peter Kenny, Nicholas Vincent; Monmouth County Historical Association, Lee Ellen Griffith; Montour County Historical Society, Helen "Sis" Hause; Moravian Archives, Paul Peucker, Lanie Graf; Moravian Historical Society, Wendy Weida; Morgan Log House, Sarah Gallagher; Muddy Creek Farm Library, Amos Hoover; Museum of Fine Arts, Boston, Nonie Gadsden; Museum of Fine Arts, Houston, Michael Brown; National Gallery of Art, Charles Ritchie; National Museum of American History, Smithsonian Institution, Bill Yeingst, Stacey Kluck; National Portrait Gallery, Brandon Brame Fortune, Ellen Miles; New-York Historical Society, Margie Hofer, Roberta Olson; Newtown Square Historical Preservation Society, Chris Driscoll; Northampton County Historical and Genealogical Society, Andria Zaia; Old Economy Village: A Property of the Pennsylvania Historical and Museum Commission, Mary Ann Landis; Old Salem Lutheran Church, Lebanon, Pa., Lila Lebo; Old Salem Museums & Gardens, MESDA, Robert Leath, Daniel Ackermann, Johanna Brown, Sally Gant, June Lucas, Zara Phillips; Old Zion Church, Sallie Gregory, Ginny Gillespie, John

Kraft, Russell Pettyjohn; Peabody Essex Museum, Dean Lahikainen; Pennsylvania Academy of the Fine Arts, Anna Marley; Pennsylvania German Society, Tom Gerhart, Carolyn Wenger; Pennsylvania Historical and Museum Commission, Barbara Franco, Jennifer Glass; Pennsylvania State Archives, Brett Reigh; Pennsylvania State University, Simon Bronner, Gregg Roeber, Anne Verplanck; Pennsylvania State University Libraries, Sandy Stelts; Peter Wentz Farmstead, Dianne Cram, Kim Boice, Morgan McMillan; Philadelphia Museum of Art, David Barquist, Alexandra Kirtley, David deMuzio, Bret Headley, Shelley Langdale, Peggy Olley, Chris Storb; Phillips Museum of Art at Franklin & Marshall College, Carol Faill, Claire Giblin; Pottsgrove Manor, Amy Reis; Primitive Hall Foundation, Trish Scott; Reading Public Museum, Vasti Deesch; Rock Ford Plantation, Cindy Trussell; Rockwood Museum, Philip Nord; Schwenkfelder Library & Heritage Center, Dave Luz, Candace Perry, Hunt Schenkel, Allen Viehmeyer; Shelburne Museum, Jean Burks, Katherine Taylor-McBroom, Erin Corrales-Diaz; Smithsonian American Art Museum, Eleanor Harvey, Betsy Anderson; Diplomatic Reception Rooms, U.S. Department of State, Marcee Craighill; State Museum of Pennsylvania, John Leighow, Beatrice Hulsberg; Stenton, Laura Keim; Swarthmore College, Pat O'Donnell, Chris Densmore; Thaddeus Stevens College of Technology, Steve Latta; Tyler Arboretum, Betsey Ney; University of Delaware, Ritchie Garrison, Kasey Grier; University of Maine, Liam Riordan; Upper Octorara Presbyterian Church, Barbara Zorn; Ursinus College, Peter Luborsky; Virginia Historical Society, Jim Kelly; Virginia Museum of Fine Arts, Sylvia Yount, Kathy Gillis; Westmoreland Museum of American Art, Barbara Jones, Doug Evans; Westtown School, Mary Brooks; Wright's Ferry Mansion, Thomas Hills Cook, Meg Schaefer; Yale University Art Galleries, Pat Kane, Katherine Chabla, John Gordon; York College of Pennsylvania, Karen Rice-Young; York County Heritage Trust, Joan Mummert, Cindy Brown, Lila Fourhman-Shaull, June Lloyd, Jennifer Royer, Becky Roberts; Young Center for Anabaptist and Pietist Studies at Elizabethtown College, Jeff Bach.

At Winterthur, the development of the publication and exhibition has been a true team effort. Nicole Belolan, Patty Edmonson, Alyce Perry Englund, Brenda Hornsby-Heindl, and Katie Wood provided research assistance as part of their coursework in the Winterthur Program in American Material Culture; curatorial interns Sara Jatcko, Laura Johnson, Katie Knowles, and Heather Hansen fielded inquiries during our many absences; and Brock Jobe gave sound and thoughtful advice based on his most recent exhibition experience. From the initial fundraising to the final stretch, the Development Office has extended enormous effort, and we thank Bob Davis, Jennifer Mackey, Scott Mangieri, Matt Thurlow, Susan Wendle, and former staff members Armand Battisti, Val Stewart, Martha Mitchell, Robin Sarratt, Lynn Calder, Rob Rudd, and Emily Davis. The daunting task of dealing with loans and lenders, from paperwork to pickup, has been handled by our capable Registration Office, Beth Parker-Miller, Katie Orr, Lonnie Dobbs, William Donnelly, Julia Hofer, Kathan Lynch, Matt Mickletz, and Matt Stiles. The Conservation Department skillfully examined each object, treating and scientifically analyzing items where necessary; for their efforts we thank Greg Landrey, Lois Price, Stephanie Auffret, Anna Friedman, Joy Gardiner, Joan Irving, Sara Lapham, Jennifer Mass, Catherine Matsen, Mary McGinn, Bruno Pouliot, and Richard Wolbers. A special thank you to Mark Anderson, head furniture conservator, for his observations and considerable efforts throughout the project. Research at Winterthur was made easy with the assistance of the library staff, including Rich McKinstry, Heather Clewell, Emily Guthrie, Laura Parrish, Helena Richardson, Jeanne Solensky, and former librarian Cate Cooney. The Finance Department carefully tracked the budget thanks to Rob Necarsulmer, Denise Adams, Hugh McVeigh, and Deb Shaw. The Public Programs staff has lent their assistance in the interpretation of the exhibition, and we thank Jeff Groff, Debbie Harper, Janis Kraft, Rosemary Krill, Jeanie McCuskey, and former staffers Jody Cross, Anna Hanusa, and Mary Jane Taylor. The advertising and promotion of the project has been ably handled by Holly Victor, Lynne Boyle, Mary

Anne Casey, Ida McCall, and former staffer Vicki Saltzman. We also thank Steve Donahue and his Public Safety staff.

The publication *Paint, Pattern & People* has involved the talents and expertise of many individuals. Our deepest appreciation goes to our editor, Onie Rollins, who kept the project on schedule and carefully guided the manuscript from rough draft to finished volume with painstaking attention to detail. We thank Bernie Herman and Sumpter Priddy for their insightful comments on the draft of the manuscript and designer Peter Blaiwas at Vern Associates for transforming the words and images into an artful presentation. We gratefully acknowledge the Pennsylvania German Society for naming *Paint, Pattern & People* the 2011 selection in their distinguished annual volume series and thank Luke Beckerdite and Chipstone Foundation for dedicating the 2011 edition of *American Furniture* to additional research on southeastern Pennsylvania furniture.

The photography for *Paint, Pattern & People* was a major undertaking. Our heartfelt thanks to photographer Laszlo Bodo, who worked wonders in the Winterthur studio and on numerous road trips, agreeing to our endless requests for "just one more shot." Jim Schneck assisted us with infrared photos of elusive inscriptions; Gavin Ashworth and Graydon Wood also provided photographic work; and Tom Willcockson created the detailed maps. The Landis Valley Museum and Chester County Historical Society graciously allowed the use of their facilities for photo shoots, and we thank them for their support. Finally, Winterthur's Susan Newton in Photo Services cheerfully organized the images and prepared them for the designer.

For the masterful exhibition design we are deeply indebted to Keith Ragone, who worked tirelessly to revise plans as we refined the interpretive scheme. The elegance of the presentation was his vision, and the installation was ably carried out by Felice Jo Lamden and her staff: Nat Caccamo, Amy Marks Delaney, Doug McDonald, and Artie Petersen. We also thank Jay Ruth for creatively producing the video accompanying the exhibition.

Our friends and family have traveled the long road with us. To fellow curators Linda Eaton, Leslie Grigsby, and Ann Wagner; former colleagues Pat Halfpenny, Don Fennimore, and Anne Verplanck; and former Director Leslie Greene Bowman, our warmest thanks for all your valuable advice. A special note of thanks as well to Silvio and Kate Minardi, who happily provided home-cooked meals on many occasions while tolerating their daughter's absence from numerous family gatherings.

Finally, the Southeastern Pennsylvania Furniture Project could not have flourished without the considerable encouragement and support of Winterthur Director Dave Roselle and Director of Museum Affairs Tom Savage. For their steadfast belief in our vision, we are most thankful.

Wendy A. Cooper
Lois F. and Henry S. McNeil
Senior Curator of Furniture

Lisa Minardi
Assistant Curator of Furniture
for the Southeastern Pennsylvania
Furniture Project

INTRODUCTION

In 1748, two years after their marriage at the London Grove Meeting in southern Chester County, Robert and Ann Lamborn acquired a spice box. Inlaid on the door with their initials and the date, the box was similar to ones owned by other Quaker couples in the area.

FIGURE I
Detail of spice box in fig. 3.19.
Collection of Mr. and Mrs.
Chester Bartoli

In 1788 James McDowell commissioned Jacob Brown, joiner of Nottingham, to make a case for the clock movement he had bought from Benjamin Chandlee Jr. Although Brown struggled to complete the work because of "feaver" among the boys in his shop, he managed to fashion a walnut case with broken-scroll pediment and numerous locally distinctive carved features.

FIGURE 2
Detail of tall-case clock in fig. 2.77.
Collection of Mr. and Mrs. John
McDowell Morris and Family

FIGURE 3
Detail of chest-over-drawers in fig. 3.48. Collection of Carl and Julie Lindberg

Nineteen-year-old Christina Benter of New Hanover Township, Montgomery County, received a paint-decorated chest in 1791 for the storage of her personal possessions. Three years earlier, her older sister Elisabeth had been given a similar one. Both chests have a brilliant blue ground, embellished with floral decoration and the names of the owners written across the front.

FIGURE 4

Portrait of Grace Peel, by
Benjamin West, probably
Philadelphia, 1756–60.
Winterthur Museum purchase
with funds provided by the
Henry Francis du Pont
Collectors Circle

policy of religious tolerance attracted people of various faiths and ethnic backgrounds, making Pennsylvania the most culturally diverse of the thirteen colonies. By examining this mixed multitude through its objects and inhabitants, the region's great diversity comes into focus. Well-documented furniture provides the key to shaping this understanding by identifying specific people and places as points of reference from which to begin the exploration.

For most of the 1700s, only about 10 percent of Pennsylvania's inhabitants lived in Philadelphia.[2] The remaining 90 percent resided in smaller settlements outside the city. Although the stylish furniture owned by elite Philadelphians often influenced production in the surrounding counties, many creative localisms flourished in areas unbound by the restraints of more formulaic urban modes of expression. It is the examination of those locally specific furniture forms, construction techniques, and ornament that defines this particular study.

FROM REGIONAL TO LOCAL

Although this work focuses on the production of the counties beyond Philadelphia, select examples of Philadelphia objects are included to illustrate the influence of the city's artisans on their environs. Wealthy, sophisticated consumers who lived in other areas frequently patronized the city's merchants and craftsmen. For example, Lancaster resident Grace Peel (1740–1814) had her portrait painted by Benjamin West (1738–1820), most likely in Philadelphia between 1756 and 1760 (fig. 4).[3] Born and raised in Chester County, West began painting by the age of fourteen. After a brief stay in Lancaster, 1755 to 1756, during which time he painted family portraits for attorney George Ross and gunsmith William Henry, West moved to Philadelphia. There his style continued to mature. His time in Lancaster may have inspired the Peel family to seek him out in Philadelphia; both Grace and her sister Elizabeth had their portraits painted by West before he went abroad in 1760.[4]

The influence of Philadelphia can also be seen in a Chester County dressing table (fig. 5). The early history of the table is unknown, but

Robert and Ann Lamborn, James McDowell, and Christina Benter—all early residents of southeastern Pennsylvania—had relatively little in common, but the furniture they owned shares one significant element. Although different in appearance, the objects all embody distinct local expressions. These "localisms" of form, ornament, and construction were influenced by a variety of factors, including ethnicity, religious affiliation, personal taste, socioeconomic status, and the skill of the craftsman. The larger southeastern Pennsylvania region in which the objects and their owners existed was diverse and characterized by local pockets of settlement. To understand the furniture of the area, one must acknowledge the influence of local expressions within the broader regional context. "We shall have a great mixt multitude," predicted Quaker merchant Jonathan Dickinson of Philadelphia in 1717.[1] William Penn's

the piece does have an inscription that places it in that locale. One of the drawer sides is inscribed in chalk "J [?] Larkin," possibly associated with joiner William Larkin (d. 1763) of Bethel Township and his wife, Jane (Smedley) Larkin.[5] The table is one of several examples possibly associated with the vicinity of West Chester, the county seat.[6] At first glance, its overall form and proportions do not strongly suggest Philadelphia prototypes, but the square ball-and-claw feet, carved shells on the knees with strong scrolling volutes, and shape and carving of the central shell reveal the inspiration of Philadelphia work. A possible local feature is the tail-like motif carved beneath the shells, which is also found on a distinctive Chester County tea table (see fig. 2.60).

Further influence of Philadelphia's stylish production can be seen by comparing the rococo case furniture of the city with that produced sixty miles west in the town of Lancaster.

Settled in 1730, Lancaster was the major supply center for the Pennsylvania backcountry throughout the eighteenth century and the largest inland city in North America at the time of the Revolution.[7] Well-to-do residents were familiar with, and even owned, furniture produced in Philadelphia, as was the case with attorney Jasper Yeates, whose possessions included a card table and looking glass.[8] A prosperous businessman, Yeates had ties to wealthy Philadelphians, including the Shippens and Cadwaladers.[9] While in the city in December 1776, Yeates wrote to his wife to inform her that "Col. John Cadwalader has requested Leave of me to store a part of his most valuable Furniture in our House. If it should come to you in my Absence," he directed, "you will please to have it put up in the Garret & have the Room locked up."[10] Through the presence of such furniture in Lancaster, local cabinetmakers and carvers would have been aware of

FIGURE 5

Dressing table, possibly William Larkin, possibly Bethel Township, Chester (now Delaware) County, 1750–75. Collection of Edward T. Lacy

FIGURE 6

High chest of drawers, owned
by Michael and Miriam Gratz,
Philadelphia, 1760–75. Winterthur Museum, gift of Henry
Francis du Pont

the Philadelphia rococo taste. Some may even
have apprenticed in that city. Ultimately, however, they fashioned their own expressions,
giving a unique Lancaster style to the carving,
proportions, and scale.

A comparison of two high chests of drawers, one made in Philadelphia and one in Lancaster, illustrates this point. Lancaster merchant
Joseph Simon, one of the wealthiest residents,
was the leader of the borough's small Jewish
community.[11] In 1769 his daughter Miriam married Michael Gratz of Philadelphia. An elaborate Philadelphia high chest of drawers and
dressing table owned by the couple are among
the finest examples of Philadelphia rococo furniture known (fig. 6). Michael, an immigrant
from Silesia, was well on his way to becoming
one of Philadelphia's leading merchants at the
time of his marriage to Miriam. Their elaborate
high chest contains many features that made
it an expensive and desirable object in its day:
highly figured mahogany; pierced brasses in the
Chinese manner coated with a tinted lacquer to
resemble gold; and heavily carved foliate-and-
shell designs on the tympanum, skirt, and legs.
An impressive original cartouche crowns this
triumph of Philadelphia furniture.[12]

In contrast, Lancaster resident Matthias
Slough (Schlauch), a German Lutheran, proprietor of the White Swan Tavern and member
of the Pennsylvania Assembly, was the owner of
a Lancaster high chest of drawers made about
1770 (fig. 7).[13] At first glance Slough's high chest
may appear to closely resemble the Gratz piece,
but further examination reveals a number of
differences. The carving emulates the naturalistic foliage and shells on the Philadelphia example, but its character and execution are quite
different. The Lancaster piece is more profusely
carved, covering the entire skirt and tympanum, and the carving was done from the solid
wood rather than made separately and applied,
as was most of the carving on the Philadelphia chest. It is unclear how or why this technique of carving from the solid developed, but
it does appear to be a Germanic tradition and
has been traced to the areas of Lorraine, Hessia, and Württemberg.[14] In fact, the Lancaster
carving style has been described as a fusion of

the Philadelphia rococo and German baroque.[15] Matthias Slough's high chest provides evidence of the level of sophistication achieved by Lancaster cabinetmakers, who, instead of copying the Philadelphia style, took inspiration from it, transforming the technique and design conventions to fit their perceptions of beauty.

The Gratz and Slough high chests epitomize the essence of this study. Beyond Philadelphia, towns such as Lancaster, York, Reading, and West Chester as well as small villages made southeastern Pennsylvania a prosperous and thriving region with local furniture traditions as diverse as its inhabitants. The area defies the usual definition of a cultural region in which people share a common ethnic background, language, and material culture. Instead, it was divided into a series of "intensely local sub-regions," each reflecting distinctive localisms of people, land use, architecture, speech, foodways, and material culture. As a result, the "local" became a significant factor in the cultural process that influenced the look of objects. Although a regional cohesiveness gradually emerged following the American Revolution, local identities remained strong well into the nineteenth century.[16] This endurance suggests that localism, more so than regionalism, may be a more relevant organizing concept for the study of American history and material culture.[17] The cultural diversity of the Mid-Atlantic region also argues for its having greater significance than Puritan New England or the plantation South as a model for modern America's development as a pluralistic society.[18] As one of the three "major cultural hearths" from which traditions diffused outward, the Mid-Atlantic's central position between New England and the South may have enabled it to have the most widespread influence of all three regions.[19]

THE REGIONAL PERSPECTIVE

Southeastern Pennsylvania is not a precisely defined geographic region; the very diversity for which it is noted challenges those who seek to describe its borders. Regional and local boundaries are formed more by the "mental maps" of the inhabitants than through the tools of a professional cartographer.[20]

FIGURE 7

High chest of drawers, made for Matthias Slough, Lancaster, Lancaster County, 1770–85. Heritage Center of Lancaster County

Political borders generally have little meaning when it comes to the decorative arts and material culture, as people, ideas, and goods move easily across them. For the purposes of this study, southeastern Pennsylvania is defined as the counties of Adams, Berks, Bucks, Chester, Cumberland, Dauphin, Delaware, Lancaster, Lebanon, Lehigh, Montgomery, Northampton, Northumberland, Philadelphia, Schuylkill, and York. The initial three counties, Bucks, Chester, and Philadelphia, grew rapidly over time, causing new counties to be carved out of earlier ones (fig. 8). When people moved beyond Pennsylvania's borders into Maryland, Virginia, the Carolinas, Ohio, and even Ontario, southeastern Pennsylvania's cultural influence spread far beyond its political boundaries.[21]

Within the region, a network of roads developed to carry people and goods between Philadelphia and the surrounding areas. County seats were established, generally in the geographic centers of counties, and attempts were made to situate them within a day's journey of each other by wagon, about thirty miles. Following the French and Indian War, southeastern Pennsylvania was swept with a town-building fever that spurred the founding of nearly thirty new settlements in the back-

country alone between 1756 and 1765, more than had been established in the entire colony the previous seventy-five years. Existing towns such as Lancaster, York, and Carlisle also became more commercially developed during this time, strengthened by their ties with Philadelphia.[22]

The geography and geology of southeastern Pennsylvania played a major role in its cultural and economic development. As settlement progressed, the good farmland, moderate climate, and plentiful natural resources enabled many to accumulate substantial material wealth. Major waterways, including the Delaware and Schuylkill rivers near Philadelphia and the Susquehanna in the central region, provided a means of transportation for agricultural and mining products. These same waterways and their numerous tributaries supplied power to milling operations, including gristmills and dozens of sawmills in operation by the mid-eighteenth century to convert logs into lumber for use in furniture and architecture (see fig. 4.22).[23] Among Pennsylvania's natural resources were plentiful iron ore deposits that fueled the development of a thriving iron industry that produced everything from cast firebacks and stove plates to cannon barrels and cooking vessels. Investors

FIGURE 8
Southeastern Pennsylvania counties in 1820 (in blue), with county seats noted.

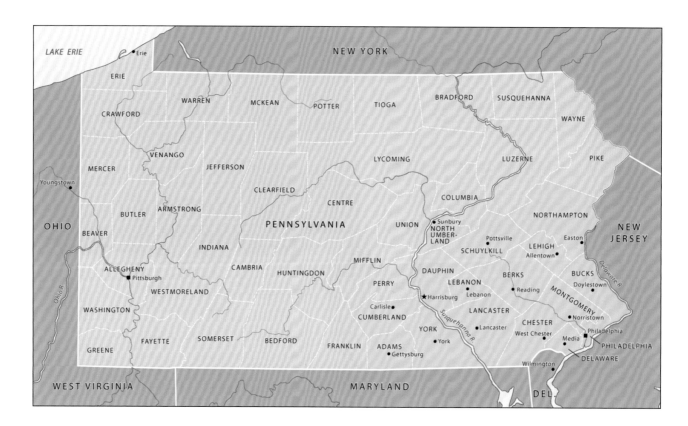

FIGURE 9.
*The Little Village of Sumney-
town*, by George Wunderlich,
Montgomery County, 1858–75.
Schwenkfelder Library & Her-
itage Center, Pennsburg, Pa.

in iron furnaces, such as entrepreneur Michael Withers of Lancaster County (see fig. 2.68), could accumulate vast fortunes that allowed them to patronize local artisans. Other rural industries developed, with tanyards; distilleries; potteries; and weaving, blacksmith, and woodworking shops dotting the countryside (see fig. 4.21).[24] Local quarries provided stone for various structures, including large bank barns, houses, mills, and workshops for a range of artisans. The region's fertile soil was invaluable for the crops it yielded, feeding both urban and rural populations and supporting livestock to work the fields. A traveler in 1836 noted that the Pennsylvania countryside was unsurpassed in its "cultivation, fertility and beauty" and "occupied by a thrifty and industrious population . . . whose comfortable farm houses, and substantial and capacious stone barns are scattered in every direction."[25] In 1833 Philadelphia antiquarian John Fanning Watson made an excursion through Montgomery County. Stopping in Sumneytown, he described it as "a German settlement of but few houses, situated at the junction of two creeks—branches of the Perkioming [Perkiomen]—it is pretty much surrounded by high & rocky & woody hills."[26]

A mid-nineteenth century view of Sumneytown calls to mind this description (fig. 9). Standing in the foreground is a large brick dwelling, built in 1757 by Daniel Hiester (who immigrated in 1737) and reputed to be the earliest brick house in the area. The interior reflected its outer grandeur, featuring elaborate chair rails, paneled end walls, and a fireplace overmantel with crosseted corners. Hiester's Germanic heritage was also evident in the flat, vasiform stair balusters, large built-in cupboards, and iron stoves for heating.[27]

Based on comments of immigrants and travelers, Pennsylvania's forests were one of its most noteworthy features, providing raw materials for the woodworking trades. In 1683 William Penn himself described the flora of his colony, noting

*The Natural Produce of the Country . . .
is Trees, Fruits, Plants, Flowers. The Trees
of most Note are the Black Walnut, Cedar,
Cyprus, Chestnut, Poplar, Gumwood,
Hickery, Sassafrax, Ash, Beech, and Oak
of divers Sorts, as Red, White, and Black;
Spanish Chesnut, and Swamp, the most
Durable of all: Of All which there is Plenty
for the Use of Man.*[28]

In 1754 German schoolmaster Gottlieb Mittelberger noted that Pennsylvania's forests were surprisingly dense, with "beautiful, smooth, thick and tall trees," including poplars having "soft wood which looks snow-white inside." The poplar to which Mittelberger referred was likely tulip-poplar (*Liriodendron tulipifera*), which, although not a true poplar was referred to as such in contemporary accounts. Both tulip-poplar and pine were indigenous to southeastern Pennsylvania and were common woods for painted furniture. Mittelberger also commented that walnut trees were "exceedingly plentiful," continuing, "this beautiful coffee-brown and hard wood is precious and useful, because all sorts of fine and elegant household furniture are made of it."[29] Walnut was the primary choice in native hardwoods for unpainted furniture, followed by cherry and maple. Because the wood from which a piece of furniture was made affected its value, probate inventories often specify woods. A study of Chester County inventories found that prior to 1800, the most common types cited were walnut (32 references), poplar (17), cherry (13), oak (8), and pine (5).[30]

    Southeastern Pennsylvania's plentiful resources enabled many to prosper, especially entrepreneurial gentlemen farmers. In 1785, with the founding of The Philadelphia Society for the Promotion of Agriculture, men focused on improving the cultivation of crops, the breeding of livestock, and the development of more efficient farming implements. By the 1820s that society and a competing offshoot, The Pennsylvania Agricultural Society, began to hold annual agricultural exhibitions—awarding premiums for everything from cattle to crops and butter to cheese.[31] The second exhibition sponsored by the Agricultural Society was held in 1824 at Chester, along the Delaware River. A painting by John A. Woodside Sr. (1781–1852) dated the same year (fig. 10) may represent this two-day exhibition, which included a display of the latest farming implements as well as prize sheep, pigs, and Durham shorthorn cattle.[32] Plowing matches were also part of these gatherings, as depicted by Woodside in the field to the left. A wooden stand between two trees on the right holds award-winning goods and produce. The Conestoga wagon by the barn is poignantly juxtaposed with a steamboat moving along the river. Woodside worked in Philadelphia and when he died was noted as "one of the best sign painters in the state, and perhaps in the country."

FIGURE 10

A Pennsylvania agricultural fair, by John Archibald Woodside Sr., Philadelphia, 1824. Private collection

He was a contemporary of Edward Hicks (1780–1849); the similarity between their work is striking, though it is not known if they ever worked together.[33]

DISCOVERING SOUTHEASTERN PENNSYLVANIA

Henry Francis du Pont was an early and enthusiastic collector of southeastern Pennsylvania arts, furnishing his Chestertown House on Long Island in the 1920s with painted furniture, hooked rugs, and other country antiques (fig. 11).[34] Many of the pieces came from dealers such as Francis Brinton, Clarence Brazer, Edgar and Charlotte Sittig, Asher Odenwelder, and Joe Kindig Jr., who acquired the objects from descendants of the original owners. In December 1929, Lancaster County dealer Hattie Brunner wrote to du Pont regarding an exciting discovery (fig. 12):

> *Am enclosing photo of a miniature chest which I bought last week, out of the original family, who had cherished it all these years, always kept it stored in a large chest, is in wonderful condition for the age. A unique piece. Dated 1773 made by Johannes Mosser who was one of our first settlers in this section. Was a shoe maker by trade. The old lady that owned it gave me the whole history of the piece. Did not like to part with it, but needs the money to live on. It was inlaid with the same old putty as that walnut Kass I sold you this spring. Will send it on approval if interested.*

Du Pont replied that he found the chest very attractive but "rather high in price and I wonder if you could not quote me a better figure," to which Brunner replied:

> *. . . the price $1,000 is the best I could consider . . . and when you stop to think that it is a pre-Revolutionary piece, and in such wonderful condition, I really think it is a good buy at that . . . however if you do not like it I shall gladly take it back. As it is one of those pieces I enjoy having around.*

Du Pont hastily wrote back that he was keeping the chest and would send payment.[35] Although he may not have realized its importance at the time, the sulfur-inlaid chest he purchased was a prime example of a distinct local furniture tradition with a well-documented history. Earlier that same year, du Pont had stunned the collecting world at the Howard Reifsnyder sale by paying a record $44,000 for a Philadelphia high chest, outbidding newspaper magnate William Randolph Hearst. The sale also contained some exceptional rural Pennsylvania material, including an inlaid chest of drawers and box made for Sarah Smedley of Chester County in 1737 (see figs. 3.13, 3.15).[36]

From iconic Pennsylvania German painted chests to inlaid spice boxes of Chester County Quakers, the furniture of the region has long been of interest to antiquarians. In 1876 Philadelphia's sprawling Centennial International Exhibition stirred interest in local family heirlooms with its "Pennsylvania Room." Fifty years later, the Sesquicentennial International Exposition, also in Philadelphia, included several pieces of painted furniture from the Mahantongo Valley of Northumberland

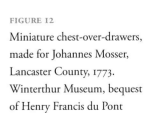

FIGURE 11
Chestertown House interior, Southampton, Long Island, 1927. Winterthur Archives

FIGURE 12
Miniature chest-over-drawers, made for Johannes Mosser, Lancaster County, 1773. Winterthur Museum, bequest of Henry Francis du Pont

FIGURE 13

Mrs. Enoch Rohrbach, by H.
Winslow Fegley, Sigmund,
Upper Milford Township,
Lehigh County, 1903. Schwenk-
felder Library & Heritage
Center, Pennsburg, Pa.

FIGURE 14

Ruth Abbott, by Gilbert Cope,
Chester County, 1913. Chester
County Historical Society,
West Chester, Pa.

County (see fig. 2.55).[37] As early antiquarians focused their attention on southeastern Pennsylvania, many local historical societies were founded and scholars began publishing county histories and genealogies. In the late nineteenth and early twentieth centuries, the region underwent a period of rapid change as automobiles, electricity, telephones, and other new technologies were introduced. While some tried to preserve the disappearing past through the collecting of relics, photographers such as Berks County native H. Winslow Fegley sought to capture it with their cameras. Fegley, whose photos were largely for a local Pennsylvania German audience, created romanticized scenes such as that of an elderly woman posed with an antique spinning wheel in front of a bake house in 1903 (fig. 13).[38] Gilbert Cope of Chester County took a similar interest in local Quaker history, co-authoring with J. Smith Futhey a *History of Chester County* in 1881 and photographing old Quaker documents and people such as eighty-nine-year-old Orthodox minister Ruth Abbott in 1913 (fig. 14).[39]

The early decades of the twentieth century saw some of the first studies on Pennsylvania

fraktur, pottery, architecture, and furniture, including Esther Stevens Fraser's pioneering work on Pennsylvania German painted chests in 1925.[40] During the 1930s, the Works Progress Administration hired artists to create the Index of American Design, which included a number of eye-catching Pennsylvania objects.[41] Museums also began to install period rooms, including a Pennsylvania German kitchen from the Millbach House of Lebanon County at the Philadelphia Museum of Art (fig. 15) in 1926 and a Morgantown, Berks County, interior at New York's Metropolitan Museum of Art in 1934.[42] By the 1940s, southeastern Pennsylvania and its distinctive arts attracted the interest of not only scholars but also decorators and tourists. In June 1941, *House & Garden* magazine produced a special double issue on the Pennsylvania Dutch (fig. 16).

Early antiquarians had also begun to place their collections of Pennsylvania decorative arts and household objects on public view by the late 1800s. In Lancaster County, Manheim resident George Danner (son of woodturner Daniel Danner, see fig. 3.51) opened a

FIGURE 15
Millbach kitchen installation, 1929, at the Philadelphia Museum of Art.

museum of local artifacts as early as the 1870s, and brothers Henry and George Landis established a museum near Lancaster known today as the Landis Valley Museum. Beginning with a single exhibition in 1897, Dr. Henry Mercer of Doylestown, Bucks County, would build a seven-story concrete museum to house his voluminous collection of local artifacts before his death in 1930.[43] Meanwhile, J. Stodgell Stokes of Philadelphia and York County native Titus Geesey began acquiring Pennsylvania objects, with many eventually gifted to the Philadelphia Museum of Art. Emily Johnston de Forest gave her collection of Pennsylvania decorative arts to the Metropolitan Museum of Art. In Lower Merion Township, Montgomery County, Dr. Albert Barnes installed Pennsylvania German painted chests and ironware amid Impressionist paintings at his museum.[44]

More recent studies have focused on specific forms, counties, and ethnic groups, augmenting the work of these early antiquarians, collectors, and scholars. In 1966 Margaret Berwind Schiffer published *Furniture and Its Makers of Chester County, Pennsylvania*, a meticulously researched survey of woodworkers based on documentary evidence and physical objects.[45] John J. Snyder

Jr. published a series of articles in the 1970s on the high-style carved furniture of Lancaster.[46] In 1978 Monroe H. Fabian produced a detailed study of Pennsylvania German painted chests that remains a standard reference.[47] In 1982–83 the groundbreaking exhibition and publication entitled *The Pennsylvania Germans: A Celebration of Their Arts, 1683–1850* was organized by

FIGURE 16
House & Garden, June 1941. Printed Book and Periodical Collection, Winterthur Library

Charles F. Hummel of Winterthur Museum and Beatrice B. Garvan at the Philadelphia Museum of Art in conjunction with the 300th anniversary of permanent German settlement in America. Also published at that time was *Arts of the Pennsylvania Germans*, with essays by Scott T. Swank, Benno M. Forman, Frederick S. Weiser, and others on a wide range of subjects, including furniture.[48] Lee Ellen Griffith also produced several studies of Chester County Quaker furniture in the 1980s, including the exhibition and publication *The Pennsylvania Spice Box: Paneled Doors and Secret Drawers* in 1986 and her 1988 doctoral dissertation on line-and-berry inlaid furniture, a portion of which she published in 1989.[49] Most recently, the 1999 exhibition and catalogue *Worldly Goods: The Arts of Early Pennsylvania, 1680–1758*, by Jack L. Lindsey, explored furniture and decorative arts from the earliest decades of settlement.[50]

Building on these studies and others, this publication takes a fresh look at the furniture of southeastern Pennsylvania and the people who made, owned, inherited, and collected it. Indeed, the people of the region become the essential component and are the threads from which the story is woven. Unlike previous publications, this study investigates the substantial range of both the English- and German-speaking segments of the population as well as their religious affiliations. The confusion surrounding the early population is addressed by considering Quakers of Irish, Welsh, and English background; Scots-Irish Presbyterians; and Germanic peoples ranging from the non-conformist minorities such as the Mennonites and Moravians to the predominant Lutherans and Reformed.[51]

The principal goal of the project was to identify distinct localisms based on well-documented examples in which the maker or family history is known. This approach has enabled us to go beyond loose attributions to one county or another and vague classifications that have long prevailed. From the beginning, it was clear that well-documented furniture would provide an original context to understand the objects as fully as possible and place them within specific locations. Consequently, we excluded many fascinating objects with only initials, inconclusive family histories, or unclear origins. In some cases, however, exceptions were made for those that serve as important examples of particular forms or decoration. Even when objects do carry legible owners' or makers' names and dates, positive identification is often difficult because of incomplete documentation and the repetitive naming patterns in the period. The frequent redrawing of political borders in the eighteenth and nineteenth centuries also hampered the documentation of precise locations.

Debunking and correcting some long-standing myths about the furniture and people of southeastern Pennsylvania was another goal of the project. One of the most common misunderstandings is the meaning of the term "Pennsylvania Dutch." It does not refer to the Holland Dutch of the Netherlands nor is it a corruption of the word *Deutsch*, or German. In fact, "Dutch" is a historically accurate term used during the period when referring to German-speaking people; however, most scholars today prefer the term "Pennsylvania German" to avoid confusion.[52] Similar misguided assumptions abound about the furniture itself. Many associate the Quakers with plainness and therefore assume that their furniture is without ornament.[53] Applying the religious concept of plainness to tangible material goods is problematic, however, as a wide range of factors influenced the appropriateness of an object for Quaker owners, including economic status. Numerous misunderstandings also exist regarding the so-called dower chests associated with the Pennsylvania Germans. As will be discussed more fully in chapter three, these chests were made for both men and women, and there is scant documentation to support the interpretation of their painted decoration as holding overt religious or symbolic meaning.

Although the objects presented in this publication have been looked at inside and out for clues about makers and owners, this work is not about dovetails and glue blocks. It is about the furniture and what it can tell us about the people who made and owned it as well as the culture and craft production of the areas in which it originated. It is not a comprehensive

FIGURE 17

The Troutman brothers, by H. Winslow Fegley, probably Berks County, 1900–1910. Schwenkfelder Library & Heritage Center, Pennsburg, Pa.

survey of the furniture of southeastern Pennsylvania, but rather one based on furniture with histories and the people associated with those objects. Such items tend to survive because they were expensive, highly ornate, or personalized with an ancestor's name. Our perceptions are inevitably informed by what survives. During the course of everyday life, many objects were worn out, repurposed, burned for firewood, repaired, repainted, or otherwise altered. No doubt hundreds of plain, unmarked, or unornamented objects have disappeared over the years. Even decorated objects were lost when they fell out of style and were relegated to attics, cellars, and barns—such as the painted schrank photographed around 1905 by H. Winslow Fegley that stands under the forebay of a barn, with bricks supporting it and rakes hanging on one side (fig. 17).[54] Some objects, particularly clocks and desks, are among the most likely to descend in a family as cherished heirlooms. On the other hand, painted chests and spice boxes—among the most common forms to have identifiable names or initials and dates on them—have rarely been found within the families for whom they were made, probably because of early collecting interests in these forms. Although numerous objects in this study were costly and owned by the well-to-do, others were inexpensive and belonged to ordinary people. These everyday objects, which might be extraordinary in their decoration, include items such as small painted boxes, slat-back chairs, and spinning wheels.

Furniture is one of many vehicles for transporting us into the lives of our ancestors. It is important for anyone interested in history and the material remains of the past. The well-documented objects presented here provide a foundation on which to build new interpretations of the region's furniture and people. This work is only the beginning of an ongoing discussion, however, and it is our hope that future scholars will continue to advance the study of southeastern Pennsylvania's art and culture, yielding fresh insights and a deeper understanding of its rich and diverse heritage.

CHAPTER ONE

PEOPLE: A GREAT MIXED MULTITUDE

We find there Lutherans, Reformed, Catholics, Quakers, Mennonists or Anabaptists, Herrnhuters or Moravian Brethren, Pietists, seventh Day Baptists, Dunkers, Presbyterians, Newborn, Freemasons, Separatists, Freethinkers, Jews, Mohammedans, Pagans, Negroes and Indians.

—Gottlieb Mittelberger, 1754 [1]

Gottlieb Mittelberger, a Lutheran schoolmaster who traveled to America in 1750 and returned to Germany in 1754, published an account of his journey that, although largely critical of life in southeastern Pennsylvania, offers insights into the region's great ethnic and religious diversity. Mittelberger commented that "Pennsylvania is the heaven of the farmers, the paradise of the mechanics, and the hell of the officials and preachers." Although this expansive diversity united the region to some extent, it also divided it. Most immigrants tended to settle with others of similar backgrounds, resulting in local clusters of like-minded individuals.

PENN'S WOODS

In 1681 Charles II of England granted William Penn a large tract of land in the New World in repayment of a debt the Crown owed Penn's late father. Thus Penn (1644–1718) became the sole owner of a vast territory positioned between New Jersey, New York, and Maryland. To promote his new colony, which was named Pennsylvania, or "Penn's Woods," he financed the publication of *A Map of the Improved Part of the Province of Pennsilvania in America* in 1687 (fig. 1.1). Developed by his surveyor, Thomas Holme, the document was aimed at potential investors from Europe and England. Depicted on the map are the three initial counties—Philadelphia, Bucks, and Chester—divided into their respective townships and individual tracts. Although few buildings are shown, the locations of county seats and towns are noted, as are waterways and other natural features.[2] Penn specifically targeted the German Palatinate as a source of immigrants. During his four visits there, the last in 1677, he observed firsthand the region's poverty and devastation from warfare but also its model agricultural practices. He commissioned pamphlets that were distributed

in the region to promote his colony; he further encouraged settlement by offering a 10-acre lot in Philadelphia to purchasers of at least 500 acres. He also enticed immigrants to bring servants by offering them 50 acres for each servant transported to Pennsylvania.[3]

From the beginning, Penn intended his colony to be a place of religious freedom in accord with Quaker principles of peace, love, and tolerance. Believing that it was possible for religious, ethnic, and economic diversity to exist without the warfare that had plagued Europe for centuries, he sought to use Pennsylvania as a "Holy Experiment." Penn himself was Quaker, having converted as a student at Oxford. Quakers believe that people are inspired directly by God through an "inner light," without need of a minister or priest to interpret God's word. This belief also encourages a strong sense of equality regardless of gender, socioeconomic standing, or race. Other key tenets of Quakerism include a refusal to swear oaths or participate in violence of any kind.

Pennsylvania's religious tolerance and abundant resources attracted immigrants of various ethnic and religious backgrounds, becoming the

FIGURE 1.1

A Map of the Improved Part of the Province of Pennsilvania in America, surveyed by Thomas Holme, engraved by Francis Lamb, published by John Thornton and Robert Greene, London, 1701–5. Winterthur Museum, bequest of Henry Francis du Pont

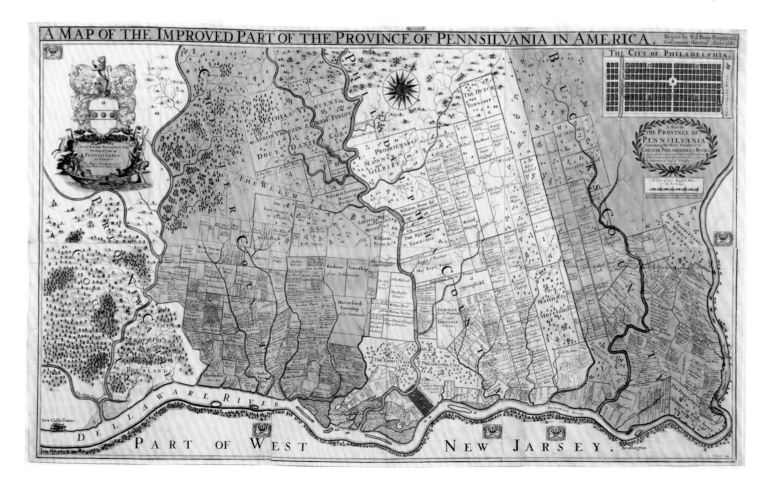

most culturally diverse of the thirteen colonies. Swedish, Finnish, and Dutch settlers as well as members of the native Lenni Lenape tribe were already living on the land when Penn received his grant. Hundreds more settlers immigrated during the 1680s in response to the announcement of Penn's policies, including English, Welsh, and Irish Quakers. In 1683 a small group of German Quakers and Mennonites established the community of Germantown. By the 1690s Pennsylvania's inhabitants totaled about 8,000—most of them English. From 1681 to the early 1800s, the composition of southeastern Pennsylvania's population evolved greatly. The early immigrants were predominantly British, largely English and Welsh Quakers until the early 1700s, followed by small numbers of Anglicans and Irish Quakers. From 1718 to 1729, Scottish Presbyterians from the province of Ulster in northern Ireland (Scots-Irish) became the largest group of immigrants to the American colonies (fig. 1.2). Impoverished conditions caused by severe drought from 1715 to 1720, exorbitant food prices, and a wave of rent increases by landlords in 1717 prompted more than 5,000 to leave for Pennsylvania in 1717, followed by a second wave in 1728–29 in the wake of another famine.[4] Established Quakers such as James Logan grew alarmed at the influx, declaring the colony "invaded by those shoals of foreigners," including "strangers from the North of Ireland that crowd in upon us." Most of these Scots-Irish immigrants settled on the western frontier, then in Lancaster County.[5]

German-speaking people formed another large segment of the expanding population, representing diverse European origins and religious backgrounds (fig. 1.3). The majority were Lutheran, followed by German Reformed, and came from the Palatinate region of southwest Germany, as did French Huguenots or Protestants, who had sought refuge in Germany following the reemergence of Catholic leadership and revocation of the Edict of Nantes in 1685. The remainder consisted of sectarian groups including the Amish and Mennonites, who came largely from the German-speaking cantons of Switzerland; the Moravians, primarily from Bohemia and Moravia; and the Schwenk-

FIGURE 1.2

British origins of English-speaking immigrants to Pennsylvania (in blue).

FIGURE 1.3

European origins of German-speaking immigrants to Pennsylvania (in blue).

felders, predominantly from Silesia (part of modern-day Poland).[6] German immigration occurred in three phases. After the settlement of Germantown in 1683, few Germans arrived in America for more than two decades, probably no more than several hundred before 1710. A second wave followed, prompted by a disastrously harsh winter in 1709.[7] The third and largest phase of German immigration began in the early 1720s and continued until the Revolution, peaking from 1749 to 1754, when some 35,000 arrived in Pennsylvania. More than 80,000 Germans came directly to Pennsylvania, comprising the vast majority of the total Germanic immigrant population in North America (about 111,000 by 1775).[8] The majority were not religious minorities fleeing persecution but rather those seeking land and better economic opportunities.[9] So intense was the German immigration that English speakers such as Benjamin Franklin began to fear that they would "shortly be so numerous as to Germanize us instead of our Anglifying them." In 1751

FIGURE 1.4
Pennsylvania's population in 1790.

Franklin famously complained that the "Palatine Boors" would "swarm into our Settlements and, by herding together, establish their Language and Manners, to the Exclusion of ours."[10] In addition to the English- and German-speaking inhabitants, Pennsylvania was also home to small numbers of French, Dutch, Swedish, and Finnish settlers as well as Africans and Native Americans. Over the course of the eighteenth century, the population gradually shifted from a strong English majority to a nearly equal English-to-German ratio, with a sizable Scots-Irish minority (fig. 1.4). In southeastern Pennsylvania, people of Germanic heritage actually outnumbered the English by the end of the century.[11]

Estimates of southeastern Pennsylvania's population by religious affiliation are more difficult, but in 1790 approximately 7,500 (2 percent) were Anglican; 8,000 (2 percent) were Catholic; 20,000 (6 percent) were Mennonite; 30,000 (9 percent) were Quaker; 60,000 (19 percent) were Presbyterian; and 85,000 (26 percent) were German Lutheran or Reformed.[12] Though never a majority, Quakers had dominated Philadelphia society and controlled Pennsylvania politics for years after its founding. By the mid-1700s, however, their pacifist principles were the source of tension in light of frontier conflicts with Native Americans and the French and Indian War. Non-Quaker colonists objected to the Quaker-dominated Assembly's lack of support and protection, ultimately leading to a loss of Quaker political control by the beginning of the American Revolution. Increasingly, Anglicans, Presbyterians, and other non-pacifists were elected to political office, including German-speaking settlers by the late 1770s (see fig. 1.94).[13]

Immigrants to southeastern Pennsylvania tended to settle with their fellow countrymen rather than mix with those of different ethnic heritage. Over time, however, there was more contact among those of diverse backgrounds—driven by dense settlement as well as business practices and political developments.[14] Writing to European friends in 1768, Schwenkfelder leader Christopher Schultz of Hereford Township, Berks County, commented,

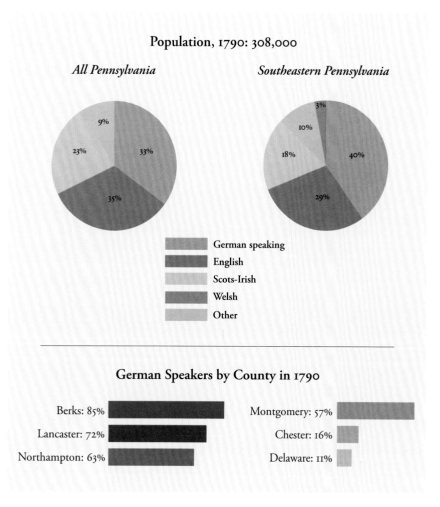

Population, 1790: 308,000

All Pennsylvania

9%
23%   33%
35%

Southeastern Pennsylvania

3%
10%
18%   40%
29%

- German speaking
- English
- Scots-Irish
- Welsh
- Other

German Speakers by County in 1790

Berks: 85%
Lancaster: 72%
Northampton: 63%

Montgomery: 57%
Chester: 16%
Delaware: 11%

FIGURE 1.5
House of Susanna Wright,
built 1738, later known as
Wright's Ferry Mansion,
Columbia, Lancaster County.
The von Hess Foundation,
Wright's Ferry Mansion

*You can hardly imagine how many
denominations you will find here . . . A
Mennonite preacher is my next neighbor
and I could not wish for a better one.
On the other side I have a big Catholic
church . . . Next to them the Lutherans
and Reformed have their congregations.*[15]

Even greater diversity existed in towns. In
1772–73 inhabitants of the blocks surrounding
Reading's Penn Square were Anglican, English Quaker, German Lutheran and Reformed,
Catholic, and Mennonite, demonstrating that
lives intersected and people coexisted despite
religious differences.[16]

Attempting to categorize and sort Pennsylvania's mixed multitude is challenging, as
religion, ethnicity, gender, language, and socioeconomic status were all factors in shaping a
person's identity.[17] Location also had a significant impact on identity, as can be seen in local
patterns of speech, foodways, and material culture that developed throughout southeastern
Pennsylvania. The sheer complexity of religious
and ethnic backgrounds also makes the study of
the region's furniture more difficult, as this het-
erogeneous mixture was reflected in distinctive
localisms of form, construction, and ornament.
Defining objects as associated with a particular cultural group can be misleading. When
evaluating why an object looks the way it does,
one must also consider that objects are a result
of conversations between craftsmen and consumers in which factors such as style, personal
taste, artisanal skill, economics, location, and
intended audience play a role.

An analysis of the construction of Wright's
Ferry Mansion in the early 1700s is representative of the difficulties encountered in attempting to assign material objects to particular
ethnic groups (fig. 1.5). Following the encouragement of James Logan, a group of Quakers
from Chester County relocated in 1729 to the
western edge of Lancaster County along the
Susquehanna River. Among them were Susanna
Wright and her family, who constructed a stone
mansion there in 1738. The single-pile, three-
room plan of the house was distinctly English.
Although the structure itself may have been a
monumental symbol of Anglo-Quakerism on
the frontier, those employed to build it were
decidedly not. As noted in the Wright papers,
craftsmen associated with projects for the family
include German stonemasons by the names of
Neif, Christ, and Stickley; a Welshman, Jemmy
Edwards, who did sawing and made shingles;
a Scots-Irish brickmaker, John McDaniel; and
Cornelius Verholst, probably Dutch, who created interior woodwork.[18]

Nonetheless, to understand the people of
southeastern Pennsylvania and their furniture,
some grouping of people into categories based
on shared characteristics is necessary. This chapter examines the two primary language groups
within the region, English-speaking and German-speaking, by subdividing them into religious affiliations. However, this is not to imply
that religion heavily influenced the look or type
of furniture. Although the Amish and more
conservative Mennonites are known today for
their plainness, in the eighteenth century their
material culture differed little from that of their

fellow Church Germans except for their style of dress and worship spaces. Only the communal religious settlements, in particular Ephrata Cloister and the Moravians, had physically distinctive material environments. Even in these instances, differences were evident. Ephrata practiced an ascetic lifestyle while the Moravians were sophisticated consumers of fine arts and cosmopolitan material culture.[19] Religion and ethnicity were critical components of cultural identity for both German- and English-speaking people in southeastern Pennsylvania. To some degree they played a part in the choices people made, but socioeconomic status, geographic location, and local craftsmanship practices were also factors that influenced the furniture a person owned and what it looked like.[20]

Contemporary travelers' accounts of southeastern Pennsylvania often made distinctions among its inhabitants based on their houses and furnishings. In 1784 Johann David Schoepf claimed he could identify English and German

houses simply by observing the placement of the chimney. If the chimney was in the center, he said, the house was likely that of a German and heated by stoves; if the house had a gable-end chimney, it belonged to an English family. Travelers also commented on outbuildings and farms in general. Many associated the Pennsylvania Germans with excellent agricultural practices and large, well-built barns. Opinions about their houses varied, ranging from disdain to admiration. The Duc de la Rochefoucauld-Liancourt, a French nobleman, found the Pennsylvania German houses sorely lacking, describing them as "small, and kept in very bad order." Their barns, however, he noted as "large, and in very good repair."[21] Quaker farms were also noted for their prosperity and orderliness. Bucks County painter Edward Hicks (1780–1849), raised by Quakers David and Elizabeth Twining, depicted the Twining's Newtown-area farmstead several times (fig. 1.6). Although he painted the picture seen here near the end of his

FIGURE 1.6

The Residence of David Twining 1785, by Edward Hicks, Newtown, Bucks County, 1846. American Folk Art Museum, New York, gift of Ralph Esmerian

THE RESIDENCE OF DAVID TWINING 1785.

life, Hicks included himself as a child, standing beside Elizabeth, who is seated in a slat-back chair and reading from the Bible. His rendition of the well-ordered landscape and its careful delineation by a hierarchy of fences presents a scene of agricultural prosperity and domestic tranquility. The arrangement of the farmhouse, barn, and dependencies, together with the health of the livestock, fields, and gardens, conveyed to observers the Twinings' success at ordering nature and controlling the landscape.[22]

Just as travelers' accounts observed ethnic differences in architecture, so too did they identify household furnishings and particular furniture forms with specific groups. For example, it was noted that Germans typically used bedsteads with side panels flanking the headboard to help hold two rows of bolster pillows, on which they slept propped up and under a feather mattress or "bed" (fig. 1.7). The English, on the other hand, complained that such heavy beds were suffocating and preferred to sleep under a thinner coverlet and sheets.[23] Travelers also commented upon the quality and quantity of furniture. Writing in 1794 about the home of German Leonard Ellmaker in Salisbury Township, Lancaster County, Theophile Cazenove observed, "The whole family (7 children) were having a very bad dinner around a very dirty little table, and the furniture in the main room was not worth 200 dollars." According to Cazenove, French farmers had "4 times as much furniture as the farmers in America generally have," including "several large wardrobes, filled with clothes and linen."[24] Of Lancaster County's German houses, Cazenove described the first floor as consisting of a kitchen and large room, which contained "the farmer's bed and the cradle, and where the whole family stays all the time; apples and pears drying on the stove, a bad little mirror, a bureau—a table—sometimes a clock; on the second floor, tiny little rooms where the family sleeps on pallets with curtains, without furniture," the latter probably indicating a mattress on the floor with no bedstead and curtains suspended from the ceiling. In the largest, most formal room he noted "an

immense stove . . . ; beds are generally without curtains, no mirrors, nor good chairs, nor good tables and wardrobes."[25]

Although some European travelers may have found the Pennsylvania German houses underfurnished and not up to their elite sensibilities, it is important not to characterize the entire region and culture on the basis of individual encounters, which tend to reflect the bias of the author. Contemporary accounts and paintings are helpful to a point but cannot accurately characterize the entire Pennsylvania landscape. Despite persistent stereotypes to the contrary, not all Quakers were good farmers and not all Germans lacked sufficient or refined furniture. To provide a more accurate interpretation of the furniture associated with particular ethnic and religious groups, it is necessary to examine objects that can be directly linked to people through solid documentation. To understand the choices people made, it is also important to know where they came from in Europe, why they immigrated to Pennsylvania, and where they settled.

ENGLISH-SPEAKING PEOPLE

Settlers from Wales, Scotland, Ireland, and England were linked by their common British heritage but were divided among several different religious affiliations, including Welsh,

FIGURE 1.7
Bedstead, probably Montgomery County, 1810–40, with reproduction and period bedding. Winterthur Museum

English, and Irish Quakers; Scots-Irish Presbyterians; and Anglicans who were members of the Church of England. Although use of the English language was a unifying factor for these immigrants, during the early years of settlement it was not absolute. As late as 1725, Anglican minister William Currie reported that many Welsh in the Radnor area did not understand English.[26]

Quakers

Denounced and persecuted by the Anglican Church as radical dissenters from the traditional establishment, Quakers would prove to be among the most prosperous of southeastern Pennsylvania's settlers. Formally known as the Religious Society of Friends, the Quakers were organized into a hierarchical series of meetings. Weekly meetings, which were centrally located within townships or settlements, consisted of silent meditation interspersed with commentary from those who felt moved to speak, having received the word of God. Two or more local worship meetings would hold a monthly business meeting to handle matters related to membership in that locale, issue marriage and removal certificates, enforce Quaker practices of discipline and social control, manage the business affairs of the meeting, and correspond with the regional quarterly meeting concerning its activities. The monthly meeting was the primary means of Quaker authority and influence—empowered to discipline those who broke the rules of conduct and disown those who refused to acknowledge and repent of their misconduct. Punishable offenses included marrying out of meeting; failure to attend meeting; immoderation in material comforts, clothing, or speech; and immoral behaviors such as cursing, excessive drinking, gambling, or sexual transgressions. Quarterly and yearly meetings were also held, which had greater authority but less direct impact on regulating the behavior of individuals.

Pennsylvania's Quakers were not a homogenous ethnic group; many came from England, but others hailed from Wales and Ireland as well as lesser numbers from the Netherlands and Germany. Most of the early immigrants were middling or poor families from Wales or Cheshire, two regions marked by small houses and farms as well as infrequent land ownership. Under such circumstances, raising children at home was nearly impossible, forcing families to send their children into servitude or apprenticeships elsewhere. William Penn's offer of cheap land in Pennsylvania, which he noted would allow a "more convenient bringing up of youth," had strong appeal to these families. In response to the complaints of Quaker leader George Fox about the number of Friends who were moving to America, Welsh Quaker leader Thomas Ellis wrote in 1685, "I wish that those that have estates of their own . . . may not be offended at the Lord's opening a door of mercy to thousands in England especially in Wales who have not estates either for themselves or children."[27]

William Penn's concept of dividing the colony into townships of 5,000 acres, with contiguous properties of 100 to 500 acres, formed a settlement pattern of farms that were large enough to support a family and keep children at home under parental supervision. Studies reveal that Quakers owned the "highest average acreage per family of any religious group in early America."[28] First-generation Quakers acquired large reserves of land for future generations. Only a small portion of these holdings were actively farmed; the remaining land lay fallow until sons of the family married, when they were given or sold a tract on which to establish their own farm. Quaker parents took great care to provide a nurturing domestic environment in which their children could grow spiritually, including ample houses furnished with material comforts. An analysis of probate inventories for the first generation of Quaker and Anglican settlers found that Quakers on average spent more money on furnishings, in particular bedding, than Anglicans of similar wealth.[29]

Welsh Quakers ⌒ Among the earliest people to settle in Pennsylvania were Welsh Quakers, who in 1684 had purchased some 40,000 acres west of the Schuylkill River from William Penn. This Welsh Tract included parts of both Philadelphia and Chester counties (a purposeful decision by the English Quaker majority to prevent the Welsh from gaining too much

FIGURE 1.8
Exeter Friends Meetinghouse,
built 1758, Exeter Township,
Berks County.

FIGURE 1.9
Marriage certificate, made for
Jonathan and Sarah Jones,
attributed to Edward Williams,
Merion Township, Philadelphia
County (now Lower Merion
Township, Montgomery
County), 1742. Rocky Hill
Collection

political influence in any one county) and included the townships of Merion, Radnor, Newtown, Haverford, and Tredyffrin.[30] By the 1730s, Welsh Quakers had moved into Berks County and established the Exeter Friends Meeting (fig. 1.8), founded by members from the Gwynedd Monthly Meeting—among them the family of legendary pioneer Daniel Boone. Some Welsh immigrants and Anglicans also settled in the Radnor area, where they built St. David's Church in 1715.[31] The Welsh immigration was not numerous and occurred largely before 1700. Few documented artifacts survive to indicate the possessions of these settlers. A marriage certificate that records the wedding of Jonathan and Sarah Jones of Merion Township, Philadelphia (now Montgomery) County on 8 day 11 month 1741/2 (January 8, 1742) is a rare survival, signed by witnesses bearing Welsh surnames such as Griffith, Evans, Lewis, and Williams (fig. 1.9). The calligraphic lettering with floral decoration does not appear on any other known Quaker marriage certificates, which are typically plain.[32]

Following their marriage, Jonathan and Sarah lived in a stone house known as Penn Cottage, built in 1695 by Robert Owen.[33] Their marriage certificate was likely made by Edward Williams, clerk of the Radnor Meeting and the son of Welsh immigrants. Not only does his signature appear on the certificate as a witness to the wedding, but his initials are beside a notation indicating that it was "Recorded in the Second Book of Records of Marriage."

A comparison of the handwriting on the certificate and related family records with that on other documents written by Williams shows a great similarity. Identified as a "Yeoman"

(farmer) in his will, Williams was a prosperous landowner whose estate totaled a substantial £875.18.6.[34]

Little furniture is known that can be firmly linked to specific Welsh Quaker families in Pennsylvania. A tall-case clock made by Thomas Thomas of Radnor Township for his daughter Margaret about the time of her marriage to Nathan Lewis in 1731 is one of the few documented examples (see fig. 3.10). Inlaid decoration of scrolling vines with leaves, tulips, and berries found on some Chester County furniture of the early to mid-eighteenth century (referred to as line and berry) relates closely to that found on Welsh furniture of the seventeenth and eighteenth centuries, suggesting a Welsh origin.[35] However, in the absence of documentation for most line-and-berry inlaid furniture, it is difficult to identify makers or owners of Welsh background. If the technique was brought over by Welsh craftsmen, it was likely adopted by others soon after its introduction, as a number of examples are linked to Irish Quaker families—suggesting that this manner of ornament was more of a local than ethnic preference.[36] Furniture forms associated with the Welsh, including large cupboards or dressers, panel-back or wainscot chairs, and settle benches, were popular in Pennsylvania. Although many such objects survive, few have firm histories that can link them to Welsh owners or makers.[37] Such a scarce survival rate may relate to the relatively small Welsh proportion of the population and intermarriage with Quakers of a different heritage as well as with non-Quakers.

Irish Quakers ⁓ The Pennock Family
Another small group of Quakers came from Ireland, with fewer than 2,000 immigrating to Pennsylvania by 1750.[38] Arriving later than most Welsh and English Quakers, many Irish Friends settled in southeastern Chester County, some twenty to thirty miles from the established seats of Philadelphia and Chester, where land was already taken. There they founded the meetings of London Grove and New Garden. By the 1730s, some families from those meetings moved into Berks County and established Maiden Creek Meeting.[39] Among the most prominent Irish Quaker settlers was Joseph Pennock, born in Ireland in 1677. His father, Christopher, of Cork, had suffered imprisonment and fines for his religious beliefs. Joseph spent two years of his childhood in Philadelphia and then moved back to Ireland in 1686. After his father's death he returned in 1701, settling permanently in Pennsylvania. He eventually became one of the largest landowners in Chester County as well as a member of the Pennsylvania Assembly and long-serving justice of the peace. In 1705 Pennock married Mary Levis, daughter of English immigrants from Leicestershire; the couple became members of the London Grove Meeting, founded in 1714 with a meetinghouse on land adjoining their property in West Marlborough Township. In 1738 the Pennocks built a brick mansion that was one of the largest in the area at the time (fig. 1.10). By the 1840s the house was known as Primitive Hall, despite its massive scale and expensive construction. Perhaps in keeping with his apparent inclination to push the limits of acceptable behavior for Quakers, Joseph Pennock was known to wear a wig, a practice uncommon for Quaker men due to its association with vanity.[40]

FIGURE 1.10
House of Joseph and Mary Pennock, built 1738, later known as Primitive Hall, West Marlborough Township, Chester County. Primitive Hall Foundation

Although no religious dictum instructed Quakers to own only plain furnishings, Friends were encouraged not to have objects that were too expensive or ornate. In 1698 the Philadelphia Yearly Meeting of Women Friends advised its members "that no superfluous furniture be in your houses," and in 1762 again discouraged "Superfluity & Excess in Buildings and Furniture."[41] Despite such admonitions, some Quakers did own ornate furnishings. Many others had objects of the finest quality and materials but plainly ornamented. Tangible signs of his prosperity abounded in Joseph Pennock's home. Silver, a clock valued at £18, five walnut chairs, and six "Black Chairs & armd Ditto" are among the items listed in his will and inventory of 1770 and 1771.[42] Possibly represented by the five walnut chairs on the inventory is a wainscot armchair and two side chairs that descended in the Pennock family with a history of coming from Primitive Hall (fig. 1.11). Another armchair and side chair identical to the documented ones are at Primitive Hall and are presumed to have come

from Pennock descendants.[43] Defined by the use of mortise-and-tenon joints to create a framework for the back panel, wainscot chairs employ rail-and-stile construction and joints similar to those in house carpentry. The Pennock armchair is a particularly impressive example of the form, with two panels instead of the more typical single panel to form the back, each surrounded by a decorative molding.[44] The shaped arms and robustly turned stretchers further distinguish it as a significant chair, meant to impress visitors with the owner's status. The crest rail with a half-round central arch flanked by pierced scrolls, together with the rounded-top stiles, are similar to examples from the west country of England, especially Lancashire and Cheshire. One of three chairs probably from the same set, the wainscot side chair has a simple cyma-curved crest rail. The hard plank bottoms of these chairs would have been softened by a cushion or squab; later the seats were sometimes cut to hold a chamber pot.

The Pennock chairs have a strong family history, but unfortunately the craftsman who

FIGURE 1.11

Wainscot armchair and side chair, made for Joseph and Mary Pennock, probably West Marlborough Township area, Chester County, 1730–50. Primitive Hall Foundation

FIGURE I.12

Spice box, probably made for Thomas and Elizabeth Hutton, London Grove Township area, Chester County, 1744. Collection of Mr. and Mrs. Joseph C. Hoopes, Jr.

among a widow's belongings; the previous year they had been listed in the inventory of her husband, Ralph Fishbourne, as a "½ doz of oaken Chaires" valued at £2.1.0. How closely these wainscot chairs resemble the later ones is unknown. Although wainscot chairs are commonly associated with Chester County owners and are usually assumed to have been made there, it is likely that the form was also produced in Philadelphia. Two joiners can be documented as having immigrated from Cheshire in 1683, both of whom were associated with Philadelphia and Chester County. Although Pennock may have acquired his chairs locally, he could also have brought them from Philadelphia. A member of the Pennsylvania Assembly at various times between 1719 and 1745, he would have had the opportunity to purchase furniture in the city.[46]

built them remains unknown, as is the case with nearly all extant wainscot chairs. The woodworkers who fashioned the paneling and turned stair balusters in Primitive Hall would have been capable of making the chairs. In fact, Joseph Pyle, a neighbor, was a joiner who later made Pennock's coffin.[45] Of course, the chairs may have been moved from another residence, as Pennock was more than sixty years old when he built the house. Wainscot chairs were certainly being made before 1738 in southeastern Pennsylvania; the earliest known reference in Chester County is a 1708 inventory that lists "6 Wainscot chairs"

The Hutton Family

Closely linked to London Grove Meeting with which the Pennocks were affiliated was New Garden Meeting, established by Irish Quaker families in 1718. London Grove became part of New Garden Monthly Meeting in 1729, further strengthening this affiliation. The Hutton family was among those associated with both meetings. Joseph Hutton, who immigrated in 1712 from County Carlow, Ireland, became the owner of 250 acres in New Garden Township. His son Thomas married Elizabeth Harry at London Grove Meeting in 1739. Five years after their marriage, the young couple acquired a spice box, its door inlaid with their initials and the date "1744" (fig. 1.12).[47] The basic spice box form was brought to America by English immigrants, likely derived from small valuables cabinets of the seventeenth and early eighteenth centuries. By the early 1700s, the form had generally ceased being made outside of Pennsylvania, where it continued to flourish among Quaker families in Chester County. Between 1684 and 1850, 358 out of 10,788 inventories from Chester County contained the term "spice box," in addition to a handful of related terms such as spice chest, spice case, and spice drawers.[48] These diminutive objects meant for storage have interiors fitted with numerous small drawers for holding valuables such as jewelry

FIGURE I.13

Spice box, made for George and Margaret Passmore, London Grove Township area, Chester County, 1744. Winterthur Museum, bequest of Henry Francis du Pont

and coins in addition to spices. Chester County resident Jacob Hibberd's inventory of 1750 lists "one Spice Box" and "Sundreys therein," including gold and silver cuff links, silver and brass shoe buckles, a pin cushion with silver chain, silver scissors, two large silver spoons, six silver teaspoons, and a pair of silver tongs, together with other "Sundrey Small things."[49] To secure the contents from the prying hands of children, servants, and would-be thieves, spice boxes were typically fitted with a lock and some even have secret drawers or compartments. Although most are plain, some were inlaid with the owners' initials and date on the doors. Inventory references reveal that spice boxes were often located in parlors on top of larger furniture. Such prominent display made them an ideal object for embellishment, with paneled doors neatly framing the inlaid ornament and initials.

Thomas and Elizabeth Hutton's spice box is one of a group associated with families in the New Garden and London Grove area of southern Chester County, distinguished by the character of the inlaid initials and dates in the 1740s set within an inlaid, arched border on the door.[50] The design on the Hutton box is unique, with ball feet inlaid beneath the frame surrounding the initials and date echoing the turned feet of the spice box itself. Closely related is a box made for George and Margaret (Strode/Stroud) Passmore in 1744 (fig. 1.13) and one made for Robert and Ann Lamborn in 1748 (see fig. 3.19). The Passmores had married in 1742 and the Lamborns in 1746, both at London Grove.[51] Like the Hutton box, the Passmore box has four hidden drawers concealed by the backboard, a long drawer behind the cornice, and three smaller drawers behind the top row of three interior drawers. Circumstantial evidence may link cabinetmaker Joel Baily Sr. (1697–1772) with the group of boxes, but no solid evidence can yet firmly document him as the maker.[52] An alternate possibility is suggested by the Hutton family, of whom several were cabinetmakers. Thomas was a cooper by trade and would have had some woodworking skills. In 1749, three years after his wife died, Thomas married Katherine Hiett, an Irish Quaker immigrant. Three of their sons—Jesse, Hiett,

and Thomas Jr.—were cabinetmakers or joiners in New Garden Township in the late 1700s and early 1800s.[53] The inventory of Hiett Hutton (b. 1756), taken in 1833, reveals a sizable workshop, containing twenty-one molding planes, chisels, a turning lathe, and other cabinetmaking tools. When Thomas wrote his will in 1786, he left the southern half of his farm in New Garden Township, containing nearly 80 acres, to Hiett. His inventory includes a spice box valued at £0.12.6, the same amount assigned to his eight chairs. This may be the same spice box listed in Hiett's inventory of 1833, valued at $1.[54] A well-built tall chest of drawers with fluted quarter columns, dentil molding, ogee bracket feet, and full dustboards was signed by Hiett on the backboards (fig. 1.14). Closely related to it is one signed by his brother Jesse and dated 1773.[55] Although Hiett's piece is more refined in its details than

FIGURE 1.14
Tall chest of drawers, by Hiett Hutton, New Garden Township, Chester County, 1780–1800. Collection of Anna Walton Myers

many examples, it represents a form that was
common throughout southeastern Pennsylvania
by 1775 and remained so long into the 1800s.
This chest descended in the Wickersham-Pusey
family. Its first documented owner was Ann
Wickersham (1818–71), who married Thomas
Pusey Jr. (1811–74) and was a member of London Grove Meeting. Likely the chest of drawers was made for an earlier generation, possibly
for her mother, Lydia Pusey Wickersham (1788–
1863) or grandmother, Elizabeth Jackson Wickersham (1752–1806). Once the chest came into
Ann's possession, it descended in the family to
the present owner, not moving more than a few
miles from the London Grove area.

Hiett Hutton or one of his brothers is the
likely maker of a spice box for cousin Mary
Hutton about the time of her marriage to Nicholas Hurford in 1788 at New Garden Meeting
(fig. 1.15). The Hurfords' marriage certificate
was signed by Hiett as well as Jesse and numerous other Huttons.[56] By this date spice boxes
had largely ceased being made, so Mary's box
may have been a revivalist commission based
on the 1744 example in the family. The inlaid,
arched design surrounding the date and initials
strongly recalls that on the earlier box; however,
the use of ogee bracket feet instead of turned
ball feet indicates the later date of the 1788 box.
The feet also relate to those on the tall chests

made by Hiett and Jesse Hutton. Another atypical facet of this box is that it is the only known
Chester County spice box with a history and
inlaid date that correspond to a marriage; all
other documented examples were made several
years after their owners' marriage.[57]

A blue-and-white plate bearing the initials "T H E" and date "1738" was likely made
for Thomas and Elizabeth (Miller) Hiett, parents of Katherine Hiett, who was the second
wife of Thomas Hutton (fig. 1.16). Alternately,
the plate may have been ordered by Thomas
and his first wife, Elizabeth, in anticipation
of their marriage the following year. The plate
links the Hietts and Huttons to several other
prominent Irish Quaker families associated
with Concord, Kennett, London Grove, and
New Garden meetings, all of whom owned
related plates. This distinctive group (fig. 1.17)
was made of tin-glazed earthenware (delftware),
probably in England.[58] All bear the date of 1738
and the initials of their respective original owners: John Allen, William Beverly, Joseph and
Sarah Dixon, Thomas and Dinah Gregg, William Gregg, and William and Elizabeth Levis.
Although in most cases only single examples
are known from each individual service, these
plates were originally part of larger sets. At least
six from William Gregg's set are known; John
Allen's inventory in 1771 included "a Duzon of
Delf pleats" probably in reference to his set.[59]
Spice boxes were personal objects of public
display, but plates enabled owners to partake
literally and figuratively in the ways of the com-

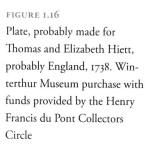

FIGURE I.17
Group of plates, owned by John Allen, William Beverly, Joseph and Sarah Dixon, Thomas and Dinah Gregg, William Gregg, and William and Elizabeth Levis, probably England, 1738.
(clockwise from top left)
Chester County Historical Society, West Chester, Pa. (3); Private collection; Rocky Hill Collection; Private collection

munity. Even when not in use, their display signified one's membership within this local group of elite Irish Quakers. The distinctive ornament of the plates and spice boxes conveyed meaning to informed observers, enabling the objects to indicate their owners' membership in the local *sensus communis*.[60] Despite their emphasis on each individual's relationship with God, Quakers also stressed the importance of social contact, particularly with those of the same religious persuasion. This group life was enacted

FIGURE 1.18
Datestone on house of
William and Margery Gregg,
built 1737, New Castle
County, Delaware.

within meeting and at home, aided by a shared
material culture.

In the case of both the spice boxes and
plates, clearly it was important to members of
the London Grove and New Garden Meetings
to convey through material goods their membership in a distinctive and close-knit community using dates and marks indicating names
and associations. Perhaps not coincidentally,
a study of Chester County datestones cites
London Grove Township as having the largest number, most in the gable ends of houses.[61]
Throughout southeastern Pennsylvania and
parts of southern New Jersey, brick houses
associated with elite Quakers (as well as stone
houses built by their German-speaking neighbors) often carried a prominent, public display
of the owners' initials and date of construction.[62] William Gregg, owner of a set of the
1738 delft plates, occupied a large brick house
just south of the current Pennsylvania border in
New Castle County, Delaware.[63] Built in 1737,
the house includes a datestone bearing his initials
and those of his wife (fig. 1.18). Gregg, a wealthy
miller, is thought to have been the original owner
of a bookstand (fig. 1.19) with an adjustable
frame. Such a stand would have been evidence
his education, literacy, and means sufficient
enough to purchase books.

English Quakers ⌒ The majority of Quakers
in Pennsylvania were of English heritage. From
the time of William Penn, they received more
desirable land grants, in part because they were
among the first to arrive. By the 1730s many
had gained significant wealth through land

investments, milling operations, and farming.
Joseph England, a prosperous farmer and miller,
immigrated from Staffordshire, England, in
1723 with his family, including his two-year-
old daughter Joanna. He acquired substantial
landholdings, including 250 acres in East
Nottingham, Chester County, and 400 acres in
New Castle County, Delaware, where he built
a gristmill on the White Clay Creek. In 1730
he joined the East Nottingham Meeting (also
known as the Brick Meeting House and located
in what is now Calvert, Maryland), and two
years later became a minister. By 1747 he had
accumulated enough wealth to build a large
house of glazed header brick. His daughter had
married John Townsend (b. 1716 in Thornbury
Township, Chester County) on December 31,
1741, at East Nottingham Meeting. The young
couple acquired a chest bearing their initials and
marriage date, which, together with the profusely
inlaid top, is the antithesis of the supposedly
plain furniture owned by Quakers (fig. 1.20).
On the front, two horses flank a central
cartouche containing the initials "I ᵀ I" over a
heart; undulating lines terminate in grapelike
clusters of eight berries. The top features a central
female figure surrounded by more line-and-
berry designs, with a sun and moon in the upper
corners and two animals at the bottom, one of
them a stag (fig. 1.21). An inlaid herringbone
border surrounds the top, front, and drawer
fronts. Removing the two drawers provides access
to a long, narrow central drawer, which in turn
conceals a small hidden drawer at the back of the
chest. The chest is supported on straight bracket
feet connected by an inverted broken-arch skirt
that, although unusual, has every indication

FIGURE 1.19
Bookstand, probably owned
by William Gregg, probably
Chester County, 1725–45.
Private collection

FIGURE I.20
Chest-over-drawers, made for John and Joanna Townsend, probably Nottingham area, Chester County, 1741. Winterthur Museum, bequest of Henry Francis du Pont

FIGURE I.21
Detail of top in fig. I.20.

of being original. As Joanna was the only one of Joseph England's daughters to marry, her father may have commissioned this elaborate chest for her as a wedding present. In 1748 she was bequeathed her father's "Negro Girl Named Ann" in addition to £10.[64]

After their marriage, John and Joanna Townsend settled in East Bradford Township, Chester County. Their ten children married members of other prominent local families, including those with the names Lamborn, Darlington, Jefferis, and Sharpless. An engraved profile portrait of an elderly John Townsend is believed to be the same John Townsend who owned the chest (fig. I.22). In 1826 descendants

FIGURE I.22
Portrait of John Townsend, drawn and engraved by Louis Lemet, Philadelphia, about 1800, inside album in fig. I.24. Winterthur Museum purchase with funds provided by the Henry Francis du Pont Collectors Circle and funds donated in honor of Anne Verplanck

FIGURE I.23

Miniature chest-over-drawers, owned by Wistar P. Brown, Chester County, 1780–1810. Rocky Hill Collection

FIGURE I.24

Silhouette album (one of two), compiled by Caroline Morris Pennock, Philadelphia, 1830–40. Winterthur Museum purchase with funds provided by the Henry Francis du Pont Collectors Circle and funds donated in honor of Anne Verplanck

FIGURE I.25

Looking glass, probably owned by Hannah (Townsend) Sharpless, labeled by John Elliott Sr., Philadelphia, 1762–67. Private collection

of John and Joanna had a family register printed to document their ancestry. According to the register, Joanna died in 1786 "at their ancient dwelling in East Bradford," and John died in 1803. The inventory of his estate includes an "Old Chest" valued at $1, in addition to limited furnishings consisting of a bed, desk-and-book-case, two chairs, and two tables.[65] A miniature walnut chest with ogee bracket feet (fig. 1.23) was likely first owned by granddaughter Lydia Painter Townsend (b. 1784), who married William H. Brown. The chest is inscribed on the underside: "Wistar P. Brown from his Grand / Mother Lydia P. Brown Pugh / Town Chester County Pa. / Bought 1812."[66]

John Townsend's profile was later compiled in the silhouette albums of Caroline Morris

Pennock (1811–82), two of about twenty such albums known that were produced mainly by members of prominent Quaker families (fig. 1.24). Although Quakers generally refrained from having portraits made, silhouettes were a popular means among Friends for preserving likenesses. From about 1800 to 1840, many Pennsylvania Quakers commissioned, exchanged, and assembled their silhouettes into albums for safekeeping and viewing, reinforcing family and community ties.[67]

In 1741 John Townsend's sister Hannah (1718–90) married Nathan Sharpless. A diminutive looking glass (fig. 1.25) bears their name and marriage date on the back, written on the German-English label of John Elliott Sr. of Philadelphia (see fig. 4.23).[68] Hannah was also the owner of an English slip-decorated dish (fig. 1.26) that descended in her family. Bearing a scene that recalls the transformation of Lot's wife into a pillar of salt, the dish may have been owned first by Hannah's parents, Joseph and Martha (Wooderson) Townsend.[69]

The distinctive, profuse inlay of the Townsend chest is highly unusual among Pennsylvania furniture—Quaker or otherwise. The only known related object is a hatbox, shaped to hold a man's tricorn hat, that features the inlaid inscription "HUGH BOYD ESQ[r]" on the top (fig. 1.27) together with grape-like clusters of berries like those found on the Townsend chest. The close relationship of the inlay on these two pieces suggests that they were made by the same hand, probably in the Nottingham area. The original owner of the hatbox is thought to have been Hugh Boyd of West Nottingham, Chester County (now Cecil County, Maryland); he was most likely Presbyterian. In his will of September 16, 1754, he mentioned his wife, Margaret, and six children: Rose McCord, Anne Meek, Jean Findly, Mary Boyd, Francis Boyd, and Alexander Boyd. Robert Finley was named as one of his executors, probably the husband of Boyd's daughter Jean. Finley was related to Irish immigrant and Presbyterian minister Rev. Samuel Finley.[70] Although Hugh Boyd signed the will with only a mark, he died possessed of "6 Old books," which suggests that he could read. His inventory includes farming implements as well as a loom, quilling wheel, great wheel (for spinning wool), and thirty-two pounds of wool. Though there is no date on the hatbox, its close relationship to the 1741 chest suggests that a date before Hugh's death in 1754 is probable.[71] Although most objects embellished with line-and-berry inlay were made for Chester County Quakers, Boyd's likely Presbyterian faith indicates that the inlay on his hatbox was probably a reflection of local preference rather than religious affiliation.

Embellished with initials, dates, inlaid decoration, or other ornamentation, objects such as wainscot chairs and spice boxes were tangible signs of membership in the highest levels of Quaker society. Although in theory all Friends were equal, in practice there was a sense of rank influenced by socioeconomic status, religious piety, gender, and age. The Quaker faith promoted a humble lifestyle that was "in the world but not of it" and censured Friends who strayed too far from this tenet and into the realm of worldliness; that did not, however, preclude the attainment of wealth as a result of honest work. The Quaker principle of plainness was not rigidly defined; its enforcement varied significantly over time and from meeting to meeting—to some degree constituting a localism unto itself. Thus, owning a finely made piece of furniture was not inherently in contradiction with Quaker beliefs, even when decoratively embellished.

FIGURE 1.26
Dish, owned by Nathan and Hannah Sharpless, made by Samuel Malkin, Burslem, Staffordshire, England, 1726. Winterthur Museum purchase with funds provided by the Henry Francis du Pont Collectors Circle

Friends who demonstrated their sincere piety in other ways, such as attending meeting, making financial contributions, and serving in leadership positions, tended to receive more leniency in subjective matters such as material goods—especially when they were wealthy enough to afford them. In the end, the spiritual state of the owner was more important than the physical appearance of the object itself.[72] Excessive displays of worldliness might

FIGURE 1.27
Hatbox, made for Hugh Boyd, probably Nottingham area, Chester County, 1745–55. Collection of Jay Robert Stiefel

at times strain Quaker ideals of humility and plainness, but such prosperity could also be interpreted as a sign of possessing good moral discipline and virtue. In contrast, poor Quaker households were often perceived as morally failing and lacking proper discipline and spirituality. The Quaker social hierarchy also tended to reward economically successful Friends with positions of social and religious leadership—including committee appointments and attendance at quarterly and yearly meetings. Thus, wealthy Friends frequently became "weighty" Friends.[73] The corporate nature of the Quaker meeting system itself created a hierarchical structure, as each congregation had ministers, elders, overseers, and a clerk—all wielding varying degrees of authority. By the mid-eighteenth century, it was apparent that the Quaker ideal of theoretical equality had practical limits and that a more stratified, class-based social order was developing.[74]

In addition to having their religious principles challenged because of economic success, Quakers in Pennsylvania were also being divided politically as a result of conflicts between Native Americans and white settlers on the frontier. Earlier in the century, James Logan, land agent for the Penn family, and the Quaker-controlled government had promoted settlement of the Pennsylvania backcountry by non-pacifist groups in order to form a buffer between the Indians and other communities. However, increasing disorder and warfare during the French and Indian War (1754–63) presented challenges to the Quakers' political control, which was further eroded by the American Revolution two decades later. With Quaker domination on the decline, people of non-Quaker backgrounds stepped into more prominent political roles. The Quaker population was also diminishing at this time, while immigration had increased the Germanic and Scots-Irish Presbyterian population. In Philadelphia, the so-called Quaker City, only about one in seven was Quaker by the 1770s. At the same time, the Religious Society of Friends was becoming stricter about enforcing discipline. In 1797 and again in 1806, the Philadelphia Yearly Meeting published revised versions of the *Rules*

of Discipline, codifying types of misconduct: marrying out of meeting or even attending a non-Quaker wedding; supporting military activities of any kind including providing supplies, paying fines, or arming oneself; failure to attend meeting; and immoral behaviors such as gambling, swearing, or excessive drinking. As the nineteenth century began, Quakerism sought to better define itself and reassert its communal solidarity by adopting concepts such as the wearing of gray or drab-colored clothing. Ultimately, continued differences about worldliness, governance, and other theological matters led to dissension within the Society of Friends, which in 1827–28 resulted in the Orthodox-Hicksite schism.[75]

Scots-Irish Presbyterians

In 1719 Philadelphia merchant Jonathan Dickinson observed, "This summer we have had 12 or 13 sayle of ships from the North of Ireland with a swarm of people."[76] Aboard these vessels were some of the first Scots-Irish immigrants to Pennsylvania—Scottish Presbyterians who, because of discrimination in their own country, had lived for some time in the northern counties of Ireland (especially Ulster) prior to leaving for America. "Scots-Irish" was a term used in colonial America, as noted by Edmund Burke in 1757: "These are chiefly Presbyterians from the Northern part of Ireland, who in America are generally called Scotch-Irish."[77] Beginning in 1718 and peaking in 1729, thousands of Ulster Presbyterians immigrated to America—more than 100,000 by 1775. Most went to New England, but many settled in Pennsylvania, where the demand for Irish linen was high. Philadelphia merchant Samuel Powel noted in 1743 that "so much linen [was made] by the back Irish inhabitants" that they sold it as far away as Rhode Island.[78] Many of these immigrants had been involved with the linen-weaving industry in northern Ireland, which had been hurt by poor harvests, severe winters, a marked decline in the linen trade, and increases in both tithes and rents as many long-term leases came up for renewal beginning in 1717.[79] Because Pennsylvania flaxseed was exported to Ulster in great quantities, a trading link for goods was already

established.[80] Reports from earlier immigrants were encouraging, such as one by James Murray, who wrote to his former minister, "This is a bonny country . . . and aw Things grows here that ever did I see grow in Ereland." Murray also noted that a shortage of labor meant "a Lass gets 4 shillings and 6 Pence a Week for spinning on the wee Wheel."[81] In addition to written communication with the old country, some Scots-Irish immigrants tangibly preserved their heritage by noting it on their gravestones.

The cemetery of the Octorara United Presbyterian Church, founded in 1753 near Quarryville, Lancaster County, contains several markers like that of James Simpson (fig. 1.28) and Thomas Alexander, noting their respective birthplaces as Scotland and Ireland. At the Donegal Presbyterian Church in Lancaster County, the tombstone of longtime minister Colin McFarquhar (d. 1822) identified him as "a native of Scotland." A similar reference can be found on a slate sundial inscribed "WEST-TOWN" on one side of the dial and "IRELAND" above the central heart (fig. 1.29), referring to either Westtown Township in Chester County or the Quaker-run school of the same name founded in 1799 by the Philadelphia Yearly Meeting. Children from many prominent Chester County Quaker families attended the school, including the Pennocks. Joseph Pennock's great-granddaughter Sarah W. Pennock (1792–1832) attended West-Town, where she stitched a needlework extract of verse. Surrounded by a simple foliate border, this piece is closely related to those worked by other young girls at the school (fig. 1.30).[82]

Early Scots-Irish settlement in Pennsylvania was initially concentrated on the western frontier of Chester and Lancaster counties, directed there by James Logan. Fearful that conflict with Native Americans was likely as European settlement expanded, Logan felt the Scots-Irish would be a valuable buffer between the pacifist Quakers and the Indians if violence broke out.[83] As he explained to Thomas Penn, "I therefore thought it might be prudent to plant a Settlement of fresh men . . . as a frontier in case of any Disturbance."[84] Discrimination and prejudices against the

Scots-Irish ran deep among the Germans and English, inflamed by newspaper stories and rumors concerning drunkenness, murder, rape, counterfeiting, theft, and general ignorance. Johann David Schoepf noted that the Germans, being "better and more orderly economists, look down with a peculiar pride and arrogance" on the Scots-Irish.[85] In western Lancaster County, place names such as Done-

FIGURE 1.28
Tombstone of James Simpson (d. 1813). Octorara United Presbyterian Church, Bart Township, Lancaster County

FIGURE 1.29
Sundial, possibly made for, or by, Benjamin Housekeeper, probably Westtown Township, Chester County, 1816. Chester County Historical Society, West Chester, Pa.

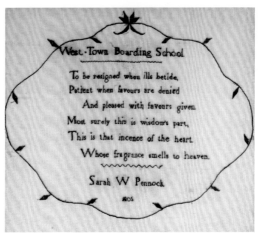

FIGURE 1.30
Sampler, by Sarah W. Pennock, Westtown Township, Chester County, 1805. Primitive Hall Foundation

gal, Londonderry, Drumore, and Colerain still in use today bear witness to the area's early settlers. The Donegal settlement—just a few miles east of the Susquehanna River—became known for the hot tempers of its inhabitants. Physical altercations, drunkenness, and other misdeeds proliferated without a court system to address them. In 1732 the Donegal Presbytery was created, which included congregations stretching from Nottingham, Brandywine, and Octorara up to Donegal, Derry, and Paxton. Finding ministers to serve these remote congregations was difficult; thus, supply ministers alternated between churches and often traveled long distances to preach.[86]

In 1723 George Gillespie, supply minister at the Donegal Presbyterian Church, wrote, "There are a great many congregations erected and new erecting; for within the space of five years . . . near to two hundred Families have come into our parts from Ireland, and more are following: They are generally Presbyterians." The Ulster immigrants favored a simpler, unadorned manner of worship, and

a less hierarchical church structure without bishops.[87] This preference was reflected in the architecture of early Presbyterian churches in Pennsylvania, which were usually well-built but plain. The stone church constructed around 1740 at Donegal features a gambrel roof and meetinghouse-style interior (fig. 1.31).[88] Among its furnishings is a walnut communion table, likely made for use in the original log church (fig. 1.32). The legs of the table feature bold, distinctive cup-and-baluster turnings connected by a turned stretcher base. Because of the remoteness of the church and early date of the table, it seems probable that it was made by a member of the congregation—possibly carpenter James Murray, who died in 1747 possessed of saws and molding planes.[89] Accompanying the table is a pewter communion service of two flagons and four two-handle cups made by William Eddon and a set of four fluted plates, or patens, made by Richard King, both of London.[90] Using this table and service, the Donegal congregation likely practiced a Scottish style of com-

FIGURE 1.31
Donegal Presbyterian Church, built about 1740, photo about 1905, Mount Joy, Lancaster County. Collection of Mr. and Mrs. Michael Emery

munion, held once or twice a year. The week prior to the service, church elders circulated among the congregation to produce a list of communicants' names and look into reports of misbehavior. The session then considered the list and called for any sinners to atone for their misdeeds before they could receive communion. Those who were deemed eligible for communion were given a token, sometimes of pewter or silver, as proof of their eligibility.[91]

By the 1740s, the Donegal settlement had begun to prosper. The minister, James Anderson, owned four enslaved servants, operated a mill and ferry service, and counted a £6 clock, chest of drawers worth £1.10, three feather beds, and £40 of books among his possessions when he died in 1740.[92] In 1739 another settler's inventory listed an oval table, six walnut chairs, four wigs, and "a walnut bed stead with a poplar board at the head of it." Thomas Wilson, who died in 1746, had an estate valued at £48 and owned a walnut table and chest; Joseph Work possessed three feather beds and three chests. James Murray owned silver buttons and a silk hat when he died in 1747 and left a bequest to his brother in Ireland.[93] Although none of these objects are known to survive, clearly there was a degree of material comfort and refinement in some Scots-Irish households even at this early date. In 1792

FIGURE I.32
Communion table of Donegal Presbyterian Church, probably Lancaster County, 1720–45; pewter communion service, London, 1720–35, 1745–75. Donegal Presbyterian Church, Mount Joy, Pa.

FIGURE I.33

Portrait of Eliza and Rebecca Wilson, by William Clarke, possibly Lancaster County, 1792. Collection of Stephen and Dolores Smith

a portrait of Eliza and Rebecca Wilson was painted by William Clarke (fig. 1.33). According to family tradition, their father, the Reverend James Wilson, was a Presbyterian minister in Lancaster County.[94] The portrait miniature worn by one of the girls in the painting may well be James's image. Around 1807, Rebecca married William Ramsey (b. about 1763 in East Nottingham). The couple lived in Bart Township, Lancaster County, and the portrait descended in their family.[95] Nothing in the painting hints at the Scots-Irish Presbyterian heritage of the girls; their filmy white dresses were fashionable at the time, and the unusual tall black hats resemble, if anything, a Welsh style of female headdress.[96] The family of James Wilson, like that of other ministers, was part of a clerical elite not totally representative of how their parishioners lived; thus, care must be taken not to infer too much from objects such as the Wilson portrait.

An extraordinary quilt made in 1787 by nineteen-year-old Rachel Mackey (1768–1841) of New London Township, Chester County, also speaks to the lack of distinction between objects made and owned by Quakers and Presbyterians. Five crewelwork panels worked by Rachel for the center of the quilt (fig. 1.34) relate it to a distinct group of embroidered pieces made by young Quaker women in Chester County, including Lydia Hoopes (1771); Elizabeth Jefferis (1777); and Sarah Smedley (1788, see fig. 3.17). Rachel was the daughter of David and Agnes (Correy/Curry) Mackey; her grandfather John Mackey (McKee) was a delegate to the Constitutional Convention of 1776. Her great-uncle was the Reverend Francis Allison, an Irish immigrant and Presbyterian minister who founded New London Academy, the forerunner of the University of Delaware.[97]

For most Scots-Irish Presbyterians, their frequent mobility and lack of financial wherewithal during the initial years of settlement no doubt affected the extent of their material possessions, as few objects can be documented to these early inhabitants. Life on the frontier had challenges that took precedence over niceties beyond the basics of material goods, and the remoteness of communities such as Donegal left many vulnerable to Indian raids.[98] What possessions early settlers did have were likely centered on linen production. Dr. Alexander Hamilton, a physician trained in Edinburgh who kept a journal of his travels in Pennsylvania in 1744, observed that many Scots-Irish raised flax, "and in every house here the women have two or three spinning wheels a going."[99] Probate inventories often listed meager possessions along with substantial linen yardage and spinning accoutrements, though few households had looms.[100] Even decades after their arrival, Scots-Irish homes may have had less furniture in general than those of their English and German neighbors. Alexander Marshall, who was raised in a Scots-Irish household in western Chester County, recalled from his youth around 1810, "The smaller children sat on the floor to eat their meals until they were large enough to stand at the table and handle a knife and fork or spoon, and when they had grown large enough to sit on a common chair and eat like other people, they were permitted to do so at the table."[101]

FIGURE 1.34
Detail of quilt, by Rachel Mackey, New London Township, Chester County, 1787. Rocky Hill Collection

Although the extent to which Irish material culture influenced the Ulster Presbyterians is not well understood, studies of Irish furniture suggest that even wealthier farmers had sparse furnishings. Oral histories note that tenant farmers feared that buying even a single piece of furniture might encourage landlords to demand rent or seize the furniture as payment. Tables were conspicuously absent from households; instead, a long flat basket was commonly used as a movable dining surface. In some houses a wooden baking board doubled as a table top, which evolved into "falling tables"—essentially a board hinged to the wall. When in use, the board would be propped up by a single leg hinged to the underside. In addition to a lack of Irish vernacular furniture, common Irish furniture forms also tend to be indistinct from those used by other ethnic groups, making them difficult to distinguish.[102]

This was also likely the case in Pennsylvania. An impressive wainscot armchair (fig. 1.35) owned by Thomas and Elizabeth Willson of West Fallowfield Township, Chester County, closely resembles wainscot chairs made for Quaker families. Unlike other known examples of this form, however, the Willson chair is inlaid with a date, "1739 40," and the names of the owners on the crest rail. Though much of the inlaid wood in the names is now gone, the carved-out channels that held it show that the lettering was unusually fine and script-like. Thomas Willson was most likely Presbyterian; his parents, Joseph and Janet (McCrea) Willson, were Irish immigrants, and the co-executor of his will was Upper Octorara Presbyterian Church minister Adam Sterling. The inventory of Willson's belongings, taken in 1766, includes "9 new Chairs & 5 old" valued at £1.7.6; "1 large and 2 small Chairs" worth £0.5.6"; "a true history of the Church of Scotland"; and "a parcle of Carpenter tools & Sundries."[103] It is therefore possible Willson was connected with the woodworking trade. In addition, his sister Margaret married joiner William Dickey of Upper Oxford Township, Chester County.[104]

Relatively little extant furniture is known that can definitely be associated with the Scots-Irish, though objects such as the Willson armchair and a tall-case clock made for James McDowell of Chester County (see fig. 2.77) document furniture owned by wealthier Scots-Irish. High mobility, minimal economic means, and the instability of frontier life have continued to the paucity of identifiable pieces. In 1759 the Presbyterian Synod of Pennsylvania observed of its own people: "The Inhabitants are inconstant and unsettled, and are always shifting their Habitations, either from a Love of variety, or from the fair Prospect of more commodious Settlements on the Frontiers."[105] By the mid-1700s, many Scots-Irish were moving even farther westward and south, down the Great Wagon Road into the Shenandoah Valley of Virginia. By 1750 the Donegal area had nearly as many German-speaking inhabitants as it did Scots-Irish, comprising a wide range of religious faiths and European origins.

GERMAN-SPEAKING PEOPLE

Defining the Pennsylvania German community that evolved from 1683 into the early 1800s is fraught with challenges, as the German-speaking settlers were extraordinarily diverse in their European origins and religious beliefs. Germany itself did not exist yet in the sense of a unified nation-state but was divided into smaller duchies, principalities, and kingdoms. The presence of strong regional dialects made even the language the immigrants spoke an uncertain commonality. Most immigrants came from the Palatinate region of southwestern Germany, traveling via Rotterdam at the mouth of the Rhine River (see fig. 1.3). The vast majority, approximately 90 percent, were Lutheran or Reformed. About 10 percent were divided into sectarian groups that included the Mennonites, Amish, Schwenkfelders, Moravians, and Brethren or Dunkards (so-called because of their practice of full-immersion baptism).[106] During the seventeenth and eighteenth centuries, the Pietist movement became influential. It encouraged individuals to make Christianity part of their everyday lives by stressing the importance of personal conversion, daily Bible study, and religious experience. Pietism was taken to its most intense levels by several movements that would have an impact on settlement in Penn-sylvania, in particular the Moravians and the Society of Ephrata. The diversity of religions practiced by the German-speaking immigrants was noted by former Pennsylvania Governor George Thomas in a letter to the Anglican bishop of Exeter in 1748: "The Germans have imported with them all the religious whim-sies of their country, and . . . have sub-divided

since their arrival."[107] Ministers such as Henry Muhlenberg, who was sent from Germany in 1742 to organize the scattered Lutheran churches, were appalled at the lack of order and chaotic fragmentation of their fellow Germans in the region.

Over time, the disparate Germanic popu-lation began forging a shared identity that combined elements of their European heri-

FIGURE 1.35
Wainscot armchair, made for Thomas and Elizabeth Will-son, probably West Fallow-field Township area, Chester County, about 1740. Collection of Dale E. Hunt

tage with their experiences in America. In 1772 Muhlenberg remarked, "The old Germans, who are otherwise discerning, spoil the English language and in time produce a third language, which is neither English nor German."[108] Having emigrated thirty years earlier, Muhlenberg had lived among the Pennsylvania Germans and was a keen observer of daily life. His commentary reflected a shift among the descendants of the original immigrants to Pennsylvania. At the time of the 1790 census, German-speaking people constituted about 33 percent of the population, proportionately less than at midcentury, when immigration peaked. People of English heritage constituted 35 percent, while the Scots-Irish accounted for about 23 percent. In southeastern Pennsylvania, the concentration of German speakers was higher—about 40 percent—compared to 29 percent English and 18 percent Scots-Irish.[109] Given the almost equal number of Germans and English in the state, it seems inevitable that these cultures would have had an influence on each other. Though Germans retained significant aspects of their heritage—such as foodways, architectural building practices, and clothing styles—over time their culture was changing, incorporating some elements from English-speaking neighbors while adapting to new conditions in America. Some historians have argued that German-speaking immigrants had essentially three choices: complete rejection of, or complete assimilation into, the supposedly dominant English culture or a more gradual assimilation or "controlled acculturation" in which they adopted some elements of English culture while maintaining other Germanic ones.[110] Recent scholars have challenged these assumptions and put forth a different interpretation, arguing that the Germanic culture in southeastern Pennsylvania evolved into something new and different following the American Revolution—something that was "neither English nor German."[111]

Early German Furniture
Most German-speaking immigrants made the ocean voyage to the New World with their belongings in a chest; however, fewer than

ten chests are known to survive. These, such as the one owned by the Amweg (Amwäg) family (fig. 1.36), were built for travel, with corners reinforced by wrought-iron straps to protect against breakage and theft. The Amweg chest retains two paper labels, one inside the top and one on the till, identifying it as the property of the family with the date 1737 (fig. 1.37).[112] Hans Martin Amweg settled in Rapho Township, Lancaster County, where he died in 1768. In his will, in addition to the usual widow's thirds, he left his wife, Barbara, a bequest of £30, "together with my Bed and Bedstead (in my Chamber) with all its furniture." The inventory of his estate includes "Two old Cheests" valued at £1.10.0, one of which was likely this immigration chest.[113]

Unfortunately, immigrant chests were subject to mishaps. In 1749 the *Pennsylvania Berichte* reported that a ship had arrived several weeks before carrying a number of chests that had been broken open. Repeated incidents such as this prompted Germantown printer Christopher Sauer in 1755 to write to Governor Robert Morris, decrying the difficulties of immigrants in transporting themselves and their belongings. To maximize profits and space, ship captains would first fill their vessels with passengers and goods for resale, sometimes leaving the passengers' chests behind or sending them on other ships. Sauer noted: "The poor people depended upon their chests, wherein was some provision . . . as dried-apples, pears, plums, mustard, medicines, vinegar, brandy, gammons [ham or bacon], butter, clothing, shirts and other necessary linens, money and whatever they brought with them; and when their chests were left behind, or were shipped in some other vessel they had lack of nourishment."[114] The inventory of Lucinda Keyser, an immigrant who died shortly after her arrival in Philadelphia aboard the *Neptune* in 1753, consistes of her "Chist" valued at two shillings and, presumably, its contents: clothing, bedding, a psalm book and Bible, copper kettle, tin basin, and two earthen pots.[115] Hans Durstein, who came with his three children and died shortly after his arrival in 1749, brought with him some 800

needles, 12 small iron kettles, linen yardage, and other goods totaling more than £75.[116] In 1773 John Frederick Whitehead reported going into the town of Rotterdam with his cabin-mates prior to disembarking "to buy ourselves a Chest and Tea Kettle, Spoons and Utensels, and also Sugar, Tea, Coffee &c."[117]

Along with precious items such as Bibles, books, and personal documents, chests continued to be useful in America and retained sentimental value. The inventory of Henry Wireman of Buckingham Township, Bucks County, taken in 1781, includes "a large Sea Chest" valued at £1.5.[118] In 1803 George Neiman of Douglas Township, Montgomery County, bequeathed to his granddaughter Polly his "chest, &c. which came from Germany."[119] Although most documentation of furniture mentions only chests, it is possible that wealthier immigrants may have also brought larger furnishings. Sometimes clock movements were imported from Europe, with cases made for them in Pennsylvania (see fig. 3.36). During the Mennonite immigration of the mid- to late nineteenth century, the objects most commonly brought continued to be chests and clocks.[120]

Although the early immigrant chests speak to the presence of some European-made furniture in Pennsylvania, surviving examples bear

little relationship to the more typical household furniture made here. Most chests made in Pennsylvania lack the distinguishing features of those from Germany, such as paneled tops and bottom boards that extend beyond the sides to form the base molding, although their construction details often show Germanic techniques. In the absence of imported models, craftsmen had to rely on their memories of furniture forms, decoration, and construction. One of the challenges about furniture research in southeastern Pennsylvania is that few objects associated with German settlers survive from before the 1760s. The earliest known example is a tall-case clock (fig. 1.38) with the date "1740" inlaid on the top rail of the bonnet door frame. The works are an earlier European lantern-clock movement, which did not require a case and probably functioned

FIGURE 1.36
Chest, owned by Hans Martin Amweg and family, probably Germany, about 1737. 1719 Hans Herr House & Museum

FIGURE 1.37
Detail of label on underside of top in fig. 1.36.

for many years without one.[121] Inlaid on the door of the case are the initials "I M C" along with foliate designs.

Closely related to the inlay on the clock is that on a *Kleiderschrank* (clothes cupboard), or schrank, dated 1741 (fig. 1.39). Unfortunately, neither piece has survived with a family history, making it impossible to assign them to any region with certainty. Because of their sophistication and early date, however, they may have been made by a German craftsman in Germantown or Philadelphia. The polychrome inlaid birds on the doors of the schrank (fig. 1.40) relate in style, though by a different hand, to inlaid birds on two tall-clock cases of 1745–55 with Germanic construction features and movements by Augustin Neisser of Germantown and Joseph Wills of Philadelphia.[122]

The schrank comes apart into separate pieces: cornice, base, two doors, side panels, and backboards, allowing it to be more easily maneuvered through narrow hallways, staircases, and doors. The cornice and base are each a separate piece, to which the sides are secured with large wedged tenons. Pintle hinges on the doors allow them to be removed. The interior, like most schranks, is divided so that one side has pegs for hanging clothing, and the other has shelves for storing folded textiles. Locking drawers at the bottom provide additional, secure storage for small objects. The four interchangeable drawers are inlaid with the date "1741" and the initials "M I" and "A M." Most schranks bearing names or initials are for the husband, or both spouses; very few have only a woman's name.[123] Following this logic, the most likely order of the initials on the 1741 schrank is "MI AM." In keeping with the use of initials to represent abbreviated forms of full names on other pieces of furniture (such as a schrank inlaid "DV HS" for David Hottenstein; see fig. 3.33), these initials most likely stand for a Michael _____. One possibility is Michael Amenzetter (Omensetter) of Germantown, whose name appears in the records of St. Michael's Lutheran Church in 1756.[124] Another candidate is Michael Amweg (Omwake), a weaver in Cocalico Township, Lancaster County, who died in 1779. A prominent member of the Muddy Creek Reformed Church, Amweg's estate was valued at £1049.10.3 and

included a loom worth £80 and various woodworking tools. No schrank is listed, but the furniture in the inventory is limited, which may indicate he was living with one of his children.[125]

Probably due to their cost and substantial size, schranks were usually made for well-established and financially secure households—not at the time of marriage as is often assumed.[126] Chests were the more common storage form for young people, acquired during their teenage years for keeping personal effects and later used when setting up housekeeping. Schranks were used in Pennsylvania German households into the nineteenth century, but declined in popularity as built-in closets and chests of drawers became popular.[127]

In addition to the 1740 clock and 1741 schrank, about a half-dozen other pieces of Pennsylvania German furniture are known dated prior to the 1760s; nearly all have been associated with Lancaster County, in most cases through their design characteristics and not family history.[128] A tall-case clock made in 1745 for Andreas Beierle (Andrew Beyerle) and his wife, Catharina, is a rare exception (fig. 1.41); their names and the date are carved on the bonnet door and case. Beierle was a baker and innholder as well as carpenter by family tradition. Doubtless the work of a German-trained émigré craftsman, the carved ornament on the clock reflects its early date and close ties to European precedents. The carving on the case is an unusual combination of motifs. Two cherubs, or *putti*, grace either side of the hood, flanking a central finial, now missing. On the upper part of the pendulum door is a baroque floral design and glass bull's-eye. Beneath this are three carved motifs representing Beierle's trade as a baker: at the top is a pretzel (a traditional baker's symbol), followed by two *Manchet* (lemon-shape rolls) and milk bread, a special roll that is baked in pairs; both types represent the finest sort of white bread eaten at the table.[129] The Germanic technique of relief carving from the solid wood used on the Beierle clock, which would reach its zenith in Lancaster rococo furniture several decades later, is an important link between Old and New World craft traditions.[130] The clock contains an eight-day English movement that appears to be an old replacement; it likely had a thirty-hour German movement originally.[131]

FIGURE 1.38

(*opposite*) Tall-case clock, movement probably England, 1680–1700, case possibly Germantown, Philadelphia County, 1740. Rocky Hill Collection

FIGURE 1.39

Schrank, possibly Germantown, Philadelphia County, 1741. Rocky Hill Collection

FIGURE 1.40

Detail of inlay on door of fig. 1.39.

Born in Rohrbach im Kraichgau, Germany in 1713, Andreas immigrated in 1738 on the *Charming Nancy.* He settled in Lancaster by 1743, when he and his wife, Maria Catharina, are recorded as the sponsors for two baptisms at Trinity Lutheran Church. Following her death, he married Beatrix Kuhl, with whom he had four children. After her death he married Phoebe Gulden. In 1754 the family left Lancaster for Westmoreland County. Prior to their departure he sold the contents of his tavern to Bernhard Hubley for £100, including: eight bedsteads, "One large walnut press . . . four long tables and benches; One dozen of chairs . . . Two dozen of bakers tinns . . . [and] Four dozen of small and large looking glasses."

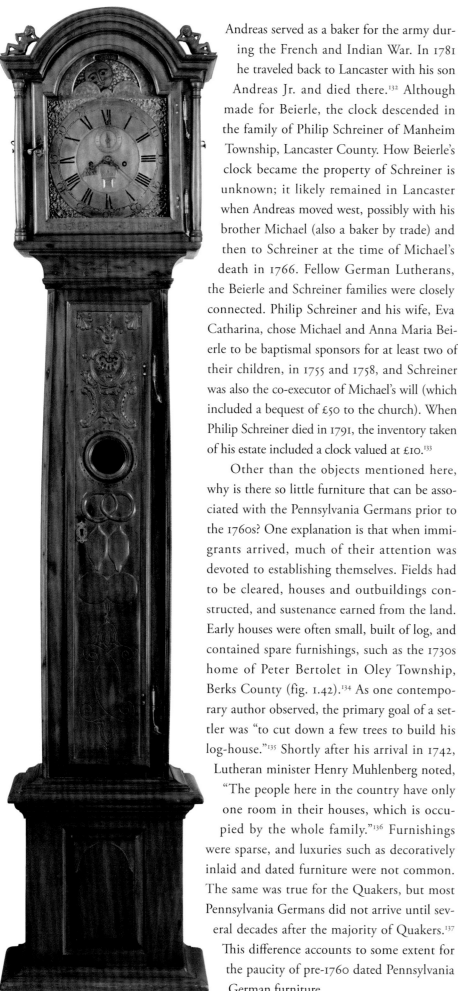

Andreas served as a baker for the army during the French and Indian War. In 1781 he traveled back to Lancaster with his son Andreas Jr. and died there.[132] Although made for Beierle, the clock descended in the family of Philip Schreiner of Manheim Township, Lancaster County. How Beierle's clock became the property of Schreiner is unknown; it likely remained in Lancaster when Andreas moved west, possibly with his brother Michael (also a baker by trade) and then to Schreiner at the time of Michael's death in 1766. Fellow German Lutherans, the Beierle and Schreiner families were closely connected. Philip Schreiner and his wife, Eva Catharina, chose Michael and Anna Maria Beierle to be baptismal sponsors for at least two of their children, in 1755 and 1758, and Schreiner was also the co-executor of Michael's will (which included a bequest of £50 to the church). When Philip Schreiner died in 1791, the inventory taken of his estate included a clock valued at £10.[133]

Other than the objects mentioned here, why is there so little furniture that can be associated with the Pennsylvania Germans prior to the 1760s? One explanation is that when immigrants arrived, much of their attention was devoted to establishing themselves. Fields had to be cleared, houses and outbuildings constructed, and sustenance earned from the land. Early houses were often small, built of log, and contained spare furnishings, such as the 1730s home of Peter Bertolet in Oley Township, Berks County (fig. 1.42).[134] As one contemporary author observed, the primary goal of a settler was "to cut down a few trees to build his log-house."[135] Shortly after his arrival in 1742, Lutheran minister Henry Muhlenberg noted, "The people here in the country have only one room in their houses, which is occupied by the whole family."[136] Furnishings were sparse, and luxuries such as decoratively inlaid and dated furniture were not common. The same was true for the Quakers, but most Pennsylvania Germans did not arrive until several decades after the majority of Quakers.[137] This difference accounts to some extent for the paucity of pre-1760 dated Pennsylvania German furniture.

Mennonites

Among the earliest German-speaking people to arrive in America were the Mennonites, who came largely from the cantons of Bern and Zurich in Switzerland and from southern Germany.[138] Widely respected today for their peaceful and plain lifestyles, Mennonites were then viewed by many as dangerous radicals. Thousands suffered imprisonment, torture, and death because of their practice of baptizing adults rather than infants; their belief in the separation of church and state; and their nonresistant practice of turning the other cheek. Mennonites were also called Anabaptists, or re-baptizers, in reference to many being re-baptized as adults after leaving the state churches in which they had been baptized as infants. Known as Mennists and eventually Mennonites, after former Catholic priest Menno Simons, who became involved with the Anabaptist movement in the Netherlands in 1536, many had moved north from Switzerland into the German Palatinate. Hardships continued during the War of Palatine Succession (1688–97), when the region was overrun by the French army and concessions that had been granted by King Ludwig ceased with his death in 1685.[139]

On October 6, 1683, a group of German Mennonites and Quakers from Krefeld (who converted during a visit by William Penn to the Palatinate in 1677) landed in Philadelphia aboard the *Concord*, along with Francis Daniel Pastorius, agent for the Frankfurt Land Company. This mixed group established Germantown some six miles northwest of Philadelphia. The first perma-

FIGURE I.41
(*opposite*) Tall-case clock, made for Andreas and Catharina Beierle, movement (replaced) by Edward Sanders, Pool, England, 1730–65, case probably Lancaster, Lancaster County, 1745. Private collection

FIGURE I.42
House of Peter Bertolet, built 1730–40, Oley Township, Berks County. Daniel Boone Homestead, Pennsylvania Historical and Museum Commission

FIGURE I.43
Detail of clock dial in fig. 1.44.

FIGURE I.44
Tall-case clock, movement by George Miller, case by William Bomberger, 1765, Germantown, Philadelphia County. Collection of James L. Price

nent German settlement in North America, Germantown soon became a diverse community that attracted people of various religious persuasions and ethnic backgrounds.[140] Most settlers were artisans and craftsmen, primarily linen weavers but also tailors, carpenters, and shoemakers. As time progressed, more Mennonites joined the settlement, including Dutch papermaker William Rittenhouse, who in 1690 established the first paper mill in America. By the mid-1700s, Germantown was a flourishing settlement of merchants and craftsmen, among them clockmaker George Miller. His clock movements are often distinguished by their creative and skillfully engraved brass dials featuring unusual scenes such as one with a military encampment and bust of General James Wolfe, hero of Quebec. One of Miller's thirty-hour movements (fig. 1.43) has a dial with an engraved design of a pitcher and cann flanking the date aperture, from which flowers and foliage are growing. At the top is a pair of birds. The walnut case of this clock (fig. 1.44), which retains its original ogee bracket feet and sarcophagus top with bulbous finials, was made in 1765 by William Bomberger of Germantown—rare documentation provided by a piece of paper found inside the clock that notes his name, date, and location.[141]

In the early 1700s, some of the Germantown Mennonites moved about fifteen miles north and established a new settlement called Skippack in what later became Montgomery County.[142] In 1710 eight Swiss-German Mennonite families—including the Mylins, Kendigs, Millers, Oberholtzers, and Herrs—received a 10,000-acre

FIGURE 1.45
House of Christian Herr, built 1719, West Lampeter Township, Lancaster County. 1719 Hans Herr House & Museum

FIGURE 1.46
Sampler, by Elisabeth Waner, Warwick (now Penn) Township, Lancaster County, 1817–20. Winterthur Museum

FIGURE 1.47
(opposite, top left)
Hanging cupboard, from the Jacob Musser house, built 1740–50, near Creswell, Manor Township, Lancaster County. Collection of John J. Snyder, Jr.

FIGURE 1.48
(opposite, top right)
Hanging cupboard, made for Jacob Strickler, attributed to Johannes Spitler, Shenandoah (now Page) County, Virginia, about 1800. Collection of Jane and Gerald Katcher

land grant near the Pequea Creek and Conestoga River (now Lancaster County), where the fertile soil, ample water, and level land led to great prosperity. In 1719 Christian Herr, a Mennonite minister and leading figure in the community, built a substantial stone house for his family that was also used for worship services until 1849 (fig. 1.45). The stone lintel above the front door was inscribed with his initials, "C H" "H R" and the date "1719."[143] Ten years later, the Conestoga settlement had grown to such an extent that the

Pennsylvania government created a new county, Lancaster, out of western Chester County. In 1731 a road connecting Philadelphia and Lancaster was begun, and Lancaster soon boasted a bustling outdoor market of its own, supplied and patronized by local farmers and merchants.[144]

Although Mennonite culture is often described as plain, as one commentator noted in 1770, this term more aptly describes their "great plainness of speech and dress" and use of private homes or simple meetinghouses for worship than it does their material culture.[145] Anabaptist theology did not discourage art; in fact, there is precedence in Mennonite history for the use of art to promote Anabaptist values in ways that connect tangible objects with particular values—such as their needlework and fraktur art.[146] Colorful samplers boldly embellished with birds, flowers, animals, and other motifs from nature were made by Mennonite women. Like the sampler made around 1817–20 by Elisabeth Waner of Warwick (now Penn) Township, Lancaster County (fig. 1.46), many contain the capital letters "OEH-BDDE" stitched in a circle, representing the phrase *O edel Herz bedenk dein End* (O noble heart, bethink your end), a common sentiment in Mennonite art reminding one to be prepared for death.[147] This expression is also frequently found on Mennonite fraktur. Because the ubiquitous birth and baptismal certificates made by their Lutheran and Reformed neighbors were of little use to the Mennonites, as they did not practice infant baptism, Mennonite fraktur largely relate to their parochial school system. They include such types as the *Vorschrift* or writing sample, which features a biblical verse or hymn followed by the alphabet and numeral systems. Mennonite schools were not strictly denominational. Children and schoolmasters of varying faiths were welcome, such as Lutheran Johann Adam Eyer, who in 1779 began teaching in the Mennonite schools of Perkasie and Deep Run in Bucks County. Eyer was also a gifted fraktur artist who made bookplates, writing samples, tune books, and other manuscript works for his students.[148]

Surviving furniture with solid histories of ownership in Mennonite families reveals that those who could afford to did own items of the

finest quality—sometimes with a high degree of embellishment. A walnut hanging cupboard (fig. 1.47) from the 1740s Jacob Musser house in Manor Township, Lancaster County, features a bold cornice and narrow double-fielded panel door above a small drawer with heavy molded edge. This cupboard is unusual in that the interior contains numerous small drawers in addition to the more typical shelf or two, but its basic form is one that was popular among Pennsylvania German families. A hanging cupboard of a different sort, with painted decoration of a leaping stag on the door (fig. 1.48), descended in the family of Jacob Strickler (1770–1842), who lived in the Massanutten settlement of Shenandoah (now Page) County, Virginia.[149] A Mennonite minister and fraktur artist, Strickler made a colorful drawing for himself in 1794 (fig. 1.49) on which he wrote: "Paper is my field. The quill is my plow, therefore I am so clever. The ink is my seed with which I write my name, Jacob Strickler."[150] The cupboard is attributed to Johannes Spitler (1774–1837), a fellow Mennonite who lived on a farm adjoining Strickler's along Mill Creek and was a

relative by marriage. In 1801 Spitler made a tall-case clock for Strickler embellished with both of their names beneath the hood.[151] The brilliant color of the cupboard and fraktur presents a different aspect of Mennonite arts, in contrast with

FIGURE 1.49
Drawing, by Jacob Strickler, Shenandoah (now Page) County, Virginia, 1794. Winterthur Museum, bequest of Henry Francis du Pont

the plain aesthetic so often assumed to have predominated. Small painted items were also popular; three distinctive groups illustrate this point.

In the Bucks County community of Deep Run, approximately two dozen objects dated in the 1790s that are signed by, or attributed to, John Drissell bear colorful, exuberantly painted decoration. Although little is known about Drissell, he is thought to be the carpenter Johannes Drissell (1762–1846) who attended the East Swamp Mennonite Meeting of Milford Township, Bucks County.[152] His work includes small looms for weaving tape (a narrow ribbon), slide-lid boxes for storing personal effects, salt boxes, and diminutive hanging cupboards. Many of these items were inscribed with the name of their original owner, the date, and Drissell's signature, often followed by the notation "his hand and pen." Anna Stauffer's tape loom (fig. 1.50), dated May 2, 1795, features polychrome painted floral designs and chip-carved decoration on the heddle. As Anna wove

tape on her loom, this decoration would have faced her and served as a tangible reminder of her membership in the local Mennonite community. Although paint-decorated tape looms are largely unknown elsewhere in southeastern Pennsylvania, five examples can be attributed to Drissell and were a unique part of this community's material consciousness. No two are the same size, suggesting that Drissell did not use a pattern or template. The salt box he made for Anne Leterman in 1797 has a hinged top and sides with tulip decoration (fig. 1.51). A large hole near the top of the backboard enabled it to be hung on the wall, while the extended backboard and pendant drop allowed the box to also stand on a table. Not all of Drissell's products were made for females; several do bear the names of male owners. A large slide-lid box made for Jacob Rohr is identified as a *Schreibkistlein*, or little writing chest, in a poem that Drissell painted on the top (fig. 1.52). A hidden drawer inside is accessed by removing the lid and sliding the end panel. The small hanging cupboard on which Drissell painted the name "Catharine Stauffer" and date "1800" (fig. 1.53) relates closely to one inscribed for Abraham Stauffer that bears the same date. Both cupboards have a glass door and interior shelf with cut-out slot to hold a set of teaspoons.[153]

In Lancaster County two distinct groups of painted wooden objects speak to the presence of decidedly non-plain objects among Mennonites there as well. Farmer Jonas Weber (1810–76) of East Earl and later Leacock Townships produced dozens of diminutive, paint-decorated boxes, cradles, chests, and other items

from about 1835 to 1855. Many were for family members, including his daughters and nieces. Two miniature chests (fig. 1.54) are typical of his painted decoration on this form, which often show a stylized house flanked by trees on the front. The feet on the chests, which are carved from square blocks of wood and attached with wooden pins to the underside, are another common feature on Weber's work. The hardware is simple, consisting of thin wire hinges and a tinned sheet-iron hasp. Smaller boxes by Weber have similar hardware but lack feet and are typically painted with floral motifs.[154] Another plentiful group of small boxes associated with Lancaster County features black grounds with brilliant red, white, yellow, and green decoration. Most have floral decoration on the tops and sides, although a number have small buildings painted on them as well. Related to Weber's boxes in their simple construction and hardware, these objects are known in the antiques world as "Bucher" boxes because of a misinterpretation of the name, H. Bucher, painted on one of the tops (fig. 1.55). Bucher was actually the owner of the box, not the maker. Most of the boxes are square, though some oval bentwood examples are known. Some bear initials or names, such as Liebelsperger, Roudenbush, and Keim, but few have a documented provenance. One with the initials "C H" on the top was owned by Christian Herr (1772–1846) of West Lampeter Township;

it held the deeds for the family farm. Another box, owned by the Muddy Creek Lutheran Church in Lancaster County, was used to store permits for burial plots.[155]

Ephrata

The Society of Ephrata, later known as the Ephrata Cloister, was founded in 1732 by Conrad Beissel (1691–1768), a radical Pietist mystic who advocated self-denial through fasting, limited sleep, celibacy, and plain dress as the means to spiritual enlightenment. A native of Eberbach am Neckar, Germany, Beissel immigrated in 1720 to Pennsylvania, where he spent a year in Germantown before joining a Brethren settlement in the Conestoga area of Lancaster County. In 1724 he became the leader of this group, but his extremist religious views soon resulted in a schism. Beissel and his followers moved several miles north and established a

FIGURE 1.53
Hanging cupboard, made for Catharine Stauffer, attributed to John Drissell, Lower Milford Township, Bucks County, 1800. Collection of Stephen and Susan Babinsky

FIGURE 1.54
Miniature chests, made for Isaac Messner and Jonas Weber, attributed to Jonas Weber, Leacock Township, Lancaster County, 1835–55 (*left*), 1845 (*right*). Winterthur Museum, bequest of Henry Francis du Pont (*left*); Collection of Mr. and Mrs. Paul Flack (*right*)

FIGURE 1.55
Box, made for H. Bucher, Lancaster County, 1800–1840. Winterthur Museum, bequest of Henry Francis du Pont

FIGURE 1.56

Saron (Sisters House, *left*), built 1743, and *Saal* (Meetinghouse, *right*), built 1741, Ephrata, Lancaster County. Ephrata Cloister, Pennsylvania Historical and Museum Commission

FIGURE 1.57

Der Blutige Schau-Platz oder Märtyrer Spiegel (The Bloody Theater; or, Martyrs' Mirror), printed at Ephrata, Lancaster County, 1748–49. Printed Book and Periodical Collection, Winterthur Library

monastic community named Ephrata (meaning "plentiful" in Hebrew) on the banks of the Cocalico Creek. Between 1735 and 1746, eight buildings were erected at Ephrata to accommodate the group's celibate Brothers and Sisters as well as householders (married couples who dissolved their unions to join the Society).[156] Of these structures, only the *Saron* (Sisters House) and *Saal* (Meetinghouse) remain (fig. 1.56). The *Saron* was built with a central dividing wall to house both men and women but was remodeled in 1745 for the celibate Sisters. This structure of clapboard over hewn logs, measuring about 70 by 30 feet, exudes a strong Germanic character with its steeply pitched roof and small, randomly placed windows. Attached to the *Saron* is the *Saal*, built in 1741 and used for worship. The Ephrata sisterhood was responsible for food preparation and textile-related work; the brothers farmed their 200 acres and operated a print shop as well as grist, paper, saw, fulling, and oil mills. One of the most noted products of the Ephrata print shop was *Der Blutige Schau-Platz oder Märtyrer Spiegel* (The Bloody Theater; or, Martyrs' Mirror), a book about early Christian and Anabaptist persecution compiled by Mennonite elder Tieleman Jansz van Braght and published in Dutch in Amsterdam in 1660 (fig. 1.57). In 1745 a group of Pennsylvania Mennonites commissioned a German-language translation of the book from Ephrata, which took more than three years to complete. At 1,512 pages, it was

the largest volume printed in colonial America; 1,300 copies were produced.[157] Traveler Johann David Schoepf noted that Ephrata manufactured its own woolen and linen cloth as well as leather, parchment, and "wax-lights, artificial flowers, and other small works and embroideries" made by the Sisters for sale to visitors. "All manner of crafts are carried on at Ephrata," he wrote, "diligently and skilfully."[158] Devoted to work and prayer, Ephrata members were permitted one vegetarian meal and six hours of sleep a day—which was interrupted by two hours of prayer and meditation at midnight. According to Schoepf, "Only sick persons lie on beds; all others, on hard boards with a block for pillow . . . these buildings are divided into cells, each large enough for one person; without ornament, but neat and cleanly."[159]

The *Saron* had common areas for work and food preparation on each level surrounded by individual chambers. These smaller rooms measured on average 6 by 10 feet and were sparsely furnished with a wooden bench and headrest, a shelf with peg rail, a small closet consisting of sides and no fixed door, and a hanging cupboard with a single door on wooden hinges (fig. 1.58). Although made of tulip-poplar, there is no evidence that the cupboards were originally painted. Several survive in situ within the *Saron* and were likely used for the storage of devotional books and personal possessions. Furniture made for the Society's members was utilitarian and functional—featuring simple wooden hardware and nailed rather than dovetail construction. It was not entirely plain, however, as evidenced by the gracefully curved sides of the hanging cupboard. Although there is no documentation that Ephrata had a nailery, the plentiful nails found in the construction of their furniture and buildings suggests access to one or the ability to purchase nails in great quantity. Even large doors in buildings had similar wooden pintle hinges. A three-door standing cupboard is one of two to survive at Ephrata (fig. 1.59); the paint and the molding around the doors were probably added later. The original function and location of these three-door versions is unclear although they doubtlessly were made for use as Ephrata. Records of the early inhabitants at Ephrata are scarce. One of the householders, Sigmund Landert, was an experienced carpenter involved in many of the construction projects. Celibate Brother Heinrich

FIGURE 1.58
Hanging cupboard, Ephrata, Lancaster County, 1740–60. Ephrata Cloister, Pennsylvania Historical and Museum Commission

(Ezechiel Sangmeister) and Brother Amos (Jan Miley) were also trained woodworkers. These men may have made the furnishings as well.[160] The austerity of the buildings and furnishings

FIGURE 1.59
Three-door cupboard, Ephrata, Lancaster County, 1740–60. Ephrata Cloister, Pennsylvania Historical and Museum Commission

contrasted with the elaborately decorated manuscripts produced at Ephrata, including large wall texts (fig. 1.60) containing religious verse and smaller examples hung in dormitory rooms that commemorated previous occupants. Decorated hymnals were also made, and some were presented as gifts to outsiders (fig. 1.61). Such items may have provided a degree of visual relief to the otherwise plainness of life at Ephrata.

Due to the uniqueness of its material culture and lifestyle, Ephrata attracted numerous visitors, as it does today. Its influence, however, was never widespread, although it did inspire the founding of a second settlement known as Snow Hill in Franklin County, Pennsylvania, in 1798.[161] At its peak, the Ephrata settlement totaled between 200 and 300 members, of whom fewer than 100 were celibate. Following Beissel's death in 1768, the community went into decline. After the death of the last celibate sister in 1813, the married householder members led the congregation until 1934. Following its acquisition by the commonwealth of Pennsylvania in 1941, Ephrata underwent a major restoration by G. Edwin Brumbaugh and later John Heyl.[162]

Schwenkfelders

The Schwenkfelders, another German-speaking sect, were the followers of Caspar Schwenkfeld von Ossig (1489–1561), a Silesian nobleman, scholar, and author of theological treatises. After his death, his followers were persecuted for failure to participate in the state-run church. Their numbers declined from several thousand to several hundred, concentrated in the duchy of Silesia (largely in modern-day Poland). From 1726 to 1733, 170 Schwenkfelder families took refuge on the estate of Count Nicholas von Zinzendorf, a Lutheran who would become the leader of the Moravian church. In the spring of 1734, 44 families sailed for America. After a failed attempt to acquire one large tract of land in 1784, most settled in what later became Montgomery County. They were divided into an Upper District in the northern end of the county in a region of the Perkiomen Valley known as Goschenhoppen, and a Middle District near the center of the county.[163] Numbering approximately 2,300 members today, the Schwenkfelder Church remains concentrated in Montgomery County. Common surnames include Schultz, Heebner, Kriebel, Wagner, and Krauss.

The Schwenkfelders are strong believers in education and in 1764 established schools open to children of any religious faith. Moral instruction was taught along with arithmetic, grammar, and other subjects, but religious doctrine was not. Girls as well as boys learned to read and write, skills that become evident when studying the elaborate fraktur produced by Schwenkfelders of both sexes. The artful depiction of a house and garden (fig. 1.62) made for Salome Wagner around 1810 is attributed to the prolific Schwenkfelder artist Susanna Heebner (1750–1818).[164] Although the scene is probably fictional, the six-bed garden in front represents a variation on the typical four-square Pennsylvania German garden plan.[165] An identical fraktur made for Salome's sister Christina was once pasted inside a walnut blanket chest inlaid with her initials on the front.[166]

In contrast with the inhabitants at Ephrata, the Schwenkfelders had a more colorful and varied decorative arts tradition, ranging from fraktur to painted furniture. One of the most vibrant

FIGURE 1.62

Drawing for Salome Wagner, attributed to Susanna Heebner, Worcester Township, Montgomery County, 1810–18. American Folk Art Museum, New York, promised gift of Ralph Esmerian

FIGURE 1.63

Slide-lid box, made for Ezra Wiegner, possibly by David Kriebel, Worcester Township, Montgomery County, about 1814. Collection of Stephen and Dolores Smith

examples is a small slide-lid box with the initials "E W" (fig. 1.63). Ezra Wiegner, the original owner, was born January 12, 1814, to Rosina (Kriebel) and John Wiegner. His family lived in the Schwenkfelder Middle District and attended the Central Schwenkfelder Church in Worcester. Ezra's great-grandmother, Susanna Wiegner, had come to Pennsylvania in 1734 during the great Schwenkfelder migration. According to family tradition, the box was made for Ezra as a presentation gift by his maternal grandfather, noted fraktur artist David Kriebel (1736–1815). It is possible that David may have been involved in designing or creating the painted decoration for his grandson, for it speaks to the fraktur tradition of polychrome decoration on paper.[167]

A number of boldly painted chests bearing their owners' names in large fraktur letters are also known from the Schwenkfelder community, including one made for Ezra Wiegner's

sister-in-law, Sarah Hübner (Heebner), prior to her marriage to Ezra's older brother Joel in 1833 (fig. 1.64). The letters "in" after the name Hübner are a suffix applied to women's surnames in German, both married and unmarried. The prominent lettering of Sarah's name on the front of the chest is typical of Schwenk-

FIGURE 1.64

Chest-over-drawers, made for Sarah Hübner, Montgomery County, 1826. Schwenkfelder Library & Heritage Center, Pennsburg, Pa.

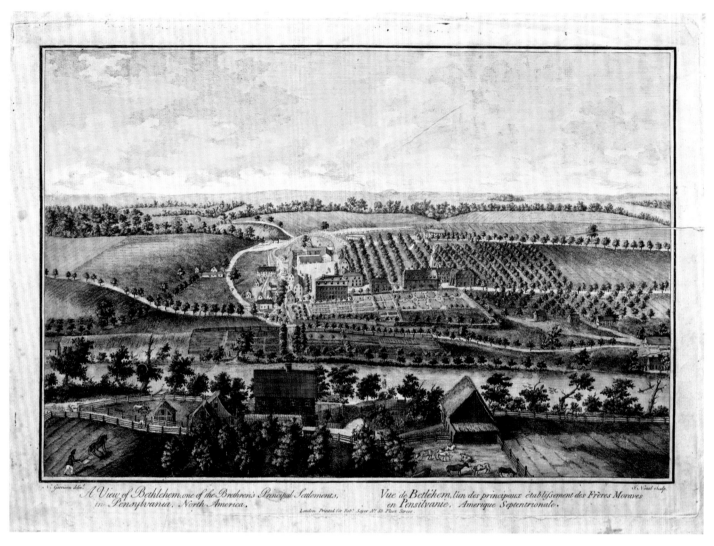

FIGURE 1.65

A View of Bethlehem, One of the Brethren's Principal Settlements, in Pennsylvania, North America, drawn by Nicholas Garrison Jr., engraved by Isaiah Noual, printed for Robert Sayer, London, about 1760. Museum of Early Southern Decorative Arts, Old Salem Museums & Gardens

felder chests; the large circular panels, however, are unusual, as most examples bear only a name and date. The palette of yellow ocher with red and blue accents remains strong. Though dated 1826, this chest with ogee-bracket feet is a stylistic continuation of examples produced several decades earlier. The stamped brass knobs and cast iron butt hinges are the strongest indicators of the later date. Sarah (1808–90) was the eldest child of Henry and Anna Schultz Heebner. Her father, grandson of David Heebner, who immigrated in 1734, was a farmer in Upper Gwynedd Township, Montgomery County. Sarah and Joel had three daughters, and the chest descended in the family of their eldest, Anna.[168]

Moravians

The Moravian Church, or Unitas Fratrum (Unity of the Brethren), was led by Lutheran noble Count Nicholas von Zinzendorf (1700–1760). His estate, known as Herrnhut, or The Lord's Watch, became a center of radical Pietism and the headquarters of the Moravians' extensive international missionary efforts. Under his leadership, the group expanded their settlements in Germany, Holland, England, Scandinavia, the West Indies, and North America—first in Georgia in 1735 and then Pennsylvania, North Carolina, Maryland, and elsewhere. In late 1741, Zinzendorf traveled to Pennsylvania to establish the Moravian community of Bethlehem, Northampton County, strategically located at the juncture of the Lehigh River and Monocacy Creek (fig. 1.65). Totaling some 500 acres, Bethlehem became the center of the Moravian Northern Synod, while Salem, North Carolina, was its counterpart in the Southern Synod. Hoping to unify the German church people, sectarians, and separatists in Pennsylvania into one Protestant movement, to be known as "The Pennsylvania Congregation of God in the Spirit," Zindendorf held a series of ecumenical councils throughout southeastern Pennsylvania to promote his vision. At the same time, Moravian missionary activity intensified, especially among the Pennsylvania German church people. Zinzendorf's dream was never achieved, in large part because of the arrival of Lutheran minister Henry Muhlenberg in 1742 and his indefatigable efforts to organize the Lutheran congregations, build churches, and provide them with suitable pastors. In 1746 Reverend Michael Schlatter arrived to do the same for the German Reformed Church.[169]

Despite Zinzendorf's grand vision, the Moravian Church in Pennsylvania was never large; in the 1790s there were approximately 400 members in Bethlehem and 1,200 total, including those in Nazareth, Lititz, York, Lancaster, and Oley. Nonetheless, their impact on southeastern Pennsylvania culture was significant. Unlike other German-speaking groups in the colony, the Moravians had aristocratic connections through Zinzendorf and others who were part of the lesser European nobility. They also drew members from central Europe rather than primarily the Palatinate. Many were skilled craftsmen and artisans, such as John Valentine Haidt (1700–1780), who immigrated to Bethlehem in 1754 and painted portraits and religious scenes. Haidt's portrait of an unknown young Moravian girl (fig. 1.66) speaks to the sophisticated fine and decorative arts that were present in the settlements. She is wearing a typical eighteenth-century Moravian costume: a brown dress, white apron and neckerchief, and the distinctive white *Haube* or cap. The red ribbon fastening her cap and bodice denotes her status as a member in the young girls' choir. The Moravian Church is divided into choirs based on sex, age, and marital status; during the communal life period most choir groups lived, worked, worshipped, and were buried together. Most of Haidt's portraits depict only the sitter's head and shoulders. This work is highly unusual, showing the gracefulness of the young woman's hands and slender waistline.[170]

For the first twenty years after its founding, Bethlehem operated as a self-sufficient, communal society under a "General Economy" system in which food, shelter, and other necessities were provided to members in exchange for their labor. It was planned as the capital and industrial center, while Nazareth ten miles to the north was

the base of agricultural operations. The Bethlehem settlement included substantial stone buildings such as the Brothers House. Some were designed by master builder Henry Antes, whose grandson was noted architect Benjamin Henry Latrobe.[171] Unlike the communal buildings at Ephrata with their randomly placed windows and log construction, those of the Moravians offered a symmetrical arrangement and impressive stone architecture, imparting a sense of formality and organization—perhaps a reflection of the well-ordered lives of the inhabitants. Numerous trades and industries soon developed along the Monocacy Creek, including blacksmith and nailsmith shops, a pottery, cabinetmaking and woodturning shops, water works, an oil mill, three buildings for the tanning of leather, and a slaughterhouse, grist mill, and flax house.[172] By 1747 as many as thirty-two trades were active in Bethlehem. Nearly fifty years later, Theophile Cazenove visited and noted the presence of "one large flour-mill, one large lumber mill, one large

FIGURE 1.66
Young Moravian Girl, by John Valentine Haidt, probably Bethlehem, Northampton County, 1755–60. Smithsonian American Art Museum, Washington, D.C./Art Resource, N.Y.

individuals.[174] A report prepared in 1756 of the trades practiced in Bethlehem noted those of turner, cabinetmaker, gunstock maker, carpenter, and spinning wheel maker. The carpenters' and joiners' shop was in a small log structure built onto the cooper shop until 1754, when it moved into the lower level of the single Brothers House. Annual inventories of the woodworking shop taken during the 1760s and 1770s reveal a large stock of walnut, tulip-poplar, oak, pine, and cherry but mention little of furniture products. In 1774 the inventory listed seven walnut chairs; in 1780 it noted a low commode and armchair. The 1785 inventory mentions one "grandfather chair," possibly a reference to a type of leather-upholstered easy chair thought to be Moravian in origin (fig. 1.67), although most have no specific history of ownership or documentation.[175] Typically, these chairs have upholstered wings attached to the upper portions of the rear stiles. The design of the legs can vary, from turned to square to cabriole with slipper or pad feet. The shape of the arms also varies somewhat, though most are curved and upholstered. Seven of the chairs known have almost identical vasiform-splat shaped arm supports and curved rear stiles, strongly suggesting that they were produced in

FIGURE 1.67
Armchair, probably Bethlehem, Northampton County, 1750–80. Collection of H. Rodney Sharp on loan from the Historic Odessa Foundation

FIGURE 1.68
Plank-bottom chair, used in Sisters House at Nazareth, probably Nazareth, Northampton County, 1750–85. Rocky Hill Collection

oil press, one large tobacco factory, one large factory to full cloth, a boarding-school, where there are 80 students from all parts of the States, . . . a brewery, a seminary for men, one for widows and one for girls, a bakery, a tan-yard, a store where all kinds of merchandise from England and from Germany are sold at retail, a large inn for strangers; shoemakers, tailor, locksmith and carpenter."[173]

Moravian Furniture ⌒ Probably due to their communal lifestyle, little is known about individual Moravian craftsmen. Annual inventories of the trade shops list the name of the master, but it remains nearly impossible to attribute extant objects, including furniture, to the same shop. Other known chairs have more variation, probably due to their production in other Moravian communities.[176]

One of the functions of these chairs was likely to provide comfortable seating for those who were invalid, disabled, or otherwise ill, as suggested by one at Bethlehem that has the words *"KRANKEN STUBE"* (sick room) spelled out on the front seat rail in brass nails, along with the date "1788." A reclining armchair owned by the Wachovia Historical Society in North Carolina is believed to be the "armchair for the use of the sick" made in Salem according to a design received from Bethlehem. This chair was purportedly used in the single Brothers or Sisters House to care for the sick, perhaps even for surgery, which was often performed in a sitting position.[177] The padded arms, backs, and headrests provided comfortable support, and the leather upholstery was sturdier and more serviceable than a woven material that might stain or tear.[178] Leather was also readily available. One of the first and most profitable industries established in Bethlehem was the tannery, built in 1742 along the Monocacy Creek, where there was access to water and room for the large vats in which the animal hides were processed. The upholstery could have been done by the saddler, an artisan who created a variety of leather products.[179] Another interesting detail is that at least one chair was made of red mulberry, a tree native to Pennsylvania that was used occasionally in furnituremaking. Mulberry trees were plentiful in the vicinity of Bethlehem, where attempts were made to develop a silk manufactory by the mid-eighteenth century.[180]

Another type of chair often associated with the Moravians is the *Brettstuhl* (board chair), though there is scant documentation for the contemporary use of this term.[181] The form has its origins in the Renaissance, when similar chairs referred to as *sgabelli* were fashionable in northern and central Italy. Typically built of walnut, though sometimes of a softwood, the chairs were made without the use of a lathe. Boards were sawn out for the seat and back, which was sometimes decorated with a heart-shape cutout such as that seen in a chair with a history of use in the

Sisters House in Nazareth (fig. 1.68). The craftsman then inserted two tenons from the back into corresponding mortises in the seat and drove pegs through the tenons to secure them from underneath. To prevent the seat from warping and to give it added strength, two battens were inserted into sliding dovetails on the underside; the dovetails were made with a side-cutting plane called a *Grathobel*. This tool was used almost exclusively by Germanic craftsmen well into the eighteenth century. The legs were typically chamfered with a plane or knife then inserted through holes in the battens and seat. Wedges driven into the top of the legs held them firmly in place.[182]

Chairs such as the *Brettstuhl* likely functioned as a liturgist's chair in the *Saal*, the room where religious services were held. The focal point of the *Saal* was a table and chair placed behind it from which the liturgist conducted biblical readings.[183] A small stretcher-base, walnut table with single drawer has a history in Bethlehem as a liturgist's table (fig. 1.69), though nothing in its construction or decoration would preclude it from domestic use. Indeed, most eighteenth-century Moravian furniture does not appear to have been designed for a religious setting. With the con-

FIGURE 1.69
Liturgist's table, Bethlehem, Northampton County, 1750–85. Moravian Archives, Bethlehem, Pa.

FIGURE 1.70
Central Moravian Church, built 1803–6, photo 1870–1900, Bethlehem, Northampton County. Moravian Archives, Bethlehem, Pa.

FIGURE 1.71

Pulpit of Central Moravian Church, attributed to Johann Friedrich Bourquin, Bethlehem, Northampton County, 1803–6. Central Moravian Church, Bethlehem, Pa.

struction of the Central Moravian Church in Bethlehem from 1803 to 1806, however, new furnishings were commissioned to mirror the stylish architecture of the building (fig. 1.70). Master builder John Cunnius (1733–1808) of Reading (see fig. 4.44) designed the church in the classical style, with input from an active building committee. Atop the building a dome-roof bell tower supported by eight Doric columns and classical entablature is flanked by a Chinese railing with urns at the corners. Cabinetmaker Johann Friedrich Bourquin made much of the interior woodwork and carved decoration—including the paneled balconies, door surrounds, pulpit (figs. 1.71, 1.72), and liturgist's chair (fig. 1.73). The design of the oriel or suspended pulpit, which includes draped swags and tassels, has been attributed to Brother Benjamin Benade, and its carving to Bourquin. The pulpit was removed in 1851 and stored in the church attic until its recent installation in a stairwell in the southeast corner of the church. Born in 1762 in East Prussia, Bourquin was a cabinetmaker in the Moravian community of Zeist in Hol-

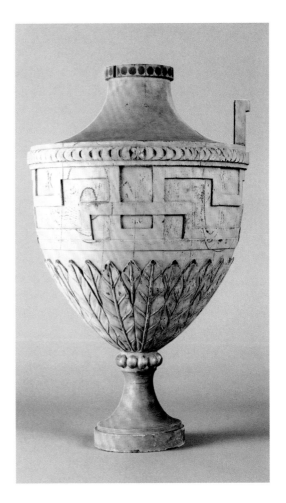

land until 1791, when he moved to Silesia. In 1800 he arrived in Bethlehem and continued to work as a cabinetmaker until his death in 1830.[184] Above the sounding board on the pulpit was a classical urn with carved acanthus leaves, gilt beading, and two angular handles—most of which are now missing. Also missing is the finial, perhaps a gilt flame, that would have topped the urn. Recorded in the minutes of the church elders' conference in 1802 is a reference to the pulpit, noting that "a pulpit with a sounding board shall be fixed above the chair of the liturgist." The official report of the dedication of the church on May 18, 1806, also noted that "Brother Loskiel preached the first dedicatory sermon and spoke from the pulpit fixed above the seat of the liturgist."[185] Exemplifying the Moravians' awareness of the latest styles, the oval-back liturgist's chair with its fluted, square tapered legs and carved details echoing the decoration on the urn speaks to the urban sophistication present in Bethlehem. The white painted surface and upholstered back and seat emulate the French taste then fashionable in Philadelphia.

Moravians and Music ~ In addition to their patronage of the fine arts, the Moravians were renowned for their music. Well-known instrument maker David Tannenberg fashioned many organs for Moravian churches.[186] Brass instruments were also prominent and were typically played for funerals, outdoor festivals, and announcements. Brass music was practical for such events, as the instruments functioned regardless of weather and their sound carried over great distances. Horns, trumpets, and especially trombones became popular—the trombone having special meaning as the instrument named in Luther's German translation of the Bible

FIGURE 1.72

Urn from pulpit sounding board of Central Moravian Church, attributed to Johann Friedrich Bourquin, Bethlehem, Northampton County, 1803–6. Central Moravian Church, Bethlehem, Pa.

FIGURE 1.73

Liturgist's chair from Central Moravian Church, attributed to Johann Friedrich Bourquin, Bethlehem, Northampton County, 1803–6. Moravian Archives, Bethlehem, Pa.

FIGURE I.74

The Trumpet Players from Lititz, by Lewis Miller, York, York County, 1828. York County Heritage Trust

FIGURE I.75

Trombone, by Johann Joseph Schmied, Pfaffendorf, Germany (now Rudzica, Poland), 1774. Lititz Moravian Congregation, Lititz, Pa.

as accompanying the word of God. Over the course of the eighteenth century, brass music was increasingly used at most Moravian settlements and, where possible, trombone choirs were organized, including one in Bethlehem by 1754 and Lititz in 1771. Moravian trombone choirs typically consisted of four parts: soprano, alto, tenor, and bass. During a funeral service, the choir led a procession of mourners and a coffin to the gravesite.[187] In 1828 the trombone choir from Lititz played at the consecration of a new church in York and was sketched by Lewis Miller (fig. 1.74). Trombones were typically imported from Europe, such as the one made by Johann Joseph Schmied of Pfaffendorf, Germany, in 1774 and used in Lititz (fig. 1.75).[188] To facilitate the playing

of trombones, the Moravians developed a special type of Windsor chair with legs several inches taller than usual, enabling the sitter to play the instrument without its hitting the floor. Some chairs have footrests as well. A bow-back example used in Lititz measures twenty-four inches tall at the seat (the average seat height is about eighteen inches) and features elongated baluster legs with tapered feet, stretchers with swelled ends, and a shallow seat associated with Windsor chairs from Lancaster County (fig. 1.76). Windsors were typically constructed from a combination of different woods, one of the reasons they were painted. The most common color is green, seen on this chair as well as others of the trombone Windsor form.[189]

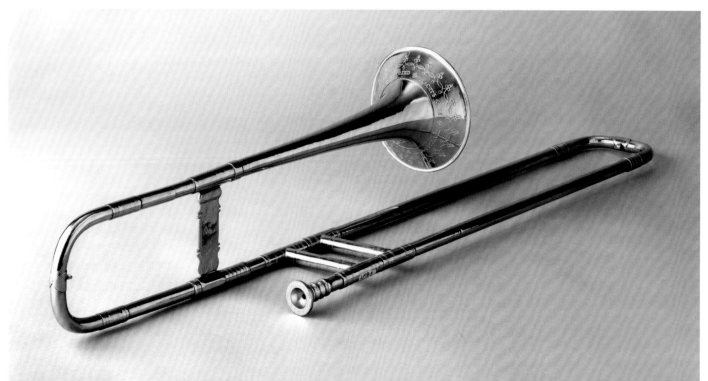

Music was also part of the educational offerings of Moravian schools, which took in Moravians and non-Moravians alike. Young ladies attending the girls school at Bethlehem learned needlework, music, painting, reading, writing, and arithmetic. Nazareth was home to the boys school, where young men were taught music, drawing, and multiple languages in addition to reading, writing, math, history, geography, and literature. In Lititz a girls school known as Linden Hall was founded in 1746; it became noted for its distinctive needlework. In

FIGURE 1.76
Windsor chair, probably
Lititz, Lancaster County,
1800–1825. Lititz Moravian
Congregation, Lititz, Pa.

1824 fourteen-year-old Hannah Mary McConaughy of Gettysburg entered Linden Hall,
where the following year she stitched a silk
needlework picture (fig. I.77) depicting the
characters Palemon and Lavinia from the 1730
poem *Autumn* by James Thomson. Adapted
from the biblical story of Ruth and Boaz, the
lovers converse with each other amid a sce-
nic rural landscape, where a Pennsylvania-style
bank barn lends a touch of realism. The picture,
made with silk and chenille thread and metallic spangles on a silk ground, retains its original gilt frame. In 1832 Hannah married Moses
McClain, who later served as a representative in
Congress.[190]

Firearms ⌇ In addition to their notable
decorative and fine arts traditions, the
Moravians also produced some of the finest
early long rifles in southeastern Pennsylvania—
the foremost center of their manufacture in
colonial America. The long rifle was essential
to pioneer families in settling the frontier,
enabling them to procure food and ensure

protection. Many rifles were embellished
with intricate carving, engraved metalwork,
and other artistic details.[191] One of the earliest
Moravian gunsmiths in America was German
immigrant Johann Andreas Albrecht (1718–
1802). Trained as a gunstock maker in Europe,
he supervised the gunsmith shop established in
1762 at Christiansbrunn (Christian's Spring),
a small settlement of single men founded in
1749 near Nazareth that included a 1,500-acre
farm, mill, and brewery. The Christiansbrunn
settlement was never large; it closed in 1796
due to a "deplorable extent" of intemperance
among the single brothers.[192] Albrecht had
left Christiansbrunn in 1766 to manage the
Sun Inn in Bethlehem; in 1771 he moved
to Lititz and took up his trade once again,
appearing in tax records from 1780 to 1800 as
a gunsmith.[193] Albrecht and other Moravian
gunsmiths, including his son Henry Albright;
Jacob Dickert; William Henry Sr. and Jr. (who
apprenticed with Albrecht in Lititz), were
an important part of the Lancaster school of
gunmaking.[194]

An unusual coffee mill with a history of
ownership in the Lititz Moravian Church is
likely an example of Andreas Albrecht's work
(fig. I.78). Coffee played an important role in
Moravian love feasts—religious events held to
celebrate special occasions such as the birthday of a prominent church leader. They typically included observance of the early Christian
practice of foot-washing followed by the serving of coffee or tea and buns.[195] Engraved on
the brass hopper of the coffee mill is the date
"1772" and the initials "A A." The body is a
dovetailed walnut box that contains a drawer
for collecting the ground coffee. A small, sliding wooden cover holds the drawer inside; it is
fastened by a metal spring lock typical of those
on firearms with sliding wooden patch boxes.[196]
The foliate carving on the cover also relates to
this type of patch box, as seen in a comparison
with the one on a long rifle owned by Edward
Marshall (figs. I.79, I.80).[197] Infamous for his
role in the Walking Purchase of 1737 in which
the Delaware Indians lost their homeland territory, Marshall (1715–89) lived in Easton,
Northampton County, and later on an island

in the Delaware River near Tinicum, Bucks County. It is not surprising that Albrecht would make a coffee grinder, as many gunsmiths were versatile craftsmen capable of working in a variety of media; indeed, repair work on guns, coffee mills, and other metal objects was commonplace for a gunsmith.[198] An inventory of the Christiansbrunn gun shop in 1781 included four coffee mills, and Albrecht owned two at the time of his death in 1802.[199]

Following Albrecht's move to Bethlehem in 1766, the gunshop was taken over by his former apprentice, Christian Oerter (1747–77). Born in Frederick Township, Montgomery County, and educated at a Moravian boys school, Oerter made a long rifle in 1775 that included both a sliding wooden patch box and brass wire inlay; during the American Revolution this gun was acquired by a British cavalry officer and later presented to the Prince of Wales for the Royal

Armory collection. Oerter made at least two other long rifles with wire inlay the same year. One featured wire inlay on its wooden patch box and stock;[200] the other (fig. 1.81) is more elaborate, with silver and brass wire inlay; an engraved silver star on the cheekpiece; and carving of a griffin with beak and claws of inlaid horn on the buttstock (fig. 1.82). The brass patch box is engraved "W M," believed to stand for Edward Marshall's son William II (1737–1823), a member of Buckingham Friends Meeting in Bucks County.[201] Despite the small size of the Moravian Church in eighteenth-century Pennsylvania, its members interacted with people of other faiths. This long rifle, made by Moravian gunsmith Christian Oerter for Quaker William Marshall, sheds light on just one of the ways in which interactions occurred between those of various religions and ethnic backgrounds.[202]

FIGURE 1.78
Coffee mill, attributed to Andreas Albrecht, Lititz, Lancaster County, 1772. Lititz Moravian Congregation, Lititz, Pa.

FIGURE 1.79
Detail of carving on coffee mill in fig. 1.78 (*top*) and long rifle in fig. 1.80 (*bottom*).

FIGURE 1.80
(*above*) Long rifle, made for Edward Marshall, possibly Northampton County, 1760–70. Mercer Museum of the Bucks County Historical Society

FIGURE 1.81
(*below*) Long rifle, probably made for William Marshall II, by Christian Oerter, Christian's Spring, Northampton County, 1775. Private collection

FIGURE 1.82
Detail of carving on fig. 1.81.

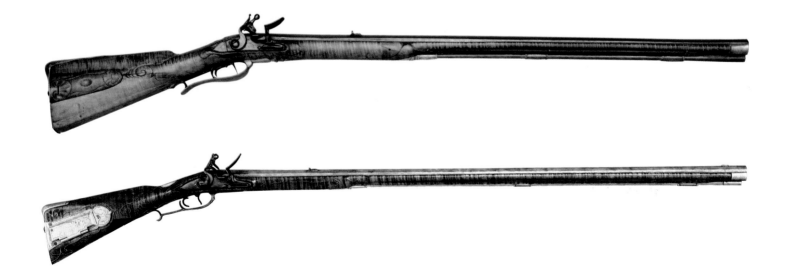

Peter Mori's Schrank ⌒　In 1791 an extraordinary schrank was made for Peter Mori (Mohry) of Upper Saucon Township, Northampton (now Lehigh) County, which lies about fifteen miles southwest of Christiansbrunn. The schrank features the highly unusual use of brass inlay to form the owner's name and date, which flank an eight-point star in the frieze (fig. 1.83).[203] Between the two doors are brass inlaid foliage and a geometric floral design that was cut from cast sheet brass and let into the front. Although the star inlaid on the schrank is not unlike that used on long rifles at Christiansbrunn and elsewhere, the image is found on a wide variety of media. It is tempting to think that the star motif and the unusual use of brass inlay on the schrank might suggest some familiarity with firearm ornament, but it is unlikely that a gunsmith would be involved in building furniture (though some did foundry work including brass and silver casting).[204] Brass ornament is extremely rare on Pennsylvania German furniture (only two other examples are known),[205] but it was executed by German craftsmen in Europe, including Moravian cabinetmaker John Frederick Hintz of London who advertised brass-inlaid furniture for sale in 1738.[206]

The inspiration for the brass inlay on Peter Mori's schrank is unknown, as is the name of the craftsman who made it. But it is evident that the schrank was an expensive one. In addition to the inlay, details such as the fluted quarter columns and five drawers would have added to the price. Cabinetmaker Abraham Overholt of Bucks County noted in his account book that he charged £9 for a painted schrank with two rows of drawers and quarter columns; the walnut used in Mori's schrank would have made it more expensive.[207] When Mori died in 1828, his inventory included a "Clock & Case" worth $30, desk worth $13, and "cobard" valued at $10. The high value of the "cobard" suggests that it is the schrank (which means cupboard in German). In his will of 1821, Mori bequeathed to his widow numerous furnishings, which after her death were directed to his son John: "one stove with the pipes, one Clock and Case, one Table, one large Cupboard, one Milk Cupboard, and four Chairs." Judging by the extensive listings

of grain (valued at $465), livestock (including twelve head of cattle, nine sheep, and hogs), and farming implements, Mori was an active farmer at the time of his death. Although he identified himself as a yeoman in his will, he owned blacksmith tools worth $13.50, which may suggest he also had a specialized skill. Numerous bequests of money, land, and personal property to his widow and children indicate his prosperity.[208]

In 1791, the same year the schrank was made, Mori and his wife attended the baptism of Peter Buchecker by Lutheran minister Jacob van Buskirk. A birth and baptismal certificate made to commemorate the event (fig. 1.84) reveals their role as godparents, or baptismal sponsors. Parents often looked to friends or relatives to serve as sponsors—a sign of respect that was often reinforced by naming the child after his or her sponsor, as was the case here. Young Peter Buchecker was named after Peter Mori.[209] Although the Mori family lived in close proximity to the Moravians, they remained members of the Lutheran and Reformed congregation in Upper Saucon, about seven miles from Bethlehem. Because of a frequent shortage of ministers, some members of this congregation had their children baptized by the Moravians, as noted by Lutheran minister Henry Muhlenberg, who wrote after the departure of Pastor Jacob Loeser

FIGURE 1.83
Schrank, made for Peter Mori, probably Northampton County, 1791. Rocky Hill Collection

FIGURE 1.84
Birth and baptismal certificate of Peter Buchecker, decoration and handwriting by Friedrich Krebs on a form printed by J. Schneider & Co., Reading, Berks County, 1797. State Museum of Pennsylvania, Pennsylvania Historical and Museum Commission

in 1749: "One or two Brethren from Bethlehem have already crept into various houses and baptized children."[210] Given the distances between churches and shortage of ministers, it was often difficult to adhere strictly to a particular faith.

German Lutherans and Reformed

The majority of Pennsylvania's German-speaking inhabitants were members of the Lutheran and Reformed churches.[211] By 1793 the region was home to 249 Lutheran congregations and 236 Reformed.[212] Although derived from separate Reformation traditions, the two churches had much in common, and intermarriages between followers were frequent. Both retained two of the seven sacraments of Roman Catholicism, baptism and communion but, unlike the Quakers and most plain German religious groups, did not believe in nonresistance or lay ministry.[213] The Lutheran Church grew out of efforts by Martin Luther (1483–1546) to reform the Roman Catholic Church. Much disagreement surrounded the changes and degree to which they were necessary. In Switzerland, Ulrich Zwingli (1484–1531) and John Calvin (1509–54) founded a second Protestant movement that adhered to the Heidelberg Catechism of 1563 and became known as the Reformed Church. Conditions in Pennsylva-

nia, in particular the scarcity of ministers as well as the difficulty and expense of building churches, encouraged Lutheran and Reformed congregations to share churches. By 1776 nearly half of all the Pennsylvania Lutheran and Reformed congregations made use of union churches, with alternate Sundays reserved for worship services by one or the other of the two congregations. Typically there was also a shared school and burial ground.[214]

Given their numerical superiority, the German Lutherans and Reformed were the predominant consumers and producers of material goods among the Pennsylvania Germans. The Laubach and Keely families of Chester County provide an informative case study of one family's material world. In 1748 twenty-year-old Johannes Laubach (Laubaugh) arrived in Philadelphia on the *Two Brothers*. He purchased 154 acres in Pikeland Township, Chester County, in the northern region of the county where a number of German-speaking people settled.[215] The Laubachs were members of the East Vincent Reformed Church, which began as a union church around 1750. In 1758 the congregation built their own church.[216] Johannes and Anna Catherina (Schumeny) Laubach's first child, Henry, was baptized there in 1753, as were many of their other nine children. Johannes became a substantial landholder and leader in the

FIGURE 1.85

Chest-over-drawers, made for Margaret Laubach, probably Pikeland Township area, Chester County, 1781. Winterthur Museum purchase with funds provided by Robert and Bobbie Falk and the Henry Francis du Pont Collectors Circle

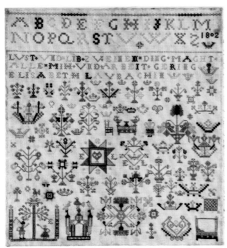

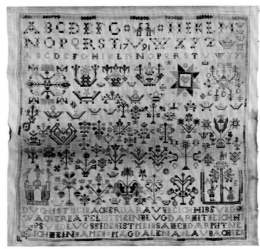

Clockwise from top row, left:

FIGURE 1.86
Birth and baptismal certificate of Margaret Laubach, decoration and handwriting attributed to the Pseudo-Otto Artist on a form attributed to the Ephrata print shop, Lancaster County, about 1788. Collection of Ronald and Nancy Harper and Douglas Harper

FIGURE 1.87
Birth and baptismal certificate of Magdalena Laubach, decoration and handwriting attributed to the Pseudo-Otto Artist on a form attributed to the Ephrata print shop, Lancaster County, about 1788. Chester County Historical Society, West Chester, Pa.

FIGURE 1.88
Sampler, by Magdalena Laubach, Pikeland Township, Chester County, 1791. Chester County Historical Society, West Chester, Pa.

FIGURE 1.89
Sampler, by Elisabeth Laubach, Pikeland or Uwchlan Township, Chester County, 1802. Collection of Mr. and Mrs. Stephen D. Hench

congregation; according to tradition he presented the church with a communion service "made out of Mexican silver dollars" at the first communion held in the new church in 1758. He also left a bequest of $66 in his will of 1808.[217]

A sizable number of objects associated with Johannes and his family survive, including furniture, textiles, and fraktur. A chest made for his daughter Margaret features an inlaid cartouche on the front bearing her initials and the date "1781" (fig. 1.85). It is one of a group of nearly twenty related chests, the majority probably local to the northern Chester County region. The group is distinguished by the use of inlaid initials on the front surrounded by a rectangular frame with ovolo ends made of alternating trapezoidal-shape inlay. Some also have inlaid hearts or tulips on the front. Eight chests in the group were made for owners with a surname beginning with L, including one for "C L" in 1781 that may have belonged to Margaret's sister Christina (1762–1823) or Catherine (1760–1819). The chest for Margaret has straight bracket feet with an ornate shaping to the inside edge, associated with the group. An unusual feature is that one of the drawers has a wooden spring lock; the other has an iron lock requiring a key. A fraktur (fig. 1.86) prepared for Margaret Laubach records her birth on July 6, 1758, and her subsequent baptism and confirmation. A similar certificate was made for her younger sister, Magdalena, born in 1769 (fig. 1.87). In 1782, the year after she acquired the chest, Margaret married Conrad Keely of Vincent Township, Chester County. A marriage certificate was prepared for them and signed by her parents and husband; Margaret made only her mark on the paper.[218]

FIGURE 1.90
Portrait of Henry Melchior Muhlenberg, 1788. Rare Books and Manuscripts, Special Collections Library, the Pennsylvania State University Libraries

FIGURE 1.91
Augustus Lutheran Church, built 1743, Trappe, Philadelphia (now Montgomery) County.

In 1791 Magdalena Laubach worked a random-type sampler (fig. 1.88) on which she stitched, "Fabric is my field, on it I sew beautifully and alertly; Needle is my plow, with it I sew beautifully and cleverly; Silk is my seed, with it I sew my name." In 1802 Elisabeth Laubach, daughter of Margaret and Magdalena's brother Henry, copied many of the motifs from Magdalena's sampler in making one of her own (fig. 1.89). Elisabeth attended the Pikeland school in 1795, when she was given a musical tune book by her schoolmaster, fraktur artist Johann Adam Eyer.[219]

The Muhlenbergs ⌒ Although the number of surviving artifacts that can be associated with the Laubach family is unusual, they and their material possessions are fairly representative of a typical Pennsylvania German farming family. There are exceptions, however. Most Pennsylvania Germans were involved with agriculture, but others were craftsmen, merchants, artisans, scholars, doctors, and politicians. Some were poor and could not afford luxuries. At the opposite end of the spectrum, a few families such as the Muhlenbergs ranked among the region's well-educated elite. In 1742 Henry Melchior Muhlenberg (1711–87) was sent to Pennsylvania by Lutheran officials at the University of Halle, in the German state of Saxony-Anhalt, to bring order to the widely scattered Lutheran congregations. A devoted minister, Muhlenberg (fig. 1.90) served as pastor of the main congregation in Philadelphia as well as those in New Hanover and Trappe,

Montgomery County.[220] He also oversaw the construction of new churches, including Augustus Lutheran Church in Trappe (1743), with its distinctive gambrel roof and three-sided apse (fig. 1.91); St. Michael's Church in Germantown (1743–48), whose congregation included more than five hundred heads of household; and Zion Lutheran Church in Philadelphia (1766–69), an elegant brick edifice designed by Robert Smith. Rebuilt in 1794 following a fire, Zion was the largest church in Philadelphia when it was the site of George Washington's memorial service in 1799.[221]

Muhlenberg's legendary devotion to his congregations has resulted in his recognition as the patriarch of the Lutheran Church in America. Though the ministry was not a viable means of obtaining wealth in colonial Pennsylvania, there was a degree of "clerical gentility" associated with it that generally afforded ministers a higher level of social status than their economic situation might otherwise warrant.[222] In 1745 Muhlenberg, "most meritorious Lutheran minister," was fortunate enough to marry Anna Maria Weiser, "Daughter of the highly honored Justice" Conrad Weiser, a prominent justice of the peace in Berks County and government treaty negotiator with the Iroquois. Not only was this marriage strategically helpful to Muhlenberg in his efforts to regain Lutherans from the Moravians, it also provided him with the financial support of his new father-in-law, who gave the young couple £240 toward the furnishing and construction of a new house in Trappe. Built in 1745, this substantial two-story stone house, in marked contrast with the one-room log dwellings occupied by most of their neighbors, made a strong statement about how Muhlenberg intended to be seen by the Lutheran community.[223]

Three of the Muhlenberg sons were sent to Germany for their education in 1763. Seven years later upon his return, their middle son, Frederick (1750–1801), was ordained a Lutheran minister. His first call was to a church in Schaefferstown (known first as Heidelberg, the town was laid out in 1758 by Alexander Schaeffer), Lebanon County, whose inhabitants his father had referred to as "wild forest people" only seven years earlier.[224] Built of gray limestone with contrasting red sandstone quoins and detailing, St. Luke's Church was an imposing edifice that took two years to construct. Henry Muhlenberg preached at its dedication in 1767 and remarked upon the substantial stone architecture, noting that it was "one

of the best in this land, built of massive stones, large, well laid out, and adorned with a tower." The new church had arisen out of a controversy between factions who supported rival ministers, prompting the wealthier members to construct a church in the center of Schaefferstown as a tangible sign of their faith. Although the new church did not resolve the schism in the congregation, it did make an imposing statement. Set into the cornice of the long side facing the main street were three winged angel heads of carved wood (fig. 1.92), one in the center and one in each corner. A photograph of the church prior to its renovation in 1884 shows the angels in situ (fig. 1.93). These carvings were removed when the church was remodeled, a factor that accounts for their remarkable state of preservation.[225] The carpenters who built the church were Heinrich and Philip Pfeffer, who inscribed their names on the back of the pulpit sounding board, though the angels may have been carved

FIGURE 1.92
Three winged angel heads from St. Luke's Lutheran Church, Schaefferstown, Lancaster (now Lebanon) County, about 1767. Collection of Katharine and Robert Booth

FIGURE 1.93
St. Luke's Lutheran Church, built 1765–67, remodeled 1884, photo about 1880, Schaefferstown, Lancaster (now Lebanon) County. Historic Schaefferstown, Inc.

FIGURE 1.94
Portrait of Frederick Augustus Conrad Muhlenberg, by Joseph Wright, New York, 1790. National Portrait Gallery, Smithsonian Institution

by someone else.[226] The survival of eighteenth-century American sculpture is rare (see fig. 4.39), making these angels all the more noteworthy and indicative of the parishioners' aspirations.[227]

After serving in Schaefferstown for several years, Frederick Muhlenberg accepted a call to New York City in 1773. He returned to Penn-sylvania in 1776 but soon left the ministry to enter politics. After serving in the Continental Congress, he was elected to the Pennsylvania General Assembly and made speaker. In 1789 he was elected as a representative to the first Federal Congress and made Speaker of the House. That news was eagerly received within the Pennsylvania German community, which, despite its significant numbers, had received little representation in politics. German-language newspapers boldly proclaimed, "The blood of the grandchildren of our grandchildren will proudly well up in their hearts when they will read in the histories of America that the first Speaker . . . was a German, born of German parents in Pennsylvania," while the *Pennsylvania Packet* announced, "The German gentleman has been honored with the chair of speaker of the legislature."[228]

Having become one of the most well-known Germans in the country and a leader of the fledgling American government, Frederick Muhlenberg was now a man of two worlds. His bilingual and bicultural competence within the German- and English-speaking communities enabled him to function as a cultural intermediary, helping his fellow Pennsylvania Germans to understand the political and legal systems of their government while also representing them in that government. Muhlenberg took this role seriously, serving from 1790 to 1797 as president of the German Society of Pennsylvania, a charitable organization that assisted German-speaking immigrants. In July 1790 his portrait was painted by Joseph Wright (fig. 1.94), depicting him in his new political role as speaker, well dressed yet not grandiose. Status is imparted instead by the distinctive chair (one of two commissioned for the Speaker of the House and President of the Senate) and the official documents he is signing—emphasizing his political achievements, authority, and superior status.[229] The portrait is also important as an indicator of the complexity of ethnic identity, not in the expression of it but rather the absence. It is a reminder and counterbalance to claims of Pennsylvania German uniqueness and ethnic distinctiveness, as nothing about it suggests the sitter is of Germanic heritage.

Although a traditional interpretation would take this as evidence of Muhlenberg's assimilation into English-speaking culture, an alternative view is that he was motivated more by notions of status and refinement than a desire to appear more English or less German. At the time of his death in 1801, Muhlenberg's household was furnished with luxury items such as a mahogany sideboard, bust of Benjamin Franklin, and fifty-seven wineglasses—not the kinds of objects typically associated with the Pennsylvania Germans. However, Muhlenberg also patronized German craftsmen such as Philadelphia silversmith Christian Wiltberger; he continued to read and write in German; and he remained a lifelong member of the German Lutheran church. When some Pennsylvania Germans purchased English ceramics or built so-called Georgian houses, they were not necessarily becoming less German or more English—they were simply aligning themselves with elite society through such objects. Multiple socioeconomic levels existed within Pennsylvania German culture, a factor that must be considered when interpreting objects that fall outside the more traditional "folk" objects commonly associated with them.[230]

Frederick Muhlenberg's selection of sophisticated furnishings that were more in keeping with those of his affluent peers than his fellow Pennsylvania Germans reflected his personal status as well as a larger process of Americanization (rather than Anglicization) in which the diverse ethnic and religious heritage of Pennsylvania's inhabitants contributed to the creation of a new and different identity by the turn of the nineteenth century.[231] Although a larger regional consciousness slowly emerged in southeastern Pennsylvania, local identities remained strong throughout this process. Not surprisingly, distinctive localisms were reflected in the region's material culture—in particular its furniture. Regionally popular styles developed, but local preferences for specific forms and types of ornament—including inlaid, painted, and carved decoration—would have a lasting and significant impact.

CHAPTER TWO

PLACES: REGIONAL FORMS AND LOCAL EXPRESSIONS

I took my Sulky . . . to Kennets Square . . . Thence by Birmingham meeting—where was part of the Brandywine battle . . . Much liked the country from Kennetts Sqre a highly situated village, —up to West Chester . . . The country was finely cultivated. Farms indicated wealth & plenty—mostly of Friends—admired the numerous trees by the road fences & the general venerable & rural beauty of the place . . . near the Brandywine.

—*John Fanning Watson, 1829*[1]

During the 1700s and early 1800s in southeastern Pennsylvania, the great population diversity as well as local settlement patterns led to preferences for certain forms, ornament, and construction techniques. To imply that all furniture made in the region can be linked to a precise locale, however, would be misleading. Even when the original context of an object is known, there may be no distinctive visual cues to relate it to a specific place of manufacture, for regional commonalities can be found in a number of forms and details. Among these regionally similar objects are several types of seating furniture as well as utilitarian forms common to many, if not all, households, such as dough troughs, tables, and cupboards.

FIGURE 2.1

Presentation drawing
for Elisabeta Huston,
by Karl Münch,
Schaefferstown, Hei-
delberg Township,
Dauphin (now Leba-
non) County, 1799.
Collection of Mr. and
Mrs. Paul Flack

FIGURE 2.2

Detail of fig. 2.1.

FIGURE 2.3

Interior of chairmaker's shop,
[1704]. Printed Book and Periodical Collection, Winterthur
Library

REGIONALISMS: COMMON FURNITURE FORMS
Slat-back Chairs

Karl Münch's creative fraktur drawing (fig. 2.1) depicts a scene of domesticity that highlights the ever-present nature of certain forms of furniture such as slat-back chairs, Windsor chairs, spinning wheels, and kitchen work tables (fig. 2.2). Among these, probably the most frequently seen is the slat-back chair, which was derived from continental European precedents and produced throughout the seventeenth, eighteenth, and nineteenth centuries (fig. 2.3).[2] Cheaply and easily constructed of turned posts and shaped rear slats, these chairs had woven rush or wood-splint seats. Although chairs of this form were made in other regions throughout the country, southeastern Pennsylvania examples are most often distinguished by their concave arched slats (from two to six) and boldly turned front stretchers with arrow-shape ends. It is thought that slat-

back chairs were introduced to America by German craftsmen, but they were made and used by people of all ethnic backgrounds in urban and rural households.[3] Benno M. Forman's analysis of Philadelphia chairmaker Solomon Fussell's ledger details the workings of a large and sophisticated urban shop that efficiently produced quantities of slat-back chairs for various economic and social levels of Philadelphia citizens as well as some clients outside the city.[4] Additional documentation of craftsmen working outside of Philadelphia makes it clear that large quantities were also produced in non-urban areas. These chairs survive in great numbers today, but they rarely have original provenances, making it difficult to ascribe them to exact places and dates of manufacture.[5] Occasionally craftsmen's account books and cabinetmakers' inventories can help to document production of the form to specific places. When Joseph Hibberd (1700–1737), joiner of Darby Township, Chester County, died at age thirty-seven, he was presumably at the height of his career, judging from his age and the unfinished work in his shop:

Ten Elbo Chairs not finished	*£2.5.*
Twenty two five Stave Chaires not finished	*£2.20.*
32 Thirty-two 3 Stave Chaires not finished	*£ 2.10.*
106 one hundred & six four Staved Chairs not finished	*£ 8.19.8.*[6]

Of particular interest in this inventory is the reference to slats as "staves," a term occasionally found in personal inventories when rush-bottom chairs are mentioned. Cushions are rarely cited with chairs in inventories, but it is likely that they were used on many for greater comfort.

Although slat-back chairs might be thought of as the staple of common seating furniture throughout the region, they were not wanting in aesthetic appeal or color. Typically the posts and slats were made of maple. Some were finished with a coat of varnish, but period references and surviving examples document they were also painted various colors. In the 1758 inventory

elderly citizens are seated in slat-back chairs; one armchair (on the far right) was converted to a rocking chair, evidence of its continued use and change over time.[11]

A slat-back armchair was owned by the Mennonite Kulp family of Upper Salford Township, Montgomery County (fig. 2.6). Retaining what appears to be the original

FIGURE 2.4
Slat-back side chair, owned by the Kriebel family, probably Worcester Township, Philadelphia (now Montgomery) County, 1775–1800. Schwenkfelder Library & Heritage Center, Pennsburg, Pa.

FIGURE 2.5
Leidich's General Store, by John Nicholas Choate, Boiling Springs, Cumberland County, about 1876. Cumberland County Historical Society

FIGURE 2.6
Slat-back armchair, owned by the Kulp family, probably Upper Salford Township, Philadelphia (now Montgomery) County, 1770–1800. Mennonite Heritage Center, Harleysville, Pa.

of Peter Hatton of Concord Township, Chester Country, "6 Rush Bottomed Chair & one armed Chair all Read" are listed.[7] Cabinet- and clockmaker Enos Thomas of Goshen Township, Chester County, made blue rush-bottom chairs costing 12 pence in 1806.[8] The Kriebel family, Schwenkfelders who lived in Worcester Township, Montgomery County, owned at least one such chair (fig. 2.4). A sampler worked in 1809 by Schwenkfelder Rosina Schultz pictures a blue slat-back side chair.[9] The provenance of the Kriebel chair might imply that it was made in that area of Montgomery County, but the generic nature of the form suggests that it could have been taken to Worcester Township from elsewhere. The rush-bottom seat on the chair is a twentieth-century replacement, for "when it was discovered on the second floor of the Kriebel home (by Dr. H. B. Shearer of Worcester) the seat was covered with chicken wire," no doubt a make-do seat from an earlier lifetime.[10] Slat-back chairs were made well into the nineteenth century, with earlier ones being repaired, repainted, and re-rushed. Their continued use is documented in an 1876 photograph of a group of locals in front of Leidich's General Store in Boiling Springs, Cumberland County (fig. 2.5). The

woven splint hickory seat, the rear posts angle back dramatically above the seat rails in what was perhaps a conscious effort on the part of the turner to make the chair more comfortable.[12] Almost all the elements of the chair suggest quick construction, from the simplicity of the posts and plain stretchers to the thinness of the arms. However, the turner took extra care in fashioning the rake of the upper portion of the rear posts. He turned each stile off-axis to create the two-axis appearance.[13] He also added ornament with multiple scribe lines encircling the elongated balusters of the front post turnings.[14] The straight, slender arms are relieved on the underside between the front and rear posts, a so-called double-cut feature sometimes associated with Germanic stylistic conventions.[15] On the inside front portion of the proper left arm, the date "1773" is incised, perhaps by an owner. Overall, the chair suggests rural construction, but without the Kulp history, it would be impossible to know where in southeastern Pennsylvania it was made or owned.

Benches

Perhaps more common than slat-back chairs were wooden benches (fig. 2.7). Not limited to any particular ethnic or religious group, the form is almost impossible to localize without a definitive provenance. Finding a bench in its original context can help to document local features; however, benches are simply constructed and even seemingly distinctive features are generic. The ends can be shaped or plain, and construction features often reflect the Germanic practice of hammering a wedge into a dovetail pin or a through-tenon to tighten the

joint. Benches were found in homes as well as churches, meetinghouses, taverns, inns, and other public places; they were made in varying lengths and woods depending on the intended use and the pocketbook of the purchaser. Humbler households were more likely to have them because they were more affordable than chairs. In German households two benches were often built into a corner of the *Stube*, or stove room, converging beneath a wall shelf or cupboard where the family Bible and other valuables were stored. Usually located in the southeast corner directly opposite the stove, the *Heiligeck* (holy corner) was a holdover from the Catholic tradition in which a crucifix would have been displayed.[16] The 1782 probate inventory of John Clemens lists the contents of his *Stube* as having a ten-plate stove, thirty-hour clock, "black walnut clothes press" valued at £1.15 shillings, "1 dough trough" worth 15 shillings, six chairs, and two painted benches worth 5 shillings.[17] Traveler Johann David Schoepf described the furnishings of one *Stube*, noting it had a "great four-cornered stove, a table in the corner with benches fastened to the wall, everything daubed with red."[18] A rare survival of a built-in bench abutting the main staircase in a Pennsylvania German household is seen in the 1762 Valentine Vihmann house, near Millbach, Lebanon County (fig. 2.8).[19]

Dry Sinks

Another utilitarian object related in form to benches are dry sinks, whose shaped ends closely resemble those of simple benches for seating and multi-tiered ones called bucket benches by present-day collectors. Little documentation survives

FIGURE 2.7
Bench, southeastern Pennsylvania, 1750–1800. Winterthur Museum

FIGURE 2.8
Built-in bench, in the Valentine Vihmann house, built 1762, near Millbach, Millcreek Township, Lebanon County.

to describe how people washed their dishes in the period, but presumably the form appeared by the late 1700s. In 1835 Absalohn Huber noted in his account book that he made a *Spiel bank*—dish washing bench—for Abraham Mayer, costing 50 cents.[20] In 1803 Bucks County joiner Abraham Overholt noted in his account book, "I made a dough trough and a water bench for Henrich Kuendig."[21] Typically made of a less-expensive local wood like tulip-poplar or pine, they may have been painted or washed with a stain. A dry sink with shaped sides resembling those on regional benches has a history of having come from Ephrata through dealer Ada Musselman (fig. 2.9).[22] The production of dry sinks continued through the nineteenth century. Amish cabinet-maker Henry Lapp (1862–1904), who was deaf, created a notebook of watercolor illustrations of his products to show customers. In that diminutive book he drew three versions of a dry sink, which he called a "water-bench," with drawers and doors in various configurations. Lapp's sinks were lined with copper or tin, sometimes painted green, and had a raised section to the left as a place for draining and drying.[23]

Dough Troughs

A form common to most eighteenth- and nineteenth-century homes throughout the region, regardless of ethnic or religious persuasion, was the dough trough or dough tray (fig. 2.10). Since bread was made in almost every non-urban household, it is not surprising that many inventories list them. Nearly every joiner, whether of German or British heritage, whose account or daybook survives, lists dough troughs.[24] Enos Thomas of Goshen Township, Chester County, recorded making seventeen "dough troughs" between 1791 and 1801. In 1792 he charged £0.15.0, and six years later his price had increased to £0.18.9.[25] Given their relative low cost (in 1792 he charged £1.15.0 for a card table), these may have been simple, lidded, rectangular canted-side boxes dovetailed or nailed together and intended to be placed on a table. Abraham Overholt working in Plumstead Township, Bucks County, recorded making both "dough trays" and a "dough tray table." In 1796 he charged Johannes Detweiler

for a "dough tray table and painted it brown."[26] That one probably stood on legs with a stretcher base and removable top. The tops on troughs with legs consisted of a large board that served as a work surface. So that the tops did not move while the dough was being worked, battens were fastened to the underside and positioned to fit within the frame of the trough. The manner in which these pieces were used helps to explain the sturdiness of the construction. Period recipes confirm that the dough for bread, cakes, and cookies was mixed in a trough or tray.[27]

Although the trough seen here may be sturdier and more ornate than those in the references above, the basic form is the same: a canted-side box attached to a frame with turned legs joined by rectilinear stretchers. The block-and-baluster legs of this trough are exceptional, with detailed turnings and molded edges. The use of side stretchers joined by a medial stretcher is distinctive, as the more common arrangement has four stretchers joining the legs in a box shape. Made of tulip-poplar, the heavy construction of the base may suggest a Germanic craftsman. Even in instances of distinctly detailed examples like this one, however, it is impossible to establish specific dates and places of manufacture without a provenance.[28]

FIGURE 2.9
Dry sink, Ephrata area, Lancaster County, 1780–1820. Collection of Susan Fetterolf and Jeffrey Gorrin

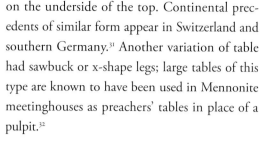

FIGURE 2.10
Dough trough, possibly
Lancaster County, 1735–75.
The von Hess Foundation,
Wright's Ferry Mansion

FIGURE 2.11
Table, southeastern Pennsylvania, 1740–1800. Collection of
James and Nancy Glazer

Tables

Another regional furniture form related to dough troughs in construction and use is the stretcher-base table (fig. 2.11). The example seen here is a diminutive version of larger ones that often have a wide and a narrow drawer.[29] The splayed legs are an exceptional feature of this design.[30] Tables of this form, with flat stretcher bases, turned or square-sawn legs, and removable tops, provided utilitarian work surfaces. The tops could be taken outside for scrubbing and even replaced when worn. These were the workhorses of the kitchen and a distinctive regional form with little indication as to precise locales. The top is secured to the sides with pegs slid through the dovetail battens

on the underside of the top. Continental precedents of similar form appear in Switzerland and southern Germany.[31] Another variation of table had sawbuck or x-shape legs; large tables of this type are known to have been used in Mennonite meetinghouses as preachers' tables in place of a pulpit.[32]

Cupboards

Cupboards are another common form for the storage of ceramics, woodenwares, pewter, and all manner of cooking, eating, and drinking vessels. Large examples with doors and shelving are frequently referred to as kitchen cupboards in period sources; they are also sometimes called dressers. They appear to have been used in both English- and German-speaking households and have origins in the British Isles, Ireland, and continental Europe. Few have been found with exact histories of ownership, so it is difficult to cite specific characteristics that pin them to precise locations. Freestanding cupboards as well as smaller hanging ones (see figs. 1.47, 1.48) were made of expensive native hardwoods like walnut as well as pine or tulip-poplar, which could then be painted or stained to appear more costly. Cupboards could be built-in or simply consist of shelves attached to the wall. If an inventory of a kitchen contains quantities of pewter, ceramics, and other equipage and yet no piece of storage furniture is listed, there is the strong likelihood that some type of built-in cupboard or shelves existed. One form in the mid- to late eighteenth century had open shelves above with doors enclosing shelves in the lower portion (fig. 2.12). Like the example seen here, some had elaborate cornices and boldly shaped sides on the upper section. Sometimes the shelves were notched along the front edges for hanging spoons, and most had rails to keep plates secure. Large and cumbersome forms, the earlier, open-front examples were often all one piece, such as the one knocked over when a steer ran into Jacob Laumaster's kitchen in York (fig. 2.13). Lewis Miller's detailed illustration provides clear documentation as to what might have been placed on the shelves of such a cupboard.

By the late eighteenth and early nineteenth centuries, cupboards were common in a broader

FIGURE 2.12
Kitchen cupboard, southeastern
Pennsylvania, 1750–1800, with
ceramics and metalwork.
Winterthur Museum, bequest
of Henry Francis du Pont

FIGURE 2.13
*Jacob Laumaster's Kitchen Cup-
board upside down*, by Lewis
Miller, York, York County, 1809.
York County Heritage Trust

economic range of households. Many had paneled doors below and glazed doors above and
were made in two parts to facilitate moving
(see fig. 4.60). One that Quaker cabinetmaker
Enos Thomas made for Phineas Massey in 1796
was described as "a large Poplar Cupboard with
a glass door above and double Panel do below .
. . painted mahogany."[33] Exactly where Massey
placed this cupboard is unknown, but the fact that
it was painted to resemble mahogany suggests that
it might have been in a more formal room.

LOCALISMS IN SEATING FORMS: CHESTER COUNTY
Settles

Although many furniture forms are difficult to document to specific locations, some have more definite links. Quakers in Chester County, for example, preferred several seating forms derived from British precedents. In addition to wainscot chairs, one of the earliest forms popular among the more affluent Quaker families was the paneled or leather-back settle.[34] Traveling in Chester County in 1830, antiquarian John Fanning Watson noted one settle with "a very high back of plain boards, and the whole was of white pine, generally unpainted and whitened well with unsparing scrubbing . . . They were a very common article in very good houses."[35] A massive piece of furniture made to shelter one from cold drafts, settles with high backs recalled wainscot armchairs owned by wealthy Quakers in Philadelphia and Chester County. Like their British precedents, some settles were made to open into a type of box bed for additional sleeping accommodations. Joseph and Mary Pennock owned a walnut settle bed (fig 2.14) that survives at their 1738 house now known as Primitive Hall (see fig. 1.10), in Chester County.[36] The large scale of this piece suggests that it may have been made about the same time as their house, or shortly thereafter. The six fielded vertical panels across the back and three horizontal panels across the front are a design seen on other Chester County examples. The leather upholstered seat appears to be original, with brass nails ornamenting the edges. Iron hooks at either end of the front seat rail unlatch from the front posts to allow the seat and paneled front to fall forward, forming a box to accommodate a mattress. Joseph Pennock's prominence as a longtime member of the Provincial Assembly and justice of the peace meant that there were frequent overnight visitors at his residence, making a versatile piece like this useful. One of Pennock's neighbors, fellow Irish Quaker Samuel Beverle (Beverly), also owned a "settle bed" when he died in 1751.[37] Leather was a popular seat covering for settles

FIGURE 2.14

Settle bed, made for Joseph and Mary Pennock, probably West Marlborough Township area, Chester County, 1730–50. Primitive Hall Foundation

FIGURE 2.15
Couch, owned by the Darlington family, probably Chester County, 1725–50. The Dietrich American Foundation

and can be found on one dated 1758 with the initials "I ᴾ E" for Isaac and Elizabeth (Darlington) Pyle, who also lived in West Marlborough Township.[38] Since no settle appears in Isaac's 1794 inventory, this may have been the "Couch" noted by the appraisers.[39]

Rush-bottom Couches

Another seating form popular among the more affluent English-speaking people in Chester County (perhaps influenced by those made or owned in Philadelphia) was the rush-bottom couch (fig. 2.15). Today this form is often called a daybed, although that term was not used in the period. With Anglo origins in the late 1600s, couches probably first appeared in America soon after that as a cane-back and seated version, with many imported from London.[40] By at least the 1720s, as rush-bottom, slat-back chairs became one of the cheapest and most common seating forms, couches were also made, perhaps en suite, as were their caned predecessors. The typical Chester County examples are distinguished by stocky cylindrical legs with bulbous turnings above and below, and ball- or baluster-turned stretchers with arrow-shape ends. The design of the back varied depending on the date and fashion—from solid arched crests above a series of molded banisters to shaped or yoked crests above one or more vasiform splats, sometimes flanked by molded banisters. These couches usually had a long mattress on the seat and cushions at the back. Some, like the example seen here, were constructed so the back could recline slightly when adjustable chains at the top of the rear stiles were released, allowing the framework of the back to pivot on the tenons of the rear rail. These rear stiles could be straight or canted backward above the seat rail for greater comfort. Usually made of walnut or maple, couches were painted or simply varnished. Like the one illustrated, several survive with original blue paint, indicating the vibrancy they would have provided in a dimly lit interior. The 1770 inventory of John Carter of East Bradford Township, Chester County, lists "one Leather Couch" as well as "One Blue rush Bottom Couch."[41] A number of couches can be documented to Chester County: the one illustrated descended in the family of Abraham Darlington (born 1757) of Thornbury Township; another comes from the family of Daniel Sharples (1710/11–75) of Ridley Township, Chester (now Delaware) County, and is attributed to Sharples, who apprenticed in 1728 to joiner Joseph Hibberd of Darby Township.[42]

Much of the early furniture owned in Chester County resided in rural farmsteads. As depicted in the painting of Lownes Taylor's farm about a mile north of West Chester, the landscape was one of rolling hills covered with acres of forests and fields (fig. 2.16). Commissioned in 1832 from artist Bass Otis (1784–1863), the image shows a prosperous farm and mill complex with an extensive number of outbuildings, similar to many farms in southeastern Pennsylvania. A Taylor descendant described this picture as "Didcot—named for the Taylor ancestral farm in England. Mill Race at Bot-

tom of yard, facing west, showing old Benjamin Taylor's Mill property in lower left."[43] The painting retains its original frame with elaborately ornamented corners of painted and stenciled gilt shells and foliage outlined with a band of gold leaf. Taylor was billed $20.00 for the work; in the same year he paid Otis $60.00 more for portraits of himself and his wife and three other family members. Taylor died in 1833 at the age of forty-one, leaving his wife a considerable estate.[44]

LOCALISMS IN ORNAMENT: LINE-AND-BERRY INLAY OF CHESTER COUNTY

By the early 1700s a type of ornament now known as line-and-berry inlay was being used to embellish furniture (fig. 2.17). Most likely this workmanship was introduced by Welsh Quakers who came to Philadelphia and moved into areas of Chester County. A related type of ornamental inlay made in southern Wales in the late seventeenth and eighteenth centuries was documented by Lee Ellen Griffith in her thorough

FIGURE 2.16
Lownes Taylor farm, by Bass Otis, West Goshen Township, Chester County, 1832. Chester County Historical Society, West Chester, Pa.

examination of this southeastern Pennsylvania localism.[45] Although no specific Welsh émigré craftsmen can be cited as having brought this distinctive style of ornament to Pennsylvania, there is little doubt about the inspiration for line-and-berry ornament.[46] The drawer fronts of a dressing table of Welsh make have inlaid compasswork lines that terminate in a single large, round berry. The front is also veneered to form a decorative striped border, related to the herringbone veneer banding found on some Chester County examples.[47] The earliest known examples of line-and-berry inlaid furniture in America include a wainscot chair with inlaid back and a date of 1704 (later changed to 1714), and a small chest of drawers (two drawers side by side over two long drawers) inlaid on the top "IB / 1706" in an oval with clusters of berries flanking the initials.[48] It is probable that line-and-berry ornament was first used on early Philadelphia furniture; however, to date no such examples can be firmly documented.

Although the Welsh primarily used oak for their inlaid furniture, a ready supply of black walnut in southeastern Pennsylvania made it the wood of choice for such pieces. Occasionally cherry or red cedar was used. The higher value of these local hardwoods, as well as the additional labor and cost for the inlay, made these objects more expensive and therefore mostly commissioned by people of greater means. The circular or arc-like line motifs that form the decoration were first scribed on the surface with a compass. Using a combination of circles and arcs, a craftsman could create a wide range of motifs, employing a straightedge if a rectangular surround for a date or initials was desired. Once the decoration was laid out, the maker used a narrow gouge or chisel to carve a shallow channel where the inlay was inserted. Holly was likely the wood used for the line inlay, as it was native and light enough in color to contrast with the walnut. The places for the berries were probably cut with a center bit, or wimble; two different color woods, usually red cedar or maple, were often used to create contrast in these motifs.[49] Although no cabinetmaker's patterns for line-and-berry inlay have been discovered, occasional scribing on the inside surfaces of an object suggests that masters

FIGURE 2.17
Detail of inlay on desk-and-bookcase (fig. 2.23), made for William Montgomery, Nottingham area, Chester County, 1725–40. Rocky Hill Collection

or apprentices experimented with their tools and motifs before executing the final design.

More than 125 pieces of line-and-berry furniture are known; chests of drawers, spice (or valuables) boxes, and small lidded boxes were the most popular forms. Furniture embellished with such inlay was favored primarily by Quakers in southern Chester County, and almost all of it was made prior to the American Revolution. Determining exactly where specific pieces were made, and by whom, is challenging since so little of this work was ever signed by the makers. Objects with initials, dates, and in rare instances a name are particularly helpful, especially when a family history identifies the original owner. A group of pieces with histories or associations in the southern Chester County areas of East and West Nottingham, New London, and London Britain townships may define a local style of inlay. Included are several spice boxes, a small lidded box,[50] three slant-front desks, a high chest, a desk-and-bookcase, and a tall-case clock.[51] In addition to related designs, several distinctive features of the inlay found on these objects are the use of single or double light and dark diagonal banding, three tightly clustered berries, two-petal tulip motifs, and initials formed with double lines.

An exceptional walnut spice box with inlaid tulips as well as light and dark banding

outlining the door and central motif is said to have come from a family in London Britain Township, east of New London Township and on the Delaware border (fig. 2.18).[52] Even the sides of this box are banded and inlaid, and applied pieces of cherry beneath the cornice molding on the front and sides contrast with the walnut, echoing the arch of the door with two smaller arches on each side piece. The straight bracket feet suggest a date in the 1740s or 1750s. An earlier-style square spice box with ball feet (fig. 2.19) and a history of ownership in the Hartshorn (Hartshorne) family of West Nottingham has related inlay details and is attributed to joiner Thomas Coulson (1703–63). The writing on several drawer bottoms appears to be "John Coul…," presumably for John Coulson (1737–1812), Thomas's son, who was also a joiner and probably apprenticed to his father at the time this box was made. Thomas was born in the village of Hartshorne, Derbyshire, England, in 1703, and married Martha Wiley in 1725, probably in Nottingham. It is not known when he arrived in America, where and with whom he trained, or when he came to Nottingham. When Thomas died in 1763 he left "to my son John Coulson all the Utensils of Husbandry on said Place and Two Horses and Two Cows and half my Joyners Tools."[53] When John died at the age of seventy-five in

1812, he may no longer have been working as a joiner since only some "old plains" and "Half Inch poplar Boards" are noted in his inventory.[54] The extent of the listing, which includes a desk-and-bookcase, numerous books, a tea table, a flowered teapot, and two cream jugs suggests a level of refinement in his household. Living in the same community, and perhaps having come at the same time from the village of Hartshorne in England, it is not surprising that there were close ties between the Coulsons and the Hartshorns.[55]

Two elaborate slant-front desks with similar inlay on the drawer fronts were the first line-and-berry objects to be associated with a known maker—Scots-Irish Presbyterian carpenter and wheelwright of Nottingham, Hugh Alexander (1724–77). The basis for the attribution comes from the tradition that one of the desks, still owned in the family, was made by Hugh for his brother James in 1757. This information is recorded in an 1878 history of the Alexander family and is noted on a brass plaque on the fall front of the desk. The other almost identical desk (fig. 2.20) was given to Henry Francis du Pont by collector Mrs. Giles Whiting in 1961.[56] No provenance accompanied the desk to du Pont, but a chalk inscription on the side of one of the interior drawers reads "Elizabeth Phillips." She may be the Elizabeth Phillips of West Nottingham (b. 1816) descended from Welsh

immigrant William Phillips (1701–60) who settled there. Another chalk inscription on the side of the proper right document drawer reads "[ill.] Draw / 1747/8," which is likely the date of manufacture. Both desks have nearly identical interiors; the Winterthur example (fig. 2.21) was carefully crafted with eleven secret drawers and compartments.[57] One of the distinctive features of these desks is the light and dark herringbone banding around the drawer fronts. Recent examination and wood analysis have determined that the light, shimmery yellowish wood in the banding and the five center drawer fronts and the prospect door trim in the interior is sumac.[58] This strikingly different wood contrasts well with the red cedar on the four drawers flanking the center section of the interior. The slant front on Winterthur's desk appears to be a replacement and has no inlay; however, the slant front on the desk made for James Alexander was elaborately inlaid although only the top portion remains.[59]

Brothers Hugh and James Alexander were born to John Alexander of Lanark and Margaret Glasson of Glasgow, Scotland. In 1736 the family immigrated to America and settled in West Nottingham Township, Chester County. There Hugh learned and practiced the trades of carpenter and wheelwright, along with agricultural pursuits. Little is known of his life and work in West Nottingham, but an indenture of October 13, 1757, noted that William Brown, son of James Brown, was apprenticed to Hugh Alexander, "to learn the Arts, Trades or Mysteries of a Carpenter & Wheel Wright" for a term of eighteen months.[60] At that time the term "carpenter" denoted a wide range of woodworking skills.

In 1752 Hugh Alexander married Margaret Edmiston of Lower West Nottingham, Chester County. In the mid-1750s he traveled northwest, perhaps following the lead of his father, John, who had gone to Carlisle, Cumberland County, and later to Chambersburg in Franklin County to buy land. Hugh purchased a farm of about 1,100 acres in Sherman's Valley, Tyrone Township, Cumberland (now Perry) County. Some of the earliest settlers in that area were the Alexander, Brown, McDowell, McNitt, Reed, and Taylor families from the Notting-

ham–New London area of southern Chester County. As war with Britain drew near, Hugh went to Philadelphia in June 1776 as a deputy from Cumberland County to the Committee of Safety.[61] By March 1777, he had died there. It was reported that "he was a tall, strong, dark-haired man, and had no fear about him." When Alexander's estate was inventoried in 1778, the listing of carpenter, joiner, turner, and

FIGURE 2.20
Desk, attributed to Hugh Alexander, Nottingham area, Chester County, 1745–60. Winterthur Museum, gift of Mrs. Giles Whiting

FIGURE 2.21
Detail of desk interior in fig. 2.20.

shoemaker tools indicated that he was a mul-titalented craftsman. Among his woodworking tools were:

> To Compasses Coopers adzs & drawing knife
>
> To 2 Turning heads . . . Compasses & manuel
>
> To Tools for Turning
>
> To 20 plains and four adze
>
> To 3 pieces of blister Steel
>
> To Joiners Tools
>
> To 2 hand saws
>
> To files
>
> To more Carpenter Tools
>
> To more Turners Tools
>
> To the Irons of a Saw Mill .....£ 10
>
> To more Vaner Tools [62]

As evidenced by this inventory, Hugh Alexander was well prepared to provide for his family in what was Pennsylvania's frontier at that time. With ample land, livestock, and tools, he was a true pioneer. Interestingly, among his household items was one desk valued at £7.0.0, a relatively high sum compared to other items in the inventory. Perhaps future research will uncover furniture that Hugh made when living in Cumberland County.

The discovery in the late 1980s of a line-and-berry flat-top high chest added a form not previously known to this group of superbly inlaid objects (fig. 2.22). Found in Peach Bottom, along the Susquehanna River in southern Lancaster County (due west of Nottingham), this piece is probably by Hugh Alexander, based on the inlay pattern on the drawer fronts.[63] Although the drawers lack the herringbone inlay found on the desks, the line-and-berry inlay is identical. No history accompanied the high chest, but the most recent owner, Joseph S. Terrill, was a direct descendant of the Gatchell family of East Nottingham. Inlaid on the topmost long drawer are the double-

FIGURE 2.22

High chest of drawers, probably made for Jeremiah Gatchell, probably by Hugh Alexander, Nottingham area, Chester County, 1750–60. Rocky Hill Collection

line initials "I G," likely for Jeremiah Gatchell (1734–1802). The grandson of prominent land-owner and justice of the peace Elisha Gatchell Sr., Jeremiah married Hannah Brown in 1753. The high chest was probably made about that time. Although Jeremiah died intestate, the inventory of his property taken in 1802 includes a "Case of Drawers Walnut" valued at $6."[64]

A stylistically early form with line-and-berry inlay, presently known in only one complete example, is the double dome-top desk-and-bookcase.[65] Made in one piece and of cherry, as opposed to walnut and the usual two-part form of desk-and-bookcases, this styl-ish urban piece descended through the Mont-gomery family (fig. 2.23). At the top of the door panels are double-line inlaid initials "W" and "M," presumably for the original owner, with an "A" inlaid in the center of the cornice molding at a later time.[66] Although the pattern of inlay on the drawer fronts differs from that on the slant-front desks and high chest, it does relate directly to a group of early rail-and-stile chests.[67] The desk interior is similar in overall format to the interiors of the slant-front desks attributed to Hugh Alexander, but the strik-ing organization of the rail-and-stile door pan-els and the inlay on them is unique. The most likely original owner of this piece was Wil-liam Montgomery (1665/6–1742), a Scots-Irish Presbyterian immigrant who came to America about 1722 and settled in northern Delaware. One of his sons, Alexander Montgomery, was likely the next owner, which could account for the initial "A" that was later inlaid on the cor-nice. Both Alexander Montgomery and his wife, Mary McCullough, died in 1747; their son William (1736–1816) is believed to have been the next owner. Because he was orphaned at an early age, William was placed under the guardianship of neighbor Evan Rice, who was a fellow member of the White Clay Creek Presby-terian Church. In 1777 William moved to Nor-thumberland County, where he helped found the town of Danville (now in Montour County) and spent the rest of his life. During the Ameri-can Revolution, he was colonel of the 4th, or "Elk," Battalion, which included Captain James McDowell's company (see fig. 2.77). Promoted

FIGURE 2.23

Desk-and-bookcase, made for William Montgomery, Nottingham area, Chester County, 1725–40. Rocky Hill Collection

later to major general, William was also a judge, land surveyor, state senator, and U.S. representative. In his will of 1816, he specified that "the Clock, Desk and Bookcase and the parlour cupboard shall continue annexed to the house." The house passed to his son Alexander (1777–1848) and remained in the family into the early 1900s.[68]

Although the original owner of the desk was most likely William Montgomery the immigrant, the maker is less certain, though the family history and line-and-berry inlay point to a southern Chester County origin. The maker may have been Hugh Alexander, but there were other artisans in the area capable of its manufacture. The possibility even exists that it was made by one craftsman and inlaid by another. With more research and new discoveries, the answer may eventually be revealed.

Tall Chests

Another distinctive group of Chester County furniture consists of tall chests of rail-and-stile construction with paneled sides. They date between the 1720s and the 1760s. Configured with three narrow, arched-head drawers across the top, some of the chests have line-and-berry inlay on two or more of the drawer fronts (fig. 2.24).[69] Depending on the date and style, the type of feet range from a simple continuation of the stiles to front ball feet and rear stile feet to straight or ogee bracket feet. On some of the chests the stiles are the primary weight-bearing members for the case. Rather than metal locks, the five narrower drawers at the top are often secured by simple wooden spring locks, sometimes incorrectly referred to as Quaker locks but also found on some Germanic furniture (fig. 2.25). An undecorated chest with two rectangular panels on either side and three arched-head drawers across the top tier is signed by maker Adam Glendenning (d. 1812) of West Fallowfield Township, Chester County, abutting the Lancaster County border. This chest has a distinctive dentil cornice with punched center circles between the dentils and an applied board just below the cornice echoing the arched drawers on the front.[70]

As noted in chapter one, both English- and German-speaking people had a penchant for placing initials and dates on furniture, dishes, textiles, and even houses. Whether done to identify ownership, status, or something else, the practice can be helpful but frustrating. If firm histories survive with marked and dated pieces, a wealth of information is often revealed; but without a history, the task of identifying an original owner can be hopeless. Within this group of paneled-side tall chests with arched-head drawers a number have owners' initials and dates inlaid across the two narrow drawers in the second row from the top. They are placed within rectangular surrounds, flanked by arched stems with three

FIGURE 2.24

Tall chest of drawers, London Grove Township area, Chester County, 1746. The Dietrich American Foundation

berries at each end. The dates on these chests range from 1746 to 1766.[71] On two, the maker added the initials but before inserting the inlay scribed over the surname initial with a different one. The chest seen here has the initials "E S" on the left-side drawer and the date "1746" on the right (fig. 2.26). Upon close examination one can see that the maker originally incised a "C" instead of an "S" for the surname. Perhaps this change was made because the purchaser wished a married surname initial placed on the chest instead of a birth surname. The other tall chest had a change in both initials. It is dated "1758" on the right-hand drawer front, and faint incised marks indicate that the maker intended to inlay an "M" and "K" on the left-side drawer front. The actual inlaid initials on the 1758 chest are "S M," correlating with its being owned by Sarah Miller of New Garden Township, and having descended through six generations of the family into the twentieth century.[72] Based on the similarity of all the initials, numerals, surrounds, and open spacing of the three berries, it is reasonable to suggest that these chests were made in the same locale, if not by the same craftsman.

Though it is not yet known who made the tall chests, two diminutive versions with similar arched-head drawers and related inlay have histories of ownership that help place this group in a specific locale. Made of highly figured walnut, one example has the initials "H D" and the date "1747" inlaid on the front (fig. 2.27) in a manner closely resembling that of the "E S" tall chest and other related chests. This chest was probably made for Hannah Darlington (1729–95), daughter of Abraham Darlington the elder (d. 1776), of Birmingham Township. It presumably descended through the Jefferis, Seal, and Bailey families of Chester County, who lived in the London Grove, New Garden, and West Marlborough Township area. In 1752 Hannah married William Jefferis of East Bradford Township.[73] Her sister, Mary Darlington, married joiner Moses Pyle (d. 1784) at New Garden Meeting in 1736. When Moses died in Little Britain Township, Lancaster County, he owned "Joyners Tools," "a walnut chest part done," and "46 foot of walnut Boards," further confirming

FIGURE 2.25
Detail of spring lock. Winterthur Museum

his occupation.[74] The attribution of this chest to Moses Pyle is further supported by its direct relationship to a small chest made the year before for his daughter; it is inlaid on the front with her name, birth date, and the year it was made: "Hannah : Pyle : was / Born : the 25 : 8M : 1742" and "1746." Hannah was the daughter of Moses and his second wife, Mary Cook, who married at London Grove Meeting in 1741.[75] As a joiner, Moses is the most likely maker of the chest for his daughter, who was four years old in 1746. Given the close similarity of this piece to the "H D" example, it is likely that Moses made the "H D" chest a year later for his sister-in-law, Hannah Darlington. Also related to this group is a box in the collection of the Chester County Historical Society with inlaid initials "H C" and

FIGURE 2.26
Detail of inlay on fig. 2.24.

FIGURE 2.27
Small chest-over-drawers, probably made for Hannah Darlington, probably by Moses Pyle, London Grove Township area, Chester County, 1747. Winterthur Museum partial purchase and partial gift of William R. Smith and sons in memory of Marjorie B. Smith, wife and mother

the date "1744" in a rectangle surrounded by similar trailing vines and berries; it descended in the Carlyle family of London Grove Township.[76] In light of the histories of the objects discussed above, it is logical to conclude that this group of dated and initialed line-and-berry pieces was made in the vicinity of East and West Marlborough, London Grove, and New Garden townships.

A Southern Connection

As the eighteenth century progressed and later generations sought land of their own, there was a continuous migration of people from southeastern Pennsylvania through western Maryland and into Virginia's Shenandoah Valley and the North Carolina Piedmont.[77] In 1872 one historian observed:

> Had a traveler from Pennsylvania visited, about forty or fifty years ago, portions of the present counties of Alamance, Guilford, Davidson, Rowan, . . . in the State of North Carolina, he might have believed himself to have unexpectedly come upon some part of the old Keystone State. His ear would have been greeted with sounds of the peculiar dialect of the Pennsylvania-German language, familiarly known as "Pennsylvänisch-Deutsch."[78]

Both English- and German-speaking people settled in the southern backcountry, creating an ethnic and religious diversity similar to that in southeastern Pennsylvania.[79] Quaker meetinghouses and Presbyterian churches were founded along with Lutheran and Reformed churches. Likewise, the furniture forms favored by these southern settlers echoed those popular among their ancestors and relatives in Pennsylvania, including slat-back chairs, kitchen cupboards, hanging cupboards, painted and inlaid chests, and tall chests of drawers. How much of this likeness can be attributed to the cultural diversity and material possessions brought by those of English, Welsh, Scots-Irish, Swiss, and German background is still unclear. However, a starting place for finding the answers can begin with well-documented furniture such as the tall

chest of drawers made in 1796 for George and Barbara Faust (Foust) of Stoner's Church in Orange County (now Alamance), North Carolina (fig. 2.28). This piece exhibits a fascinating combination of design and ornament associated with furniture made and owned by both English- and German-speaking people.

At first glance this tall chest, with its three arched-head drawers across the top row, resembles the Chester County examples discussed above. To make this story more complex, though, the inlaid initials and date (fig. 2.29) are executed with sulfur inlay instead of light wood, as a Quaker craftsman from Chester County would have done.[80] As will be discussed below, in southeastern Pennsylvania, sulfur inlay is found almost exclusively on Germanic pieces from Lancaster County and the surrounding areas. A study of architecture in the North Carolina Piedmont reveals a similar amalgam of distinct Germanic features on buildings that are otherwise English in their appearance, not unlike the use of sulfur inlay on an otherwise English-looking chest of drawers. Such examples speak to the cross-cultural influences on objects when a locale is settled by diverse groups.[81] Other sulfur-inlaid pieces from this part of Orange County and other areas are known, including four blanket chests with similar devices outlining the initials.[82] A closer look at the Faust tall chest reveals significant design and construction aspects that support its later date: the case is a dovetailed box rather than the rail-and-stile construction with paneled ends; the feet are ogee instead of straight bracket; and the brasses (replacements that approximate the witness marks of the originals) are in the Chippendale style rather than the earlier Queen Anne type seen on the 1746 tall chest made for "E S." All these features reflect the date of "1796" inlaid on the chest.

George Faust (1756–1836) was the son of Johannes Faust (1719–89) of Hessia, Germany, who immigrated through Philadelphia to Bern Township, Berks County, in 1733. In 1764 George and his family moved to North Carolina, where, in 1778 he married Barbara Kivett, who was likely born in Randolph County, North Carolina, around 1761. Eventually George

FIGURE 2.28
Tall chest of drawers, made
for George and Barbara Faust,
Orange (now Alamance)
County, North Carolina, 1796.
Museum of Early Southern
Decorative Arts, Old Salem
Museums & Gardens

FIGURE 2.29
Detail of inlay on fig. 2.28.

and Barbara settled near Bellemont in Orange County and were among the founders of Stoner's Church, whose members were primarily from the southeastern Pennsylvania counties of Schuylkill and Berks.[83]

Understanding the diverse demographics of this area of Piedmont North Carolina is critical to understanding the Faust tall chest. In the second half of the eighteenth century, the inhabitants of Orange County included German Lutherans, Quakers, and Scots-Irish Presbyterians. About twelve miles south of Stoner's Church, near Snow Camp, the Cane Creek Monthly Meeting was founded in 1751 by Friends from the Exeter Meeting in Berks County. It was the first monthly meeting of Friends in central North Carolina, where 150 Quakers had settled by 1759.[84] In 1754 the New

Garden Monthly Meeting was established just west of Greensboro, in Guilford County. It is likely there was a connection between this meeting and the New Garden and London Grove meetings in Chester County, since local names like Beeson, Mendenhall, and Dicks were among the original membership of the North Carolina New Garden Meeting.[85] Did a Quaker from southern Chester County take a tall chest to the Cane Creek or the New Garden Meeting area, and was that form copied by a German craftsperson? Or might a Quaker craftsman familiar with the earlier form have been asked by George Faust to make a tall chest for him? Until more is known about the background of specific craftsmen in the North Carolina Piedmont, these questions will remain unanswered.

LOCALISMS IN ORNAMENT: SULFUR INLAY OF LANCASTER COUNTY

Sulfur inlay, used to ornament and sometimes identify the owner and date of a piece of furniture, appears to have had its earliest roots in Lancaster County, spreading quickly to other counties in the region. Presently no European furniture with sulfur inlay is known, though there are sixteenth-century examples of Italian furniture with an inorganic composition inlay that resembles sulfur.[86] More than fifty years ago, folk art historian Frances Lichten wrote about a masterpiece of sulfur-inlaid furniture—the elaborately ornamented schrank made for Georg Huber and dated 1779, now in the collection of the Philadelphia Museum of Art.[87] Lichten unknowingly stated that the inlay "is composed of humble substances: powdered white lead and beeswax," relating it to a German technique called *Wachseinlegen*, meaning wax inlay.[88] In 1977 Smithsonian curator Monroe Fabian shed more light on the subject, and with assistance from colleagues in the analytical field he identified the material as sulfur. At that time he had found twenty-two pieces of sulfur-inlaid furniture.[89] A recent focused study has now identified more than one hundred examples.[90]

By the end of the twentieth century, extensive analytical work on this unusual inlay material presented important information about its composition and the technique of inserting it into wood.[91] The application of pure sulfur into V-shape channels cut into wood is a relatively easy process. Depending on the ability of the craftsman, results can range from rudimentary to highly ornate. Because powdered sulfur melts and liquefies when heated just above the boiling temperature of water and expands upon cooling, it is a perfect inlay material. Molten sulfur can be poured into incised decoration; when it has cooled to the consistency of wax, the excess can be removed with a chisel. When the molten sulfur is poured into the channels, tiny air bubbles rise to the surface leaving holes. The resulting look is that of a fairly strong yellow against the dark wood. Over time the yellow sulfur fades to a creamy off-white.

The recorded pieces of sulfur-inlaid furniture from southeastern Pennsylvania and

the South range in date from 1764 to 1844, with a schrank dated 1764 and a chest and tall clock both dated 1765 being the earliest known examples (fig. 2.30). The 1764 schrank and 1765 chest, along with two other schranks dated 1768 and 1775, were owned by descendants of Swiss Mennonite immigrants Christian and Maria Bamberger. The Bambergers and their eight children came to America in 1722, settling first in the Pequea area of Lancaster County before moving about twelve miles north to Warwick Township. The schrank dated 1764 was owned by daughter Anna, who married John Kauffman, a well-to-do farmer and owner of extensive lands in East Hempfield Township. When he was nineteen, their son Michael received a walnut chest with sulfur-inlaid foliate cartouche surrounding the "M 17 65 K" flanking the escutcheon plate.[92] These objects signify the wealth and status of the Kauffmans. The foliate inlay on Michael's chest is almost identical to that on the great paneled doors of Winterthur's sulfur-inlaid schrank made for Emanuel and Mary Herr of Lancaster Township and dated February 17, 1768 (fig. 2.31).[93] Who made these pieces remains a mystery.

The Pequea Valley, southeast of Lancaster, was home to a number of families who fled religious persecution abroad. The French Huguenot Ferree and Lefever families were among the earliest settlers there. Silk weavers of lesser nobility, the family came from lower Normandy. Following the revocation of the Edict of Nantes in 1685, they sought refuge in the Palatinate, then Bavaria, and eventually London, where the indomitable widow, Mary (Marie) Ferree, managed to secure a land grant of 2,300 acres from William Penn and Queen Anne.[94] In 1708 the family journeyed to America, staying first at New Paltz in the Hudson Valley with other refugees from the Palatinate. By 1710 the Pennsylvania lands they were granted had been surveyed, so in 1712 they traveled to Philadelphia and on to the far reaches of what was then Chester County (now Lancaster). The tract along the Pequea Creek that land agent Martin Kendig transferred to them for the sum of £150 was no doubt a rich and fertile land as described in 1754:

FIGURE 2.30
Tall-case clock, made for Peter Feree, movement by Rudolph Stoner, Lancaster, Lancaster County, 1765. Rocky Hill Collection

FIGURE 2.31
Schrank, made for Emanuel and Mary Herr, probably Manor Township area, Lancaster County, 1768. Winterthur Museum, bequest of Henry Francis du Pont

FIGURE 2.32
Detail of clock hood in fig. 2.30.

. . . the beautiful Pequea Valley. The vale is formed by the Valley Hill on the south and the Welsh Mountain on the north . . . Pequea affords a pleasant prospect— a rich landscape–farmhouses surrounded with apple and peach trees. The farmers, proprietors, not tenants. On every farm a lime-kiln, and the land adapted for the best wheat. On inquiry, the finest farms are all owned by Switzers. Land of farms sells readily at three pounds an acre. On the east side of the hills at five pounds per acre.[95]

The monumental tall clock made for Peter Ferree in 1765 is one of the earliest and most ambitious of all known sulfur-inlaid clock cases. The boldly inlaid hood is an obvious statement of ownership, wealth, and status (fig. 2.32). Clocks were an expensive item, marking heri-

tage and history as they passed from generation to generation. Peter was born about 1730 in the Strasburg area of Lancaster County, a grandson of Daniel Ferree, son of Mary and one of the first Pequea-area settlers. A Peter Ferree "living at Pequay" in 1764 paid £14.18.8 for an indentured servant named George Munganus Radle (Ridle) for two years of work.[96] This sum included the cost of passage, suggesting that Ferree was a wealthy man. The well-to-do landowners and farmers who commissioned these early pieces of sulfur-inlaid furniture seem to have been primarily Mennonites of French and Swiss lineage.[97] When Peter Ferree died in Lampeter Township in

1795, the most costly item in his inventory (other than livestock and grains) was his "One eight-day Clock and Case" valued at £8.[98] In December that year his estate was sold at auction and the clock was bought by his fourth son, Jacob, for £18.2.0. In his will, Peter had left his plantation in Lampeter Township to that son.[99] At Peter's sale, Jacob was by far the most successful bidder, purchasing almost all of the household goods and much of the livestock and implements, including one lot of "joiners tools."[100]

An almost identical tall-clock case with similar sulfur inlay, dated a year later, has a movement probably made by George Hoff of Lancaster. Like the Ferree case, it is inlaid in sulfur with the name of the owner, Christian Schwar, and the date "1766." A third clock in a related but not identical case, made for Daniel Besore (Boshaar) and dated "1768" in brass inlay, has a signed Hoff movement.[101] Given the locations of the owners (Ferree lived southeast of Lancaster, and Schwar lived northwest in East Hempfield Township), the sophistication and similarity of the clocks, and the

fact that at least two of the three have movements by Lancaster makers, it is possible that the cases were made in Lancaster.

The eight-day movement with moon-phase dial in Ferree's clock is engraved on the brass dial "Rd[lph] Stoner" for Moravian artisan Rudolph Stoner (1728–69). His origins and training are not known, but he was most likely of Germanic ancestry. Stoner was among the earliest clockmakers to practice his trade in Lancaster and appears in the tax records as early as 1755. By 1760 he had purchased a brick house just north of Center Square, an ideal location for a rising young artisan of thirty-two. His life was cut short in mid-career, however, when he died at the age of forty-one. By that time he had built a sizable business with an upper-class clientele that included Lancaster attorney and businessman Jasper Yeates. Judging from Stoner's inventory, valued at £604.19.2, his shop was full of highly specialized equipment, suggesting that he may have made most parts of the movements and dials, presumably with the assistance of an apprentice. He spoke both German

FIGURE 2.33
Chest-over-drawers, Lancaster County, 1783. National Museum of American History, Smithsonian Institution

FIGURE 2.34
Detail of till inside fig. 2.33.

and English and was a charter member of Pennsylvania's third subscription library, the Juliana Library Company, chartered in 1763. In his estate he left two violins and a clavichord, indicating that he was a man of stature and culture.[102]

The most elaborately ornamented sulfur-inlaid chest known to date is not marked with a name or initials but has a sulfur-inlaid date of "1783" on a removable panel covering the drawer compartment beneath the till (figs. 2.33, 2.34).[103] Tills are usually located on the left side, less often on the right; rarely is there one on each side. They can have one or more drawers, which may be exposed or hidden behind the front board, which then slides up to reveal the drawers. This chest has an early provenance in Lancaster County, which was noted in a 1910 letter from Ephrata dealer W. H. Spangler to Mrs. M. H. Harrington of Germantown, the purchaser:

> *The chest was a bridal gift to the owner
> (Mrs. Dietrich) when she was 17. I
> bought it from her son who was an old
> man. Mrs. Dietrich lived in the country
> about 9 or 10 miles from here and is dead
> many years ago.*"[104]

A pencil inscription inside the top of the chest reads "D W Dietrich / June 22nd 1876,"
further confirming Spangler's statement. This information does not provide enough detail to determine the original owner, but it does give a general location for the origin of the chest. Assuming it was made in 1783, it likely descended through three generations of the Dietrich family by the time Spangler acquired it. Highly architectural with detailed columns having capitals and bases, it was no doubt designed and executed by a skilled craftsman, possibly with a design source or pattern book at hand. Though not identical to any other documented sulfur-inlaid work, the foliate ornament is suggestive of that on the cartouche on the "M K" chest and the Herr schrank (see fig. 2.31). The double band of line inlay outlining the drawer fronts is identical to that on the schrank made for Georg Huber and dated 1779, and the unusual stippling within the leaves is also similar. The ends of this chest are elaborately inlaid, simulating columns flanking a doorway; the lower panels imitate the line inlay on the drawer fronts with the addition of floral inlay where the brasses would be if they were drawer fronts. The extra labor for the inlay, plus the addition of drawers, brasses, and the side carrying handles, most likely made this piece a more expensive product than any other known sulfur-inlaid chest.

FIGURE 2.35
Tall-case clock, movement by George Hoff, Lancaster, Lancaster County, 1790. Private collection

FIGURE 2.36
Detail of inlay on door in fig. 2.35

The use of sulfur inlay continued into the 1800s, though by the 1790s the ornate foliate motifs were replaced by simpler designs. A tall clock with a thirty-hour movement by well-known Lancaster clockmaker George Hoff (1733–1816) is one such example (fig. 2.35). The choice of a thirty-hour movement was presumably that of the purchaser and was likely based on economics, as it was less expensive than an eight-day movement.[105] The flat-top case with deep cornice molding suggests a date earlier than the "1790" inlaid in sulfur on the case door, but that choice also may have been related to cost or personal preference. The "IO SC" inlaid on the case (fig. 2.36) is probably an abbreviation of the first and last names of the owner. The inlaid initials, date, and bird bear a close relationship to those on a twenty-two-inch straightedge dated "1800" with initials "I S" (fig. 2.37). Straightedges were used by a variety of artisans. It is likely that one as personalized as this was made by a craftsman for himself. Might these initials provide a clue to someone working with sulfur inlay?

George Hoff, one of the most influential eighteenth-century clockmakers in Lancaster, settled there in 1769, shortly after Rudolph Stoner's death earlier that year. He was trained in Grünstadt, Germany, and arrived in Philadelphia in August 1765 with his wife and two-year-old daughter. During his life and career in Lancaster, he held numerous public offices and served as a warden and elder at Trinity Lutheran Church. In 1776 he was a private in Jasper Yeates's Company of the Militia,

and was elected for three terms as an assistant to the burgesses of the borough. He owned a stone and brick house on West King Street with a separate brick kitchen and frame stable as well as other properties in Lancaster, indicating that he was a successful craftsman and respected member of the community.[106]

Hoff was part of a prosperous community of middle-class artisans, including the talented artist Jacob Eichholtz (1776–1842), who was also a coppersmith and sign painter. Living just a block away from each other on West King Street, the elderly Hoff had his portrait painted by Eichholtz in late 1815, just eight months before his death (fig. 2.38). The only entry referencing this work in Eichholtz's daybook is on January 1, 1816, when he notes that Hoff's son John bought a frame for his father's portrait. Though

FIGURE 2.37
Straightedge, probably Lancaster County, 1800. Collection of Stephen and Dolores Smith

FIGURE 2.38
Portrait of George Hoff, by Jacob Eichholtz, Lancaster, Lancaster County, 1815. Collection of LancasterHistory.org, Lancaster, Pa.

FIGURE 2.39
Conestoga Creek and Lancaster,
by Jacob Eichholtz, Lancaster,
Lancaster County, 1833. Penn-
sylvania Academy of the Fine
Arts, Philadelphia, gift of Mrs.
James H. Beal

there appears to be no entry for the painting,
in September 1816 John Hoff recorded an order
from Eichholtz for an eight-day spring-powered
clock for $70, possibly in exchange for the por-
trait done months earlier.[107] This image of the
respected patriarch of three generations of Lancaster clockmakers signifies the wealth and status
he achieved over decades of work and service to
his community. Looking like a sage elder with his
hand resting on a book, the image suggests Hoff's
knowledge and learning.[108]

From its settlement in 1730, Lancaster was
a bustling metropolis, market town, and capital of the commonwealth from 1799 to 1812.
The countryside remained an agricultural oasis,
with the Conestoga River snaking through the
land. In 1833 Eichholtz captured this rural landscape in a painting for his married daughter,
Catharine Lindsay, then living in Philadelphia
(fig. 2.39). As he was working on the painting he wrote to her noting that he was taking
it from "Kreider's Hill." In the far distance, he
included a view of Lancaster.[109]

LOCALISMS IN ORNAMENT: PAINTED DECORATION
The Compass Artist

Distinctive local expressions of paint-decorated objects could be found in rural communities throughout the counties of southeastern
Pennsylvania. Ranging from small, slide-
lid storage boxes to colorfully decorated
chests and monumental paneled and painted
schranks, these objects were made for men and
women of all ages. They were plentiful and
often inexpensive. Those that have survived
today are prized as family heirlooms and collectors' pieces. A meticulously decorated group
of boxes and chests known as the Compass
Artist group includes more than sixty objects
with distinctive compasswork and freehand
decoration. Recent study has yielded significant information, although no specific artisans'
names can be associated with the objects.[110]
The most popular form is the dome-top box
with hinged top made in a wide variety of
sizes with consistent construction techniques

(fig. 2.40). A hinged-top salt box, two doll-size cradles, and five full-size chests have also been recorded. Small slide-lid boxes were also made, some with divided interiors to hold trinkets or perhaps spices. These forms were usually constructed of tulip-poplar and painted with a Prussian blue or vermilion (or red lead) ground with contrasting motifs of white, red, or blue. Early collectors of folk art such as Elie Nadelman, Henry Francis du Pont, Emily Johnston de Forest, and Titus Geesey acquired Compass Artist pieces in the 1920s and 1930s.

The decoration on the pieces was first scribed with a compass, or "pair of compasses" as they were called at the time. A standard tool in many craftsmen's inventories, a compass was used to lay out designs. Of all the boxes examined, few have the same dimensions or exact decorative patterns or combinations of motifs. On some the decorative elements are dense; on others they are spaced farther apart. The hardware on all is consistent, with hinges, hasps, and escutcheon plates simply made of tinned sheet iron. Three of the largest boxes painted with a blue ground have drawers (fig. 2.41) and would have cost slightly more because of the size and time involved in making the drawer. A slide-lid box with compasswork decoration of a different sort (fig. 2.42) illustrates the variety a craftsman could achieve with this tool. Decorated with a series of radiating arcs on the top and scribed motifs of speckled flowers and birds on the sides, the color palette remains nearly as vibrant as when new. Based on the close relationship of the box to a dome-top example with slit-through hinges like those used on the Compass Artist boxes of similar form, this box may be from the same region, albeit made by a different hand.[111]

None of the boxes bear names or dates on the exterior; however, inscriptions have been noted on several, providing the best clues as

FIGURE 2.40
Group of three boxes, attributed to the Compass Artist, owned by Jacob and Jonas Nolt (*left*), William Bechtel (*middle*), and S [ill.]le Miller (*right*), Lancaster County, 1800–1840. Winterthur Museum, bequest of Henry Francis du Pont (*left, middle*); Collection of Stephen and Dolores Smith (*right*)

FIGURE 2.41
(*below, right*) Box-over-drawer, attributed to the Compass Artist, Lancaster County, 1800 1840. Private collection

FIGURE 2.42
(*below, left*) Slide-lid box, possibly Lancaster County, 1800–1840.Collection of Jane and Gerald Katcher

to early, if not original, owners and, hence, a place of origin. Surnames written on the bottoms and interiors of several include Nolt, Hunsicker, Ulrich, Brubaker, and Knabb, all found in Lancaster County. Research on the inscriptions indicates that many of the people who owned or inherited these pieces lived in the border region of Lancaster and Lebanon counties. The owners belonged to a variety of Protestant faiths, including Mennonite, Dunkard, Lutheran, and German Reformed. The most fully documented item in the group is a small blue (now dark green) slide-lid box (fig. 2.43, *right*). Written on the bottom is what may be an almost complete history of ownership: "Christian Hunsicker's Box/ died in his 82nd year, Birthday 177[6] / Now Jos Hunsicker Box Ex[r] of C. H. / died in his 89th year Birthday 1803/ Now W. H. Hunsicker Box Ex[r] of J. H." (fig. 2.44). Christian Hunsicker was born March 26, 1776, and died August 5, 1857.[112] He was buried in the graveyard of Wolf's Union Church, Bethel Township, Lebanon County. His son Joseph was born in 1803 and died in 1892. William H. Hunsicker was born about

1842 and died between 1920 and 1930. According to the 1850 census for Bethel Township, Joseph was head of a household occupied by his seventy-four-year-old father Christian and eight-year-old son William. By the time of the 1880 census, Joseph lived with William and his wife in Bethel Township. William was still there in 1920, but no reference to him occurs in the 1930 census.[113] He is likely the same William H. Hunsicker who served on the building committee of the Union Meetinghouse in Bethel Township in 1913. The religious groups who used the original meetinghouse included German Baptists (also known as Dunkers/Dunkards or Brethren), so it is possible that the Hunsickers were members of that faith.[114] Unfortunately, the probate inventories of the Hunsicker men do not list small items in detail.[115]

Five full-size Compass Artist chests are known; one has the date "1788" and initials "C H."[116] All the chests conform in construction, with flattened ball feet attached with a round tenon set into a batten on each side, tenoned through the bottom board of the chest, and then wedged for tightness (fig. 2.45). This consistency of construction suggests they were made in the same shop.[117] The drawer under the till in one chest is similar in construction to those on the smaller boxes, with the bottom attached with small wooden pins; those across the grain are closer together. Like the smaller boxes, each chest is decorated differently. The fronts are organized with three arched panels, the center one being narrower. Motifs such as tulips and tulip petals were drawn with templates. An unusual feature of the chest seen here is the large mermaids drawn in chalk on the underside of the top, flanking each hinge (fig. 2.46). Chest tops were frequently marked with inscriptions, most often with tally marks that recorded amounts of money or time, sometimes with owners' names or dates. It is impossible to know the meaning of these chalk images or who might have drawn them and when. Depictions of mermaids and mermen can be traced to ancient times, and such likenesses appeared in print in the eighteenth century, including a number on fraktur.[118] In particular,

FIGURE 2.43

Slide-lid boxes, attributed to the Compass Artist, made for Christian Hunsicker (*right*), Lancaster County, 1800–1840. Winterthur Museum, bequest of Henry Francis du Pont (*left*); gift of Larry M. Neff in memory of Frederick S. Weiser (*right*)

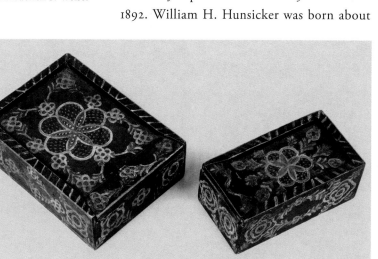

FIGURE 2.44

Detail of inscription on underside of box (*right*) in fig. 2.43.

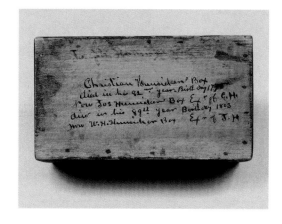

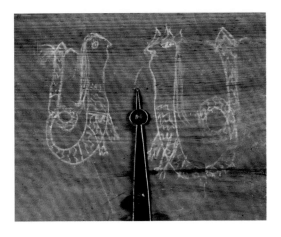

the mermaids rendered in chalk closely resemble those made by Friedrich Speyer on fraktur printed in Ephrata and Reading.[119] Is it possible that whoever drew the mermaids inside the top of the chest may have seen such a fraktur, or even owned one by Speyer? Given what is already known, as additional Compass Artist pieces come to light more clues may point to the makers of these colorful pieces of everyday furniture.

The Jonestown School

As settlers moved into the backcountry, small communities were established close to waterways and rich agrarian land. By 1761 the village of Williamstown (renamed Jonestown in 1771), was founded northwest of Lancaster. Among the earliest inhabitants were the Seltzer and Ranck families. Christian Seltzer (1749–1831) had immigrated with his parents from the Kra-

ichgau region of the northern Palatinate in 1752; the Ranck family was of French Huguenot origin and had arrived in Pennsylvania in 1728–29, settling first in Earl Township in northern Lancaster County. About 1777, some of the second generation of Rancks (including brothers Johannes and Peter) moved farther north to Jonestown, then in Lancaster County.[120] As the population grew, new counties were formed; in 1785 Dauphin County was established from the western portion of Lancaster County, and in 1813 Lebanon County was created from both Lancaster County and Dauphin counties. In 1829 Philadelphia antiquarian John Fanning Watson described this area as a

> romantic looking country of alternate woods and farms, along the margin of the Swatara. I everywhere found more cultivation than I had expected . . . Afterward I passed a well-finished bridge at Jones'town. About forty houses in Jones'town and a steepled church on a level ground. Some locust trees before old houses . . . Went through Stumptown, and a small log-house town, rich and cultivated, in the county of Lebanon. All Germans—none along the road could answer me in English.[121]

It was in Jonestown that some of the first-recognized and best-documented Pennsylvania painted chests were made by members

FIGURE 2.45
Chest, attributed to the Compass Artist, Lancaster County, 1785–1820. Collection of Dr. and Mrs. Donald M. Herr

FIGURE 2.46
Detail of underside of top of chest in fig. 2.45.

FIGURE 2.47

(below) Chest, by Christian Seltzer, Jonestown, Bethel Township, Dauphin (now Lebanon) County, 1796. Winterthur Museum, gift of Henry Francis du Pont

FIGURE 2.48

Detail of inscription on chest in fig. 2.47.

FIGURE 2.49

Chest, made for Henry Winter, probably by Peter Ranck, Jonestown, Bethel Township, Dauphin (now Lebanon) County, 1800–1810. Westmoreland Museum of American Art, Greensburg, Pa., gift of the William A. Coulter Fund

of the Seltzer and Ranck families (fig. 2.47). These chests first attracted the attention of scholar Esther Stevens Fraser in 1925, when she authored a two-part article entitled "Pennsylvania Brides Boxes and Dower Chests."[122] Fraser was particularly attracted to the Seltzer and Ranck chests: "There is one unique thing about Dauphin County chests which, almost to the day that this study went to press, caused me much speculation. This curiosity is the scratching of a name and sometimes a date in the wet paint of a flower vase" (fig. 2.48). Fraser realized the daunting task of identifying and making attributions as she wrote that "the subject is too new a field of research for me to do more than blaze a somewhat imperfect trail."[123] By 1927 she had written three articles comparing the decoration on the chests signed by Christian Seltzer, his son John, and brothers Johannes and Peter Ranck.[124] Fraser made subjective judgments about the quality of the painting on various signed chests, postulating about the makers' training, apprenticeships, competition, and competence.

The existence of this large group of related chests with inscribed signatures is an amazing resource for study, but in 1967 an equally important part of the story was discovered when Winterthur Museum acquired the account book of Peter Ranck, kept between 1794 and 1817. Since only a handful of eighteenth- and early nineteenth-century account books of carpenters or joiners are known, this purchase added significant insight to the context and understanding of the work of the Seltzers and Rancks. Although the accounts shed light on Peter's work and his clients, to date no signed examples of his chests are known.[125]

The names of Ranck and Seltzer are well known and examples of their work and that of the so-called Jonestown School can be found in many museums with Pennsylvania German decorative arts; yet, we know relatively little about the apprenticeships and working relationships of these men. We also do not know for certain whether the name scribed on the vases is that of the painter, joiner, or both. From a construction standpoint, there is great similarity between Christian Seltzer's chests and those of Johannes Ranck. In terms of their decorative schemes, the same is true. The overall format consists of two or three painted panels containing an urn

or vase at the base with a central stem bearing five flowers, but there is great variety in the interpretation of the pots and flowers, making it difficult to know who painted the ones that are not signed and dated. Some chests appear to have other names scratched in the vases, and these may indicate the owners.[126]

Today these chests may not command great attention because of the number that survive and their formulaic nature, but as a body of work they provide the most comprehensive group of documented chests from a specific locale. Knowing the heritage of the Seltzers and Rancks, when they arrived in America, the places they settled, where they worked, and their client base brings us closer to learning more about the artisans who made and painted furniture. Much still remains unknown, including the source for the painted motifs and whether the makers of the chests were also the decorators. What we do know may present a fairly typical scenario for rural craftsmen: making chests, painting them, and doing a variety of other jobs, from farming to innkeeping. Christian Seltzer was described as a yeoman (farmer) in his will, but he clearly was also a cabinetmaker, as was Johannes Ranck.

Although Peter Ranck's account book documents his making furniture in the early part of his career, by about 1804 he was a merchant and tavern keeper as well as a landowner renting farmland. By 1814 he had given up cabinetmaking and joinery, and from then on his wealth and status increased. He was a frequent witness to documents and sold alcohol for great profits. Although the work of Christian Seltzer and Johannes Ranck has been identified, that of Peter Ranck remains a mystery. One chest inscribed inside the top of the till with the name "Henry Winter," presumably the owner, is likely his work (fig. 2.49). The front and overall painted decoration on the piece differ significantly from the documented work of the Seltzers and Johannes Ranck. However, Henry Winter was a client to whom Peter Ranck sold a chest, bedstead, kitchen dresser, table, and dough trough in 1804 as well as chest, dough trough, and table in 1810. At that same time Winter also purchased a gill of whiskey

from Ranck and paid for it in part with two barrels of cider. This Henry Winter had a son named Henry (b. 1791), who was the likely owner of this chest (fig. 2.50).[127] There is an oral tradition that chests with this overall decorative scheme of three arched panels and a surround of alternating blue and red diamonds are from the Jonestown area. The bold red, white, and blue ornament might well be an alternate design to the typical Seltzer-Ranck urns and flowers, perhaps executed by another artisan in the same area. Another equally interesting aspect of this chest appears inside the top, where two brilliantly colored paper and wool rosettes with crimped edges are attached

FIGURE 2.50

Birth and baptismal certificate of Henry Winter, attributed to Johann Conrad Trevits, East Hanover Township, Dauphin (now Lebanon) County, about 1800. Winterthur Museum purchase with funds provided by the Henry Francis du Pont Collectors Circle

through their centers with brass upholstery
nails. Suspended between the rosettes is a blue
and white checkered woven tape. Oral tradition
refers to these tapes as "stocking strings," presumably for hanging personal items belonging
to the owner. Careful examination of numerous chests has discovered nail holes just above
the tips of the hinges inside the tops of chests
or forged nails with fragments of thread or
tape beneath them. The remarkable survival of
this stocking string and rosettes documents the
added creativity and color imparted by such a
simple, utilitarian detail.

Wythe County, Virginia

In considering the migration of Pennsylvania
Germans into Virginia and North Carolina, one
of the mysteries that remains is the relationship
between the typical Jonestown School of painted
chests and those produced in Wythe County, in
southwestern Virginia. Over the years, numerous painted chests resembling the work of the
Seltzers and Rancks, but with a distinctive aesthetic, have surfaced in Wythe County (figs. 2.51,
2.52). Did someone from Jonestown take the idea
of this design, or more likely a chest, to Wythe
County, which had residents of Germanic as well
as Scots-Irish ancestry? Scholarship in the early
1980s noted twenty-two chests in this group, and
today more than thirty are known.[128]

Like the Ranck-Seltzer chests, the decorative schemes of the Wythe County chests vary,
and similarly some have drawers and some do
not. However, the woods (tulip-poplar) and construction are quite consistent. Known examples
are dated between 1808 and 1829. The earliest
recorded one has the name of "Georg Bittinger
[?]" and the date "1808" in a smaller central
panel flanked by two arched-head panels with
floral and urn motifs typical of Wythe County
work; this chest is the only one of this format
known.[129] The name of "Johannes Hudel" is
inscribed on the urn of two other chests.[130] John's
brother, Henry Huddell (variously spelled Hudel
and Hottel in the period), has also been associated with the group. Brothers John (1772–1839),
Henry (1768–1846), and Gideon (1770–1833)
were the children of John (d. 1771) and Elizabeth (Pfeiffer) Huddell, and are buried in the

Kimberling Church Cemetery, several miles north of Rural Retreat in Wythe County. The Huddell brothers were originally from Shenandoah County, but their family moved to Wythe County by 1781 following their widowed mother's marriage to Peter Spangler Jr. They were subsequently raised by a step-uncle, Jacob Spangler, who most likely was a woodworker and trained them in that trade. The large number of joiners tools and materials in all their inventories, greater than in most farmers' inventories, suggests that woodworking was one of both Spangler's and the Huddells' primary means of livelihood.[131] Two of Henry Huddell's daughters married Duttons and at least one of the known chests descended in the Dutton family.[132]

It is unknown whether the Huddells had any connection with Jonestown in Lebanon County, but the recent discovery of a family that did migrate from there to Wythe County is informative.[133] A Jacob Tobler Jr. (Dobler) was born in Jonestown in 1764 and died in Wythe County in 1820; he is buried in the Kimberling Church Cemetery.[134] Might the Tobler family have taken a painted chest with them when they moved to Wythe County? When Jacob Tobler Jr., made his will in December 1817 he appointed Henry Huddell as his executor.[135] This connection between Tobler, born in Jonestown, Pennsylvania, and Huddell, who presumably made several Wythe County chests, is worthy of note. While Tobler's occupation is not known, it would seem that he was at least farming given the significant amount of livestock and agricultural implements in his inventory. Although there is no specific indication that Tobler was a craftsman of any type, he did have 100 pounds of iron in his inventory as well as 162 feet of walnut plank and 390 feet of pine plank. Also of interest in connection with the Huddell and the Tobler/Dobler names is the observation that four of the locks on these chests have the engraved initials "J. D." (Jacob Dobler/Tobler?) and one hinge has the punched initials "J. H." (John Huddell?).[136] While the mystery is not yet solved, more clues to the relationships and occupations of these men may yield firmer documentation for the authorship of the Wythe County chests and their connection with Jonestown, Lebanon County, Pennsylvania.

Conestoga Wagons

As settlement in the eastern counties of southeastern Pennsylvania became denser and younger generations desired farms of their own, the population moved farther west and south into the backcountry. Over mountain ranges and through fertile valleys, the principal vehicle used by settlers was the Conestoga wagon, the same type of conveyance that carried wheat and other local products between Philadelphia and regions westward. These mammoth wagons were the tractor trailers of their time between county seats and the ports of Philadelphia, New Castle, and Baltimore. They were named for the Conestoga Valley near Lancaster, and southeastern Pennsylvania was their main place of manufacture, using the talents of both woodworkers and blacksmiths. York was well known for its production of the wagons, and Lewis Miller, the carpenter-artist of York, often depicted them on the streets of the town. On one drawing he noted, "The wagons made in York had a good praise, for the good work done to them at our place, in the woodwork, and the iron work, done–by the–blacksmith shops." In a more formal manner, Philadelphia artist Thomas Birch painted a bucolic scene of a wagon on the Pennsylvania Turnpike in 1816 (fig. 2.53). As the primary route westward, the turnpike had been incorporated in

FIGURE 2.53
Conestoga Wagon on the Pennsylvania Turnpike, by Thomas Birch, Philadelphia, 1816. Shelburne Museum, Shelburne, Vt.

1792 by Philadelphia and Lancaster merchants who lobbied for a good road between the two cities. Indeed, the weighty Conestoga wagons would have left the roads in deplorable condition. In 1792 five merchants each from Philadelphia and Lancaster formed a commission to oversee construction of the turnpike as a toll road.[137] Upon completion, the highway was said to be the best in the nation:

> [At the] General Paoli tavern, I met a family who had landed a few days before in Philadelphia, and were now on their way to Ohio. . . . Altogether they had the appearance of a stout, hardy race, and in the company, I understand there were four generations. The master of the inn informed me that he had every reason to believe they had a very large property with them in the wagon in which they traveled.[138]

An informative illustration of this mobility and westward movement is recorded on the birth and baptismal certificate of David Landis (fig. 2.54). The inscription notes that he was born in Donegal Township, on the western edge of Lancaster County, in 1804, and baptized in 1823 in York County. The colorful document that records all of this, however, was made in Westmoreland County (near Pittsburgh) by artist George Busyaeger in 1825.[139] Although the fraktur is written in English, Busyaeger made an almost identical birth and baptismal certificate in German for his daughter Martha in 1846.[140]

Schwaben Creek and Mahantongo Valley

In addition to the early publication of the Jonestown School chests, the 1920s also saw the discovery and marketing of colorfully painted and decorated furniture from the Schwaben Creek area of the Mahantongo Valley region in Northumberland County. In December 1926 Bethlehem dealer A. H. Rice placed an illustrated two-page ad in *The Magazine Antiques* offering eleven pieces of furniture for sale for $7,300, proudly announcing that "all this Furniture was collected by me personally in Remote Sections of Pennsylvania." The remote sections were in the Mahantongo Valley area. Three of the pieces listed in his ad were at the time on exhibit at Philadelphia's 1926 Sesqui-Centennial International Exposition, including a desk with the date "1834" and name "Jacob Maser" painted on the rail beneath the fall front (figs. 2.55, 2.56). The desk had been inherited by Maser's son Felix and then passed on to his son Charles, who lent it to the Sesqui-Centennial, apparently before selling it to Rice. The initial attempt by Rice to market the furniture in one lot was unsuccessful, but within the next few years he sold the items separately. Not surprisingly, the superbly decorated desk that Rice pictured in his ad was sold by the time Henry Francis du Pont's interest was piqued, so du Pont purchased a chest of drawers and another desk instead. On January 1, 1930, Rice billed him for "1 Penna dutch decorated desk $350.00" and one chest of drawers for the same price. It was not until April 1946 that du Pont acquired the Maser desk for $1,000 from Connecticut collector Gale H. Carter, who had purchased it from Rice.[141]

FIGURE 2.54

Birth and baptismal certificate of David Landis, by John George Busyaeger, Westmoreland County, 1825. Westmoreland Museum of American Art, Greensburg, Pa., The Joy and R. David Brocklebank Collection through the William Jamison Art Acquisition Fund

The first extensive scholarly examination of this colorful furniture did not occur until 1973, when Mary Hammond Sullivan and Frederick S. Weiser published a study of nearly five dozen pieces.[142] Between that publication and a second more detailed one in 1980, Sullivan and Weiser recognized that most of the furniture they were studying came from the long, narrow Schwaben Creek Valley that backs up against the south face of Line Mountain. Even today this area remains largely unaltered, as Schwaben Creek Road winds past early nineteenth-century brick farmhouses, Himmel's Union Church, and Jacob's Cemetery.

Weiser and Sullivan's study was followed in 1987 with an exhibition and publication by Henry M. Reed.[143] Both publications recognize two distinct groups of furniture from this region. The first is a group of painted (sometimes grained) chests-over-drawers with rectilinear, astragal-end panels on the front containing the owner's name and a date, usually in fraktur lettering. The floral decoration of these chests is minimal, limited to small flowers in the panels containing the name and date. The chests date between about 1798 and 1828. The second group is more varied. The most numerous form is the chest of drawers, in addition to several chests, desks, kitchen cupboards, and three hanging cupboards that range in date from 1827 to 1841. Their decoration is much more colorful and profuse than that of the earlier chests. In their analysis, Sullivan and Weiser postulated that there were as many as twelve decorators involved with painting this group. They created an extensive list of joiners and carpenters from the immediate area but did not find sufficient documentary or physical evidence to identify any of those craftsmen as makers of specific pieces. Following their study, Reed attributed various pieces to a number of the listed joiners and carpenters in the Schwaben Creek/ Mahantongo Valley region.[144] In addition to Maser and his desk, one name can be firmly linked to a chest of drawers; "John Mayer" is written on one of the drawers twice. Mayer (1794–1883) is noted in the Upper Mahanoy Township tax lists between 1817 and 1840 as

FIGURE 2.55
Desk, made for and probably by Jacob Maser, Mahantongo Valley, Northumberland County, 1834. Winterthur Museum, gift of Henry Francis du Pont

FIGURE 2.56
Detail of interior of desk in fig. 2.55.

a joiner and carpenter, so he can definitely be included as one of the craftsmen constructing this furniture. There is also reason to believe that men such as Johannes Braun, Johannes Haas, Jacob Maser, Johannes Mayer, William Otto, and Samuel Swinehardt were some of the craftsmen responsible for these objects, but limited evidence of their authorship of specific examples exists. The account book of Johannes Haas (1814–56) survives as the only remaining written documentation of cabinetmaking in the Mahantongo Valley between 1835 and 1856. From this it is clear that he owned a lathe and was painting pieces as well as making them. This account provides an important glimpse at not only what he made, which was wide-ranging, but also the nature of the work of many others in that locale.[145]

The Mahantongo furniture reveals its "remote" origins by the sturdy construction and simple decoration. Many of the case pieces are of rail-and-stile construction, like that used by joiners and house carpenters in architectural woodwork. The stock is typically thick, and the woods are primarily local white pine and tulip-poplar, with walnut battens on some of the chests.[146] The ground paint colors on most of the pieces are a combination of Prussian blue, chrome yellow mixed with Prussian blue, or chrome green, with additional decoration in vermilion, chrome yellow, and black.[147]

A smaller number of pieces that appear as a darkish red were painted with a red iron oxide ground (which was cheaper than vermilion), and then decorated with black, chrome green, and chrome yellow.[148] As chrome yellow and chrome green did not become commercially available until about 1818, it is significant how quickly they came into use in this rural region. Recent research regarding early nineteenth-century chromium mines informs our knowledge of the introduction of these colorful paints.[149] Much of the decoration was likely made with templates or stencils; small rosettes were probably stamped with a piece of cork.[150] Common motifs include birds, angels, trees, flowers, praying children, compass-drawn designs, quarter-round fans, and horses. The inspiration for some of the images was taken from printed fraktur of the period, including the distinctive praying children of printer Joseph Schnee of Lebanon.[151] The horses on the Maser desk and on a diminutive chest (fig. 2.57) are different in execution, suggesting two different hands (or stencils), but both may have been inspired by the same printed and published source such as a fraktur or broadside.[152]

Examining the contents of Jacob Maser's (spelled later as Masser) inventory taken after his death, the subsequent auction listing (with purchasers noted), and nineteenth-century genealogical and biographical notes, we can be certain of Maser's authorship of some pieces in the group. Although Reed argued it was unlikely that Maser could have made his own desk in 1834 at age twenty-two, it is nonetheless possible.[153] In the same year noted on Maser's desk, he married Catharina Christ (1816–90), with whom he had fourteen children. His was among the leading families of the area, along with those named Rebuck, Geist, Reitz, Brosius, and Braun. When Maser died in June 1895, his inventory noted "Carpenters tools" valued at $5, a "Desk" appraised at $1.50, and an "organ" appraised at $21.[154] At the vendue of his estate, numerous planes, chisels, augers, lumber, and planks were sold, along with a carpenter's bench and a planing bench. In 1911 it was noted in the *Genealogical and Biographical Annals of Northumberland County* that Maser

FIGURE 2.57
Chest, Mahantongo Valley, Northumberland County, 1830–50. Collection of Katharine and Robert Booth

was born Oct. 29, 1812, on his father's farm, where he was reared. He lived and died on the farm now owned and occupied by his son Felix C. Masser, to whom he willed it, a property consisting of 128 acres of rolling, fertile land, on the south side of Line Mountain in Upper Mahanoy township, . . . Jacob Masser was not only a successful farmer but also an excellent mechanic, in which line he was particularly well known. He learned the carpenter's trade and being called upon to make many coffins followed undertaking also, conducting many funerals in his day. He made considerable furniture, of all kinds, and his son Felix has a cupboard of his make which is a most creditable sample of his workmanship. He made a cupboard for each of his daughters. He died May 29, 1895, after a life of over eighty-three years in which he had enjoyed unusually good health, having been sick but once, shortly before his death. He was a well-built and vigorous man, a good walker, and energetic all his days.[155]

In addition to the pieces already noted, at least three large two-part kitchen cupboards with glazed doors, one corner cupboard, and three hanging cupboards from this region survive today (fig. 2.58).[156] The paint and decorative details of the hanging cupboards vary significantly, suggesting that they were made by different craftsmen. The alternating lunettes that create a rope-twist motif down either side of the door are seen on at least one other piece.[157] The cupboard seen here bears a faint inscribed date on the front edge of the top shelf: "August 3d 1848." Interestingly, for years this cupboard hung upside down as that inscription verifies, as does the fact that the ogee molding and the deeper top rail below that molding signify the "head" or top of the cupboard. Sometime in the early twentieth century the interior was over-painted with a lead white paint, which covered the original red lead that appeared as a strong salmon color.[158] Since the white paint was unable to be

removed without damaging the original red beneath, in 2009 a barrier coat was placed over the white, assuring reversibility, and the interior was painted to match the original color. The stock of the door with four divided lights is about one-eighth of an inch thicker than the rest of the wood of the cupboard (except the shelves); hence, the maker had to notch the edges of the shelves for the door to close. This could indicate that the maker was also involved in house joinery and used the standard stock he would have employed when making divided light windows, perhaps not realizing at the outset that there would be a difference when the door was installed.

Some of the rarest objects that survive from the Mahantongo Valley region are the small, personal items that held everything from knitting needles to sugar and spices (fig.

FIGURE 2.58
Hanging cupboard, Mahantongo Valley, Northumberland County, 1830–50. Winterthur Museum, promised gift of Mrs. George P. Bissell, Jr.

2.59). A lidded box with black ground has the incised date "1842" and initials "A S" on the underside, thought to represent Annjulein Stiehly or her mother, Anna. A red sugar bowl is dated "1831" on the side, and a tall green box was likely used for knitting needles. Skillfully turned on a lathe and painted with floral decoration, these items may have been made by John Mayer or his son-in-law Jared Stiehly.[159] The simple decoration of these boxes echoes that of the interior motifs on the Maser desk (see fig. 2.56). Johannes Haas is another likely candidate for maker, as he owned a lathe and painted objects. His account book notes that in 1841 he made a salt box for 50 cents and a pepper box for 25 cents; in 1846 he turned a candlestick for 12½ cents.[160] Of course, there were numerous other joiners and carpenters in the region. Much has been written about the objects from the Mahantongo Valley, but much remains to be discovered. Until more signed pieces are found, the names of other makers and painters will remain a mystery.

LOCALISMS IN ORNAMENT: CARVED DECORATION
Chester and Berks Counties

The eighteenth-century fashion for carved ornament on furniture was by no means lim-

ited to urban centers along the Atlantic coast. Local consumer tastes no doubt guided the work of craftsmen, and those employed in the counties beyond Philadelphia may have felt free to exercise their individual creativity to the extent that their clients were willing to pay for it. The absence of carving on many pieces may reflect a fiscal limitation or a personal preference. Since the custom of tea drinking was enjoyed by various levels of society, exploring less-urban versions of tea tables in terms of their localisms is illuminating.[161] County centers and larger towns within rural regions did produce decidedly local expressions of tea tables. Although firmly documented examples have proven difficult to identify, several groups can be associated with specific locales based on the relationship of design, ornament, and construction details to other forms known from those regions.

The craftsmen, or shops, that produced a distinctive group of Chester County tea tables has not yet been identified, though oral tradition relates that a number of the tables have been found in the Downingtown area, west of the county seat of West Chester (fig. 2.60). Distinguished by their circular birdcages (between the table top and pillar), most of the tables are made of native black walnut or curly maple, usually with a three-board

FIGURE 2.60
Tea table, possibly
Downingtown area,
Chester County,
1780–1800. Winterthur
Museum purchase
with funds provided
by Robert and Bobbie
Falk and the Henry
Francis du Pont Col-
lectors Circle

FIGURE 2.61
Detail of fig. 2.60.

top with concave molding around the edge.[162]
The pillars are typically a baluster shape, with
an incised line around the most bulbous portion and flattened ring beneath, and a narrow
ring on the shaft above the ball. Another subtle but distinguishing feature of the tables is a
noticeable taper at the top of the pillar where
it engages with the upper plate of the birdcage
(fig. 2.61). The pad feet are usually high and
rounded, often with a slim plate beneath. The
legs usually have a defined shoulder and epau-
lette-like device at the top where they join the
pillar. The illustrated table has simple, carved
fluting on the epaulette and a tapering tail-like
device down the top of the legs. On several,
including this example, the craftsman paid

a feature that is exceedingly rare on even high-style American tea tables.[165] The relief carving on the pillar and legs consists of simple four-petal flowers, tulips, and leaves, all with distinctive veining and a stippled background to disguise tool marks, as the ornament was carved from the solid. This carving relates closely to a group of case furniture also believed to be from Berks County, including two painted slant-front desks, a chest, and several tall-case clocks containing Reading movements that have quarter columns with related floral carving.[166] Established in 1752, Berks County was largely German (85 percent in 1790), although some Quakers and Anglicans lived there. Outside the county seat of Reading, much of the landscape remained unchanged into the late 1800s. A stone farmhouse, which later became a tenant house on the Berks County almshouse property, was painted by Charles C. Hofmann around 1870 (fig. 2.64). The painting shows a traditional raised-bed garden like that drawn by Susanna Heebner more than a half-century earlier (see fig. 1.62).[167]

FIGURE 2.62
Tea table, probably Berks County, 1780–1810. Winterthur Museum, promised gift of John J. Snyder, Jr.

FIGURE 2.63
Detail of fig. 2.62.

special attention to the iron spider (or three-part brace) that adds support to the join of the legs and the pillar: it is set into the underside of the legs and base of the pillar so that it is not visible.[163] Tea tables of similar form, without circular birdcages, are also found in Chester County in greater numbers.[164]

Quite different from the Chester County tea tables is a small tea table, or stand, from Berks County, a rural expression striving for the sophistication of urban examples (figs. 2.62, 2.63). Indicative of objects made and used by people in the area, this diminutive table is constructed of tulip-poplar and was originally painted red. The scalloped top, also seen on British tables, is

Lancaster County

As the largest inland urban center at the time of the American Revolution, it is not surprising that Lancaster, settled in 1730 just 60 miles west of Philadelphia, attracted skilled craftsmen capable of extraordinary workmanship. The mercantile connections between the two locales were strong. In 1794 Theophile Cazenove commented on the architecture of Lancaster, describing the German Lutheran church as "very well built, of brick, and its steeple is the best built and the most elegant one in the United States." He continued, "There is a large town-hall and several very good brick houses . . . and a large

number of log houses in the less conspicuous parts." Cazenove also described the women of Lancaster, noting, "The young ladies here are very well dressed, very much like Philadelphia ladies. Generally the young women and girls . . . have a rather pretty figure, good carriage, beautiful teeth and hair."[168]

The fact that some wealthy Lancaster residents such as attorney Jasper Yeates purchased furniture from Philadelphia craftsmen may have encouraged artisans to settle in Lancaster, where there was an elite clientele. There is little doubt that the influence of stylish Philadelphia furniture in the rococo taste had a significant impact on the demand for, and production of, similar furniture in Lancaster. A puzzling piece of documentation that illustrates the high-style Philadelphia taste translated by a craftsman of Germanic heritage, presumably in Lancaster, is found in the account book of Peter Ranck. Included are drawings with annotations and descriptions in German (in a hand other than Ranck's) of high-style carved rococo furniture, including a dressing table, tall clock, and the upper part of a desk-and-bookcase (fig. 2.65).

An inscription in the book "Daniel Arnd His Book . . . Lancaster March 22, 1791" may reveal the author of the drawings, though why they are in Ranck's account book is unknown. Who was Daniel Arnd; what was his relationship to the Rancks; how did Ranck get this book; and did anyone ever execute these pieces and where? Over the years a number of possibilities have been proposed, but to date there are no firm conclusions.[169] Nevertheless, the drawings and inscriptions do suggest that a craftsman familiar with Philadelphia furniture made them. Certainly the quality and

FIGURE 2.64
Stone house of the Berks County almshouse, attributed to Charles C. Hofmann, Berks County, 1870–80. Historical Society of Berks County Museum and Library, Reading, Pa.

FIGURE 2.65
Drawing of desk-and-bookcase pediment, attributed to Daniel Arnd, Lancaster County, 1791. Joseph Downs Collection of Manuscripts and Printed Ephemera, Winterthur Library

FIGURE 2.66
Tea table, made for Jacob and Anna Neff, probably Lancaster, Lancaster County, 1770–90. The Dietrich American Foundation

FIGURE 2.67
Detail of fig. 2.66.

quantity of rococo furniture made in Lancaster supports this conclusion, and its distinctive differences from Philadelphia examples further confirms a specific localism.

In contrast to the tea tables from Chester and Berks counties, the walnut example owned by Mennonite minister Jacob Neff and Anna (Brackbill) Neff of Strasburg, Lancaster County, who married in 1755 (fig. 2.66), echoes Philadelphia workmanship but reflects a distinctive local style.[170] The overall design is bolder, with the large ball that dominates the pillar having strong foliate carving that is less naturalistic and flowing than Philadelphia workmanship. In places the carving is almost linear in its execution, with a stylized quality.

The stippled background of the carving on the ball is a characteristic of Lancaster pieces (fig. 2.67). The ball-and-claw feet are also distinctive with rigid, pointed knuckles on the talons and an egg-shape ball that comes to a point at the back. The top of the table is made up of three boards with a simple molded edge much like Chester County examples.

The furniture and craftsmen of Lancaster have been thoroughly researched over the years. Initially much of the furniture was attributed to the Bachman family of Strasburg, but in 1974 John J. Snyder Jr. ably refuted this through his study of Bachman account books.[171] A year later he wrote about Lancaster's carved case furniture, introducing the makers of various organ cases—George Burkhart, Peter Frick, and Conrad Doll—and for the first time presented his discovery of "M [?] Lind" written in red chalk on a drawer bottom of the elaborately carved Lancaster high chest now in the Diplomatic Reception Rooms of the Department of State.[172] Michael Lind (1725–1807), thought to be from Sweden, arrived in Philadelphia in 1752 and by the next year had set up shop as a joiner on Orange Street in Lancaster. Snyder had previously identified a slant-front desk with the name "Conrad Lind" inscribed on a drawer; Conrad was one of Michael's seven children and one of three sons who became a joiner. The desk is of the simplest form with straight bracket feet; the only carved work is found on the prospect door, which has a simple fan-like shell featuring the typical Lancaster carving techniques of stippling the ground between the rays and deeply incising an arc around the shell. This desk was owned in the Kready family, who lived in northern Lancaster County and earlier in Manor Township.[173] It may typify the kind of furniture that wealthy farmers from the surrounding area came to Lancaster to purchase.

Although the names of Lind, Burkhart, Frick, and Doll are known, and church organs by the latter three exist, little work of theirs has been documented. Their shops were within two blocks of one another, and all went to the First Reformed Church. Typical of relationships among craftsmen, Lind is mentioned in Burkhart's estate papers with regard to transac-tions between 1783 and 1791. But are these joiners the carvers of this distinctive furniture? Accounts for various carvers working in Lancaster have been discovered, including Michael Stump (w. 1750), Christian Myer (w. 1787–92), and Daniel or David Hostetter (w. 1796–99), all of Germanic heritage. Still no known work by any of them has been identified that would aid in attributing the carving on certain objects to specific hands. Like the London-trained carvers who came to Philadelphia, were these artisans trained on the continent or perhaps by masters in Philadelphia?[174]

One of the most ambitious statements of Lancaster carving and cabinetwork is the cherry desk-and-bookcase made for Michael Withers (1733–1821), a gunsmith and, more significantly, wealthy iron forge owner of Strasburg, Lancaster County (fig. 2.68).[175] In 1952 Henry Francis du Pont purchased the piece from Edgar and Charlotte Sittig, noted antiques dealers from Shawnee-on-Delaware, Pennsylvania. The $8,500 bill to du Pont noted that it was for "One Bachman Secretary Desk from Dr. Wither's Family of Strasburg, Penna."[176] The Sittigs had purchased the desk from Elizabeth Withers Shertz (b. 1876), the great-great-niece of Michael Withers. When Withers died in 1822, his will revealed that he owned extensive real estate and shares in three iron forges: Sadsbury, Conowingo, and Mt. Eden. His nephews Michael and George (sons of his brother George) were his principal beneficiaries. Exactly how this treasured family heirloom descended to Elizabeth W. Shertz is unclear, but presumably it was through her mother, Catharine Withers, who married John J. Shertz in 1868.[177]

Of the three known highly carved Lancaster desks with bookcases, the Withers example was likely the most costly at the time it was made.[178] The amount of superior carving, finely executed interior, carved pendant below the base molding, and carving on the ogee bracket feet all suggest a special commission. The choice of native cherrywood, whether desired by Withers or suggested by the craftsman, would also have affected the cost. The other two desk-and-bookcases known are made of walnut (perhaps a little more costly than cherry), although more expensive imported mahogany was also used in

Desk-and-bookcase, made for
Michael Withers, Lancaster,
Lancaster County, 1770–90.
Winterthur Museum, gift of
Henry Francis du Pont

Lancaster case furniture and tea tables.[179] The symmetrical relief carving on the pediment (fig. 2.69) is representative of the best Lancaster workmanship.[180] The pendant thistle (or tassel) motif in the pediment carving is an unusual design element in Lancaster carving; the source or inspiration is unknown. The extravagance of five carved shells in the interior, four on drawer fronts, and a central one on the prospect door suggests that the owner wished to make his affluence known when his desk was open (fig. 2.70). The detailed workmanship of the molded drawer fronts beneath the pigeonholes further enhances the aesthetic impact of this extraordinary interior.[181]

FIGURE 2.69
Detail of desk pediment in fig. 2.68.

FIGURE 2.70
Detail of desk interior in fig. 2.68.

FIGURE 2.69

FIGURE 2.70

FIGURE 2.71

Small chest-over-drawers, descended in the Ensminger family, probably Manheim, Lancaster County, 1770–90. Private collection

FIGURE 2.72

Portrait of Samuel Ensminger, Jr. and Portrait of Mrs. Samuel Ensminger, Jr. (Elizabeth Summy) and child, attributed to Jacob Maentel, Manheim, Lancaster County, 1831. Collection of Stephen and Dolores Smith

Smaller urban centers in Lancaster County such as Lititz and Manheim also had clientele who demanded quality and creativity from craftsmen. A diminutive carved cherrywood chest-over-drawers has a foliate relief-carved front and sides (fig. 2.71) and a history of ownership in Manheim, northwest of Lancaster.[182] The flowing, slender, carved tendrils are different in character from Lancaster rococo carving and represent a distinctive school of Manheim carved ornament. Several other small carved walnut chests of related form are known, but they have different carving that is more closely related to Lancaster craftsmanship and appears to be by a less-skilled hand.[183] One aspect of the front on the Manheim chest that distinguishes it from any of the other small chests is that the carving is set within a rectangular field that has been entirely relieved so that the foliate motifs will stand proud of the background. The fully carved quarter columns and the end panels with exquisite carved shell motifs distinguish this chest as one of the most singular examples of its kind.

This chest has a tradition of having descended in the Ensminger family of Manheim, and although the original owner is not certain, Samuel Ensminger Sr. (1763–1840) might be a likely candidate. By 1803 he had opened an apothecary business in Manheim and held many prominent civic positions. His son, Samuel Jr. (1801–66), like his father, was an entrepreneurial businessman who continued to run the local apothecary. Portraits of Ensminger and his wife

(fig. 2.72) were painted in 1831 by Jacob Maentel (1778–1863?), a German immigrant and itinerant folk artist.[184] Samuel is shown standing at his writing desk with ledgers lining the shelves of the bookcase above. When Ensminger died in 1866 his inventory attested to both his profession and wealth. It includes "1 Writing Desk"; "1 Book-case"; numerous books were listed by title; and "a lot of Medical, Anatomical, Law & Miscellaneous Books." Following that listing are the contents of his shop: "Drug Store–Drugs, Medicines, Bottles, jars, Counter, Showcase, Shelving, & c."[185] Whether Samuel is in his shop or his home is unclear; nevertheless, this vibrant and immensely detailed watercolor is strong evidence of the visual impact of paint and pattern in interiors of the period. Samuel is seen at work, while Mrs. Ensminger is seated outdoors in a Windsor chair with, presumably, young son John Henry (1829–46) on her knee.[186] Maentel painted the portraits of dozens of Pennsylvania German families, many in the Lebanon and Schaefferstown area. Rendered with exceptional clarity and detail, the Ensminger portrait provides an intimate glimpse into the lives of this prominent family.

A number of tall-case clocks with movements by Manheim makers Christian Eby and John Heinzelman have similar carving in their pediments and relate to several desks and desk-and-bookcases from Manheim.[187] John Hiestand (1766–1834), the original owner of an impressive eight-day clock, was a well-to-do farmer in East Hempfield Township, Lancaster County, south of Manheim (fig. 2.73).[188] The case, with a door of highly figured crotch walnut, features a base panel with shallow relief carving and motifs typical of Manheim craftsmanship (fig. 2.74). Similar to Lancaster carving that is worked from the solid, it is characterized by narrow curvilinear lines that define the vine motifs and outline the shell and the heavily stippled background. This case may have been made for John by his first cousin Jacob Hiestand (1767–1834), who was a cabinetmaker in nearby Mount Joy Township. The white-painted dial bears the name of Lancaster clockmaker George Hoff and may have been lettered by noted Lancaster artist Jacob Eichholtz (see fig. 2.38). In Eichholtz's account

FIGURE 2.73
Tall-case clock, made for John Hiestand, movement by George and John Hoff, Lancaster, Lancaster County, 1797, case possibly by Jacob Hiestand, possibly Mount Joy Township, Lancaster County, about 1797. Collection of John J. Snyder, Jr.

FIGURE 2.74
Detail of carving on base of fig. 2.73.

FIGURE 2.75
Tall-case clock,
probably made for
Roland Rogers,
movement by Ben-
jamin Chandlee Jr.,
Nottingham area,
Chester County,
1750–75.
Winterthur
Museum purchase
with funds pro-
vided by the Henry
Francis du Pont
Collectors Circle

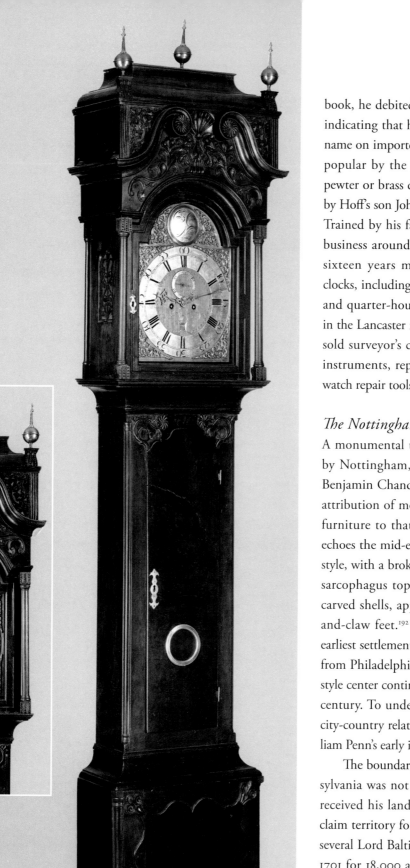

FIGURE 2.76
Detail of clock
hood in fig. 2.75.

book, he debited Hoff for "painting his name," indicating that he was probably painting Hoff's name on imported white clock faces, which were popular by the 1790s and less expensive than pewter or brass dials.[189] The movement is signed by Hoff's son John (1776–1818) and dated "1797." Trained by his father, John Hoff went into the business around this time and during the next sixteen years made more than one hundred clocks, including thirty-hour, eight-day, musical, and quarter-hour chiming. His advertisements in the Lancaster newspapers indicate that he also sold surveyor's compasses, other mathematical instruments, replacement glass, and clock and watch repair tools.[190]

The Nottingham School

A monumental tall-case clock with movement by Nottingham, Chester County, clockmaker Benjamin Chandlee Jr. (fig. 2.75) has led to the attribution of more than a dozen pieces of case furniture to that locale.[191] The elaborate clock echoes the mid-eighteenth century Philadelphia style, with a broken-scroll pediment beneath the sarcophagus top (fig. 2.76), pierced fretwork, carved shells, applied foliate carving, and ball-and-claw feet.[192] This is not surprising, as the earliest settlement of that region was by Quakers from Philadelphia, and ties to that major urban style center continued throughout the eighteenth century. To understand the background of this city-country relationship, one must look to William Penn's early involvement with the area.

The boundary between Maryland and Pennsylvania was not clearly delineated when Penn received his land grant in 1681. In an effort to claim territory for Pennsylvania, in dispute with several Lord Baltimores, Penn granted a deed in 1701 for 18,000 acres, all of which lay in Chester County. After the completion of the Mason-Dixon Line in 1768, 1,300 acres remained in Chester County and 16,700 acres were allotted to Cecil County, Maryland.[193] Penn divided this tract into thirty-seven lots of about 500 acres each, which were drawn by those interested in settling on this frontier. These were called the "Nottingham Lotts"—presumably commemorating Penn's own home in Nottinghamshire, England. The area was rich in natural resources,

including fertile fields and heavily wooded for-ests of oak, walnut, chestnut, and hickory. It pre-sented a fine opportunity for new settlers, and Penn encouraged both Quakers and Scots-Irish Presbyterians to move there. The original lots were settled by fifteen families, some of whom owned more than one lot, and Penn kept 3,000 acres for his own use. In 1710 there was a second wave of settlers, including the England, Cop-pock, Gatchell, and Chandlee families. Many of these early Quaker settlers transferred their mem-bership to Nottingham from meetings such as the Chester Meeting.[194] Additionally, in 1724 the New Castle, Delaware, Presbytery directed two pastors to serve the people in the Nottingham area at the mouth of the Octoraro Creek, which forms the western boundary of Chester County with Lancaster County.

A joiner's name long associated with the Nottingham area is that of Jacob Brown. The Brown family, including brothers James and Wil-liam, was one of the earliest to settle in Notting-ham. Nearly fifty years ago, Margaret Berwind Schiffer published a walnut tall clock (fig. 2.77) with movement by Benjamin Chandlee Jr. and a case by Jacob Brown, made for Irish immigrant James McDowell (1742–1815) of Oxford.[195] Let-ters from both Chandlee and Brown to their patron have been preserved by McDowell's descendants along with the clock. Schiffer cited these and listed a Jacob Brown, born in 1724, as the likely joiner.[196] These letters provide valuable documentation about Brown, but they also raise questions. Brown wrote to McDowell on Octo-ber 24, 1788:

> *Friend James Mc Dowel I am Sorry That I*
> *have Disapointed you So much About your*
> *Clock Case if I had thought I Could knot*
> *Served you Beter I would knot under took*
> *for to have Done it I am Sorry for to inform*
> *you that 3 of my Boys have all got the feaver*
> *and cant Work one Stroke for me and 3 of*
> *my own Chil Dren is onwell Likewise But*
> *we will Lay all those maters aside If I keep*
> *my own health you Shall Have your Clock*
> *Case Some Day Next Week from your Dis-*
> *apointed friend to Serve*
> *   —Jacob Brown Joyner*

FIGURE 2.77
Tall-case clock, made for James McDowell, movement by Benjamin Chandlee Jr., case by Jacob Brown, Nottingham area, Chester County, 1788. Collection of Mr. and Mrs. John McDowell Morris and Family

FIGURE 2.78
High chest of drawers,
Nottingham area, Chester
County, 1760–80. Collection
of Katharine Draper Schutt

FIGURE 2.79
Desk-and-bookcase, made for
Joseph Coudon, Nottingham
area, Chester County, 1760–
80. Private collection

A careful reading of this letter demands a rethinking as to whether the Jacob Brown born in 1724 would have had young children at home in 1788, when he was sixty-four years old. Although possible, it seems more likely that there was a younger Jacob Brown who made the clock case. Indeed, a look at Cecil County probate records yielded the answer. Another Jacob Brown (1746–1802), the son of William and Phebe Brown, married Elizabeth Cook at London Grove Meeting in 1772 and had at least eight children, some of whom were probably "onwell" in 1788. Brown was an active joiner in West Nottingham, and the lengthy listing of his possessions sold at public vendue following his death confirm this fact. An extensive stock of various woods, numerous and sundry joiner's tools, and unfinished pieces and parts of furniture, including three "Clock cases not finished," further attest to an active shop.[197]

Who Brown trained with is presently unknown, but stylistically, this Nottingham group of furniture suggests that it was likely produced by two generations of joiners. Winterthur's clock and a number of other pieces, including an ambitious high chest and desk-and-bookcase (figs. 2.78, 2.79), are stylistically earlier. Although there is no early provenance for the high chest, family history states that Winterthur's clock was first owned by Roland Rogers (1717–87) and then by John Price (d. 1816) of Nottingham.[198] The clock descended in the Price family until 1849, when Millicent R. Price married Judge James McCauley; from then it passed through that family until purchased by Winterthur in 2003. Rogers may have acquired his clock in the 1750s, so it would not have been made by Jacob Brown but perhaps by his master.[199]

The high chest is in the full-blown rococo style, yet its proportions are not typical of Philadelphia examples. The boldly scrolled pediment, large pinwheel rosettes, almost oversize upper case, and large peanut-shape cartouche all belie its nonurban origins (fig. 2.80). The creative shape of the skirt with central carved shell, along with the carved

FIGURE 2.80

Detail of high chest pediment in fig. 2.78.

knees, are unlike that on any other group of objects from the Mid-Atlantic region. Even the trapezoidal drawer in the tympanum is unusual—echoing rectilinear drawers in early Philadelphia high chests. The pseudo-rococo carved ornament on these pieces is distinctive in design and execution, with the relief and intaglio ornament embellished with naive gouge and veiner work. The artisan who made this florid carving drew chalk sketches on several of the interior boards of the clock and high chest before the cases were assembled.[200]

The monumental desk-and-bookcase also descended directly through the family of the original owner.[201] Perhaps second only to clocks, desk-and-bookcases were frequently mentioned in wills as specific bequests (often to a son). This particular piece relates closely to Nottingham-area case furniture. Joseph Coudon (Cowden, 1742–92), the original owner, was of French Huguenot descent and a teacher, lay preacher, and eventually an Anglican clergyman. He spent most of his life in Cecil County, Maryland, which was part of Chester County, Pennsylvania, until 1768. Coudon was minister of St. Mary Anne's Anglican Church (built 1743) in North East,

Maryland, from 1785 until his death in 1792. The inventory taken following his death reinforces the fact that he was an educated man of means. Both his "Walnut Desk & Book Case" and "All the Books and Pamphlets of the Decd." were valued at £9, the second highest amount for household goods after the "49 oz 3 dwt Silver Plate" listed at £20.9.4.[202] This desk-and-bookcase, while striving toward the Philadelphia rococo style, has ornamental features relating it to the high chest discussed above as well as the early tall clocks. The broken-scroll pediment, cartouche, and rosettes are singular, with echoes of related pieces seen in the rosettes, openwork dentils, and central peanut motif. Most remarkable are the elaborately arched and molded paneled doors of the upper section, a surprisingly sophisticated expression for such a rural region. The desk interior relates to those of several slant-front desks that also have narrow drawers as fall-front supports and nearly identical feet with large scrolled spurs on the brackets that curve toward the ogee foot to form a closed, or almost closed, circle. Collectors and dealers often call this type of foot an "Octoraro type" referring to the Octoraro Creek.

The tall clock case that Jacob Brown made for James McDowell in 1788 reflects a later and more restrained style than the earlier clock, high chest, and desk-and-bookcase. Since the publication of McDowell's clock by Schiffer, a number of other clock cases—most with Chandlee movements—have been identified with similar design features. Having survived remarkably intact with original feet and two original finials, the base panel relates closely to that on Winterthur's earlier model; though the upper portion is wholly different (fig. 2.81). The central keystone panel in the pediment, the pinwheel rosettes, and the fluting and gouge carving on the plinths and flanking the fretwork are all signature Nottingham features that are repeated in variations on other cases from this area.

Three generations of Quaker Chandlee clock and instrument makers have long been known to collectors.[203] As evidenced by families such as the Chandlees, the relationship between Nottingham and Philadelphia was strong. Benjamin Chandlee Sr. (1685–1745) emigrated in 1702 from Ireland to Philadelphia, where he was apprenticed to English clockmaker Abel Cottey and married his daughter Sarah.[204] After Cottey's death in 1711, the Chandlees moved from Philadelphia to Nottingham on land purchased by Cottey in 1703. Their son, Benjamin Jr., was born there in 1723 and trained with his father, becoming a renowned maker of clocks as well as scientific and mathematical instruments, sundials, telescopes, scales, steelyards, and other metalwork. In 1750 he married Mary Folwell, daughter of a Wilmington, Delaware, goldsmith. When he died in 1792, the sale of his estate included more than 750 pounds of iron and 170 of brass.[205]

Cumberland County

An impressive example of carving in a frontier area can be seen in the case of a sophisticated tall clock with movement by Jacob Herwick of Carlisle, Cumberland County (fig. 2.82). Founded in 1751, Carlisle rapidly became the regional center for political and military activity. Its location on a major road westward made it a strategic site and gathering point during the French and Indian War, the American Revolution, and the Whiskey Rebellion of 1794. Fifty miles northwest of Lancaster, Carlisle was also a center of trade for backcountry products. Much of its population was Scots-Irish Presbyterian, some of whom established Dickinson College in 1783.[206] When French traveler Cazenove stopped in Carlisle in 1794, he noted that "the inhabitants are generally Irish, and a few Germans, who gradually are coming to live here."[207]

Little is known of Jacob Herwick, but supposedly he was born in York in the early 1750s and was of Germanic heritage. His father may have been the Jacob Herwick listed as a baker in Carlisle tax records from the 1750s

FIGURE 2.81
Detail of clock hood in fig. 2.77.

FIGURE 2.82

Tall-case clock, movement by Jacob Herwick, Carlisle, Cumberland County, 1780–1800. Collection of James L. Price

through the 1770s. Who Jacob apprenticed with is unknown, but it likely occurred in York. It is tempting to think that he may have learned the art of engraving and clock- and watchmaking from the renowned horologist, painter, and woodcarver John Fisher.[208] By the 1770s he was in Carlisle, first listed in 1774 as a freeman over twenty-one, and in 1779 as a clockmaker in the Cumberland County tax records. About 1774 or 1775 he married Barbara Holtzbaum of York.[209] In 1786 Herwick advertised his new location on Pomfret Street, where he continued to make and repair "all sorts of Musical, Spring and Common Clocks—makes and repairs all kinds of watches—also the Silvers-smith's business carried on in its various and different branches—all which he will execute at the most reasonable prices and shortest notice."[210] Herwick may have had a feisty personality, for he was involved in several legal suits. In 1798 he sent a brief, but beautifully penned, note to prominent Carlisle lawyer James Hamilton requesting that he come speedily to the Carlisle jail, as he was illegally confined and needed Hamilton to bail him out.[211] About 1780 Herwick made a fine tall-case clock for Hamilton, so perhaps he called on him often for help in such matters.[212]

Herwick's skill and creativity are demonstrated in his unusual handling of the face, particularly in the arched head above the dial, which appears to be a unique design and execution (fig. 2.83). The applied brass name plate in this arch is exquisitely engraved with Herwick's surname encircled in a calligraphic manner, a "J" to the left and whimsical pseudo-animal face beneath. He playfully embellished the letters in "Carlisle" and noted to the right that this clock was "N 39." Beneath his name he engraved "Amor Honor et Justitia" (Love Honor and Justice), a Masonic motto.[213] Although the client who commissioned this clock is not known, the names of the two rearing horses depicted on the dial—Figure and Nettle—may be a clue to the original owner. Those names are known in horse breeding and racing circles of the Revolutionary War period. A horse named "Young Figure" from Bucks County was advertised for stud service near Carlisle in 1789, but to date any connection to a person who might have been Herwick's patron has not surfaced.[214] The horses as well as the three sheaves of wheat seem to be directly drawn from the Pennsylvania coat of arms, although the amusing bovines flanking the wheat, carefully depicted as a bull and a heifer, are not part of the arms.

There seems to be little doubt that both the movement and case for this clock were a special order, but the maker of the case remains unknown. That said, the finely fashioned piece is a perfect match for the movement. Far more high style than one would ever expect to see deep in the Pennsylvania backcountry near the end of the eighteenth century, it clearly strives to approach the refinement of Philadelphia work and may have been made by an artisan who knew such craftsmanship firsthand. The

extraordinary quality is first reflected in the superior walnut; a great piece of crotch wood was selected for the door and lower panel. From the urn and flame finials to the feet, the case is framed by engaged fluted columns, and colonettes with carved Corinthian capitals flank the face. The applied foliate carving on the tympanum and the carved molding outlining the broken-scroll pediment complete this statement of sophisticated taste on the Pennsylvania frontier.

From the earliest Quaker settlements in Chester County to the Carlisle frontier, regional forms developed that reflect a wide range of skill and inspiration and define the furniture of southeastern Pennsylvania. Distinctive expressions of ornament—from inlay to paint to carving—shaped the localisms of the region. The people who made and owned this furniture left a great material legacy.

FIGURE 2.83
Detail of clock dial in fig. 2.82.

CHAPTER THREE

FAMILIES: OWNERS AND INHERITORS

I Give and Bequeath to my Grand Daughter Elizabeth Maris . . .
my Feather Bed whereon I now lies . . . my Clock, one pair of High
Case of Drawers standing in the Great Chamber, one large Walnut
Oval Table standing in the House or Common Hall, my Black
Walnut Cloaths press and two large Silver spoons . . . I Give and
Bequeath to my Grand Daughter Sarah Howell . . . my Case of
Drawers in the Parlour and a new Case of Drawers spoke for but
not yet made . . . one dressing Table and dressing Box.

—Elizabeth Bartram, 1771[1]

The romance and nostalgia for the past was captured by Thomas Hicks (1817–90) in his painting of a kitchen interior in 1865 (fig. 3.1), presumably depicting a Quaker home in his native Bucks County.[2] Propping open the door is a Philadelphia armchair, probably more than a century old. Once a treasured heirloom but now an old-fashioned relic with a broken splat, the chair is a lingering reminder of a proud past. Many such objects were handed down from generation to generation, valued by some for their association with ancestors but disregarded by others as old fashioned, only to be rediscovered by another generation and revered as treasured heirlooms. Over time, many were refurbished, refinished, or otherwise restored to make them more presentable or valuable.

As objects become further removed from their original owners, either by descent to successive generations or sale out of the family, histories are often lost. Thus, the rare objects that do survive with excellent family histories take on larger roles in identifying distinctive localisms of form, ornament, and construction. When a group of objects from a particular house or family survives, a more complete understanding of the context of the objects is possible.

The Bartram, Coppock, and Pancoast Families
One of the earliest known pieces of furniture that was carefully preserved by generations of one family in southeastern Pennsylvania is the massive drop-leaf table made for James and Elizabeth (Maris) Bartram at the time of their marriage in 1725 (fig. 3.2). Although other early gateleg tables are known, this is the only one that bears an inlaid date and the initials of the original owners, confirming the locale in which

FIGURE 3.1
Kitchen interior, by Thomas Hicks, possibly Bucks County, 1865. The Dietrich American Foundation

FIGURE 3.2
Drop-leaf table, made for James and Elizabeth Bartram, possibly by James Bartram, Marple Township area, Chester (now Delaware) County, 1725. Winterthur Museum, promised gift of Mr. and Mrs. John L. McGraw

FIGURE 3.3
Detail of inlay on fig. 3.2.

it was owned and presumably made (fig. 3.3). The line-and-berry design that frames the date and initials is unique among tables of this date and size.[3] Inlaid at the top edge of one of the table leaves, the design is clearly visible when the leaf is down. Only one other drop-leaf table of similar date, though smaller in scale, is known with line-and-berry inlay, and that design appears on a drawer front.[4] Of the nearly dozen early southeastern Pennsylvania gateleg tables extant, the Bartram example has distinctive turnings, with a ring, flattened ball, and a cuplike form beneath the heavy baluster. Three

FIGURE 3.4
Dressing table, made for Elizabeth Maris (later Bartram), possibly by James Bartram, Marple Township area, Chester (now Delaware) County, 1724. Philadelphia Museum of Art, bequest of R. Wistar Harvey

other related tables have histories of ownership in Germantown (Ashmead family); West Marlborough Township, Chester County (Pennock family);[5] and Pennsbury Township, Bucks County (Penn family).[6] The turnings on those tables are generally similar, but no two are identical. The shaping of their skirts also varies, reinforcing the conclusion that no well-defined local styles of this form can be ascertained. A comparison of the turned elements on gateleg tables with turnings such as stair balusters also fails to identify distinctive local turning traditions.

James and Elizabeth Bartram died in 1771 within months of each other, and their estate inventories indicate they had accumulated con-

siderable wealth. James's "Purse and apparel" were appraised at £48.22.0; he also owned a watch valued at £4 and a clock worth £12. The household furnishings included a corner cupboard, walnut clothespress, desk, "pair of high case of drawers" (probably a chest-on-chest), silver spoons, china and glassware, table linens, and curtains. Elizabeth's will specifies bequests to her three granddaughters, including "my Case of Drawers in the Parlour and a new Case of Drawers spoke for but not yet made" to the youngest, Sarah Howell.[7] Sarah also received "one dressing Table and dressing Box." That table is the one bearing the initials "E M" and date "1724" that was made for Elizabeth Maris in 1724, the year before she married James Bartram (fig. 3.4). The inlay on the top of the dressing table is distinctive (fig. 3.5), specifically the unusual style of initials and date as well as leaf terminals of vines and three clustered berries, which is identical to the inlay on the Bartram table.[8] The singular nature of these inlays not only relates them to each other but may indicate an early localism in Marple Township, Chester (now Delaware) County. In 1927 this dressing table was sold at auction from the estate of Hannah P. Lawrence, who was the great-great-great-granddaughter of James and Elizabeth Bartram. Her great-grandmother was Elizabeth (Howell) Maris, the sister of Sarah Howell, who inherited it from her grandmother Elizabeth. Exactly how the dressing table came to descend from Elizabeth Maris is not known; however, her sister Sarah married Nathan Gibson in 1773 and died soon after in 1779, possibly without issue.[9]

James Bartram (1701–71) was the younger brother of noted naturalist John Bartram (1699–1777). Their father, William, and his parents came to Pennsylvania in 1682 with William Penn and settled in Darby. In 1696 William married Elizabeth Hunt, and they had two sons: John, who married Mary Maris in 1723, and James, who married her sister Elizabeth in 1725. The Maris sisters were the daughters of Richard and Elizabeth (Hayes) Maris of Marple Township.[10] Mary Bartram died in 1727, leaving two children. The same year Elizabeth Bartram gave birth to her only child, a daughter named Mary (possibly after her late aunt), who died in 1756. When Elizabeth died, the inlaid table made for her marriage nearly fifty years earlier was described in her will as "one large Walnut Oval Table standing in the House or Common Hall." She bequeathed the piece to her eldest granddaughter, Elizabeth, wife of Isaac Maris, along with a clock, walnut clothespress, bedstead and bedding, high chest of drawers, and two large silver spoons. The table then descended through the family until its sale at auction in 2002.[11]

The year after James and Elizabeth Bartram married, they purchased a "Messuage & tenement and Tract of Land" of 240 acres along Darby Creek in Marple Township from

Bartholomew Coppock (1681/2–1761) and his wife, Phebe. The Bartrams paid only five shillings; why Coppock gave them such a bargain is unknown.[12] An early two-story stone house (fig. 3.6) survived on the property into the mid-twentieth century, when it fell into ruin and the interior was salvaged. When Bartram acquired the property in 1726, he was identified in the deed as a "joyner."[13] The extent of his cabinetmaking is not known, although it has been

FIGURE 3.5
Detail of inlay on top of fig. 3.4.

FIGURE 3.6
House of Bartholomew and Phebe Coppock, then James and Elizabeth Bartram, built 1700–1725, photo about 1960, Marple Township, Chester (now Delaware) County. Rocky Hill Collection

FIGURE 3.7

High chest of drawers, by Seth Pancoast, Marple Township, Chester (now Delaware) County, 1766. Winterthur Museum, promised gift of John J. Snyder, Jr.

speculated that he made the great inlaid table for his marriage. If this is the case, then he was also the likely maker of the dressing table the previous year. Several receipts do survive that document payment to him for making coffins in the 1740s. From 1748 onward, Bartram was listed in Marple Township tax assessments as a yeoman, or farmer. Given the size of his land-holdings and personal estate, which included livestock, farming rather than cabinetmaking was likely his primary occupation. His inventory, however, does include "Joyner Tools" valued at £2 and "Smith Tools" of the same value, but no lathe is listed. It is likely that he owned a sawmill, as his will includes a bequest of "two acres and an half adjoining thereunto called the Saw Mill Land."[14]

An intriguing link between Bartram and several other woodworkers comes through Bartholomew and Phebe Coppock. Two of the Coppock daughters married joiners: Sarah married Daniel Sharples (1710/11–75), who apprenticed under Joseph Hibberd (1700–1737) of Darby; Esther married Seth Pancoast (1718–92) in 1741.[15] Born in Burlington County, New Jersey, to English Quakers William and Hannah (Scattergood) Pancoast, Seth presumably served his apprenticeship in Chester County, where he met and married Esther. To whom he apprenticed is unknown, though James Bartram and Joseph Hibberd are likely candidates. Not only did Pancoast witness James Bartram's will, he also served as an inventory taker for both James and Elizabeth following their deaths in 1771.[16]

In Bartholomew Coppock's will, made in 1761, he bequeathed his 180-acre plantation in Marple Township to Esther and Seth Pancoast.[17] Five years later, Pancoast made and signed a curly maple high chest of drawers (fig. 3.7). The high chest has no provenance, but a matching dressing table has a history of having descended in the Coppock family, and it is possible that they were made as companion pieces (fig. 3.8).[18] Both suggest that Pancoast was familiar with the urban products of Philadelphia artisans. The overall format of the high chest's broken-scroll pediment; central drawer

in the tympanum; meticulously detailed, carved rosettes; shells on the knees; and exaggerated trifid feet are distinctive and accomplished details (fig. 3.9). In addition, the highly fig-ured curled maple, while not as costly as wal-nut or mahogany, was a fashionable selection. It was also more difficult to work because of the grain. A closely related high chest attrib-uted to Pancoast has similar curled maple, pediment, central drawer, and carved rosettes but differs in the drawer arrangement of the top tier. It also lacks the carved shells on the knees and has slipper feet raised on thick pads.[19] Pancoast's son Samuel was also a joiner, as his signature and the date "1772" appear on a flat-top high chest with ball-and-claw feet that descended in the family into the mid-twentieth century.[20] Pancoast probably trained his son, and they worked together in Marple Township.

FIGURE 3.8
Dressing table, descended in the family of Bartholomew Coppock III, attributed to Seth Pancoast, Marple Town-ship, Chester (now Delaware) County, 1765–75. Collection of Mr. Curtis Fenstermacher and Family

FIGURE 3.9
Detail of carving on knee of fig. 3.7.

FIGURE 3.10

Tall-case clock, made for Margaret Thomas, movement by John Wood Sr., Philadelphia, about 1731, case attributed to Thomas Thomas, Radnor Township, Chester (now Delaware) County, about 1731. Collection of Irvin and Anita Schorsch, Jr.

FIGURE 3.11

Detail of clock hood in fig. 3.10.

The Thomas, Lewis, and Smedley Families
The identification of an important group of early and unusual inlaid case pieces began with the study of a tall-case clock with movement by noted Philadelphia clockmaker John Wood Sr. (fig. 3.10).[21] In 1943 the owner of the clock, Mrs. Roger Williams of Merion, Pennsylvania, pasted a typed note inside the door relating its history:

> *The clock came from a member of the Lewis family in which it had descended, according to the family legend, from the time it was made a wedding present from Thomas Thomas to his daughter Margaret, who married Nathan Lewis at Radnor Meeting on July 1ˢᵗ, 1731. Thomas Thomas, the father of Margaret, was one of the early settlers of Radnor Township.*

By identifying the father and daughter represented by the initials "TT / ML" inlaid on the door of the clock case, this note presented the opportunity to learn more about the giver, receiver, and a larger group of related furniture. A distinguishing feature of the clock case is not only the checkered inlay of the initials but also the elaborate diamond inlay around the cornice and top of the sarcophagus hood (fig. 3.11). The Thomas family was Quaker and originally from Flintshire, in northern Wales. In 1686 they immigrated to America with the Lewis family from the parish of Illan, Glamorganshire, Wales. After settling in Radnor, where Thomas Thomas was born in 1687, they relocated to adjoining Newtown Township.[22] Thomas eventually moved to Radnor Township, where he was listed in tax records as a joiner. When he died in 1774, his estate was valued at £233.11.8 and included "Carpenter and Turning Tools."[23] Although it is unusual to find a father and daughter's initials combined on a piece of furniture, this is explained by the fact that Thomas probably made the clock case for Margaret and chose to inlay their initials to signify the gift (fig. 3.12). Thomas himself owned an eight-day clock that he left to his grandson Levi, along with his tools.

The tall clock belonging to Nathan and Margaret Lewis stood in a stone house they inherited. It had been built by his grandfather,

William Sr., and left to his father, William Jr., in 1704. Nathan may have been associated with one or more Lewises who were woodworkers in Chester County during the eighteenth and nineteenth centuries. In 1777, during the Revolutionary War, the Lewis house was a surveillance outpost occupied by Major John Clark, who sent a series of important dispatches to General Washington.[24] The inlaid initials on the Lewis clock case are distinctive. Alternating light and dark squares of wood bordered by a thin line of light-wood inlay and pronounced triangular serifs give a checkered effect to the letters. Related checkered inlay is seen on Welsh furniture of the later eighteenth century, but it remains a mystery as to where Thomas learned this style of ornament.[25] Perhaps his father was a joiner or Thomas was apprenticed to a Welsh émigré joiner. The initials are separated with diamonds inlaid in light wood with a dot in the center, echoing the more complex inlaid and checkered diamond motif in the cornice and around the uppermost section of the sarcophagus top. As the sides were less visible than the front, a simpler version of this diamond motif appears there.

The diamond motifs and checkered lettering relate the Thomas/Lewis clock case to a number of other objects, including a chest of drawers and box made for Sarah Smedley in 1737. According to family tradition, the chest of drawers and box, both dated "1737" and inlaid with the initials "S S," were made for Sarah as part of her wedding furniture (figs.

FIGURE 3.12
Detail of inlaid initials on clock door in fig. 3.10.

FIGURE 3.13
Chest of drawers, made for
Sarah Smedley, possibly by
Thomas Thomas, Radnor
Township area, Chester (now
Delaware) County, 1737.
Private collection

FIGURE 3.14
Detail of inlaid
initials on fig.
3.13

in America originated with George Smedley (d.
1723), who immigrated from Derbyshire, England in 1682 or 1683. He married widow Sarah
Goodwin (d. 1709) in 1687 and lived along Ridley Creek in Middletown, about one mile northwest of Media. They had two sons, Thomas and
George, as well as a daughter named Sarah. She
married John Williamson of Newtown before
the box and chest were made, however, exclud-
ing her as a viable candidate.[27] George Smedley
Jr. had a daughter named Sarah, born in 1737/8,
but given the high rate of infant mortality it
would have been most unusual to commission
a chest of drawers and box for a young child;
thus, she is also not a likely candidate. Thomas
Smedley married Sarah Baker (d. 1765) in 1710 at
Middletown Meeting, and they had a daughter
named Sarah, born in 1717. The chest and box
were likely made for this Sarah, as she would have
been twenty years old in 1737, the date on the
objects. She married John Minshall in 1739/40 at
Goshen Meeting and died in 1801. Although her
wedding date is not an exact match to the date
of 1737, the box and chest of drawers could well
have been made in anticipation of her marriage.
This conclusion is supported by a reference in the
1901 Smedley family genealogy to "a case of drawers which belonged to Sarah Smedley, mother
of Jane Longstreth, in which her initials and the
date, 1737, are inlaid in lighter wood," which was
then in the possession of Sarah's great-great-grand-
daughters, Sarah Longstreth Jones and Mary Jane
Jones of Kernstown, Virginia.[28]

The chest of drawers is constructed in an
unusual manner for the period and locale. Full
dustboards are used between the drawers (a feature typical of Philadelphia but not less-urban
furniture), and the drawers themselves have
lipped fronts and relatively thin sides. The top
center drawer is inlaid with the initials "S S,"
made with the same checkered design found on
the Thomas/Lewis clock. The drawer blades are
tenoned through the sides, with a three-part
veneer that gives the effect of a dovetailed joint,
as if the maker were attempting to copy a technique seen elsewhere. One of the drawers in the
chest is branded on the back "T S" in large letters. Although when and by whom this brand
was applied is unknown, one possibility is that

3.13, 3.15). This tradition states that they subsequently descended through the family to a Sarah
in each of several generations. The last owner of
the pieces, Mrs. Henry M. Jones of Germantown, sold them to noted Philadelphia collector Howard Reifsnyder in the late nineteenth
or early twentieth century. When Reifsnyder's
collection was sold at auction in 1929, Henry
Ford purchased the box for his museum in Dear-
born, Michigan, and William Randolph Hearst
acquired the chest of drawers.[26] Genealogical
research has identified several Sarah Smedleys in
the first half of the 1700s. The Smedley family

FIGURE 3.15
Box, made for Sarah Smedley, possibly by Thomas Thomas, Radnor Township area, Chester (now Delaware) County, 1737. Collection of The Henry Ford Museum

FIGURE 3.16
Detail of inlaid top of box in fig. 3.15

it may stand for Thomas Smedley, father of the probable first Sarah to own the box and chest of drawers. Along the elaborately shaped inside edge of the straight-bracket feet and pendant drop is a solid light-wood inlay border. The date "1737" is inlaid within the drop with a solid light wood rather than the more complex checkered inlay used for the initials. This simplification may have been made since the date is located near the floor and not as visible as the initials. The maker used the opposite approach on the top of the box (fig. 3.15), however, going to great effort to inlay elaborate motifs, as on the front. The box likely sat on top of the chest of drawers, where such complex workmanship would have been appreciated. Although frequently referred to as a Bible, or document, box, this form was probably called a dressing box in the period. It held valuables and personal items. Checkered inlay outlines the shaped bracket base and forms the date "1737" in the pendant drop; across the front of the box diamond inlay almost identical to that on the Thomas/Lewis tall clock flanks a four-point star. On the top the craftsman used both light wood and checkered inlay to create a large geometric design, which contains a heart and the initials "S S."

The tall clock made for Margaret Lewis and the box and chest of drawers belonging to Sarah Smedley represent a distinctive local inlay tradition from the Radnor and Newtown areas of eastern Chester County. Closely related to the Smedley box is one dated 1739 bearing the initials "H P," but without any provenance.[29] Two other boxes without elaborate inlay but bearing checkered initials—one with the initials "S T" supposedly made for a Sarah Thomas, and one

"E C" with no history—may one day yield additional clues.[30] Based on the inlaid initials on the clock and his work as a joiner, Thomas Thomas is a strong candidate as the maker of the clock case. Whether he also made the box and chest of drawers for Sarah Smedley or the related boxes is difficult to determine. Even without this information, the family histories of the Thomas/Lewis clock and Smedley pieces enable us to trace their origins to eastern Chester County and thus identify the ornament as a unique localism.

In 1788 Sarah Smedley (1772–1827), the niece of Sarah Smedley Minshall who most likely was the original owner of the "S S" chest of drawers and box, worked a large wool crewelwork picture (fig. 3.17). Nine years later she married Jonathan

FIGURE 3.17
Crewelwork picture, by Sarah Smedley, Willistown Township area, Chester County, 1788. Winterthur Museum, gift of Harold O. Ladd

Matlack at Goshen Meeting. Where she attended school and learned this distinctive needlework is unknown, but many of the motifs are similar to those on other Chester County pieces of the same period, including the quilt made in 1787 by Rachel Mackey (see fig. 1.34). The birds holding three cherries in their beaks, the two-handle vase, and the moths are all variations of motifs worked by other local young women. In addition, a related crewelwork pocketbook made by a Sarah Smedley in 1775, who also married into the Matlack family, is known.[31]

The Lamborn Family

The story of two early objects, both identified with initials and the dates of acquisition, is one of long-lost provenance and recent reunion. The paneled chest and spice box originally owned by Robert and Ann Lamborn (figs. 3.18, 3.19),

are typical of the furniture a prosperous young Quaker couple would have acquired as they started housekeeping just before 1750. In 1746 the Lamborns were married at London Grove Meeting in Chester County. Robert was the son of Robert Lamborn (b. 1697) of Berkshire, England, who came to America in 1713 and married Sarah Swayne in 1722. Ann was the daughter of Jesse Jacob and Alice (Maris) Bourne of Patuxent River, Maryland.[32] Not surprisingly, one of the first pieces of furniture Robert and Ann acquired was a storage chest, made of walnut with panels set in rails and stiles in the manner of seventeenth- and early eighteenth-century chests.[33] The five drawers with brass hardware would have added significantly to the original cost of the object. The newly married couple ordered the piece inlaid with their initials, "R L A," and the date "1746" on either side of the lock (fig. 3.20).

FIGURE 3.18
Chest-over-drawers, probably made for Robert and Ann Lamborn, London Grove Township area, Chester County, 1746. Germantown Historical Society

Although no provenance identifies the Lambo-rns as the original owners of the chest, a spice box that descended directly through the family until its sale at auction in 1995 provides convincing visual evidence of the history.[34] Inlaid on the fielded, arched panel door of the spice box are the initials "R ᴸ A" and the date "1748." The initials are rendered in exactly the same manner as on the chest, with a flaring curve to the R and a dip in the crossbar of the A; the first three numerals of the dates are identically inlaid on both pieces. Additionally, the base molding of the chest is the same as the molding at the top of the spice box, suggesting that both pieces came from the same shop in the London Grove Township area of southern Chester County.[35]

The Lamborn spice box relates to several others made in this vicinity. The inlay, particularly the sprigs surmounting the arch and shape of the numerals, is almost identical to that on the door of a spice box made in 1744 for George and Margaret Passmore, who married at London Grove Meeting in 1742, as well as one dated 1744 made for Thomas and Elizabeth Hutton, who married at London Grove Meeting in 1739 (see figs. 1.12, 1.13). The dates on these boxes suggest that a small, locked valuables box was a luxury not acquired until several years after marriage.[36] The interior configuration of the Lamborn box (fig. 3.21) reveals small drawers that retain their original brass knobs, which bear traces of a tinted lacquer that made them look like burnished gold. Two pigeonhole compartments under the arch facilitate access to three hidden drawers. The valances and divider between the pigeonholes are one unit; by pulling it forward the backboard of the chest is released and lowered to reveal three secret drawers accessed from the back.[37] Pasted on the inside of the door is a woodcut of George II; he is identified as "King of Great-Britain, France & Ireland, Defender of the Faith &c."

The Lamborns were only one of many Quaker couples to own a spice box in Chester

FIGURE 3.19
(top left) Spice box, made for Robert and Ann Lamborn, London Grove Township area, Chester County, 1748. Collection of Mr. and Mrs. Chester Bartoli

FIGURE 3.20
(bottom) Detail of inlay on front of chest in fig. 3.18.

FIGURE 3.21
(top right) Detail of interior of spice box in fig. 3.19.

FIGURE 3.22

Spice box, probably made for Mary Warford, Loudoun County, Virginia, 1791. Colonial Williamsburg Foundation, acquisition funded by the Friends of Colonial Williamsburg

County, where the form was especially popular during the 1725–50 period. As Quaker families moved beyond southeastern Pennsylvania, they took objects and material preferences with them. Period references and similar extant examples with southern histories are also known. In Charleston, South Carolina, a mahogany spice box is noted in an inventory of 1816. A walnut spice box with a Warren County, North Carolina, history has also been identified.[38] A spice box with a light-wood inlaid date of "1791" surmounted by the initials "M W" was probably made for Mary Warford (d. 1832) of Loudoun County, Virginia, in whose family it descended (fig. 3.22). When the box was acquired by Colonial Williamsburg in 2006, secret drawers behind the back panel were found to contain estate papers of her husband, John (1750–1812). Included among them was his inventory, which lists "Drawers & spice box . . . $18.00," probably in reference to the box sitting atop a chest of drawers.[39] Loudoun County, in the northern portion of the Virginia Piedmont and just sixty miles from

the Pennsylvania border, was settled as early as the 1740s by Quakers from Bucks County, Pennsylvania, who may have taken spice boxes with them.

The Miller Family

A group of remarkable objects from the Miller (Müller) family of Millbach provides a rare glimpse into the home, possessions, and lifestyle of a wealthy Pennsylvania German family. In 1752 George (1706–84) and Maria Caterina Miller built a house and mill along Mill Creek (*Millbach*) in Heidelberg Township, Lancaster County (now Millcreek Township, Lebanon County) (fig. 3.23). In 1784 their son Michael built a three-story mill (probably replacing an earlier mill) adjacent to the main house; this house-mill arrangement is associated specifically with Pennsylvania Germans. In the 1798 tax list for Heidelberg Township, Michael was one of seven mill owners. His property was the most valuable, including a house, gristmill, sawmill, still house, and barn valued at $6,900.[40] Michael is also thought to have enlarged the house his father built with a stone addition, constructed of native limestone with contrasting red sandstone quoins and segmented arches; the kicked gambrel roof created a large, two-level attic well-suited for the storage of grain. Inside was a massive staircase with flat balusters in the baroque manner (fig. 3.24). Much of the interior woodwork of the house, including the staircase, was removed in 1926 by the Philadelphia Museum of Art; the kitchen was installed as a Pennsylvania German period room at the museum. The double raised paneled shutters and doors used throughout the house relate to those on a walnut chest (fig. 3.25) with a history from the house, suggesting that the craftsmen who produced the woodwork might have also made some of the furnishings. The paneled top of the chest, unusual for Pennsylvania examples, relates more to European prototypes. Craftsmen in Pennsylvania took advantage of the availability of much wider boards and usually made single-board tops.[41]

About 1750–60, the Miller family acquired a tall-case clock with movement by Jacob Graff

FIGURE 3.23
House of George and Caterina Miller, later known as Millbach House, built 1752, expanded by their son Michael by 1784, Heidelberg Township, Lancaster County (now Millcreek Township, Lebanon County). The Millbach Foundation, Inc.

FIGURE 3.24
Staircase from kitchen of the Miller house. Philadelphia Museum of Art, gift of Mr. and Mrs. Pierre S. du Pont and Mr. and Mrs. Lammot du Pont 1926

FIGURE 3.25
Chest, probably owned by the Miller family, Heidelberg Township area, Lancaster County (now Millcreek Township, Lebanon County), 1750–75. The Millbach Foundation, Inc.

FIGURE 3.26

Tall-case clock, owned by the Miller family, movement by Jacob Graff, Lebanon, Lancaster (now Lebanon) County, 1750–60. Winterthur Museum, bequest of Henry Francis du Pont

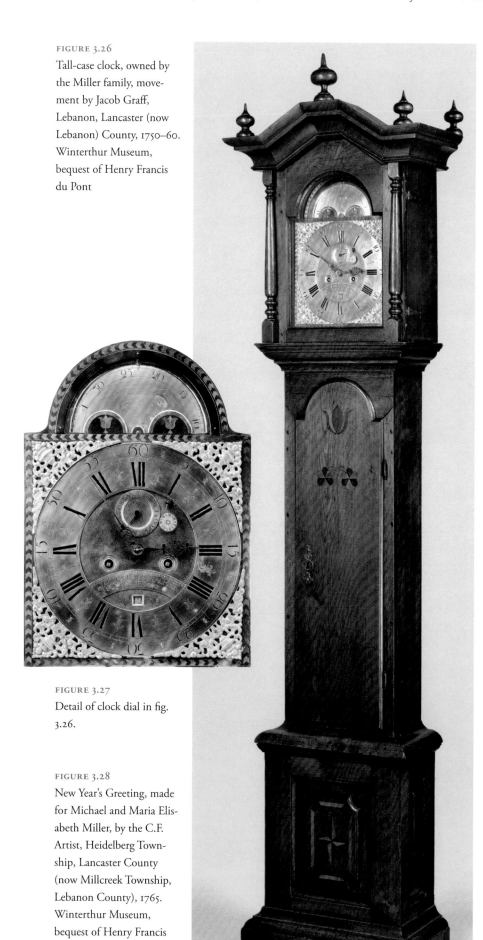

FIGURE 3.27

Detail of clock dial in fig. 3.26.

FIGURE 3.28

New Year's Greeting, made for Michael and Maria Elisabeth Miller, by the C.F. Artist, Heidelberg Township, Lancaster County (now Millcreek Township, Lebanon County), 1765. Winterthur Museum, bequest of Henry Francis du Pont

(1729–78) of Lebanon (fig. 3.26). Four clocks by this skilled artisan are known, including one with a musical movement.[42] Graff first appears as a clockmaker in the Lebanon tax list of 1750; when he died in 1778, he left his clockmaking tools, valued at £40, to his eldest son, John. The Miller clock has an eight-day movement with a moon-phase dial and date aperture; it also has an additional disc to indicate the day of the week.[43] The cast pewter spandrels on the brass and silvered dial may have been gilded originally. The inscription "JACOB GRAFF MACHET DIESES" on the arched name plate translates as "Jacob Graff Made This" (fig. 3.27). Inlaid on the door of the clock are tulip and pinwheel motifs, while a stylized shell is inlaid on the hood. The unusual hood relates closely to a miniature bracket clock made about 1770 with movement by Samuel Meyli of Lebanon, who is thought to have trained under Graff.[44]

The Miller's Germanic heritage was also celebrated in several brilliantly painted fraktur. In 1765 Michael and Maria Elisabeth Miller received an elaborate New Year's Greeting (fig. 3.28) embellished with flowering vines, rampant lions, and trumpeting angels.[45] To commemorate the birth and baptism of their daughter, Maria Elisabeth, ten years later, the Millers commissioned a certificate (fig. 3.29) from schoolmaster and noted fraktur artist Henrich Otto.[46] Designs from this fraktur appear on a walnut chest made for Maria Elisabeth in 1792 (fig. 3.30); an applied panel on the front with inlaid floral designs bears her name and the date in fraktur lettering. Some of the inlaid designs, in particular the pomegranate motif and the seven-petal flower, relate closely to those on the fraktur. Most important, however, is the intricate fraktur lettering on the chest done in ink; the shaping of individual letters, in particular the "M" in Maria, the "17" in 1792, and the calligraphic scrolls, relate closely to characters found on her baptismal certificate, making it tempting to speculate that Henrich Otto had a hand in the chest's design. In the late 1780s, however, Otto moved to Northumberland County, as he is listed there in the 1790 census, so it seems more likely that whoever made the chest copied the motifs from the fraktur.[47]

The unusual configuration of the chest with the additional four small drawers set within the main storage compartment is singular. The short ogee bracket feet are attached to an oak batten that runs from front to back on either side. Maria Elisabeth Miller (1775–1843), married Henry Schultz (1774–1824; grandson of Lutheran minister Henry Muhlenberg); they had no children. No mention of the chest is con-

tained in Maria's will, but it likely passed to her niece Catherine, eldest daughter of her younger brother, John Miller (1776–1848). Catherine married Jacob Weigley in 1810; they occupied the Millbach house until her father's death in 1848. She likely gave the chest to her eldest daughter, Mary Weigley (1811–98), who never married. Mary left the chest to her niece Emma (1865–1925), as documented by a revealing entry in a

FIGURE 3.29

Birth and baptismal certificate of Maria Elisabeth Miller, by Henrich Otto, Heidelberg Township, Lancaster County (now Millcreek Township, Lebanon County), about 1775. Rare Book Department, Free Library of Philadelphia

FIGURE 3.30

Chest-over-drawers, made for Maria Elisabeth Miller, Heidelberg Township area, Lancaster County (now Millcreek Township, Lebanon County), 1792. Private collection

ledger kept by Mary's brother, John A. Weigley (1832–92) and his son Walrow (1868–1933). On March 15, 1894, the ledger states, "Emma got great-grandfather Miller's sister's chest from Aunt Mary."[48] The extraordinary survival of architecture, furniture, and family documents associated with the Miller family permits a look at the relationships of objects within the household of this affluent rural family.[49]

The Hottenstein Family

In 1783 David and Catharina Hottenstein built a large center-passage stone house (fig. 3.31) along Easton Road, two miles north of Kutztown, Berks County. Filled with academically inspired architectural details, the interior included pedimented doorways, fluted pilasters, and moldings that even continued up the stair rail. The paneled walls and fireplace surrounds were painted with blue-and-white grained decoration. The woodwork from the large second-floor room was acquired in 1950 by antiques dealers Edgar and Charlotte Sittig and sold to Henry Francis du Pont, who installed it at Winterthur the following year as a room for the display of fraktur and other Pennsylvania German decorative arts (fig. 3.32). Born in 1734 to immigrant parents, David Hottenstein was one of the wealthiest men in Berks County at the time of his death in 1802. The inventory of his estate totaled an astonishing £10,812.18.11. Included in his household furnishings were six bedsteads (two with curtains), twenty chairs, seven wal-

FIGURE 3.33
Schrank, made for David
Hottenstein, Kutztown area,
Maxatawny Township, Berks
County, 1781. Winterthur
Museum

FIGURE 3.34
Detail of inlay on schrank in
fig. 3.33.

nut tables, a clock, kitchen dresser, and a dough trough. Also listed was a "Cloath Dresser" (or schrank) valued at £5.5, the single most expensive piece of furniture he owned.[50]

The massive schrank (fig. 3.33), inlaid with David Hottenstein's initials and the date "1781" in the cornice, remained in the house until 1950. At that time it was purchased by collector Asher Odenwelder, a good friend of the Sittigs, who had told him about the piece. The Sittigs accompanied Odenwelder to the house, where the schrank was standing in the large upstairs chamber. After Odenwelder's death in December 1957, the Sittigs purchased the schrank from his estate and sold it to du Pont, who reunited it at Winterthur with the room in which it had stood for nearly 170 years.[51] The classically inspired schrank is made of walnut but is not painted, as one might expect given the painted interior of the house. Of extraordinary width, it includes a vertical row of drawers beneath a small cupboard between two large doors. Inlaid on the front are a series of sand-shaded floral and shell designs (fig. 3.34), including an unusual insect that appears on several pieces of furniture from the same area.[52] The survival of the schrank is especially informative. Had it not survived, one would logically assume that David Hottenstein's costly "Cloath Dresser" bore more of a relationship to the boldly painted interior decoration of the house.

The Importance of Clocks

One of the most expensive objects in eighteenth- and nineteenth-century households was a tall-case clock.[53] Because of their value

FIGURE 3.35
Wedding party of Elizabeth
Landis and John Bomberger,
Lititz, Lancaster County, 1916.
Joanne (Hess) Siegrist Collec-
tion, Lancaster Mennonite His-
torical Society, Lancaster, Pa.

and universal functionality, clocks were among the most common heirlooms to be passed from generation to generation, as documented by a 1916 photograph (fig. 3.35). Taken in the Lititz, Lancaster County, home of Elizabeth Landis on the day of her marriage to John Bomberger, November 9, 1916, her family's heirloom clock can be seen in the background.[54] Because clocks often have the name and location of the maker of the movement engraved or painted on the dial and frequently descended in the family of the original owner, they can be strong convey-ors of local characteristics for both the move-ment and cases.

Clocks were expensive, whether they had thirty-hour or more costly eight-day movements. A clock in a handsome hardwood case was a powerful symbol of economic means and social status among both the English- and German-speaking populations of southeastern Pennsylva-nia. Clocks might represent up to 6 percent or more of a person's net worth.[55] They were also a reminder of one's mortality, a fact that was some-times echoed on the dials with images of Father Time or the Grim Reaper. Studies of Virginians into the 1800s found that wealthy households typically acquired clocks only after they had purchased luxury goods such as silver, ceramics, and mahogany furniture. In contrast, even many modest households in Pennsylvania included

a clock. Schaefferstown resident Martin Albre-cht, for example, occupied a one-story "bad old house" of 26 by 22 feet but owned a clock valued at £7.10.0 listed in an inventory totaling less than £66.[56] Once in place, a clock might remain in the same location for generations, through house renovations and various rounds of painting. The Bean homestead in Montgomery County has the outline of a tall clock on a wall, where the own-ers whitewashed around it for decades. The clock was positioned beside a window in the gable end of the room, where it was visible from the kitchen.[57] Another house in southern Chester County has a ceiling joist cut out to accommo-date the hood of a sarcophagus-top tall clock.

George Yunt's Clock ⌁ Some of the earli-est tall clocks in southeastern Pennsylvania were owned by people of Germanic heritage. A number of them have locally made cases with imported thirty-hour movements made by members of the Möllinger family, Swiss-Mennonites who fled to the Palatinate in the late seventeenth century. Clockworks of this type were designed to function with or with-out a case; two brackets at the back allowed them to be suspended from two large forged nails driven into the wall or the backboard of a case. Many of these clocks have histories of ownership by Mennonite families in Lancaster County, though not exclusively.[58] Lutheran farmer George Yunt (Yund/Yound/Junt), who lived several miles east of Ephrata in Lancaster County, owned an impressive tall-case clock (fig. 3.36). Yunt (1719–70) was doubtless a suc-cessful farmer, for he possessed substantial real estate in Earl Township and left £300 to each of his three daughters in his will of September 13, 1770. Inlaid on the door of the slender wal-nut case of his clock is the inscription "GORG / IUNT / ANNO / 1755" above a pair of birds seated in a tree. The hood has embellish-ments unknown on other clocks of the period, including applied canted colonettes (or balus-ters) that flank the face and are repeated on either side of the base. The boldly coved cor-nice molding is reflected in the identical base molding that rests on the floor, as the clock never had feet.[59]

The movement, which has a square, red-painted, sheet-iron dial, cast and gilt pewter spandrels, and pewter chapter ring, was probably made by Hans Jacob Möllinger (1695–1763) or his son Friedrich (1726–78) of Neustadt and Mannheim, Germany. Identical chapter rings and spandrels were used on clocks by both father and son. Hans Jacob Möllinger had a direct tie to Pennsylvania through his sister Esther (b. 1703), who immigrated to Pennsylvania with her husband Jacob Bossert in 1726. There is also the possibility that Lancaster clockmaker George Hoff may have known Möllinger; he trained in Grünstadt, only twenty miles from the Möllinger shop in Neustadt and made movements that have features similar to those of Möllinger.[60]

When he acquired the clock in 1755, Yunt was thirty-six-years old. He died in 1770 and was interred a short distance from his farm in the cemetery of the Bergstrasse Lutheran Church, where a massive sandstone gravestone marks his final resting place (fig. 3.37).[61] What happened to the clock after his death is unknown. His will directed that his land be divided among his three sons, with the youngest, George, to inherit the tract with the house. His widow, Anna Margarette, was

FIGURE 3.36
Tall-case clock, made for George Yunt, movement attributed to Hans Jacob or Friedrich Möllinger, Neustadt or Mannheim, Germany, 1745–55, case probably Ephrata area, Lancaster County, 1755. Collection of Earle H. and Yvonne Henderson, Jr.

FIGURE 3.37
Tombstone of George Yunt (d. 1770), Bergstrasse Lutheran Church, Ephrata Township, Lancaster County.

to be permitted to continue living there. Yunt
also directed his wife to "sell the Rest of my
Moveables which she will not keep for her Use
and the Use of her Family, that is my Household Utensils."[62] Whether she sold the clock
or bequeathed it to a descendant is unknown,
as no vendue records or will for her have been
located. Were it not for the inlaid name and
date on the case, the history of George Yunt's
clock might have been lost forever.

William Dishong's Clock ⁓ Clock cases
marked with an owner's initials or name, like
George Yunt's, are uncommon but not rare in
southeastern Pennsylvania. Only infrequently,
however, is the dial of a clock marked with an
owner's name rather than that of the maker. In
1811 Lancaster clockmaker John Hoff noted in
his account book that Rudy Kaufman "bespoke
an eight-day clock, clock, & dial marked with
his name."[63] Perhaps with an eye to posterity
or personal pride, William Dishong (d. 1807)
of Ephrata had not only his name painted on
the white dial of his clock but also his initials
prominently inlaid on the case flanking the top
of the door (figs. 3.38, 3.39). Perhaps this was
a statement that he was more important than
the maker of the movement, Jacob Gorgas Sr.
(1728–98), who was his brother-in-law.[64] The
Dishong family immigrated to Philadelphia
in 1752 and 1753, with William and Matthias
(probably a brother) sailing on the *Two Brothers*
in 1753. Soon after his arrival, William settled in
Germantown, where he appears in the account
book of Alexander Mack Jr. (1712–1803), a
stocking weaver and Brethren church leader, in
an entry dated May 26, 1760:

> *Figured with William DiSchong for the*
> *stockings that he sent to his father in win-*
> *ter, there were, first, 4 dozen, each dozen*
> *50 [05 s] sh / Also 4 pair men's and 2 pair*
> *women's stockings / and the 4 caps.*

In the same year Mack calculated room and board
for William and Matthias, deducting against it
what they wove in stockings and caps. William
developed a close relationship with Mack and
became a foreman in his weaving shop. According
to a provision in Mack's will of 1785, he wrote,

*My loom must first be offered to Dear
Brother William DuSchong, according
to a promise I made to him that he may
pay whatever he sees fit. If he doesn't wish
to buy it himself, he will presumably give
the best advice on how best to sell it.*[65]

Mack's reference to Dishong as a "Brother" indicates that he was a fellow member of the Brethren or Dunkard faith. By the time Mack wrote his will, William was living in Ephrata, Cocalico Township, Lancaster County. He had married Hanna Mack, daughter of Johann Valentin Mack (d. 1755) and the niece of his former employer. The date of their marriage is unknown, but it occurred prior to 1761, when they are mentioned in a document related to the disposition of Valentin's estate.[66] Valentin had married Maria Hildebrand in Germantown in 1730; nine years later they moved to Ephrata along with other Germantown Baptists to join the Ephrata Community, where Valentin died in 1755. His daughter Elizabeth (1732–82) never married; she lived at the Cloister and was known as Sister Constantia. A third daughter, Christina, married Jacob Gorgas Sr., who made the clock movement for William Dishong. Born in Germantown to John Gorgas, a Mennonite preacher, and Psyche Rittenhouse, Jacob's first cousin was David Rittenhouse, the noted Philadelphia clockmaker, astronomer, and scientist. Jacob and Christina (Mack) Gorgas moved to Ephrata by 1749, where they were householder members of the Ephrata Society.[67]

Exactly when William Dishong ordered this elaborate walnut tall-case clock is not known, though it was between the early 1780s, when white dials came into use, and the death of Gorgas Sr. in 1798. Dishong was clearly an entrepreneurial sort, involved in both stocking weaving and storekeeping. He was listed in the Cocalico tax records of 1792 as a storekeeper; in 1796 as a stocking weaver with a fulling mill; and in 1800 as a storekeeper.[68] When he died in 1807, his estate was valued at $6,315.82, including various debts and bonds owed to him; wearing apparel worth $45; two watches valued at $32; and a desk worth $20. His clock, however, had the highest value of all his furniture,

an impressive $53.[69] There is little doubt that Gorgas Sr. made the movement for the clock, but the maker of the case is unknown. It does bear some relationship to several less-ornate cases containing movements by Reading clockmaker Daniel Rose; those cases have similarly carved ruffles on the body just above the arched door opening as well as scrolled inset carving in the upper corners on the front of the base.[70] The Dishong case is by far the most elaborate example in the group, featuring ornately carved foliage with piercing in the tympanum, ornate rosettes, and inlaid initials with shaded ruffles echoing the C-scrolls and the ruffle carving above the door opening. Even the frieze on the sides of the hood has finely carved foliate C-scrolls flanked by three flutes as seen on either side of the carving in the arched head or tympanum. The front of the base is inlaid with light-wood scrolls across the top and sides. Given the great expense and pride of ownership

FIGURE 3.39
Detail of clock hood in fig. 3.38.

evidenced by William Dishong's clock, it is no surprise that it remained a highly valued heirloom that was passed through generations of the Kemper and Fishburn families until 1994, when it was donated to the Historical Society of the Cocalico Valley in Ephrata.

Thomas and Sarah Downing's Clock ⌐

Like William Dishong's clock, the one made by Chester County clockmaker Isaac Thomas (1721–1802) of Willistown Township descended through the family of the original patron to the present owner (fig. 3.40). In the late 1800s a history-minded descendant recorded the names of all previous owners on a note that was placed inside the door; the names of subsequent owners were then added over the years. The first owners of the clock were Thomas and Sarah (Smith) Downing, Quakers who married in 1786 and were members of Uwchlan Meeting. The handwritten note states that the clock was "Purchased by Sarah Smith Downing, wife of Thomas Downing, about 1792." In her will, dated 1835, Sarah directed: "I give and bequeath my Clock to my daughter Elizabeth."[71] In 1858 Elizabeth passed the clock to her daughter Anna Valentine Edge. Forty years later, it was inherited by her son Jacob Valentine Edge, who is probably the one who recorded the history of ownership. The clock has remained in the Edge family to the present day. Because of the great respect and care taken by each generation, it has survived totally intact, retaining even the original finials and feet, the two parts that are often broken or removed over time.

Thomas Downing (1691–1772), the first of the family to immigrate, arrived in 1717 from Bradninch, Devonshire, England, and settled in Concord Township, Chester (now Delaware) County. By the mid-1730s, he was living in a village on the Brandywine Creek, halfway between Philadelphia and Lancaster. Initially called Milltown because of the many mills along the creek, by the time of the Revolution the community was referred to as Downing's Town; in 1812 it was officially named Downing-

town. Thomas Downing's sons Richard (1719–1804) and Joseph (1734–1804) became successful mill owners, which proved to be a lucrative line of work. Joseph's eldest son, Thomas (1758–1829), married Sarah Smith, and they were the first owners of the clock.[72]

Not surprisingly, the well-to-do Downings chose prominent clock- and cabinetmaker Isaac Thomas to make their clock movement and likely the imposing case as well. Like the Downings, Thomas was a Quaker. His grandfather, Peter, of Wales, had settled in Pennsylvania by 1685.[73] By 1697 the family had acquired a tract of more than 500 acres in Willistown Township along Crum Creek, where Isaac's father, Peter, was born. Following Isaac's marriage to Mary Townsend at Birmingham Meeting in 1745, they settled on the family property on the west side of Crum Creek. Isaac became a successful and multitalented craftsman, listed in tax assessments as both a joiner and clockmaker. As early as 1764 he owned and operated a saw mill on his property, a valuable asset for his cabinetmaking activities.[74] In 1774 he built a large grist mill, another lucrative venture.[75] Active Friends in Newtown Preparative Meeting and Goshen Monthly Meeting, Isaac and Mary had eleven children. Two of their sons, Enos and Mordecai, followed their father into the trades of cabinetmaking and clockmaking.[76]

When Isaac Thomas died in 1802, his inventory was taken by cabinetmaker Benjamin Garrett, along with Joseph Thomas and [?] Grubb.[77] Included among his possessions were:

Cherrytree Desk and Breakfast table	*$29*
Ten Clocks and three Cases	*276*
Several Cupboards Spice box and Tables	*21.50*
Clock Shop Tools and Joiner Shop Tools	*140*
Surveying Instruments Chain Desk & Stove	*32.70*
A Stove Gears Shaving Instruments	*21.00*

Although it was not typical for a craftsman to make both clock movements and their cases, Isaac Thomas was not the only rural artisan to do so. Enoch Jones of Schuylkill Township, Chester County, died in 1833 possessed of "one box of clock tools," "one chest of carpenters tools," and a "lot of Millwright tools."[78] The production of both clocks and cases by the Dominy family of East Hampton, Long Island, has also been extensively documented.[79] When Isaac Thomas wrote his will in 1801, the numerous bequests he left specifically to his wife provide an indication of the affluence and sophistication of their household:

> *I give and bequeath to my wife Mary Thomas . . . .the first built Part of the house being the west End except half the big Seller and the new kitchen and its furniture and her Needfull househould Goods. She shall have two fether beds of her Choice two cases of drawers of her Choice her Cubbard and Teaware and Pewter and the Largest Looking Glass and Chears, sufficient. A Cherrity dining Table and Cherrity Tea Table and her Little Chamber Clock and watch and Spinning wheels and her Riding Creture and One Cow kept Sumer and winter and a Reasonable Right in the Orchard And Garden and firewood Redy Cut Near her door, and that my Son Mordecai Shall Nurish and Cherrish his Loving Aged Mother Untill her few day in this world be Over.*[80]

His wife's "Little Chamber Clock" is believed to be a walnut shelf clock now owned by Chester County Historical Society (fig. 3.41). It has a silvered brass dial marked with twenty-four, instead of the usual twelve, hours and an experimental thirty-hour movement—designed so that the clock does not stop running while it is being wound.[81] Like the Downing clock and several others by Thomas, the shelf clock has a circular dial framed within a circular opening in the door of the hood. The inspiration for this unusual feature is unknown; according to tradition these round-dial clocks were made for members of the Thomas family.[82] Unless the Smiths or Downings were related to the Thomases, however, their clock seems to contradict this tradition.

Thomas and Sarah Downing's clock was probably a special request, as the dial is particularly large, measuring sixteen inches across

instead of the standard twelve (fig. 3.42). Like all known clocks by Isaac Thomas, this one has a brass dial, which Thomas may have made and engraved himself.[83] The chapter ring on the Downing clock obscures part of the "I" in Isaac, the "s" in Thomas, and some of the foliate engraving, suggesting that Thomas may have engraved the dial and then assembled the other parts without precise measurements. The walnut case exhibits a number of characteristics found on other clock cases with Thomas movements and may be distinctive features of the Thomas cabinetmaking shop or an indication of localisms. On either side of the hood, circular openings echo the round dial of the face. The size of the dial and accompanying hood give the clock a monumental presence that is accentuated by the height above the dial, creating a deep tympanum beneath the broken-scroll pediment. This aspect of the case design is seen consistently on other Thomas cases, as are the flat, shaped extensions at the rear of the hood and the distinctive carved rosettes with center cross-hatched buttons and narrow petals. Also typical of other Thomas clock

FIGURE 3.40
(opposite) Tall-case clock, made for Thomas and Sarah Downing, movement and probably case by Isaac Thomas, Willistown Township, Chester County, 1790–95. Collection of Paul S. and Caroline Edge Beideman

FIGURE 3.41
(above) Shelf clock, probably made for Mary Thomas, movement and probably case by Isaac Thomas, Willistown Township, Chester County, 1770–1800. Chester County Historical Society, West Chester, Pa.

FIGURE 3.42
Detail of clock hood in fig. 3.40.

cases are the two-part finials, consisting of a large round ball with a separate flame carved with precisely defined, spiraling grooves. The waist of the clock is bordered at the top and bottom with a narrow scalloped band seen on other Thomas cases as well as on case pieces thought to be from Chester County.[84]

Owner and Maker:
Lydia Harlan and Samuel Morris

It is rare to find a piece of furniture signed and dated by the maker, but it is even more so when a separate inscription also reveals for whom the piece was made. Although the client may have asked the maker to sign the piece, more likely it was pride of workmanship that compelled joiner Samuel Morris (d. 1809) to sign the back of a drawer with the large inscription, "Samuel Morris / Joiner of Logtown / 8 mo 5 1793."[85] When this commanding tall chest-on-frame (fig. 3.43) and inscription (fig. 3.44) were published in 1966 by Margaret Berwind Schiffer, the less-visible inscription "For Lydia Harlan" on the inside of the backboard of the same drawer went unnoticed. Discovered during a reexamination of the piece in 2007, this notation has brought additional meaning to the history of the chest and its owner.

Born June 12, 1763, Lydia Harlan was a lifelong Quaker. Thomas Harlan (1725–1824), her father, was a farmer in Kennett Township. His second wife, Mary Baily, of London Grove Meeting, was Lydia's mother. After Thomas Harlan's death, his widow married Samuel Mendenhall and in 1768 took a certificate of removal from Kennett to Concord Monthly Meeting for herself and her children: Thomas, Lydia, and Israel.[86] Daughter Lydia never married, and at the time of her death, August 24, 1825, she was living in the Kennett Township home of Elizabeth (Harry) Harlan, the widow of her late brother Thomas (1759–1824). Although Lydia was a spinster, she was not shunned by members of her Quaker faith; indeed, some unmarried women even became ministers.[87] Lydia's will and inventory indicate that her material possessions were minimal, consisting of clothing and bedroom furnishings, which she left to her sister-in-law. Included

among these items was one "case drawers," valued at $4. Lydia did have significant resources in bonds and interest due to her, totaling nearly $700. The final bequest in her will also indicates some level of material wealth: "I give and bequeath to my niece Lydia Harlan daughter of Israel Harlan my six silver tea spoons marked with the initials L. H. and my riding whip."[88] Lydia was buried at London Grove Meeting with other members of her family.

Little is known of Samuel Morris, the joiner who signed the drawer and identified himself as a "joiner of Logtown." The manner in which Morris wrote the date, "8 mo 5 1793," suggests that he was most likely a Quaker. His place of residence is uncertain, as at least two communities were historically known as Logtown: Chester Heights, a borough within Aston Township, Delaware County, and the village of Hamorton in Kennett Township.[89] When Morris died in 1809, he was living with his friend John Craig Sr. in Kennett Township. Morris began his will by noting his occupation as a cabinetmaker. He appears to have had Philadelphia connections, as he refers to a house and lot on Stamper's Alley in Philadelphia that he had sold to the Reverend Robert Blackwell.[90] Morris left his real and personal estate "in the City of Philadelphia or whereforever it may be found" to Craig, whom he also named his executor. Craig, along with Joshua Peirce and William Passmore, took the inventory of the estate. It included "one Desk part finished" valued at $8.00, suggesting that Morris was still an active cabinetmaker.[91]

The tall chest-on-frame that Morris made for the thirty-year-old Lydia Harlan is one of a number of similar examples from Chester County cabinetmakers. The form consists of a tall chest of drawers resting on a separate frame with short cabriole legs and paneled trifid feet. Morris used full dustboards between the drawers of the case, suggesting he may have been familiar with Philadelphia workmanship. The paneled, trifid feet on this and other chests can be found on Irish furniture, but they are rare in English work.[92] The shaped skirt on the frame may be a local trait, as at least eight other chests-on-frame with nearly identical front skirts are known. Two

FIGURE 3.44
Detail of signature on back of
drawer in fig. 3.43.

are signed by cabinetmaker Virgil Eachus (d.
1839) and dated 1785 and 1789 respectively.[93] The
skirt shape may have originated in one workshop and been copied by apprentices or other
craftsmen. Little is known about Eachus, but in
1789 he is listed as a freeman in the Thornbury
Township tax assessment; Thornbury is adjacent to Aston Township, where a Logtown was
located during the period. Eachus may have
had some Philadelphia connections, as in 1791
he married Bathsheba Webb at Zion Lutheran
Church in the city.[94] Another chest-on-frame
with a related but not identical skirt is signed
"John W. Thomas / Cabinet Maker" "December
27th 1805." It also has a second chalk inscription,
"George Gregg" (1763–1833), a cabinetmaker who
worked in Kennett Township from 1796 to 1819.[95]

Paint-Decorated Chests

Some of the more pervasive myths about
southeastern Pennsylvania furniture involve
the paint-decorated chests owned by German-
speaking settlers and their descendants. The
most common surrounds the oft-repeated term
"dower chest," implying that these pieces were
made exclusively for young women as they
prepared for marriage. In fact, young men and
women alike were given chests, typically in
their early-to-mid teen years, for storing clothing and possessions. These chests then accom-

panied the owners when they married and set
up housekeeping; they were, by and large, not
made as dower chests. A survey quickly reveals
that numerous male as well as female names can
be found on the chests, such as the one made
for Adam Minnich of Bern Township, Berks
County in 1796 (fig. 3.45). The lions and unicorns on Minnich's chest might give the impression of its being a masculine object, but the
existence of a virtually identical chest inscribed
across the front "Marrichen (little Maria) Grim"
and also dated 1796 suggests that the decoration
was equally appropriate for a female.[96]

The inscription on Minnich's chest tell-
ing us that he lived in Bern Township, Berks
County, is most unusual. Although many
chests have an owner's name and date painted
on them, few cite a location. Even when an
owner's name is present, it is difficult to identify
the exact person, given the repetition of common names in the period. There are also many
chests with no identification at all. Some of
these are nevertheless highly detailed and beautifully painted, and a number were designed
and built with an applied front that creates
the effect of two or three recessed panels. This
architectural treatment (fig. 3.46) was achieved
by applying molded columns on either side of
each panel, topped by a long, horizontal board
cut to form the tops of the arches—with the

central arch usually pointed.[97] Although this type of chest has long been associated with Lancaster County, one example was made for Caspar Hildenbrand, who lived in southern York County. Chests of similar construction, but made of walnut rather than tulip-poplar or pine, are also associated with southern York County and northern Maryland. Another group of architectural facade chests can now be identified with the area of Windsor Township, Berks County, including one for Margaret Kern in 1788 and an undated example made for Jacob Hill.[98]

In the architectural chest seen here, the boldness of the red and blue tulips against the original white ground within the panels is complemented by the molded columns separating each panel, carefully painted with a vertical row of red and blue blocks flanking the half-round molded section with rows of dots. This artisan's minute attention to detail is most dramatically seen in the small painted dots that surround the escutcheon, echoing the beading on the perimeter of the stamped-brass escutcheon plate. The decorator of this chest must have intended for it to be viewed from the front, as the sides were painted a simple, solid red. Nonetheless, the red, white, and blue color palette (a popular

combination in the late eighteenth and early nineteenth centuries) results in a stunningly graphic statement. The bold motifs and careful execution combine to create a dramatic example of an architectural chest.

Another myth surrounding the decoration on chests is the assumption that the designs carry religious or symbolic meaning. Over the past century this has become accepted fact, despite a lack of documentation. Fortunately, numerous chests survive with excellent family histories (including some with names and dates) to help address these issues and separate fact from fiction. The notion that religious symbolism was embedded in motifs painted on these chests was promoted by early scholars such as John Joseph Stoudt, who in 1948 published the controversial *Pennsylvania Folk Art: An Interpretation* (revised and reprinted in 1966). Stoudt hypothesized that the three-petal tulip (which he claimed is a lily) represents the Trinity; unicorns symbolize chastity; birds signify the soul; pomegranates are associated with fertility, and so on.[99] Although there is a historical basis for the use of religious symbolism in art, what Stoudt and others could not prove is whether the makers and owners of these objects understood them to have such

FIGURE 3.46
Chest-over-drawers, probably Lancaster County, 1785–1800. Collection of Katharine and Robert Booth

FIGURE 3.47
Chest, made for Maria Eitenyer (b. 1789), by John Bamberger, Warwick Township,
Lancaster County, 1835. Lancaster Mennonite Historical
Society, Lancaster, Pa.

FIGURE 3.48
Chest-over-drawers, made
for Christina Benter, New
Hanover Township area,
Montgomery County, 1791.
Collection of Carl and Julie
Lindberg

meaning. Because no documentation in the form of journals, letters, or other writings has yet been found to indicate a decorator's intent or an owner's interpretation of the motifs on his or her object, we can only speculate as to the extent to which religious symbolism played a role. In the case of fraktur and sgraffito ware, there are some instances when the text and imagery clearly relate, but more often designs have no apparent connection to the text. An alternative explana-tion for images such as the lions and unicorns on Adam Minnich's chest is that many were derived from printed sources or the natural world. A rampant lion and unicorn are key figures in the British coat of arms, well known in colonial Pennsylvania on broadsides, currency, and other printed materials. The Pennsylvania state seal, adopted in 1782, also shows a pair of black horses that could have inspired decorators. Flowers and birds, seen on so many of the painted chests, were all around for inspiration. Some motifs likely did have symbolic meaning while others were merely part of an artist's design vocabulary; sometimes a tulip is just a tulip.

Chests were popular because they were useful pieces of storage furniture. In his will of 1789, John Jacob Long of Montgomery County left to his wife "that bedstead and bed with the curtain which is in the stove room together with the blew chest with all her clothes in it."[100] Chests were also a repository for personal identity—often inscribed prominently with their owner's name. Painted chests involved choices of eco-nomics, aesthetics, and ethnic preferences. Most were made of six boards, with front, sides, and back dovetailed together. The tops were usually a single board with molded battens on the ends, attached to the back-board with wrought iron strap hinges. Feet ranged from bat-ten or turned-ball feet tenoned through the base on earlier models to dovetailed straight or ogee bracket feet by the

1770s. Numerous variations in design and construction, however, make this iconic category of southeastern Pennsylvania furniture also one of the most diverse forms to be produced in the region. Though many chests have no drawers, some have two or three side by side. Drawers added to the expense because of the additional labor and hardware. Enos Thomas of Willistown Township, Chester County, typically charged £0.17.6 for a painted chest in the 1790s, but he charged £1.10.0 for a chest with drawers, locks, and brass handles.[101]

One of the best-documented painted chests is that made for Maria Eitenyer (Eitenier) (fig. 3.47), which highlights the risk in assuming that the date on a piece of furniture is the date of manufacture. On the front of the chest, a large central heart frames Maria's name and the date "1789," together with two decorative pinwheels (fylfots) and a compass star. Fortunately, the chest is signed on the underside of the bottom board by the maker, John Bamberger (1780–1861), a cabinetmaker and farmer in Warwick Township, Lancaster County.[102] Recorded in Bamberger's farm ledger are several entries pertaining to Jacob Eitenier, Maria's husband. In 1835 Bamberger sold him a peck-and-a-half of timothy seed and cider and then noted: "made for him a chest" at a cost of $3.50.[103] The 1789 date on the chest was actually the year of Maria's birth; so she was forty-six when her husband purchased the piece. Other known chests by Bamberger date primarily to the 1820s; thus, the use of Maria's birth date was likely a special request. Bamberger was one of the last cabinetmakers in Lancaster County to make painted chests in the traditional manner of the previous century. In 1815 he had a two-story stone joiner's shop measuring 24 by 16 feet on his 142-acre farm. Even so, his output was limited, documented by the fact that between 1831 and 1847, the period covered by his surviving ledger, he recorded making seven full-size chests, one clock case, and one small chest.[104]

Few painted chests have the level of documentation as that made for Maria Eitenyer by John Bamberger. Nonetheless, groupings of similarly decorated and constructed chests can sometimes allow regional or local schools

FIGURE 3.49
Detail of till and drawers in fig. 3.48.

of workmanship to be identified, as with the exquisite paint-decorated chest made in 1791 for Christina Benter (fig. 3.48).[105] It is one of four closely related examples bearing names and dates. Others include those for Elisabeth Binder, 1788; Anna Schultz, 1788; and Anna Maria Mack, 1792. A chest made for Anna Maria Muthhart in 1786 may be an earlier work by the same artist.[106] A sixth example, made for Daniel Eisz and dated 1795, is related in the overall form and writing of the name and date, but the painted decoration does not appear to be by the same hand as that of the other four, which relate in numerous ways.[107] All are of similar construction, including large bracket feet, a central pendant drop, and drawers that have beaded edges along the tops of the sides and back. There is some variation in the composition of the large paint-decorated panels on the fronts, but the floral decoration, birds, and other motifs compare quite closely from chest to chest. Painted at the top of the front on each is a long, horizontal panel containing the date and name of the owner in a flowing script. The interiors also share an unusual feature; most have hidden drawers with painted fronts under the till. These drawers are revealed when the side of the till is slid upward (fig. 3.49). The drawers on the Benter and Mack chests have simple sponged decoration, with the vertical dividers between the drawers painted a bright red. The hidden drawers on the Schultz chest, however, are painted with delicate floral imagery.

Genealogical research on the original owners indicates that the chests were made in the border region of Berks and Montgomery counties. Elizabeth Binder and Christina Benter were sisters; despite the different spelling of their surnames, they would have been pronounced the same by a Pennsylvania German. The Binders/Benters/Benders lived in New Hanover Township, Montgomery County, and were the daughters of Ludwig and Margaret Bender. They were members of the New Hanover or Falckner Swamp Reformed Church. Christina was born August 25, 1772, and Elisabeth on April 15, 1767. Anna Schultz is more difficult to identify, but Schultz was a common Schwenkfelder surname in northern Montgomery County. Anna Maria Mack was likely the daughter of Peter and Margaretha Mack, born in 1778 and baptized at the Emanuel Lutheran Church in Pottsgrove Township, Montgomery County. A Daniel Eiss was confirmed at the Oley Hill Union Church in 1791, which was an affiliate of the New Hanover parish for most of the late 1700s.[108]

The magnificent painted chest made for Magdalena Leibelsperger in 1792 is a tour-de-force of the decorator's art (fig. 3.50). The front is divided into three panels separated by black columns with painted flowers; the central panel contains floral decoration and a compass star. To either side is a large heart, containing two compass-work stars. The two drawers are painted with contrasting blue-grained borders and red trim, surrounding an ochre central section. Black frames above the panels contain the date and name (spelled Machtdalena Leübelsperger) in fraktur lettering in a contrasting red paint. Magdalena was born November 25, 1772, in Weisenberg Township, along the western edge of what is now Lehigh County. She married John Kemmerer, who is listed in tax records as a farmer in Salisbury Township. Magdalena died on April 14, 1844, and was buried in the cemetery of the Western Salisbury Jerusalem Union Church. The fact that the Leibelsperger chest represents a local product is reinforced by a related example documented to the same area. That chest was made for Michael Finck and is dated 1789. It is over three drawers and has similar large hearts and compass stars on the front, but the central panel is arched at the top and contains the owner's name.[109] Finck was probably the son of

Michael Finck, a weaver who died in 1773 in Salisbury Township. Finck Sr. was a member of the Jerusalem Union Church, where Magdalena was buried.[110]

The Leibelsperger and Finck chests have traditionally been attributed to woodworker John Bieber (1763–1825), based on a paint-decorated schrank made for Bieber's father, Jacob, in 1792.[111] The grain-painted decoration on the drawers of the schrank closely resembles that on the drawers of the chests. The drawer construction also relates in the use of a chamfered bottom board that fits into grooves on the sides and backboard instead of being nailed or pegged to the bottom of the sides and back. The numerals in the date "1792" on both the chest and schrank compare quite closely, as does Jacob Bieber's name, which is rendered in red fraktur lettering in a manner similar to that on the chest. Jacob was born in Germany in 1731, immigrated in 1744, and settled in the Oley Valley. Around 1786, he moved to Salisbury Township, Lehigh County, where he died in 1798. His son is listed in tax records in 1788 and 1789 as a joiner in Salisbury Township, and he attended Jerusalem Union Church in Western Salisbury from at least 1789 to 1799.[112] However, it is important to recognize that John Bieber was not the only woodworker in the area. Heinrich Kemmerer (1740–1801) was a carpenter living in Salisbury Township from 1770 until his death in 1801. He also attended Jerusalem Union Church, and his son John married Magdalena Leibelsperger. Other joiners in the township who might also be likely candidates for producing these chests include George Eschbach and Philip Klein.[113]

Chests were painted with imported pigments that were readily available in stores across southeastern Pennsylvania—including red lead, vermilion, Prussian blue, yellow ochre, and lead white. From 1790 to 1807 storekeeper Samuel Rex of Schaefferstown, Lebanon County, advertised that he carried Prussian blue, red, Spanish brown and Spanish white, white lead, and yellow ochre.[114] Although milk paint is thought to have been commonly used, the majority of paints were oil-based. Chrome-based pigments, which were not commercially available until about 1818, were quickly adopted because of the vibrant greens and yellows they provided. The brightness of this group of chests is a result of their having survived in remarkably good condition. Many surviving chests, however, have now darkened or faded due to the effects of varnish, sunlight, and grime; thus, our perceptions of the color palette used by our ancestors is skewed. As vivid as the colors on these chests remain, when new they would have been even brighter. They may seem garish to our modern sensibilities, but in the dark, candlelit interiors of early homes they would have shone brilliantly.

Many questions pertaining to painted decoration remain unanswered. In the absence of documentation, we can only speculate as to the role the consumer played in choosing the decoration, but an indication comes from two indentures for housewifery. Among the goods to be given upon completion of the indenture were, for one girl, a chest painted the color of her choosing, and, for the other, "one chest, either poplar or painted, or one of walnut boards."[115] Another difficult question is whether the craftsmen who built the chests also painted them. Although some decoration has been attributed to fraktur artists such as Henrich and Daniel Otto, it may have been done by an artist copying their work. Undoubtedly there was a significant difference in technique and materials between fraktur drawings done with pen and watercolor and chests painted with oils. Account books provide limited insights. Bucks County craftsman Abraham Overholt, for instance, noted only single colors for much of his painted furniture, with brown being the most common cited. The only decorated objects he made were a poplar chest with three drawers that he described in 1791 as "blue speckled" and a chest with three drawers he "painted . . . blue and the mouldings red" in 1797.[116]

FIGURE 3.50
Chest-over-drawers, made for Magdalena Leibelsperger, probably Weisenberg or Salisbury Township, Lehigh County, 1792. Philadelphia Museum of Art, purchased with the Thomas Skelton Harrison Fund, the Fiske Kimball Fund, and the Joseph E. Temple Fund 1982

Daniel Danner

Spinning wheels were a common item in most Pennsylvania households, frequently given to young women before marriage. During an almost 100-year period, 1749 through 1839, every daughter in three generations of the Clemens family received a spinning wheel as part of her dowry.[117] The upright type of wheel, known as a German or castle wheel, was popular among Pennsylvania Germans, as it took up less floor space and was more easily transported and stored than a flax or Saxony-type wheel. Upright wheels were especially common in Lancaster County, where they were made by craftsmen such as Daniel Danner of Manheim and Samuel Henry of Lampeter Township.[118] Danner (1803–81) made the upright wheel and clock reel seen here (figs. 3.51, 3.52) in 1842 for Rebecca H. Hershey (1815–50); her death within a few years of their manufacture probably accounts for their pristine condition. Rebecca was the daughter of Andrew (1778–1868) and Mary (1774–1850) Hershey, who lived near Salunga, Lancaster County. Rebecca's husband, Isaac Brubaker (1817–96), was a deacon in the Mennonite Church. After Rebecca's

FIGURE 3.51

Spinning wheel and reel, made for Rebecca H. Hershey, attributed to Daniel Danner, Manheim, Lancaster County, 1842. Private collection

death, the wheel and reel descended to her daughter Mary Ann Brubaker (1842–97), who married Jonas Mumma (1835–1921). They then went to her daughter Fannie (b. 1865), who married Jonas H. Herr (1863–1935), a merchant in Ephrata. The wheel and reel then passed to her daughter Mary Herr Hottel, who sold them at auction in 1987.[119]

Many spinning wheels and turned objects made by Danner have survived. Few, however, still carry the paper labels he often applied to his work. A comparison of the turnings on his labeled work with those on unlabeled pieces identifies him as the maker of Rebecca Hershey's wheel and reel and documents his turned elements as a distinctive localism. Danner is listed as a turner in Manheim tax records from 1831 to 1846, and his account books indicate that he made turned parts for other craftsmen, including bed posts, half-columns, and "stumps," or feet, for case furniture.[120] Such evidence is invaluable in not only identifying other craftsmen but also providing clear evidence of the interrelated nature of the work within the craft community. It is rare,

FIGURE 3.52
Detail of reel in fig. 3.51.

however, since most furniture is not identified by a maker's mark or craftsman's account book. Whether treasured by generations of one family or passed on to other owners and collectors, furniture with documented provenance is key to understanding the diverse localisms of southeastern Pennsylvania.

Lewis Miller Carpenter,
working ———— At the Trade for
Thirty Years, In South Duke Street, York, p. a.
done work for the Citizens, and County—
Commissioners—at
the Court house Jail
poor house and county
office and Bridges.
and for the — Borough
at market house &c &c
for the lutheran
congregation at the
houses and church
David Landis,
mr. Miller, weaver
Henry Ernst,
James Conley,
Abraham Greenawalt
Daniel Baumgardner
Clemens Stillinger
Jacob Schindel Jacob Frey Skoemaker

Names of work done.
George Geistweit.
John Beck.
mr. Hill
George — Jacobs.
John Gardner.
Henry Heartzog. Jacob nell
John N. Kolb.
Jacob Uffer.
miss. — Gros. widow
Henry Smyser.
william Eichelberger.
John Graber. Polly wagner
Peter Small.
John Voglesong.
Samuel Fry. Richard Porter
william Spangler.
Dr. William McIllvain
Samuel Leedy. Spangler Kuntz
Henry Sheffer.
John Kuntz.
Jacob Spangler Cooper George Spangler
Michael Welsh.
George Loucks. Miller.
George Brickel. Jacob May
Philip Waltemyer.
Michael Ash.
widow Dritt. Jacob Stair
Daniel Billmyer.
Peter Debart.
old Zellor. Mathias Strom
Joseph Kraft.
Peter Rupp.
Conrad Beck. Henry Sheffer
Richard Koch.
Benjamin Landus.
Jacob Laumaster. Joseph Kolb
John Rouse.
Lewis Getz.
nathaniel Bailey. John Kolb
Peter All.
Jacob Decker.
Mis. C. Schram. noah Kolb
Michael Bentz.
Miss. Luttman.
Jacob Gardman. Peter Armspin
Jacob Heckert.
william Rease.
Abraham Gardman. mrs. Banix
Frederick Hibner.
christian miller.
Samuel Mayer. polle wagner
John Hibner.
Adam Miller.
Jacob Rupp. william Bart
Joseph Fahs.
George Small.
Lewis Kuntz. widow Gaelhor
Jacob Busser.
Philip Small.
Youst Kuhl. Gottlieb Ziegle
George Epply.
Samuel Brooks.
Martin Boyer. Jacob baumga
Jacob Frey, tailor.
Polly Stroman.
Robert Fisher. George Bricke
Henry Wagner.
Elisabeth Billmyer.
Cooper Oram. Carle Miller
John Inebest.
Martin Spangler.
Matthew Kear. Lewis Wample
Martin Boeshor.
mr. quenly. George Sheffel
Mises. fisher widow. Aronie
Jacob neede. Samuel Klingm

CHAPTER FOUR

MAKERS: FROM CRADLE TO COFFIN

To Wit: James Ewing orders John Fischer to manufacture for his account one tall floor clock . . . to be done in the craftsmans neatest manner . . . The face of said clock to be furnished in the latest style and clearly discernible at a distance of twenty five feet. The wood to be of fine cured walnut or cherry, whichever is found to be the soundest in the hands of the joiner. John Fischer, the seller assures the buyer of the latest style and design that is to be had at the hands and mind of himself and the most skillful and renowned joiner it is his responsibility to hire.

—*James Ewing to John Fisher, 1789*[1]

In 1842 West Chester cabinetmaker Yarnall Bailey (1799–1862) proclaimed his ability to produce "all kinds of work . . . from the cradle to the coffin."[2] Some forty years earlier, painter Edward Hicks had produced a trade sign for Henry Vanhorn, "Carpenter & Joiner" of Bucks County, to show prospective customers that Vanhorn made a wide range of furniture, including cradles, chests of drawers, and coffins (fig. 4.1). In 1796 Vanhorn had opened a cabinetmaking shop in Newtown; around 1800 he moved to Lower Makefield Township, where he was recorded in the tax records as a carpenter.[3]

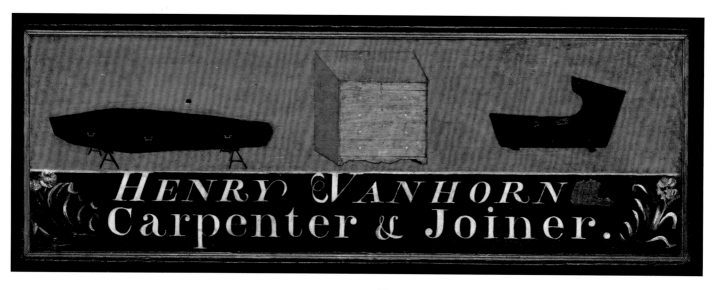

FIGURE 4.1

Trade sign, made for Henry Vanhorn, attributed to Edward Hicks, Bucks County, 1800–1805. Abby Aldrich Rockefeller Folk Art Museum, Colonial Williamsburg Foundation

The furniture forms depicted on Vanhorn's trade sign served a dual function, indicating his trade as a cabinetmaker as well as illustrating the stages of life. This theme was not uncommon, as can be seen in a watercolor-and-ink drawing (fig. 4.2) attributed to fraktur artist and schoolmaster Johann Adam Eyer (1755–1837). The drawing comprises four sections. The first, and lowest, depicts a young man in the prime of life. The next section shows him on his deathbed with a minister by his side; adding to the realism of the scene is the bedstead with pillow panels—a common feature on Pennsylvania German beds to hold the bolsters and pillows in place (see fig. 1.7).[4] The deceased man's body is represented in the next scene by a casket atop a bier, awaiting burial. The final, top, section depicts heaven, complete with angels and flow-

ers, and is the only portion of the drawing rendered in vibrant colors—a subtle commentary by the artist on the joys to be found in paradise.

Yarnall Bailey and Henry Vanhorn were typical of many cabinetmakers who fashioned a variety of objects for their customers. Some woodworkers specialized in particular aspects of the trade such as carving or turning, but many—especially those in more rural areas—willingly produced whatever their clients wanted. Although cradles survive today in far greater quantity than coffins, in the period cabinetmakers made many more coffins. One Bucks County cabinetmaker listed only two cradles in his account book from 1790 to 1833; for each he charged £0.15.0.[5] Amos Darlington of Chester County kept an account book in which he recorded making 173 pieces of furniture between 1791 and 1810; only two were cradles, one of poplar and the other of walnut.[6] A cradle might be commissioned by newlyweds in anticipation of starting a family or given to a young woman as part of her dowry furniture.[7] Cradles varied in materials and decoration; from plain to ornate, some were embellished with carving, inlay, or painted decoration. Rarely, however, were cradles personalized with names, initials, or dates—probably because of their anticipated usage by many children rather than any one individual. One cradle from Lancaster County was made for twins. Windsor-type cradles were also made, such as the one branded by John Letchworth with a history of ownership in the Valentine family of Downingtown, Chester County.[8] Not surprisingly, cradles can reflect

FIGURE 4.2

Drawing, attributed to Johann Adam Eyer, probably Hamilton Township, Northampton (now Monroe) County, 1810–25. Winterthur Museum purchase acquired through the bequest of Henry Francis du Pont

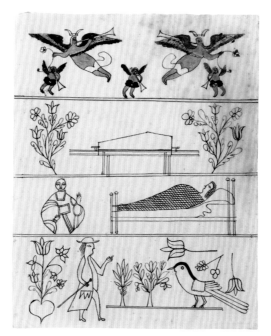

local design and construction preferences. A walnut example from Chester County of paneled construction has head- and footboards shaped like the crest rails on wainscot chairs (fig. 4.3). This cradle was made to hold a roped support for the bedding; many also have slots or holes cut in the bottom board for ventilation and easier cleaning. It also has small pillow panels attached to the headboard, like those found on Pennsylvania German beds, and shows evidence of wooden or brass knobs along the top edge of the sides for securing an infant with woven tape string.

More so than cradles, coffins were a mainstay of business for many cabinetmakers. Between 1751 and 1758, William Smedley of Chester County made 24 pieces of furniture and 21 coffins.[9] In Strasburg, Lancaster County, John Bachman II sold more than 375 coffins between 1769 and 1808, second only to bedsteads, of which he sold more than 400. Curiously, Bachman also kept a book where he noted details concerning "the death of each person for whom he made a coffin." His descen-

dants continue to operate a funeral home in Strasburg today.[10] Because coffins were needed on such short notice, many cabinetmakers kept a quantity in stock or subcontracted for them if needed. Thomas Ford, a cabinetmaker and undertaker in Coatesville, Chester County, owned 26 coffins at the time of his death, in addition to walnut, poplar, and pine boards and varnish.[11] In 1829 Amos Darlington Jr. of West Chester hired John Mickle to make 9 coffins as well as several bureaus and washstands.[12] Yarnall Bailey advertised in 1838 that he carried "sofas, sideboards, secretaries, bureaus, Tables" as well as "COFFINS of all sizes on hand (better than when made in haste)."[13] Some cabinetmakers found this line of work profitable enough to expand into the undertaking business, providing hearses and funeral arrangements as well. Cabinetmaker Samuel Lawrence of East Caln Township, Chester County, made his will in 1813, leaving to his son William "my hearse and the Gears thereunto belonging and all my Coffen Boards." Not all cabinetmakers went into the funerary business, however. Some found

FIGURE 4.3
Cradle, probably Chester County, 1740–65. Collection of Mr. and Mrs. Thomas B. Helm

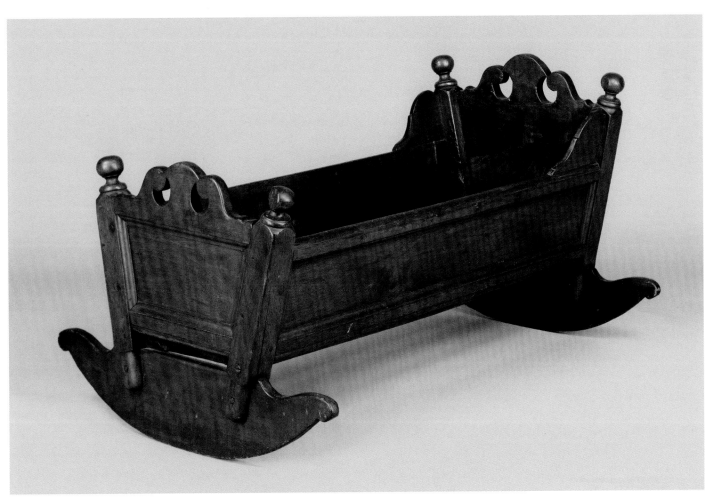

FIGURE 4.4
Bier, Bethlehem, Northampton County, 1800–1825. Central Moravian Church, Bethlehem, Pa.

it highly disagreeable, such as Allen Gawthrop (b. 1810 near Avondale, Chester County), who in his autobiography revealed his discomfort on the subject. Gawthrop was apprenticed to cabinetmaker Ziba Moore (1800–1846) of nearby London Grove Township. On his first visit to Moore's shop, he was

> much horrified at seeing the hearse standing in the yard, one of the old fashioned kind, the body in the shape of a coffin and the though[t] that I would be obliged to go to making coffins was very unpleasant to me, but I thought that after I learned the cabinet business I could do as I pleased about making coffins.[14]

Given the nature of their use, coffins from the eighteenth and nineteenth centuries are largely unavailable for study. Period descriptions are also scarce. Although construction details are not well known, the woods are often referenced in account books and other period sources. Walnut was the wood of choice for those who could afford it. German schoolmaster Gottlieb Mittelberger noted in his account of life in Pennsylvania in the mid-1700s that coffins were "made of fine walnut wood and stained brown with a shining varnish."[15] Cheaper woods such as pine and tulip-poplar were also used. In 1845 Yarnall Bailey successfully sued another man for libel who had accused him of "making poplar coffins and palming them off on poor individuals for walnut."[16]

A bier was often used to transport a coffin to the church and burial location (fig. 4.4). Most had wooden clamps for holding the coffin in place, and some had padded leather supports under the rails to ease the burden for those carrying them. The Moravians placed bodies of the deceased in a corpse house, or *Leichenkapellchen,* for three days prior to burial. This practice was described in 1794 by a visitor to Nazareth: "There is a little isolated building where the dead are kept for three days, and are often examined to prevent the burial of those who might not be dead." The writer went on to recommend this practice as preferable to the prevailing custom of burial within twenty-four hours.[17] Corpse houses could also be found in Bethlehem and Lititz; the latter, built in 1786 of dressed limestone, still stands and measures just over nineteen-feet square (fig. 4.5). Bodies were stored in the corpse house on wooden cooling

boards or corpse trays, which had handles and slots in the sides that allowed the body to be tied in place and carried (fig. 4.6). In at least some instances, biers were likely used to support corpse trays as well as coffins. A number of corpse trays survive at both Bethlehem and Lititz; they are made of painted wood with dovetailed, canted sides in a range of sizes, with the largest measuring about seventy-nine inches in length.[18]

FIGURE 4.6
Corpse tray, Bethlehem,
Northampton County,
1775–1800. Central Moravian
Church, Bethlehem, Pa.

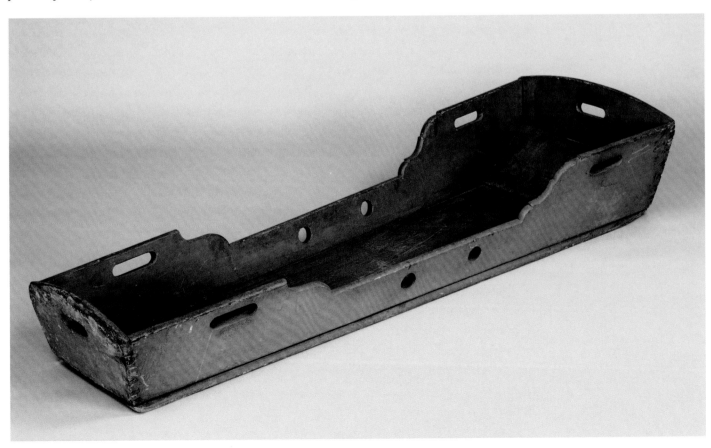

FIGURE 4.7
Self-portrait, by Lewis Miller,
York, York County, about 1845.
York County Heritage Trust

Craftsmen, Tools, and Techniques

Discovering information about individual cabinetmakers in southeastern Pennsylvania is difficult due to limited numbers of signed objects as well as scarcity of account books, receipts, tools, portraits, and other artifacts that can be associated with specific makers. Objects inherently possess a specificity of place that reflects their maker's location; those rare examples that can be linked to particular craftsmen reveal the means by which factors such as location, religion, and ethnicity help shape the contours of one's life and work. Noted York County artist Lewis Miller was a carpenter by trade. He drew a portrait of himself at his workbench, planing a board and surrounded by an assortment of tools, including handsaws, gimblets, gouges, a hammer, ruler, axe, mallet, grindstone, glue pot, and planes (fig. 4.7). Written alongside the drawing is the notation "Lewis Miller Carpenter, working At the Trade for Thirty Years, In South Duke Street, York, p.a.," along with a list of his many customers. Rare glimpses such as this help bring to life the stories of the many anonymous craftsmen in southeastern Pennsylvania.

Woodworking in southeastern Pennsylvania was practiced by a range of people; in addition to those with formal training, many found it necessary or convenient to have at least some woodworking knowledge and tools at hand to perform basic repairs. In 1800 more than half of Chester County landowners supplemented their income from farming with other pursuits; many were engaged in industries such as milling, tanning, and distilling.[19] Most Pennsylvania craftsmen lived in villages rather than on farms, despite assumptions to the contrary. Given the full-time demands of agriculture, few farmers had dedicated craft shops on their properties, but many no doubt earned additional income through other pursuits. Out of 167 farms in Heidelberg Township, Dauphin (now Lebanon) County, in 1798, for example, only 7 had craft shops; of these, some were rented to others or used exclusively for farm purposes.[20] Craftsmen were not of a standard socioeconomic status, as some trades clearly paid better than others. A study of tax records from Reading in 1773 found that clockmakers were on average assessed a tax of £7, bakers £6, and gunsmiths £5.10.0; tailors, weavers, and coopers were assessed less than £3 on average.[21]

The terminology used to refer to woodworkers in the period varied; both "joiner" and "cabinetmaker" were interchangeable for much of the eighteenth century. In the seventeenth century, however, furnituremakers employing frame-and-panel construction were called joiners; those who made dovetailed case furniture were known as cabinetmakers. Another term was that of "carpenter" for artisans who framed buildings and made architectural woodwork. In German, the term *Schreiner* was most often applied to joiners and cabinetmakers while carpenters were called *Zimmerman*. The most specialized and high-end furniture craftsmen were known as *Tischler*.[22]

Masters and Apprentices ⁓ Most woodworkers learned their trade through an apprenticeship, when they served under a master craftsman for a set period of years (typically seven). Apprenticeships provided the opportunity to learn woodworking skills but were also the

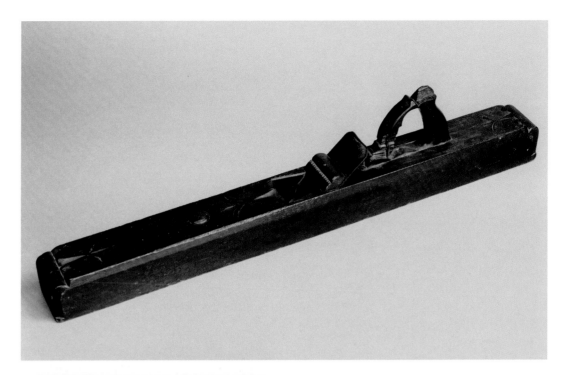

FIGURE 4.8
Jointer plane, owned by
Barnet Hillpot, Tinicum
Township, Bucks County,
1787. Collection of J. D.
Miller

FIGURE 4.9
Detail of incised initials on
fig. 4.8.

means of transmitting particular construction and decorative techniques from one generation to the next. Sometimes these characteristics are distinct enough to identify an object as the product of a particular locale, perhaps even a specific shop or craftsman on occasion. Apprenticeships were also an important means of developing social and economic connections, as apprentices frequently married into their masters' families. Such extended kinship networks promoted the formation of tightly knit artisanal communities. Upon the completion of the set time period, an apprentice became a journeyman and could work in the trade, eventually setting up as master of one's own shop when resources allowed. Sometimes the apprenticeship experience led one to seek a different profession, as was the case for John Frederick

Whitehead. In 1772 Whitehead worked under his uncle in Hamburg, Germany, "to learn the trade of a Cabinetmaker." After seven months, he reported, "I was no further advanced in learning the trade than when I began . . . the chief [thing] I did was breaking of Gimblets, bending of Chysels and Saws, spoiled boards and planes." Whitehead immigrated to America the following year and became a weaver in Berks County.[23] Formal legal agreements specified the terms of the apprenticeship, such as an 1803 indenture in which Daniel Maurrer bound himself to Emanuel Deyer of Manheim, Lancaster County, for three years to learn "the Art & Mystery of a House Carpenter & Cabinet maker." In addition to being provided with food, lodging, washing, a yearly allotment of $25, and six days off at harvest time, Maurrer was to receive a hand saw, jack plane, fore plane, and smoothing plane upon the completion of his apprenticeship.[24] Tools were essential but expensive necessities for craftsmen, who often marked them to identify ownership. In rare instances, they were decoratively inscribed, such as the jointer or trying plane owned by joiner Barnet Hillpot (1766–1848) of Tinicum Township, Bucks County, which bears his initials, "BHP," the date "1787," incised carving, and diamond motifs formed with a star-shape punch (figs. 4.8, 4.9). Tools were the

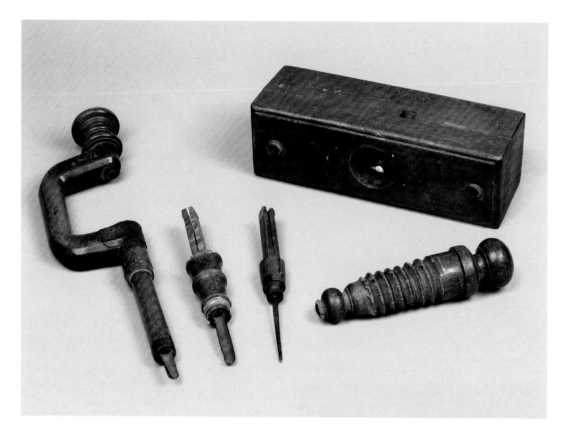

means to a craftsman's livelihood, which is no doubt what prompted the wives of Quakers Moses Roberts and Job Hughes from Berks County to attempt to hide a tool chest for fear it would be seized while their husbands were imprisoned for their pacifist beliefs. In 1780 the women petitioned Chief Justice Thomas McKean for the release of their husbands and reimbursement for their material losses of livestock, crops, furniture, saw and gristmills, and "a Chest of Carpenters tools which we were just burying under ground when the men came upon us."[25] Over the course of his working career, a craftsman might accumulate a number of tools. When Richard Armitt of Chester County died in 1789 at the age of fifty, his inventory included unfinished joiner's work along with numerous saws, chisels, gouges, and an impressive eighty planes.[26]

The most complete insights into the everyday lives of cabinetmakers are possible in the rare cases when one can link account books, drawings, tools, and furniture to known makers. One of the best-documented instances is that of two related Mennonite craftsmen working in Bucks County: Rudolph Landes (1732–1802) and his nephew Abraham Overholt (1765–1834). Landes immigrated in 1749

and settled in Bedminster Township, where he established himself as a turner, producing flax spinning wheels, spooling wheels, and other related wares. Several of his tools survive, including three bits, a brace dated "1770" that bears his initials, and a screw box for making wooden screws with an internal metal blade. The box is stamped twice "RUTHOLPH LANDES" and incised "1774 / RL" (fig. 4.10).

Overholt, very likely his uncle's apprentice, lived in nearby Plumstead Township. From 1790 until shortly before his death, he kept an account book in which he recorded his output as a turner and joiner. The book notes that he worked in hardwoods, primarily walnut and oak, as well as soft woods that he then painted—typically brown. On December 20, 1821, Overholt sold a spooling wheel (for winding thread onto quills or bobbins) to Jonas Frey at a cost of $4. The wheel, stamped twice "AOH" on the end of the bench, was purchased by Dr. Henry Mercer in 1897 from ninety-five-year-old Annie Frey, Jonas's widow (figs. 4.11, 4.12). Aside from a few minor differences in the turning, this wheel is practically identical to one made in 1787 by Landes.[27] An undated drawing in Overholt's account book shows dimensions and many of the details seen on both wheels,

FIGURE 4.11
Spooling wheel, made for Jonas Frey, by Abraham Overholt, Plumstead Township, Bucks County, 1821. Mercer Museum of the Bucks County Historical Society

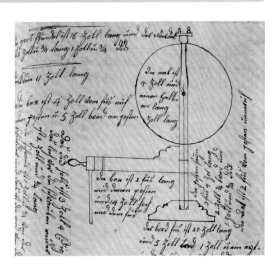

FIGURE 4.12
Detail of maker's mark on fig. 4.11.

including the scrolled footboard and sides of the box (fig. 4.13). A comparison of the turned elements on surviving wheels made by Landes and Overholt also shows a close relationship in their work. Textile equipment was Overholt's mainstay; from 1790 to 1833 he made 89 spinning wheels, 10 wool wheels, and 8 spooling wheels. He also made bedsteads (31 are recorded in the account book), dough troughs, tables, kitchen cupboards, clock cases, rolling pins, cradles, and some large case furniture, including a walnut tall chest with ten drawers for which

FIGURE 4.13
Drawing of spooling wheel, by Abraham Overholt, Plumstead Township, Bucks County, 1790–95. Private collection

FIGURE 4.14
Tall chest of drawers, by
Benjamin and probably Joseph
Garrett, Goshen Township,
Chester County, 1786. Chester
County Historical Society,
West Chester, Pa.

he charged £7.10.0. In comparison, he typically charged £0.15.0 for a spinning wheel. In 1794 he bought a 57-acre farm, and his woodworking output lessened considerably. Between 1790 and 1794, Overholt made 71 spinning wheels; over the next thirty-nine years he made only 18 more. The inventory of his estate included

a turning lathe, augers, axes, chisels, gouges, planes, saws, drawing knives, and numerous lots of wood.[28]

The master-apprentice relationship between Landes and Overholt was repeated within many families throughout southeastern Pennsylvania. Such was most likely the case with Joseph

FIGURE 4.16
Detail of floral carving on
knee of related tall chest of
drawers, attributed to the shop
of Joseph Garrett, 1780–1800.
Winterthur Museum purchase
with funds in part from Mr.
and Mrs. Richard W. Vieser

Garrett (1743–92) and his son Benjamin (1771–1856). A figured maple tall chest of drawers (fig. 4.14) was signed in chalk by Benjamin and dated "1786" on the inside backboard of the second drawer from the bottom. The inscription appears close to the edge, suggesting that it was written on the board before the drawer was made. The eldest child of Joseph—a joiner, watchmaker, and farmer who lived in Goshen Township, Chester County—Benjamin was fifteen years old when he signed the drawer. He was probably working as an apprentice in his father's shop; he later appears in tax records for Goshen Township as a joiner. Benjamin inherited his father's tools when Joseph died in 1792. The inventory includes 2,446 feet of poplar boards and 1,350 feet of maple and walnut boards; a lot of joiner's and watchmaker's tools, scales, and weights; watch keys and glasses; and a grindstone. Benjamin was also well acquainted with the family of clockmaker and joiner Isaac Thomas of nearby Willistown, as he attended the Goshen Meeting with Isaac's son Mordecai and in 1802 appraised Isaac's estate.[29]

The short cabriole legs of the Garrett tall chest are unusual in that they attach to the case with large wooden screws. To accomplish this the craftsman dovetailed the legs to a batten that runs front-to-back at either side of the case, which was then secured to the underside with two wooden screws (fig. 4.15). Approximately thirty other tall chests with this construction feature are known, although enough variation exists to indicate they were not all produced by the same shop. Frequently referred to as "Octoraro" chests in reference to the creek that flows along the western border of Chester County, the tall chest signed by Benjamin Garrett is the only documented example known and was in all probability made well east of the Octoraro in his father's workshop. Because little information exists as to the provenance of the other chests and there is little to link them stylistically to other pieces said to be made in the Octoraro region, it is difficult to substantiate this claim.[30] Several other tall chests in the group can be linked to the Garrett shop, including one with distinctive intaglio floral carving on the knees (fig. 4.16) that is otherwise nearly identical to the signed Garrett chest in overall dimensions, molding profiles, markings on drawers, and shape of the legs. The Garrett tall chest is made of striped maple, and the dense, uneven grain would have been difficult to work; most of the others are walnut.

Attaching legs with large wooden screws may have been a variation of the chest-on-frame form, where the case that contains the drawers can be separated from the more fragile legs. The case would still have been heavy to transport without the legs, but removing them helped to prevent breakage and damage. A contemporary publication noted that wooden screws ensured easy disassembly and were cheaper than metal ones.[31] The frequency with which these tall chests were disassembled and moved, however, is unclear. The condition of the wooden screws varies, suggesting that some were taken apart more often than others. A number of the thirty-some examples in the group now have metal screws supplementing or replacing wooden ones.

Where did the idea for attaching legs with wooden screws originate? One possibility is that spinning wheels, which use wooden screws as tensioning devices and threaded ends to join various components, may have provided the inspiration. Wooden screws can also be found on objects ranging from adjustable candle stands to linen presses. Spinning wheel makers often proved to be versatile craftsmen. The tape loom initialed "D W" and dated "1816" (fig. 4.17) is one of a small group with turned legs and winding mechanisms, suggesting they were made by someone who also made spinning wheels and reels.[32] Woodworkers who made spinning wheels

and case furniture might have been the ones to develop the idea of using wooden screws to secure legs onto tall chests. Although not working in Chester County, Abraham Overholt of Bucks County made spinning wheels, case furniture, and even bedsteads with screws—presumably wooden ones. Five generations of the Garrett family in Chester County, including another Joseph (d. 1770) also of Goshen Township, were weavers.[33] Joseph Garrett the cabinetmaker of Goshen, who worked as a joiner and watchmaker, is the sort of versatile craftsman who might have developed the idea of using wooden screws to attach legs. Perhaps his familiarity with textile production and furniture provided the inspiration. The signature of his son Benjamin on a tall chest with legs attached by such screws certainly indicates that Joseph's workshop produced them. In addition to spinning wheels and the group of tall chests, at least two walnut schranks are known with wooden screws holding the two main cupboard sections together.[34]

One small subgroup of tall chests with legs attached by wooden screws is thought to be from Frederick County, Maryland. By the 1760s, Chester County was so extensively settled that younger generations had to seek farmlands by moving into Maryland, Virginia, or the Carolinas. Many Chester County Quaker families settled in Frederick County, where they established meetings including Pipe Creek, Bush Creek, and Deer Creek. Surnames such as Smedley, Griffith, Bailey, Garrett, and Pusey—names common in the Goshen area of Chester County—appear in Frederick County in the 1790 census.[35] The Maryland tall chests in question are characterized by a reeded border below the cornice, quarter columns with two flutes, and vertical backboards that are nailed on. Two examples have initials inlaid with a simple line-and-berry design and are linked to Quaker families in Frederick County.[36] Closely related to the inlaid initials on the two tall chests of drawers is a chest (fig. 4.18) with the inlaid initials "S L," made for Salome Lehman (1763–1855) of Uniontown, Frederick County, shortly before her marriage to Jacob Yon. Although the chest has straight bracket feet instead of the cabriole legs of the tall

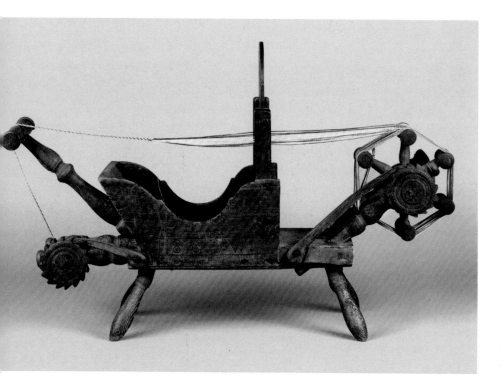

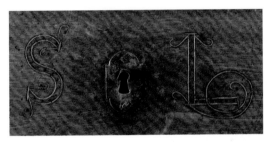

chests, its distinctive inlay (fig. 4.19) firmly links it to the Maryland group. The bracket feet may have been appropriate because of the smaller size of the chest. The Lehman chest is also remarkable because of the ornate hinges with chased ornament and inscriptions including the owner's name, the date "1787," and the name of the blacksmith, David Barnhart (fig. 4.20).

In addition to information on shop production and clientele, account books provide insight into the means by which cabinetmakers were reimbursed for their work. Payment for furniture was often made in goods, services, or labor bartered in exchange rather than cash. The account book of Philadelphia joiner John Head, kept from 1718 to 1753, recorded many payments in goods and services.[37] In 1800 clockmaker John Hoff of Lancaster began keeping a "Book of New Clocks," where he recorded those he made and payments he received, which in addition to cash included clock cases, a dining table, shoes, flour, rifle barrels, a bedstead,

and lumber.[38] Cabinetmaker Thomas Ogden of West Chester advertised in 1820 that he would "take in exchange beef, pork, fire wood, wheat, rye, corn or any kind of boards, such as he makes use of in his line."[39] Sometimes these bargains and extensions of credit became quite complicated, particularly when they involved relationships that extended beyond that of maker and owner. Patronage often followed ethnic or religious associations, which provided important economic networks but could become problematic when breakdowns in payment or quality occurred. An exchange between Lutheran minister Johann Friedrich Ernst (1748–1805) and joiner Christian Shouse of Easton, Northampton County, illustrates this point. Ernst ordered a new bedstead from Shouse in 1781, promising to pay him in grain that he anticipated receiving as part of his salary from the congregation. Both parties grew frustrated when neither the grain nor the bed arrived in a timely manner. Shouse wrote to Ernst first, complaining, "I am in great necessity for want of grain if you cannot procure the Rye you owe me you will be kind enough to send me three pounds of State money." The pastor responded by reminding Shouse that "when our bargain was making about the Bedstead . . . I could not promise payment at any

FIGURE 4.18
Chest-over-drawers, made for Salome Lehman, Frederick County, Maryland, 1787. Historical Society of Carroll County

FIGURE 4.19
Detail of inlay on chest in fig. 4.18.

FIGURE 4.20
Detail of hinge on chest in fig. 4.18, by David Barnhart, Frederick County, Maryland, 1787.

FIGURE 4.21
House and woodturning shop
of Jacob Keim, built about 1753,
Pike Township, Berks County.
Historic Preservation Trust of
Berks County, Pa.

FIGURE 4.22
Sawmill of Daniel Bertolet, built
about 1810, Oley Township, Berks
County. Daniel Boone Homestead, Pennsylvania Historical
and Museum Commission

certain time because I must wait until I should receive the Grain." Even though the bedstead was not ready as promised, Ernst said he had not pressed Shouse for it since he could not yet make payment, then concluded, "if Providence pleases I am hope[ful], by the Time you have finished the [bedstead] in the bargain finish, which you remember is to be a plain one, I shall be able to make a full Satisfaction as I expect grain in every Day."[40]

The physical space in which craftsmen worked can also yield insight into their everyday lives and means of making a living. A few woodworking shops survive from eighteenth- and early nineteenth-century southeastern Pennsylvania. The woodturning shop of Jacob Keim (fig. 4.21), built about 1753 near Oley in Rockland (now Pike) Township, Berks County, is one of the earliest still standing. A substantial two-and-a-half story structure, this building included a spring and fireplace on the lower level, workroom on the midlevel, and attic space above, typical of the Pennsylvania German preference for multipurpose ancillary buildings as opposed to the European use of small, single-purpose buildings.[41] When Keim's inventory was taken in 1799, "turning chisels," planes, a rasp, compass, "carpenters adze," "spike gimblet," and "old iron tools for making led window sash" were among his possessions.[42] Although Keim's pole lathe no longer exists, scars on the walls and ceiling indicate that it was anchored in place in the south corner; wear on the floor bears evidence of the foot treadle location. A large window on the long side opposite the entrance would have provided a light source to someone operating the lathe, while another window in the gable end lit the workbench. Built into the chimney stack is a dry kiln for seasoning wood. A similar drying chamber existed at the nearby 1740s home of joiner Wilhelm Pott, who also operated a sawmill.[43] Pott was one of many woodworkers who found it advantageous to own or share in the ownership of sawmills. By the mid-eighteenth century, dozens of sawmills such as the one owned by Daniel Bertolet of Oley Township, Berks County (fig. 4.22), were in operation, converting the region's rich timber resources into lumber for furniture and carpentry work. About 1790 organ builders John and Andrew Krauss of Kraussdale, Lehigh County, constructed a stone building of about 22 by 26 feet with first-floor workshop (identified as a "joiner's shop" in the 1798 tax list), which still retains racks for tool storage and drying racks for wood on the ceiling by the chimney.[44] In 1840 David Brown of New Garden Township, Chester County, advertised for sale "a frame Cabinet Makers Shop, 24 feet square, 2 stories high, plastered inside with a platform for drying work on attached to one end, 14 by 30 feet."[45]

Large workshops such as those used by Keim, the Krausses, and Brown were atypical, as records from the 1798 Federal Direct Tax indicate that most woodworking shops at the time were fairly small and built of log. Shops were also not necessarily suited to one trade; the property of Henry Muhlenberg in Trappe, Montgomery County, included a workshop used at different times by a blacksmith, shoemaker, and hatter. Shops tended to be either relatively square in shape or long and narrow, to allow room for planing long boards at workbenches.[46] In 1798 there were four carpenters' shops in Warwick Township, Lancaster County, measuring 13 by 20, 16 by 24, 18 by 24, and 18 by 28 feet, while Heidelberg Township, Dauphin County, had two joiners' shops measuring 18 by 12 and 27 by 18 feet. Even when built of humble materials and of limited space, cabinetmakers strove to impress their customers. In 1809 Thomas Ogden of East Bradford Township, Chester County, advertised that he "has commenced Cabinet-Making in the neatest and most fashionable

FIGURE 4.23
Detail of label on looking glass in fig. 1.25.

modern style, in the shop formerly occupied by his father." According to the tax records from 1798, when his father, Benanuel, still owned the shop, it was built of log and measured 20-feet square.[47]

Makers' Marks

Why so few furniture craftsmen signed or labeled their work, especially during the eighteenth century, is open to speculation.[48] For Quakers, the community-based nature of their faith discouraged the acknowledgment of individual contributions, in some cases quite directly. In 1768 Matthias Hutchinson, builder of the Buckingham Friends Meetinghouse in Bucks County, was denied permission to include his initials in the datestone of the building.[49] Of those objects with signatures or other inscriptions, the marks are often illegible due to abrasion, fading, and damage.[50] In the instances when a name is inscribed, it is often unclear as to whether it is that of the maker, owner, subsequent restorer, or inheritor. Retailers also occasionally put their names on objects, such as John Elliott of Philadelphia, who affixed his bilingual (German/English) label to looking glasses imported from England that he sold in his "Looking-Glass Store" (fig. 4.23). When a piece of furniture is found with a legible inscription that clearly identifies its maker, the object can become a keystone for attributing other unsigned examples and identifying

FIGURE 4.24
Chest, by Peter Rohn,
Northampton County,
1784. Winterthur
Museum purchase with
funds provided by the
Henry Francis du Pont
Collectors Circle

FIGURE 4.25
Detail of inscription inside
fig. 4.24.

FIGURE 4.26
Detail of dovetail with
wedged pin.

distinctive local groups. Such is the case with a painted chest with two large trefoil designs on the front (fig. 4.24). Written in German script on the underside of the till lid, probably before the chest was assembled, is the ink inscription: "Peter Rohn made this / the 11 March in the year / 1784" (fig. 4.25). He also wrote his surname multiple times on the underside of one of

the two small drawers under the till. Although Rohn did not include a location, he is thought to be the Johann Peter Rohn who was born January 4, 1763, and died August 21, 1834, as noted in the records of the Dryland Union Church, Northampton County. He is listed in the 1790 census as head of a household in Bethlehem, Northampton County, and in 1800 in Forks

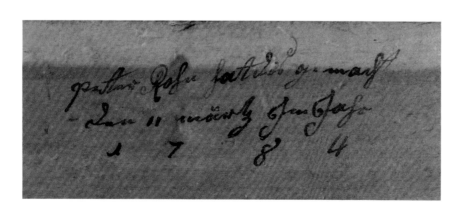

Township, Northampton County.[51] The original owner of the chest is unknown; a painted inscription on the front retains traces of her first name, "Lisbeth," and the date "1784." According to the owner of the chest in 1958, it was purchased in northern Bucks County, which abuts the Northampton County border.[52]

In addition to the inscription documenting Rohn as the maker, the chest is further distinguished by unusual construction techniques that help to identify other unsigned work by Rohn. The bottom board extends beyond the sides to form the base molding, a practice common in Europe but rarely seen in Pennsylvania.[53] The bracket feet are formed by four boards dovetailed together at the corners to form a rectangular frame that is pegged to the underside of the bottom board. This distinctive feature has not been observed on other Pennsylvania chests outside this group; also unusual is the use of a fifth bracket foot in the center of the chest. The paint losses on the front are a result of the resinous pine boards. Painted chests were typically made of less-expensive, locally available native woods such as pine or tulip-poplar. Pine, because of its knots and high resin content, can cause losses and discoloration in the painted decoration over time, so craftsmen often selected a clear piece of pine or substituted a tulip-poplar board for the front. Observation of these characteristics on several other chests, along with similar trefoil designs, has led to the identification of more examples attributable to Rohn. Some include drawers with an unusual manner of construction: the drawer sides are pegged to the sides of the drawer fronts rather than dovetailed.[54]

Highly distinctive construction techniques can sometimes identify the product of a particular maker or workshop, as craftsmen developed a workmanship of habit based on experience and repetition.[55] Most often, however, construction techniques only hint at a craftsman's background. Craft practices such as the use of wedged dovetails and wooden pegs rather than nails are commonly associated with Pennsylvania German cabinetmaking as a

craft tradition brought from Europe. However, over time these techniques were learned by non-German apprentices and other craftsmen and thus can be found on furniture of seemingly non-Germanic origin. Driving a thin horizontal wedge into the end grain of a dovetail pin spreads the wood (fig. 4.26), making a tight and efficient joint that would not loosen as the wooden boards dried and shrank.[56] This technique also enabled the craftsman to make dovetails more quickly and with wood that was not yet completely seasoned—advantages that saved time and money and were thus important.[57] Another feature often associated with Pennsylvania German craftsmanship is the use of wooden pegs to attach moldings, enforce mortise-and-tenon joints, and secure drawer bottoms, which were simply butted up and pegged to the drawer sides and back. Craftsmen with English training typically preferred nails by the mid-eighteenth century and attached their drawer bottoms by routing a groove near the inside bottom edge of the drawer sides to accept the chamfered edges of the drawer bottom, which was then slid in and nailed at the back.[58] Regardless of their ethnic background, craftsmen also used templates, patterns, and jigs when possible to create a workmanship of certainty in which the outcome was efficient and predictable. Details such as carving, which could be difficult to fix if a mistake was made, fell into the workmanship of risk. However, measures could be taken to minimize that risk, such as executing the carving on wood that was to be applied rather than carving on the front directly; if a mistake was made, it could be more easily corrected.[59]

Fancy Goods

Peter Rohn was atypical of eighteenth-century cabinetmakers in signing his chest. As the nineteenth century progressed, this practice became more common, especially with chairs, which were sold as larger sets and often branded, labeled, or stamped on the underside of the seat with the maker's name. At the same time, ornately decorated chairs became popular as part of a larger trend in the arts known as

"Fancy," noted for its bold ornament and exuberant decoration that was applied to everything from painted furniture to tinware to coverlets. Fancy goods were highly decorative but relatively inexpensive, making them accessible to an ever-growing American middle class.[60] Household interiors showed the influence of the Fancy movement, as seen in a portrait of Johann Abraham Sprenger and family of Lebanon County (fig. 4.27). Painted about 1825 by itinerant folk artist Jacob Maentel, the interior of the Sprenger parlor features colorful, boldly patterned walls and carpet. Gathered around a drop-leaf table, the family sits in bamboo-style yellow Windsor chairs with painted floral motifs on the crest rails, with two small rocking chairs for the younger children made en suite.[61] The rocking chair was a relatively new development, not

coming into widespread popularity in America until after 1815.[62] The prominent inclusion of the chairs in the foreground of the painting may have been an attempt to show that the Sprenger family was fashionable enough to own this new furniture form and had not one, but two child-size examples.

Paint-decorated Windsor chairs were the forerunners to a prolific chair-manufacturing industry that was in full force by the mid-nineteenth century in southeastern Pennsylvania. In Lancaster, John Swint was one of the preeminent chairmakers from about 1847 to 1860; he is listed in the tax records from 1841 to 1850 as a cabinetmaker and in 1847 advertised that he carried out "the Chair Manufacturing business."[63] A blue paint-decorated chair (fig. 4.28), one of a set of six, is stamped "J.SWINT / CHAIRMAKER"

FIGURE 4.27
Portrait of Johann Abraham Sprenger and family, attributed to Jacob Maentel, Schaefferstown, Lebanon County, about 1825. Winterthur Museum, bequest of Henry Francis du Pont

FIGURE 4.28
Chair, by John Swint, Lancaster, Lancaster County, 1840–50. Collection of Teresa and Richard Ciccotelli

on the underside of the seat (fig. 4.29). The vivid blue ground is accented with touches of red and white to highlight the vestigial ball turnings on the legs and front stretcher. By this time, the emphasis was on painted decoration rather than the quality of the turnings. The chair has slender, tapering spindles for the back—a feature that was a holdover from the 1820s. In contrast,

FIGURE 4.29
Detail of underside of chair in fig. 4.28.

a chair with bright green ground (fig. 4.30) features the broad, baluster-form splat that became popular around 1850. The pierced central section of the splat echoes the curves of the outer profile and resembles an abstract lyre, a fashionable motif inspired by the classical revival of the early 1800s. Under the seat (fig. 4.31) is the painted stencil inscription "G. NEES" for George Nees (d. 1882) of Manheim, Lancaster County, who

began working there around 1850.[64] Like the Swint chair, the Nees example also has a shouldered tablet-top crest rail that flares at the lower corners and is painted with stenciled naturalistic floral motifs. Some of the tools used by Nees survive (fig. 4.32), including a spokeshave, bevel, paint brushes, grain combs, feathers, and sponges in addition to a sample painted and blank crest rail (fig. 4.33). Painted chairs like those made by

FIGURE 4.30

Chair, by George Nees, Manheim, Lancaster County, 1850–60. Collection of Dr. and Mrs. Donald M. Herr

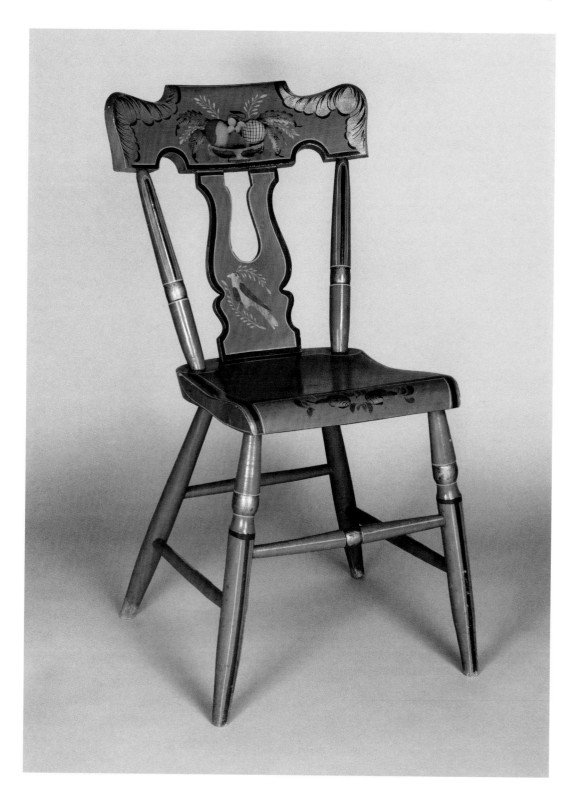

Swint and Nees were widely popular in the nine-teenth century, the equivalent to the ubiquitous slat-back chairs of the eighteenth century. In 1841 John Hartman of Chester County advertised for sale "Fancy and plain Windsor chairs" while Emmor Jefferis of West Chester sold "Settees and Chairs, of all descriptions, gay, plain, Windsor, fancy, or rush bottom."[65] In addition to making Fancy furniture, chairmakers also redecorated old furniture in the newest taste. In 1850 William Sweney of West Chester advertised "Fancy and Windsor Chairs of every variety and colour," as well as "Old Chairs repaired in splendid style."[66]

FIGURE 4.31
Detail of underside of chair in fig. 4.30.

FIGURE 4.32
Tools owned by George Nees, Manheim, Lancaster County, 1850–75. Mercer Museum of the Bucks County Historical Society

FIGURE 4.33
Crest rails, attributed to George Nees, Manheim, Lancaster County, 1850–60. Mercer Museum of the Bucks County Historical Society

A Curious & Versatile Genius: John Fisher of York

In 1800 Philadelphia merchant Thomas Cope noted in his travel diary that while in York he had called on "a German mechanic of a curious & versatile genius," to see his clocks and other inventions.[67] This genius was John Fisher (1736–1808), whose talents included clockmaking as well as sign painting, wood carving, and engraving. Free from the constraints of a specialized urban environment, craftsmen such as Fisher could pursue a variety of creative bents. York chronicler Lewis Miller depicted Fisher several times, once holding a pair of compasses (fig. 4.34) to evoke his occupation as a tradesman. Born in Germany, Fisher immigrated in 1749 to Pennsylvania and settled in York by 1756. He married Barbara Lightner of Baltimore in 1766, and the couple had three sons. The eldest, George, became a clockmaker, while John Jr. was a doctor and Charles a coppersmith.[68] Founded in 1741 along the Codorus Creek, York was a thriving market town by the time of the Revolution with a population of nearly 2,500 (fig. 4.35). More than half of the town's taxpayers in

1779 were artisans, practicing nearly forty distinct trades.[69] The inhabitants were "very largely Germans," according to German traveler Johann David Schoepf in 1783. The town's concentrated artisanal community made an impression on Schoepf, who took particular note of their clocks:

> *All manner of craftsmen and artificers are to be found in this and other similar country-towns; especially, it appears, are many wall and standing-clocks made here, at least in most of the houses along the road I saw very well designed works, with the rubric of this place.*[70]

Among the most impressive clocks made by John Fisher is one with an eight-day movement and orrery that indicates the positions of the sun, moon, and planets (fig. 4.36). The brass dial is engraved "John Fisher \ York Town" and is surrounded by mythological figures (fig. 4.37). Although parts of the orrery are missing, the engraved surround includes the zodiac signs and months of the year. Latin inscriptions from Virgil's *Aeneid* and *Georgics* are engraved on the dial near the figure of Zeus and around the orrery.[71] The massive walnut case has fluted quarter columns with brass capitals, Greek key molding on the broken-scroll pediment, applied panel on the base, and ogee bracket feet. The clock plays seven tunes; a pinned brass cylinder adjusts automatically so that a different one plays each day of the week. The musical mechanism has thirteen nested bells and eighteen hammers rather than the usual single bell and hammer design, enabling a more melodious sound. Although the name of the original owner of this impressive clock is uncertain, the piece may have been the musical clock valued at $80 in Fisher's inventory. In the twentieth century it was the property of the Aughenbaugh family of York.[72] Another clock made by Fisher in 1790 has a thirty-five day movement, astronomical dial, and planispheric map; it was mentioned in the *Maryland Gazette* in 1790 as a "curious Time-Piece . . . the astronomical part of which does the greatest honour to the inventor." The article went on to say that Fisher had also built several other clocks "by which he has gained very distinguished professional celebrity" and

FIGURE 4.38
Pennsylvania coat of arms,
by John Fisher, York, York
County, 1796. York College of
Pennsylvania

that he "possesses fine natural talents in Drawing, Painting, Engraving, &c."[73] Few of Fisher's
contemporary American clockmakers made
astronomical or musical clocks, so his achievements are all the more notable. In 1793 Fisher
advertised for an apprentice: "WANTED As
soon as possible, An active LAD of genius," the
notice began, continuing,

> *The subscriber flatters himself that from*
> *upwards of 40 years close attention to his*
> *profession, and a variety of inventions*
> *put in practice both as to the internal*
> *machinery of his Clocks, as also the*
> *beauty of the enamel and engraving of his*
> *Clock Faces, will induce some ingenious*
> *lad to apply; none need apply but such*
> *are possessed of ingenuity and sobriety .*
> *. . he will teach the method of making*
> *Musical clocks, such as chiming, also with*
> *organs, as well as to shew the motions of*
> *the Heavenly Bodies.*[74]

The advertisement reveals that Fisher's abilities
as a craftsman extended to engraving, a necessary skill for fashioning clock dials and other
objects. A pair of silver-mounted flintlock pistols signed by York gunsmith Friedrich Zorger
are thought to have been engraved by Fisher, as
the inscription "& I.F." appears beneath Zorger's name on the locks.[75] Fisher's reference to
enameling in the advertisement also indicates
he was likely painting his own white dials.

John Fisher was also a talented painter
and woodcarver. Lewis Miller sketched him
painting a tavern sign of a black bear that was
so realistic that a dog attacked it.[76] In 1796 the
York County Commissioners paid Fisher £25
for "Painting the Coat of Arms to and for the
use of the Court House" and £5 for "Carving
and Guilding the Image to the same." The oil
painting on panel Fisher executed of the Pennsylvania coat of arms (fig. 4.38) survives and features two white horses flanking a central shield
topped by an eagle, all above the state motto

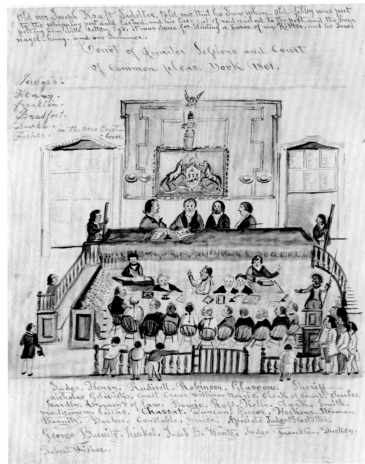

"Virtue, Liberty, and Independence."[77] Within the shield are images symbolizing Pennsylvania's heritage, including a ship under full sail, a plow, and three sheaves of wheat. This iconography is thought to derive from the seals of individual counties, which formed their own insignia by adding a distinguishing crest to the Penn family coat of arms: Chester County used a plow; Philadelphia County a ship; and Sussex County, Delaware (officially part of Pennsylvania until 1776) a sheaf of wheat.[78] Given Fisher's work as a woodcarver, he probably made the ornately carved frame for the painting as well. The coat of arms was displayed in the York County courthouse, together with a figure of Justice carved by Fisher hanging above (fig.

4.39). Although the statue is not dated, carved into the flat back near the base are the initials "I F" for John Fisher (fig. 4.40). The painting and statue were depicted in situ by Lewis Miller in a drawing of the courthouse interior (fig. 4.41).[79] Other woodcarvings by Fisher include a bust of Conewago Indian John Carlton that bears his initials and a deer head with antlers. These were no doubt the goods appraised to his widow in his 1809 inventory as "1 Carv^d Buck & Indian head."[80]

When Fisher's estate was inventoried, it revealed the many avenues his "curious & versatile genius" had taken over the course of his lifetime. From his clockmaking profession were various watch and clock parts, tools, a musical clock and case, a timepiece and case, organ clock, and two new eight-day clocks and cases. A "Chamber Organ," valued at $200, is likely the one Fisher had purchased from David Tannenberg in 1780. He may have used it to teach himself to make organs, as the inventory also includes an unfinished organ. His work as a painter and artist is represented by paints, paint pots, and gold and silver leaf. Numerous

FIGURE 4.39
Figure of Justice, by John Fisher, York, York County, 1795–1800. York County Heritage Trust with permission from the York County Law Library

FIGURE 4.40
Detail of initials on back of fig. 4.39.

FIGURE 4.41
Interior of the York County Courthouse, by Lewis Miller, York, York County, 1804. York County Heritage Trust

prints, copperplate engravings, and books such as *Engraving Book Plates* and a *Book of Flowers* probably served as design sources for his clock dials and engraving. The inventory also lists dozens of books by title, revealing Fisher's interest in astronomy; philosophy; government; military exercises; Greek, Roman, and English history; painting; and drawing.[81]

Given Fisher's talents, it would be logical to wonder if he made his own clock cases. Similar cases containing movements by other York clockmakers, however, suggest that a dedicated cabinetmaking shop was responsible. A contract between Fisher and the purchaser of a clock and case reveals that he was at least sometimes responsible for obtaining the case and giving instructions on its appearance, providing rare insight into the nature of how clocks were commissioned. Dated July 6, 1789, Fisher's contract is unusual in its detail and stipulations:

> *To Wit: James Ewing orders John Fischer to manufacture for his account one tall floor clock not to exceed 100 inches in height. Said clock to be done in the craftsmans neatest manner and on the latest approved principles equal to or of the finest English invention; and to be of the finest brass regardless; running one week after one elevation of the power weights.*

> *The face of said clock to be furnished in the latest style and clearly discernible at a distance of twenty five feet. The wood to be of fine cured walnut or cherry, whichever is found to be the soundest in the hands of the joiner. John Fischer, the seller assures the buyer of the latest style and design that is to be had at the hands and mind of himself and the most skillful and renowned joiner it is his responsibility to hire. The buyer agrees to inspect the progress of the work three times before completion. Starting of the work constitutes acceptance of the tenets of this document by the seller and the buyer. The seller being an honorable man will exert his best skills and judgment in behalf of the buyer regardless. Upon being stood in his house and found a satisfactory timepiece for seven days the sum of 31 pounds will be laid in hand as full payment.[82]*

Though special commissions might require a contract, especially for something as expensive as James Ewing's £31 clock, many arrangements may not have been specified in writing, sometimes leading to disagreements over quality and price. Lewis Miller drew York cabinetmaker George Adam Gosler in the act of hacking a clock case into splinters with a hatchet (fig.

FIGURE 4.42

Drawing of George Adam Gosler, by Lewis Miller, York, York County, 1805. York County Heritage Trust

4.42) rather than sell it to a customer who complained about its cost. In addition to bespoke work, cabinetmakers and clockmakers also stocked ready-made clocks. Thomas Ogden, a cabinetmaker of Chester County, advertised in 1824 that he had "on hand several elegant eight-day clocks of Mr. Baldwin's make." This may have been clockmaker Thomas Baldwin of Downingtown, who in 1829 advertised having on hand "Eight Day Clocks, with Mahogany cases" in addition to watches, thimbles, jewelry, and sundries.[83] Studies of store accounts in Pennsylvania reveal an absence of goods such as furniture, firearms, and silver, suggesting that consumers typically obtained these items directly from craftsmen, either as custom work or from stock.[84] For a particularly expensive item, like a tall-case clock, consumers might also travel to an urban center such as Reading, Lancaster, York, or even Philadelphia.

Architecture and Furniture

Although most furniture is moved from place to place over time, architecture, by design, is relatively permanent—a quality that makes it an enduring marker of the "local" and a basis against which to compare furniture, thus expanding our understanding of localism as a cultural process. Furniture, however, also makes use of architectural elements such as pediments, moldings, columns, and panels, a factor that led numerous woodworkers to engage in the production of architectural woodwork as well. This versatility is evidenced in a variety of surviving documents, revealing that some even functioned as master builders.[85] For example, Lutheran minister Henry Muhlenberg hired cabinetmaker Leonard Kessler to make furniture, including chairs and a coffin, as well as do miscellaneous carpentry work on the Philadelphia parsonage. In 1765 Kessler supervised alterations to the pews in St. Michael's Lutheran Church of Germantown.[86] When Muhlenberg moved back to Trappe, Montgomery County, in 1776, he hired a local carpenter to make a chest and kitchen cupboard, build partitions, repair shutters, and cut down shelving.[87] Furniture was also sometimes built as part of the construction, as documented in several extant building contracts. In

FIGURE 4.43
Building contract between Christian Hagenbuch and Jacob Kratzer, Kreidersville, Northampton County, 1783. House detail appears on the other side. Joseph Downs Collection of Manuscripts and Printed Ephemera, Winterthur Library

1783 a contract and building plans (fig. 4.43) were drawn up between Christian Hagenbuch and Jacob Kratzer of Kreidersville, Northampton County, specifying that Kratzer was to provide "On the first floor; baseboards, chair rail in the stove room-a raised panel partition in the stove room with one doorway, Two benches at the table; and a small cupboard in the wall, and all the work must be painted." Another building contract from 1791 called for "2 benches in the stove room and a wardrobe in the partition, a corner cupboard with glass . . . and two small wall cupboards."[88] The two benches referred to would have been built into the corner of the stove room, a common practice in Pennsylvania German housing at this time. The account book of joiner and carpenter Abraham Hoover (1764–1843) of Lampeter and Conestoga townships, Lancaster County, includes scaled drawings of case furniture such as a tall chest of drawers, kitchen cupboard, and slant-front desk as well as the framing of a building.[89] Built-in furniture was also found in Quaker houses, including cupboards built into walls or overmantels and closets that contained shelving and a writing surface.[90]

Moravian cabinetmakers were noted as versatile craftsmen, making everything from furniture to architectural elements such as doors, window sash, floor boards, and staircases.[91] Although not known to be Moravian, John Cunnius (1733–1808), designer of the Central Moravian Church in Bethlehem, was a noted cabinetmaker and builder in Reading. Born February 17, 1733, in Germany, Cunnius immigrated to Pennsylvania in 1749. He settled in Hereford Township, Berks County, where he married Maria Elisabeth Catherine Griesemer. In 1767 he appears as a joiner in the Hereford tax records. Five years later, the New Hanover Reformed Church in Montgomery County paid him for carpentry work on their new parsonage. Around 1790 Cunnius moved to Reading and worked on the building of Trinity Lutheran Church from 1791 to 1793. In 1792 he was again hired by the New Hanover Reformed congregation to do the interior woodwork of their new church; several years later he helped build St. Stephen's Reformed Church in New Holland, Lancaster County. In 1797 Reading clockmaker Daniel Oyster built a brick townhouse on property he had purchased three years earlier from his father-in-law, clockmaker Daniel Rose. A carved wooden keystone above the front door of this house bears not only the date, "1797," but also the co-joined initials "J C" believed to stand for John Cunnius. These same initials appear on the pendulum doors of several tall-case clocks from Reading. One example contains a movement by Oyster and has a profile bust of a man, possibly George Washington (figs. 4.44, 4.45). The inventory taken at

the time of Cunnius's death indicates a sizable workshop, including two work benches, a lathe, nearly sixty molding planes, and eighty-one chisels. Cunnius identified himself as a "house carpenter" in his will. With a repertoire ranging from clock cases to churches, his work highlights the interplay of furniture and architectural woodwork possible in a craftsman's output.[92]

Tulpehocken Manor

An excellent case study of the relationship between furniture and architecture may be seen in a house known as Tulpehocken Manor, west of Myerstown in what is now Jackson Township, Lebanon County. Myerstown was a small settlement, totaling only eighty-four inhabitants in 1779, while nearby Schaefferstown had three hundred residents.[93] In 1794 Theophile Cazenove traveled through Myerstown, arriving just as a church service finished and observed, "It seemed to me I saw people coming out of church in Westphalia, so much have these farmers kept their ancestors' costume."[94] Situated between the Tulpehocken Creek and the highway from Philadelphia, Tulpehocken Manor was on a tract of 1,000 acres in what was then Lancaster County, settled by immigrant Christopher Ley (or Loy). Two embanked stone houses were built on the property, possibly by Christopher before his death in 1741. Michael Ley (1739–1824), Christopher's son, purchased the property in 1760 for £680. Nine years later, he and his wife, Eva Magdalena (1744–1815), built a large, five-bay stone house that still stands (fig. 4.46). Although the house was greatly remodeled and

expanded in 1883, significant original elements were saved, providing a look into the relationship between furniture and architecture.[95]

On the exterior of the house, directly above the front door leading into the central hall, there was a large triangular pediment (fig. 4.47) embellished with a dentiled cornice and relief-carved ornament of a central floral design flanked by the inscription "GOTT / ALLEIN DIE EHR / MICHAEL LEY UND / EFA MAGDALENA LEYIN / CHRISTOPH UHLER 1769 VON LEBANON" (God alone the Honor; Michael Ley and Eva Magdalena Ley/Christoph Uhler 1769 of Lebanon). Passing under the pediment and into the house, observant visitors would have been struck by

FIGURE 4.46

House of Michael and Eva Magdalena Ley, later known as Tulpehocken Manor, built 1769, remodeled 1883, photo about 1885, near Myerstown, Jackson Township, Lebanon County.

FIGURE 4.47

Door pediment from Tulpehocken Manor, by Christoph Uhler, Lebanon, Lancaster (now Lebanon) County, 1769. Collection of James C. Keener, Lancaster, Pa.

the close relationship between the pediment and the interior woodwork, including a fireplace surround with triangular overmantel and dentiled cornice resembling that on the door pediment.[96] On the first floor, a built-in corner cupboard with arched, glazed doors and a brilliant blue painted exterior would have displayed ceramics and other luxury goods.[97] The cupboard's bold cornice of alternating square and triangular blocks (fig. 4.48) relates it to a large walnut schrank built for the Leys in 1771 (fig. 4.49). Highly architectural in detail, the tall and shallow proportions of the schrank give it the appearance of a freestanding paneled wall. Measuring eight-and-one-half feet tall and seven-and-one-half feet wide, the schrank has two doors with raised panels between a five-paneled frieze and a row of five drawers across the bottom. The central panel of the frieze is inlaid in sulfur with the inscription "ML / & / EML / 1771," surrounded by small tulips and stars (fig. 4.50).

house were dated "1780." In 1798 the house (then owned by Christian Ley) was described in tax records as "Well-finished" and valued at $1,500. Three tenant houses were also on the now 660-acre property, which had a total assessment of $15,482.[99]

The door pediment from Tulpehocken Manor contains an important clue to the identity of the craftsman who was likely responsible for not only the house but also the interior woodwork and quite possibly the schrank. Flanking the date of "1769" is the inscription "Christoph Uhler of Lebanon." Uhler was born in Lebanon on February 2, 1741. His father, Anastasius, immigrated from Germany in 1732 aboard the *Samuel* and settled in Lebanon by 1737, when he married Dorothea Jerg.[100] At the time of his death in 1804, Christoph was an affluent and highly respected citizen. He identified himself as a "joiner" in his will, and his inventory includes two sawmills; a gristmill; a "lott of carpenter tools" worth £4.10.0; 15,000 feet of pine boards; 500 feet of clapboards; and 6,000 shingles.[101] He was among the largest property holders in Lebanon, assessed in 1798 for owning six tenant houses in addition to his own two-story stone house with a stone kitchen wing, log barn, and a stone joiner's shop measuring 20 by 29 feet, all on more than 200 acres.[102] In 1783 Uhler was elected a commissioner of Lancaster County and served as an executor for the estate of Carl Arndt, a beer brewer in Lebanon.[103] A lifelong member of Salem Lutheran Church in Lebanon, Uhler was a church elder from 1794 to 1796, treasurer of the congregation from 1794 to 1804, and chairman of the building committee. The latter role no doubt stemmed from his reputation as the master builder of Lebanon, having supervised the construction of the Lutheran parsonage in 1783 and a new German Reformed church from 1792 to 1796. In 1796 the Salem Lutheran congregation began construction of a new church, with instructions that it "must be larger than any other building in Lebanon, and of the most substantial material and workmanship possible."[104] In addition to his significance in helping develop the architectural landscape

FIGURE 4.48
Detail of cornice of corner cupboard from Tulpehocken Manor, possibly by Christoph Uhler, possibly Lebanon, Lancaster (now Lebanon) County, about 1769. Collection of Lester and Barbara Breininger

FIGURE 4.49
Schrank, made for Michael and Eva Magdalena Ley, possibly by Christoph Uhler, possibly Lebanon, Lancaster (now Lebanon) County, 1771. Rocky Hill Collection

FIGURE 4.50
Detail of inlay on schrank in fig. 4.49.

According to family tradition, the schrank stood in the best bedchamber of the house, where George Washington slept on a visit in 1793 to thank the Leys for their financial support of his troops while encamped at Valley Forge. Because of its intrinsic connection to the house and its massive size, the schrank remained there for more than sixty years. It was moved to Bethlehem in 1834, returned in 1970, and then sold at auction some twenty years later.[98] The Leys must have found it meaningful to have their names or initials and dates inscribed on their house and its furnishings, for they continued the practice on other parts of the property. The house has a pair of datestones on the facade containing religious verse, their names, and the date "1769"; a nearby stone smokehouse has a decorative wrought-iron bar inscribed "M 1777 L"; and a pair of stone gateposts that stood near the

of Lebanon, Uhler is one of only a few wood-workers whose names can be linked to a piece of sulfur-inlaid furniture. In 1771, the same date as that on the Ley schrank, he appears in the tax records of Lebanon as a joiner.[105] Although it is not definitive that Uhler was responsible for the schrank or its sulfur inlay, the close relationship of its details to the architectural woodwork of the Ley house suggests the possibility.[106]

The Deyers of Manheim

Approximately fifteen miles south of Lebanon, in the town of Manheim, another craft shop found success in the production of both furniture and architecture. Laid out in 1762 by German ironmaster Henry William Stiegel, Manheim was home to Stiegel's glass manufactory as well as to numerous craftsmen and artisans, including the Deyer (Dyer) family of cabinetmakers and carpenters. In 1785 the

184

FIGURE 4.51

(below, top) Detail of inlay on chest of drawers in fig. 4.54.

FIGURE 4.52

(below, bottom) Detail of inlay on clock in fig. 4.53.

FIGURE 4.53

Tall-case clock, movement by Jacob Eby, case attributed to the shop of Emanuel Deyer, Manheim, Lancaster County, 1810–20. Winterthur Museum

founder of the shop, Emanuel Deyer (1760–1836), purchased land and was identified in the deed as a joiner. Thirteen years later, he was assessed for owning a brick house, log barn, and log joiner's shop measuring twenty-two-feet square. In 1803 Emanuel was identified in an indenture as both a house carpenter and cabinetmaker and is listed in Manheim tax records as a joiner from 1800 until his death in 1836. Emanuel had five sons, three of whom can be identified as cabinetmakers or joiners: George, John, and Samuel.[107] The Deyers are known to have made case furniture and clock cases as well as architectural woodwork.

Clock cases produced by the Deyer workshop are readily distinguished by their inlaid eagle in an oval surround above the clock door. Two different versions were used: one has an eagle with symmetrically spread wings (fig. 4.51); the other, more commonly found, design has both wings angled to the left (fig. 4.52). In both, the eagle typically has a striped shield for its body (often inlaid with a red or black compound); bears a banner reading "E Pluribus Unum" in its beak; and grasps an olive branch and arrows in its claws. These distinctive inlays, which compare closely as a

group and are unlike other known eagle inlays, suggest that the inlay was made in Manheim—most likely in the Deyer shop. The inspiration was probably U.S. currency. From 1801 to 1807 a symmetrical spread-wing eagle graced the reverse of the half-dollar coin; then in 1807 coins appeared with an asymmetrical eagle more like the other inlay used by the Deyers.

Several dozen clock cases are known with eagle inlays associated with the Deyer shop, most in walnut or cherry cases. One of the most sophisticated is the bow-front clock (fig. 4.53) with highly figured mahogany veneers and contrasting satinwood inlay on the case. Bow-front clocks are rare in American furniture, with most known examples linked to the Deyers.[108] The clock shares many other features associated with the Deyer shop, including French feet and a slender broken arch pediment with inlaid pinwheels (fylfots) in place of rosettes. The edges of the case and finial plinths also typically have a narrow inlaid border with diagonal, alternating light and dark stripes. Although the bow-front clock is not signed by the Deyers, it is firmly attributed to their shop based on the relationship of the construction and inlay to other documented examples, including one signed on the inside of the bottom panel by Emanuel Deyer, dated "1807," which has a symmetrical eagle inlay and movement by Samuel Hill of Harrisburg. Another example with a movement by Manheim clockmaker Jacob Eby has a case signed by George Deyer with an asymmetrical eagle inlay like that on the bow-front clock.[109] The majority of the Deyer cases house movements by Eby.[110] A Mennonite, Jacob (1776–1828) was the nephew of clockmaker Samuel Stauffer (1754–1825). By 1783 Stauffer owned property in Manheim, where he likely taught his nephews Jacob and Christian (1768–1803) the trade. Unfortunately, Stauffer fell ill and became mentally incompetent in 1794; business records indicate that Christian finished an eight-day clock Stauffer had begun. Christian was skilled enough to make at least one musical clock and may have painted his own clock dials. When

his inventory was taken in 1803, it included three books on painting and three unfinished clock faces. After his uncle's illness and his brother's early death, Jacob Eby became the preeminent clockmaker of Manheim.[111]

In addition to cases for clocks, the Deyer family also built case furniture. George made a tall chest of drawers (fig. 4.54) in 1808, which he signed "George Dyer" and dated on the underside of the top board. Flanking the escutcheon on the uppermost drawer is a pair of inlaid symmetrical eagles like those used on the clock cases; inlaid oval borders surround

FIGURE 4.54

Tall chest of drawers, by George Deyer, Manheim, Lancaster County, 1808. Philadelphia Museum of Art, gift of Hannah L. Henderson in memory of J. Welles Henderson

each drawer; and herringbone borders can be found at the top and bottom of the chest.[112] Another piece of furniture attributed to the Deyer workshop is a bow-front tall chest of drawers; the upper two drawers are faux, in reality formed by hinged doors that open to reveal an interior compartment. This unusual object speaks to the creativity of the shop, and its bow-front case recalls the construction of the clock cases.[113]

The Deyer family was also involved with architecture. In 1813 the German Reformed congregation near Brickerville, Lancaster County, hired Emanuel to construct a new brick church (fig. 4.55) to replace an older log church. Known as Old Zion, the church remains almost entirely unaltered and is one of the finest surviving examples of its type in Lancaster County.[114] The interior arrangement of the church is an open sanctuary with wine-glass pulpit surrounded by seating galleries on three sides. Directly across from the pulpit on the paneling of the second-floor gallery in *Fraktur* lettering is the painted inscription "Emanuel Deyer / October den 2 / 1813" (fig. 4.56). The current pulpit (fig. 4.57) is a reconstruction of the original, which was removed in 1890. Salvaged elements from the original feature inscriptions made by the builders,

FIGURE 4.57

FIGURE 4.57
Pulpit of Old Zion Church
(reconstructed).

including a beaded-edge board signed "George Deyer Carpenter in / the Town of Manheim Lancaster / County 1813" and another board inscribed by William, George, and Emanuel Deyer, with each name followed by the words "in Manheim." A little more than two decades after the construction of Old Zion Church, Emanuel Deyer died at the age of seventy-six. The inventory of his personal property includes "a Complete Sett of Cabinet Makers tools Consisting of plains, Chisels, Saws, & W. Screws" valued at $100.50.[115] At the vendue held to dispose of Deyer's estate, many items were sold that reflected his trade, including hammers, gimblets, a compass, square, planes, spoke shaves, chisels, gouges, a turning lathe, carpenter's bench, and a lot of cherry boards. Deyer's sons were among the buyers, including Samuel who paid 12 cents for "1 Eagle," probably a piece of inlay. Woodturner Daniel Danner purchased a "Saw Machean" for 41 cents and a clock and case for just over $20.[116]

Like Christoph Uhler, John Cunnius, and other craftsmen, the Deyers found success in making furniture and architectural woodwork. Unusually talented craftsmen such as John Fisher also pursued diverse trades. Such versatility, a necessity for many woodworkers faced with increasing competition, also reinforced the development of distinctive localisms in which details of form, construction, and ornament took on the specifics of maker and place.

From Localism to Regionalism

In 1828 cabinetmaker Jacob Blatt wrote in German script on a board he would then use as the side of a chest of drawers: "1828 13th October / In / Bern Taunschip / Berks Caunti /

FIGURE 4.58
Chest of drawers, made for Samuel Spatz, by Jacob Blatt, Bern (now Centre) Township, Berks County, 1828. Collection of Lester and Barbara Breininger

Jacob Blatt." When the case was assembled, this writing was partially obscured by one of the drawer runners. Although the turned feet on the chest of drawers (fig. 4.58) place it in keeping with furniture styles of the period, the wedged dovetails and pegged construction of the drawer bottoms are techniques that had been employed by Pennsylvania German cabinetmakers nearly a century earlier. Despite the advent of mechanized tools and factory production in the nineteenth century, the work of individual artisans using traditional craft practices was still in demand.[117] A lifelong resident of Berks County, Blatt (1801–78) was probably at work as a cabinetmaker by the early 1820s. In 1832 Jacob and Heinrich Blatt, likely a brother, made a painted chest (fig. 4.59) and signed their names on the back, noting

their location as Bern Township.[118] In contrast with the plainly painted chest of drawers, this chest was first covered with a yellow ground. Then a red paint was skillfully applied to create bold circular and fan-shape designs. This type of wildly patterned decoration was part of the Fancy movement then popular among the middle classes. Such radiating motifs were inspired by the kaleidoscope, which was patented in 1817 by Scottish inventor Sir David Brewster. It quickly became so popular that a veritable kaleidoscope craze developed in America by the 1820s, inspiring designs on quilts, painted furniture, tinware, and other objects.[119]

Apparently the Blatts and their clientele found this kaleidoscope-inspired imagery appealing, as it appears repeatedly on their

FIGURE 4.59

Chest, by Jacob and Heinrich Blatt, Bern (now Centre) Township, Berks County, 1832. Winterthur Museum purchase with funds provided by the Henry Francis du Pont Collectors Circle

FIGURE 4.60
Kitchen cupboard, by Jacob
Blatt, Bern (now Centre)
Township, Berks County, 1848.
Winterthur Museum purchase
with funds drawn from the
Centenary Fund and acquired
through the bequest of Henry
Francis du Pont

FIGURE 4.61
Back of fig. 4.60.

furniture, including a magnificent painted kitchen cupboard (fig. 4.60) signed and dated by Jacob in 1848. The cupboard survives in pristine condition, allowing its vibrant palette of a red lead ground with vermilion decoration to shine as brilliantly as when it was first made.[120] Standing in sharp contrast to the painted decoration are the five small drawers with striped maple fronts. Behind the glazed doors in the upper section are shelves with grooves and a rail for the display of dishes; notches cut in the front of the middle shelf are for holding spoons. The doors of the lower section flank a central scrolled bracket reminiscent of those used on the fronts of pillar-and-scroll chests of drawers. The back of the cupboard (fig. 4.61) reveals Blatt's attention to detail; the raised panel, rail-and-stile construction enables the backboards to shrink and expand naturally. A section of paint on the lower case shows how the artist experimented with the color and graining technique before applying it to the primary surfaces. Along the center of the rails between the paneled backboards, horizontal lines were scored to mark their alignment with the stiles. The same techniques were repeated on several other closely related kitchen cupboards, one of which bears the date 1845 and the signatures of both Jacob and Heinrich Blatt as well as the notation "Centre Township, Berks County."[121] Formed out of the eastern part of Bern Township in 1843, Centre Township is the location given for Jacob Blatt in the 1850 census, in which his occupation is identified as that of cabinetmaker.[122]

The handcraft techniques and careful construction used by the Blatts as late as the mid-1800s speak to the slow pace by which industrialization and mechanization affected southeastern Pennsylvania. Of course, craftsmen had long used new tools and techniques to gain a competitive edge by improving efficiency or the quality of their output. Nonetheless, many persisted for years in the use of traditional techniques alongside technological innovations. The tenacity of traditional furnituremaking in southeastern Pennsylvania likely stemmed from several factors: a strong ethnic and artisanal consciousness; a conservative tendency; and thriftiness that valued tried-and-true hand-tool technologies over unproven new machinery. Cost was also a significant factor. One historian studying the impact of technological innovation on furniture manufacture in the nineteenth century found that a "furniture maker who invested in the conversion from hand to machine technology could hope to save no more than 15 percent on the production of commonplace furniture and even less on expensive furniture."[123] Even when cabinetmakers had access to machine tools such as planers, circular saws, and mortisers, they did not necessarily have the capital to invest in them, an adequate source of power to operate them, or the expertise to keep them running. Thus it is little wonder that rural woodworkers such as the Blatts

continued to use traditional tools and construction techniques even as more modern technologies became available.

Change was inevitable, however, as the nineteenth century progressed. The prosperous Berks County farmstead painted in the late 1800s by John Rasmussen (1828–95) speaks to changes that had already occurred as well as those yet to come (fig. 4.62). Within the neat picket fence stands an earlier farmhouse built of gray limestone with a more recent brick addition. Beside the house is a vegetable garden; beyond it hay is being loaded on a wagon. The bank barn with its forebay shelters livestock and provides crop storage.[124] In the foreground of this pastoral scene we see a dirt road, where an open carriage, large wagon, and stage coach are traveling. Paralleling the road are the tracks of the Pennsylvania and Reading Railroad, with a steam engine chugging along in the opposite direction. Against the backdrop of the traditional Pennsylvania German farmstead and horse-drawn modes of transportation, the train is a jarring sign of man's progress and a precursor of changes to come.

Faster travel and increasing connectedness over the years made possible by trains, highways, and cars have had a profound impact on the region, bringing southeastern Pennsylvania's inhabitants into greater contact with outside influences and diminishing the important role played by its local pockets of settlement. Although the local continues to be a significant force in the form of political entities such as townships and boroughs, the highly diverse, locally specific material culture that characterized the region for nearly two hundred years has largely become a relic of the past. That rich material legacy does live on, however, through the furniture of the region as well as the people who made, owned, inherited, and collected it— the focus of this publication. It is our hope that future scholars will build on this study, continuing the task of identifying and sorting out the near-endless variety of localisms that characterized the landscape of southeastern Pennsylvania. In the words of Esther Stevens Fraser, from 1925, "The subject is too new a field of research . . . to do more than blaze a somewhat imperfect trail."

FIGURE 4.62

Berks County farmscape, by John Rasmussen, Berks County, 1879–86. American Folk Art Museum, New York, gift of Ralph Esmerian

ENDNOTES

INTRODUCTION

1   Jonathan Dickinson to John Askew, Oct. 24, 1717, Jonathan Dickinson Copy Books of Letters, 163–64; cited in Patrick Griffin, *The People with No Name: Ireland's Ulster Scots, America's Scots Irish, and the Creation of a British Atlantic World, 1689–1764* (Princeton: Princeton University Press, 2001), 101.

2   The total population of Pennsylvania in 1790 was about 308,000, of which approximately 10 percent (28,522) lived in Philadelphia; see James T. Lemon, *The Best Poor Man's Country: A Geographical Study of Early Southeastern Pennsylvania* (Baltimore: Johns Hopkins University Press, 1972), 23.

3   Grace Peel (1740–1814) married William Parr, who left her a substantial estate when he died in 1786; see inventory of William Parr, Aug. 19, 1786, inv. 1786, F001, P:097, Lancaster County Historical Society (hereafter LCHS).

4   West went abroad in 1760, settled in England, became court painter to King George III, and in 1792 succeeded Sir Joshua Reynolds as president of the Royal Academy of Arts. On West and particularly his American work, see Allen Staley, *Benjamin West: American Painter at the English Court* (Baltimore: Baltimore Museum of Art, 1989), 13–18; also Robert C. Alberts, *Benjamin West: A Biography* (Boston: Houghton Mifflin, 1978), 7–28. The portrait of Elizabeth Peel is also thought to have been painted by West, 1757–58, in Philadelphia; see Staley, *Benjamin West*, 29–30. For an image of West's portrait of William Henry, see Henry J. Kauffman, *The American Gunsmith* (Morgantown, Pa.: Masthof Press, 1998), 2.

5   At his death in 1763, William Larkin's inventory listed several unfinished pieces, including "A Desk unfinished a Table frame and a Tea Table foot . . . Two New Oval Tables . . . Wood prepared for tools patterns Molds &c." Larkin also had an apprentice with four months left to serve, further indication that he was an active cabinetmaker at the time of his death; see Margaret Berwind Schiffer, *Furniture and Its Makers of Chester County, Pennsylvania* (Philadelphia: University of Pennsylvania Press, 1966), 141. Jane Smedley (1734–82) married William Larkin, joiner. Her brother William (1728–66) was also a joiner; see Gilbert Cope, *Genealogy of the Smedley Family* (Lancaster, Pa.: Wickersham Printing Co., 1901), 50.

6   For the table in fig. 5, see Sotheby's, *Important Americana: The Collection of Dr. and Mrs. Henry P. Deyerle*, Charlottesville, Va., May 26–27, 1995, lot 420, formerly owned by Alex F. Phillips of West Chester, Pa., and his father, T. Van C. Phillips. Another dressing table in the Deyerle sale (lot 634) appears to be from the same shop. A third related table was advertised by Philip H. Bradley Co.; see *Chester County Historical Society Antiques Show Catalogue* (West Chester, Pa.: Chester County Historical Society, 2007), back cover.

7   Jerome Wood, *Conestoga Crossroads* (Harrisburg: Pennsylvania Historical and Museum Commission, 1978). Lancaster County was founded in 1729. The county seat was settled in 1730 but not established as a borough until 1742. In 1818 Lancaster became a city.

8   The card table was sold at Christie's, New York, Oct. 21, 1978, lot 291. Yeates paid £6.15.0 for the looking glass in 1774; it is not known to survive but was drawn in 1879 by David McNeely Stauffer in the Yeates house; see John J. Snyder Jr., "Federal Furniture of Lancaster Borough/City, 1795–1825," *Journal of the Lancaster County Historical Society* 101 (Spring 1999): 3–5.

9   On Yeates, see Mark Häberlein, *The Practice of Pluralism: Congregational Life and Religious Diversity in Lancaster, Pennsylvania, 1730–1820* (University Park: Pennsylvania State University Press, 2009), 126–27.

10 Cited in Nicholas B. Wainwright, *Colonial Grandeur in Philadelphia: The House and Furniture of General John Cadwalader* (Philadelphia: Historical Society of Pennsylvania, 1964), 65.

11 On Joseph Simon and the Jewish community in Lancaster, see Häberlein, *Practice of Pluralism*, 166–71.

12 Wendy A. Cooper, *An American Vision: Henry Francis du Pont's Winterthur Museum* (Washington, D.C.: National Gallery of Art and the Henry Francis du Pont Winterthur Museum, 2002), 104–7. On Philadelphia rococo furniture, see Morrison H. Heckscher and Leslie Greene Bowman, *American Rococo, 1750–1775* (New York: Harry N. Abrams for the Metropolitan Museum of Art, 1992), 182–217.

13 Born Matthias Schlauch to German immigrant parents, Slough became proprietor of the White Swan when he married the widow of former owner George Gibson. In 1776 he went into the dry-goods business. Slough served numerous positions in Lancaster government before election to the Pennsylvania Assembly in 1773. He also served in the state assembly 1780–83; see Häberlein, *Practice of Pluralism*, 152.

14 Beatrice B. Garvan and Charles F. Hummel, *The Pennsylvania Germans: A Celebration of their Arts, 1683–1850* (Philadelphia: Philadelphia Museum of Art and the Henry Francis du Pont Winterthur Museum, 1982), 96; see also Wolfgang Schwarze, *Antike Deutsche Möbel: Das Bürgerliche und Rustikale möble in Deutschland von 1700–1840*, 2d ed. (Wuppertal, Ger.: Kunst und Wohnen Verlag, 1977).

15 John J. Snyder Jr., "Carved Chippendale Case Furniture from Lancaster, Pennsylvania," *The Magazine Antiques* 107, no. 5 (May 1975): 964–75.

16 Historians such as Gabrielle M. Lanier have argued that the Revolution's disruption of deeply rooted political, ethnic, and religious affiliations was followed by a transformative period of change and "conscious nation-building" (Gabrielle M. Lanier, *The Delaware Valley in the Early Republic: Architecture, Landscape, and Regional Identity* [Baltimore: Johns Hopkins University Press, 2005], 5–6, 18, 179). Historian Steven Nolt found that in the years following the American Revolution, a distinct Pennsylvania German culture evolved in a process of "ethnicization-as-Americanization." Fashioning themselves as "representative Americans," the Pennsylvania Germans became Americanized without being assimilated, retaining distinctive foodways, language, and decorative arts traditions that remain to this day (Steven Nolt, *Foreigners in Their Own Land: Pennsylvania Germans in the Early Republic*, Publications of the Pennsylvania German Society [hereafter PGS], vol. 35 [University Park: Pennsylvania State University Press, 2002], 3–9).

17 Anthropologists such as Clifford Geertz have long recognized the importance of the local in understanding a culture; see Clifford Geertz, *Local*

Knowledge: Further Essays in Interpretive Anthropology (New York: Basic Books, 1983), 167–70. See also Liam Riordan's comparative study of three Mid-Atlantic towns in Liam Riordan, *Many Identities, One Nation: The Revolution and Its Legacy in the Mid-Atlantic* (Philadelphia: University of Pennsylvania Press, 2007), esp. 15–41.

18 See Michael W. Zuckerman, "Introduction: Puritans, Cavaliers, and the Motley Middle," in *Friends and Neighbors: Group Life in America's First Plural Society*, ed. Michael W. Zuckerman, 7–15 (Philadelphia: Temple University Press, 1982); see also Häberlein, *Practice of Pluralism*, 242–43, where he argues that the towns in the Philadelphia hinterland offer a more suitable model than New England communities for the antecedents of modern America's diversity.

19 Fred B. Kniffen, "Folk Housing: Key to Diffusion," in *Common Places: Readings in American Vernacular Architecture*, ed. Dell Upton and John Michael Vlach, 3–26 (Athens: University of Georgia Press, 1986); Henry Glassie, *Pattern in the Material Folk Culture of the Eastern United States* (Philadelphia: University of Pennsylvania Press, 1968), 34; and Henry Glassie, "Eighteenth-Century Cultural Process in Delaware Valley Folk Building," in *Winterthur Portfolio 7*, ed. Ian M. G. Quimby, 29–57 (Charlottesville: University Press of Virginia for the Henry Francis du Pont Winterthur Museum, 1972); Geographer James T. Lemon also argues that southeastern Pennsylvania was the prototype of North American development in Lemon, *Best Poor Man's Country*, 15–23.

20 Terry Jordan, "Perceptual Regions in Texas," *Geographical Review* 68, no. 3 (July 1978): 293; cited in Lanier, *Delaware Valley*, 196.

21 Nolt, *Foreigners in Their Own Land*, 13.

22 Lemon, *Best Poor Man's Country*, 29, 123.

23 The Susquehanna was broad but rocky and shallow in the lower parts, precluding it from becoming a major inlaid waterway; see John F. Walzer, "Colonial Philadelphia and Its Backcountry," in Quimby, *Winterthur Portfolio 7*, 166.

24 Paul G. E. Clemens and Lucy Simler, "Rural Labor and the Farm Household in Chester County, Pennsylvania, 1750–1820," in *Work and Labor in Early America*, ed. Stephen Innes, 110–12 (Chapel Hill: University of North Caro-

lina Press for the Institute of Early American History and Culture, 1988).

25 *A Pleasant Peregrination through the Prettiest Parts of Pennsylvania* (Philadelphia, 1836), 39; cited in Margaret Berwind Schiffer, *Survey of Chester County, Pennsylvania, Architecture: 17th, 18th, and 19th Centuries* (Exton, Pa.: Schiffer Publishing, 1984), 10.

26 John Fanning Watson, "Trip to Franconia Township," Col. 189, Watson Family Papers, Joseph Downs Collection of Manuscripts and Printed Ephemera, Winterthur Library.

27 For images of the interior of the Hiester house, see G. Edwin Brumbaugh, "Colonial Architecture of the Pennsylvania Germans," *Proceedings of the Pennsylvania German Society* 41 (1933): pls. 92–95.

28 From Penn's letter to the Free Society of Traders in 1683, cited in Rachel McMasters Miller Hunt, *William Penn, Horticulturist* (Pittsburgh: University of Pittsburgh Press, 1953), 21.

29 Carl Theo. Eben, trans., *Gottlieb Mittelberger's Journey to Pennsylvania in the Year 1750 and Return to Germany in the Year 1754* (Philadelphia: John Jos. McVey, 1898), 73.

30 Schiffer, *Furniture and Its Makers*, 278.

31 For more on nineteenth-century agricultural and livestock improvement, see Eric C. Stoykovich, "The Culture of Improvement in the Early Republic: Domestic Livestock, Animal Breeding, and Philadelphia's Urban Gentlemen, 1820–1860," *Pennsylvania Magazine of History and Biography* 134, no. 1 (January 2010): 31–58.

32 This painting was exhibited at the Metropolitan Museum of Art in 1939 and at the Philadelphia Museum of Art in 1940, when it was called "A Pennsylvania Country Fair." It was owned by Harry T. Peters and later sold from the estate of Harry T. Peters Jr. at Christie's, *American Paintings: Drawings and Sculpture of the 18th, 19th, and 20th Centuries*, New York, June 3, 1982, lot 263. With thanks to Connie V. Hershey for this citation. On Woodside, see Lee Ellen Griffith, "John Archibald Woodside Sr.," *The Magazine Antiques* 140, no. 5 (November 1991): 816–25; Virgil Barker, *American Painting: History and Interpretation* (New York: Macmillan, 1950), 371–75; also Joseph Jackson, "John A. Woodside: Philadelphia's Glorified Sign-Painter," *Pennsylvania Magazine of History and Biography* 57 (1933): 58–65. For more on the agricultural exhibitions of

the Pennsylvania Society for Agriculture, see Stevenson Whitcomb Fletcher, *Pennsylvania Agriculture and Country Life, 1640–1840* (Harrisburg: Pennsylvania Historical and Museum Commission, 1950), 349–50.

33 Carolyn J. Weekley, *The Kingdoms of Edward Hicks* (New York: Harry N. Abrams for the Colonial Williamsburg Foundation, 1999), 76, 240.

34 Joshua Ruff and William Ayres, "H. F. du Pont's Chestertown House, Southampton, New York," *The Magazine Antiques* 160, no. 1 (July 2001): 98–107.

35 Hattie Brunner to Henry Francis du Pont, Dec. 4, 1929 to Dec. 23, 1929, Folder: Brunner, Mrs. R. S., 1931–40, Antiques Dealer Correspondence Files, Box 12, Winterthur Archives, Winterthur Library. The "walnut Kass" Brunner referred to is the sulfur-inlaid schrank made for Emanuel and Mary Herr in 1768 (1965.2262; see fig. 2.31).

36 American Art Association, *Colonial Furniture: The Superb Collection of the Late Howard Reifsnyder*, New York, Apr. 24–27, 1929, lots 585, 627.

37 A. H. Rice advertisement, *The Magazine Antiques* 10, no. 6 (December 1926): 426–27.

38 On Fegley, see Alan G. Keyser and Frederick S. Weiser, comps., *Farming, Always Farming: A Photographic Essay of Rural Pennsylvania German Land and Life Made by H. Winslow Fegley (1871–1944)*, Publications of the PGS, vol. 20 (Birdsboro, Pa.: PGS, 1987); see p. 26 for a discussion of this photo.

39 J. Smith Futhey and Gilbert Cope, *History of Chester County, Pennsylvania, with Genealogical and Biographical Sketches* (Philadelphia: J. B. Lippincott, 1881); on Cope's photography and Ruth Abbott, see Mary Anne Caton, "The Aesthetics of Absence: Quaker Women's Plain Dress in the Delaware Valley, 1790–1900," in *Quaker Aesthetics: Reflections on a Quaker Ethic in American Design and Consumption*, ed. Emma Jones Lapsansky and Anne A. Verplanck, 258–61 (Philadelphia: University of Pennsylvania Press, 2003).

40 Edwin AtLee Barber, *Tulip Ware of the Pennsylvania-German Potters* (Philadelphia: Patterson & White, 1903); Esther Stevens Fraser, "Pennsylvania Brides Boxes and Dower Chests, Parts I and II," *The Magazine Antiques* 8, nos. 1–2 (July–August 1925): 20–23, 79–84; Esther

Stevens Fraser, "Pennsylvania German Dower Chests," *The Magazine Antiques* 11, no. 2 (February 1927): 119–23; no. 4 (April 1927): 280–83; no. 6 (June 1927): 474–76; Brumbaugh, "Colonial Architecture," 5–60; Henry S. Borneman, *Pennsylvania German Illuminated Manuscripts*, Proceedings of the PGS, vol. 46 (Norristown, Pa.: PGS, 1937).

41 Virginia Tuttle Clayton, Elizabeth Stillinger, Erika Davis, and Deborah Chotner, *Drawing on America's Past: Folk Art, Modernism, and the Index of American Design* (Washington, D.C.: National Gallery of Art, 2002). Clarence P. Hornung, *Treasury of American Design*, 2 vols. (1950; reprint, New York: Harry N. Abrams, 1972).

42 On the Millbach house, see Joseph Downs, *The House of the Miller at Millbach: The Architecture, Arts, and Crafts of the Pennsylvania Germans* (Philadelphia: Franklin Printing Co., 1929); on the interior at the Met, see Marshall B. Davidson and Elizabeth Stillinger, *The American Wing at the Metropolitan Museum of Art* (New York: Alfred A. Knopf, 1985), 130–31; also Marshall B. Davidson and Elizabeth Stillinger, *Pennsylvania German Arts and Crafts: A Picture Book* (New York: Plantin Press for the Metropolitan Museum of Art, 1946).

43 On Henry Mercer, see Helen H. Gemmill, *Pioneering America: A Mercer Museum Centennial* (Doylestown, Pa.: Bucks County Historical Society, 1997).

44 On Albert Barnes, the Barnes Foundation, and the interiors of Barnes's home Ker-Feal, see *House & Garden*, December 1942, 36–53; see also William Schack, *Art and Argyrol: The Life and Career of Dr. Albert C. Barnes* (New York: T. Yoseloff, 1960); and Gilbert M. Cantor, *The Barnes Foundation: Reality vs. Myth* (Philadelphia: Drake Press, 1974).

45 Schiffer, *Furniture and Its Makers.*

46 John J. Snyder Jr., "The Bachman Attributions: A Reconsideration," *The Magazine Antiques* 105, no. 5 (May 1974): 1056–65; Snyder, "Carved Chippendale Case Furniture," 964–75; John J. Snyder Jr., "New Discoveries in Documented Lancaster County Chippendale Furniture," *The Magazine Antiques* 125, no. 5 (May 1984): 1150–55.

47 Monroe H. Fabian, *The Pennsylvania-German Decorated Chest*, Publications of the PGS, vol. 12 (New York: Universe Books, 1978).

48 Garvan and Hummel, *Pennsylvania Germans*; Scott T. Swank et al., *Arts of the Pennsylvania Germans*, ed. Catherine E. Hutchins, Publications of the PGS, vol. 17 (New York: W. W. Norton for the Henry Francis du Pont Winterthur Museum, 1983).

49 Lee Ellen Griffith, *The Pennsylvania Spice Box: Paneled Doors and Secret Drawers* (West Chester, Pa.: Chester County Historical Society, 1986); Lee Ellen Griffith, "Line-and-Berry Inlaid Furniture: A Regional Craft Tradition in Pennsylvania, 1682–1790" (Ph.D. diss., University of Pennsylvania, 1988); and Lee Ellen Griffith, "The Line-and-Berry Inlaid Furniture of Eighteenth-Century Chester County, Pennsylvania," *The Magazine Antiques* 135, no. 5 (May 1989): 1202–11.

50 Jack L. Lindsey, *Worldly Goods: The Arts of Early Pennsylvania, 1680 –1758* (Philadelphia: Philadelphia Museum of Art, 1999).

51 Donald F. Durnbaugh, "Pennsylvania's Crazy Quilt of German Religious Groups," *Pennsylvania History* 68, no. 1 (Winter 2001): 9.

52 On the terms "Pennsylvania German" and "Pennsylvania Dutch," see Don Yoder, "Palatine, Hessian, Dutchman: Three Images of the German in America," in *Ebbes fer Alle-Ebber, Ebbes fer Dich: Something for Everyone, Something for You*, ed. Frederick S. Weiser, 107–29, Publications of the PGS, vol. 14 (Breinigsville, Pa.: PGS, 1980).

53 One of the first scholars to comment on the plainness of Quaker material culture was Frederick B. Tolles in his 1948 study of Quaker merchants in colonial Philadelphia, in which he wrote that Quakers owned objects that were "of the best sort but plain" (Frederick B. Tolles, *Meeting House and Counting House: The Quaker Merchants of Colonial Philadelphia, 1682–1763* [Chapel Hill: University of North Carolina Press for the Institute of Early American History and Culture, 1948], 88). More recent studies have found little evidence to support this claim, particularly for the eighteenth century; see, for example, Susan Garfinkel, "Quakers and High Chests: The Plainness Problem Reconsidered," in Lapsansky and Verplanck, *Quaker Aesthetics*, 50–89.

54 For a discussion of this photo, see Keyser and Weiser, *Farming, Always Farming*, 59.

CHAPTER 1

1 Carl Theo. Eben, trans., *Gottlieb Mittelberger's Journey to Pennsylvania in the Year 1750 and Return to Germany in the Year 1754* (Philadelphia: John Jos. McVey, 1898), 54, 63. For the original account, see *Gottlieb Mittelbergers Reise nach Pennsylvanien im Jahr 1750 und Rückreise nach Teutschland im Jahr 1754* (Stuttgart: Gedruckt bey Gottlieb Friderich Jenisch, 1756).

2 Catharine Dann Roeber, "Decoding a Historic Map," *Catalogue of Antiques and Fine Art* 9, no. 5 (Summer 2009): 182–83.

3 Sharon V. Salinger, *"To Serve Well and Faithfully": Labor and Indentured Servants in Pennsylvania, 1682–1800* (Cambridge: Cambridge University Press, 1987), 35.

4 Albert Cook Myers, *Immigration of the Irish Quakers into Pennsylvania, 1682–1750* (Swarthmore, Pa., 1902), 46–49; R. J. Dickson, *Ulster Emigration to Colonial America, 1718–1775* (London: Routledge and Kegan Paul, 1966), 10–14, 24–29, 38–42; Wayland F. Dunaway, *The Scotch-Irish of Colonial Pennsylvania* (Chapel Hill: University of North Carolina Press, 1944), 28.

5 Cited in Patrick Griffin, *The People with No Name: Ireland's Ulster Scots, America's Scots Irish, and the Creation of a British Atlantic World, 1689–1764* (Princeton: Princeton University Press, 2001), 102.

6 The term "Church Germans" refers to members of Lutheran or Reformed congregations, which were state-sanctioned institutions in Europe. The "Plain Germans" include the Amish, Mennonites, and Brethren (or Dunkards), who worship in private homes or in meetinghouses lacking the adornment more typical of churches. The Plain Germans also share a common belief in adult baptism and non-resistance. On the religious affiliations of the Pennsylvania Germans, see Donald F. Durnbaugh, "Pennsylvania's Crazy Quilt of German Religious Groups," *Pennsylvania History* 68, no. 1 (Winter 2001): 8–30.

7 Clarke Hess, *Mennonite Arts* (Atglen, Pa.: Schiffer Publishing, 2002), 16–17.

8 Aaron S. Fogelman, *Hopeful Journeys: German Immigration, Settlement, and Political Culture in Colonial America, 1717–1775* (Philadelphia: University of Pennsylvania Press, 1996), 4–8; Marianne S. Wokeck, *Trade in Strangers: The*

Beginnings of Mass Migration to North America (University Park: Pennsylvania State University Press, 1999), 37–46, 53.

9 Wokeck, *Trade in Strangers*, 14–18; Fogelman, *Hopeful Journeys*, 6.

10 Cited in Cynthia G. Falk, *Architecture and Artifacts of the Pennsylvania Germans: Constructing Identity in Early America*, Publications of the Pennsylvania German Society (hereafter PGS), vol. 42 (University Park: Pennsylvania State University Press, 2008), 53–54.

11 James T. Lemon, *The Best Poor Man's Country: A Geographical Study of Early Southeastern Pennsylvania* (Baltimore: Johns Hopkins University Press, 1972), 14, 23, 126. Aaron S. Fogelman, "Immigration, German Immigration, and 18th-Century America," in *Emigration and Settlement Patterns of German Communities in North America*, ed. Eberhard Reichmann, LaVern J. Rippley, and Jörg Nagler, 13–14 (Indianapolis: Indiana University-Purdue University at Indianapolis for the Max Kade German American Center, 1995).

12 Lemon, *Best Poor Man's Country*, 18.

13 Karen Guenther, *"Remem'bring Our Time and Work is the Lords": The Experiences of Quakers on the Eighteenth-Century Pennsylvania Frontier* (Selinsgrove, Pa.: Susquehanna University Press, 2005), 76–78.

14 Lemon, *Best Poor Man's Country*, 43.

15 Cited in Richard K. MacMaster, *Land, Piety, Peoplehood: The Establishment of Mennonite Communities in America, 1683–1790* (Scottdale, Pa.: Herald Press, 1985), 138.

16 Laura L. Becker, "Diversity and Its Significance in an Eighteenth-Century Town," in *Friends and Neighbors: Group Life in America's First Plural Society*, ed. Michael W. Zuckerman, 208 (Philadelphia: Temple University Press, 1982). Though small in number, Roman Catholic congregations were established in Reading and Goschenhoppen (now Bally) by the 1740s.

17 Sally Schwartz, *"A Mixed Multitude": The Struggle for Toleration in Colonial Pennsylvania* (New York: New York University Press, 1987).

18 On the building and plan of Wright's Ferry Mansion, see Elizabeth Meg Schaefer and Joe K. Kindig III, *Wright's Ferry Mansion*, 2 vols. (Columbia, Pa.: von Hess Foundation, 2005), 1:35–46. Bernard L. Herman presented information regarding the ethnic diversity of the workers involved with the building of the house in "Susanna among the Germans" at the conference "New World Orders: Violence, Sanction, and Authority in the Early Modern Americas, 1500–1825," McNeil Center for Early American Studies, Philadelphia, Oct. 19–20, 2001.

19 Falk, *Architecture and Artifacts*, 10.

20 Ibid., 4–5, 190–94.

21 François Alexandre Frédéric, Duc de la Rochefoucauld–Liancourt, *Travels through the United States of North America, the Country of the Iroquois, and Upper Canada, in the Years 1795, 1796, 1797, with an Account of Lower Canada*, 2 vols. (London: R. Phillips, 1799), 46.

22 Bernard L. Herman, "The Model Farmer and the Organization of the Countryside," in *Everyday Life in the Early Republic*, ed. Catherine E. Hutchins, 35–38 (Winterthur, Del.: Henry Francis du Pont Winterthur Museum, 1994); Carolyn J. Weekley, *The Kingdoms of Edward Hicks* (New York: Harry N. Abrams for the Colonial Williamsburg Foundation, 1999), 16–19, 207–8; see also Stacy C. Hollander, *American Radiance: The Ralph Esmerian Gift to the American Folk Art Museum* (New York: Harry N. Abrams, 2001), 90, 413–14.

23 Alan G. Keyser, "Beds, Bedding, Bedsteads, and Sleep," *Der Reggeboge: Journal of the Pennsylvania German Society* 12, no. 4 (October 1978): 1–28.

24 Rayner Wickersham Kelsey, ed., *Cazenove Journal 1794: A Record of the Journey of Theophile Cazenove through New Jersey and Pennsylvania (Translated from the French)* (Haverford, Pa.: Pennsylvania History Press, 1922), 42.

25 Ibid., 30, 69, 34.

26 From James Thomas Lemon, "A Rural Geography of Southeastern Pennsylvania in the Eighteenth Century" (Ph.D. diss., University of Wisconsin, 1964), 78; cited in Sara Matthews, "German Settlement of Northern Chester County in the 18th Century," *Pennsylvania Folklife* 27, no. 4 (Summer 1978): 27.

27 Cited in Barry Levy, "The Birth of the 'Modern Family' in Early America: Quaker and Anglican Families in the Delaware Valley, Pennsylvania, 1681–1750," in Zuckerman, *Friends and Neighbors*, 30–31.

28 Ibid., 44.

29 Ibid., 31, 44–45, 49–50, 55–56.

30 David Hackett Fischer, *Albion's Seed: Four British Folkways in America* (New York: Oxford University Press, 1989), 591–92.

31 Margaret Berwind Schiffer, *Survey of Chester County, Pennsylvania, Architecture: 17th, 18th, and 19th Centuries* (Exton, Pa.: Schiffer Publishing, 1984), 34–35.

32 The 1741/2 marriage date of Jonathan and Sarah Jones reflects the simultaneous use of the Julian and Gregorian calendars. Under the older Julian calendar, March was the first month of the year. England did not adopt the Gregorian calendar until 1752, so many Pennsylvanians used double dates during January, February, and March. Two related family records are known: one made for the family of James Jones of Blockley Township (once part of Philadelphia County, now defunct) and Hannah Hayes of Haverford, who were married in 1727 at Haverford Meeting; and one made for Lewis and Catharine Jones, who were married in 1732 at Merion Meeting. For an illustration of the latter, see Lee Ellen G. Chalfant, "Fraktur and Related Art in Chester County," in *Chester County Historical Society Antiques Show Catalogue* (West Chester, Pa.: Chester County Historical Society [hereafter CCHS], 1984), 9.

33 Richard Jones, ed., *The First 300: The Amazing and Rich History of Lower Merion* (Ardmore, Pa.: Lower Merion Historical Society, 2000), 29.

34 Will and inventory of Edward Williams, 1749, Philadelphia County Will Book I, no. 143, 225–27, Winterthur Library.

35 Richard Bebb, *Welsh Furniture, 1250–1950: A Cultural History of Craftsmanship and Design*, 2 vols. (Kidwelly, Carmarthenshire, U.K.: Saer Books, 2007), 2:65–79, 133, 380.

36 Benno M. Forman, *American Seating Furniture, 1630–1730: An Interpretive Catalogue* (New York: W.W. Norton for the Henry Francis du Pont Winterthur Museum, 1988), 160.

37 Paneled back or wainscot chairs may also have some Irish origins. An oak armchair with two vertical panels inset for the back descended in the Conyngham family at Springhill, Londonderry; see The Knight of Glin and James Peill, *Irish Furniture: Woodwork and Carving in Ireland from the Earliest Times to the Act of Union* (New Haven: Yale University Press for

the Paul Mellon Centre for Studies in British Art, 2007), 205; see also a mid-eighteenth-century wainscot armchair made of riven ash in the collection of the Armagh County Museum, illustrated in Claudia Kinmonth, *Irish Country Furniture, 1700–1950* (New Haven: Yale University Press, 1993), 59.

38   Myers, *Immigration of the Irish Quakers*, 41–46, 83; Salinger, *To Serve Well and Faithfully*, 21.

39   Guenther, *Rememb'ring Our Time*, 25.

40   George Valentine Massey II, *The Pennocks of Primitive Hall* (West Chester, Pa.: CCHS, 1951), 1–2, 21, 25, 28, 34–35. On the restoration and furnishing of Primitive Hall, see Clarence W. Brazer, "Primitive Hall and Its Furniture," *The Magazine Antiques* 53, no. 1 (January 1948): 55–57; also Schiffer, *Survey of Chester County*, 68–71. The first known use of the name Primitive Hall is on a quilt dated 1842, possibly made by Isabel Pennock for the birth of Caspar and Caroline Morris's daughter Sarah; it is in the CCHS collection.

41   Cited in Susan Garfinkel, "Quakers and High Chests: The Plainness Problem Reconsidered," in *Quaker Aesthetics: Reflections on a Quaker Ethic in American Design and Consumption*, ed. Emma Jones Lapsansky and Anne A. Verplanck, 63 (Philadelphia University of Pennsylvania Press, 2003); and Catherine J. McElroy, "Furniture of the Philadelphia Area: Forms and Craftsmen before 1750" (Master's thesis, University of Delaware, 1970), 5.

42   Will of Joseph Pennock, dated Oct. 10, 1770, no. 2616, vol. E, 242, Chester County Archives (hereafter CCA). Massey, *Pennocks*, 113; inventory of Joseph Pennock, taken Apr. 18, 1771, mss. no. 10527, CCHS.

43   The identical armchair and side chair (also at Primitive Hall) were illustrated by Brazer, "Primitive Hall and Its Furniture," fig. 6, and are presumed to have been acquired from Pennock descendants. An armchair with four vertical molded back slats and scalloped crest rail (now at CCHS) has also been associated with Primitive Hall; see William Macpherson Hornor Jr., *Blue Book, Philadelphia Furniture* (1935; reprint, Washington, D.C.: Highland House Publishers, 1977), pl. 10; also Brazer, "Primitive Hall and Its Furniture," fig. 8; a related example but with slightly different turnings is at Winterthur Museum (1967.1176) and another is in a private collection; see Joseph K. Kindig, *The Philadelphia Chair, 1685–1785* (York,

Pa.: Historical Society of York County, 1978), pl. 10. Two other wainscot armchairs, a pair with paneled arms and base, are said to have descended in the Pennock family; see Jack L. Lindsey, *Worldly Goods: The Arts of Early Philadelphia, 1680–1758* (Philadelphia: Philadelphia Museum of Art, 1999), 170.

44   A nearly identical armchair with a history of ownership in the Bonsall family of Chester County is in the CCHS collection and illustrated in Margaret Bleecker Blades, *Two Hundred Years of Chairs and Chairmaking: An Exhibition of Chairs from the Chester County Historical Society* (West Chester, Pa.: CCHS, 1987), 10, fig. 6, 25.

45   Margaret Berwind Schiffer, *Furniture and Its Makers of Chester County, Pennsylvania* (Philadelphia: University of Pennsylvania Press, 1966), 200.

46   Some of the more sophisticated examples of wainscot chairs may have been made in Philadelphia although no specific documentation has yet been found to prove this theory. Benno Forman notes that joiners Richard Clone and John Maddock moved to Philadelphia in 1683 from Cheshire and may have made wainscot chairs; see Forman, *American Seating Furniture*, 134–43, 154–63. For additional commentary on the making of wainscot chairs in Philadelphia, see Schaefer and Kindig, *Wright's Ferry Mansion*, 2:38–39.

47   As this spice box has no specific documentation, it is also possible that the initials stand for Thomas and Elizabeth (Miller) Hiett, parents of Thomas Hutton's second wife, Katherine. This is less likely, as such boxes were normally acquired within several years of marriage, and the Hietts were much older. Thomas Hiett's inventory of 1751, however, did include a spice box; see Thomas Hiett will and inventory, 1751, no. 1390, CCA. On the Hiett genealogy, see William Perry Johnson, *Hiatt/Hiett Genealogy and Family History* (Jesse Hiatt Family Assoc., 1951).

48   Lee Ellen Griffith, *The Pennsylvania Spice Box: Paneled Doors and Secret Drawers* (West Chester, Pa.: CCHS, 1986), 13–18; on the Hutton box, see 102–3; see also Schiffer, *Furniture and Its Makers*, 265. A drop-leaf table with inlaid drawer now at CCHS was owned by the Hutton family.

49   Inventory of Jacob Hibberd, 1750, no. 1315, CCA; cited in Griffith, *Pennsylvania Spice Box*, 15.

50   The practice of inlaying a set of initials above a date within an arched surround appears on Welsh furniture as well; see Bebb, *Welsh Furniture*, 2:406.

51   J. Smith Futhey and Gilbert Cope, *History of Chester County, Pennsylvania, with Genealogical and Biographical Sketches* (Philadelphia: J. B. Lippincott, 1881), 675.

52   On the Passmore spice box, see Griffith, *Pennsylvania Spice Box*, 100–101. Joel Baily Jr. (1732–97) was also a cabinetmaker. In 1742 the elder Baily attended the Passmores' wedding at London Grove Meeting (which he joined in 1726) and signed their marriage certificate. From this it has been speculated that he was the maker of the Passmore spice box and related ones, such as the Hutton's. However, only one piece of furniture can be firmly documented to Baily, a desk-and-bookcase signed and dated 1732 and 1747. It is tempting to infer from this circumstantial evidence that Joel Baily Sr. was the maker of these spice boxes, but it is possible that he was not, as other craftsmen were working in the same area. When the desk was first published by Margaret Schiffer, it was attributed to Joel Baily Jr., who would have been fifteen years old in 1747. Baily Sr. is the more likely candidate. Subsequent examination of the desk revealed another inscription, "I B 1732," on the inside of the same drawer, putting its date too early for the younger Baily. In addition, evidence was found to indicate that the desk originally did not have a bookcase, but that the present one was made for it later, probably in 1747. The "Joel Baily" inscription on the desk also compares favorably with the signature on the Passmore marriage certificate. Therefore, the most likely interpretation of the inscriptions is that Baily Sr. made the desk in 1732 and in 1747 made the bookcase for it, with the additional inscription. The Baily shop was no doubt capable of making furniture big and small. When Baily Jr. died in 1797, he had an extensive inventory of woodworking tools, including a lathe, a dozen chisels and gouges, and ten molding planes; on Joel Baily, see Schiffer, *Furniture and Its Makers*, 22–23; Arthur E. James, *Chester County Clocks and Their Makers*, rev. ed. (Exton, Pa.: Schiffer Publishing, 1976), 37–47; also a report prepared by Penelope Hartshorne Batcheler based on observations of Lee Ellen Griffith and Charles F. Hummel, dated May 6, 1994, Winterthur Museum Registration Office file, acc. no. 1964.965.

53 Schiffer, *Furniture and Its Makers*, 124; C. Osborn Hutton, *Descendants of the Quaker Huttons of Pennsylvania* (Mentor, Ohio, 1965).

54 Thomas Hutton will, no. 3775; Hiett Hutton will, no. 8958, CCA.

55 The Jesse Hutton chest of drawers is in a private collection; it was sold by Christie's, *Important American Furniture, Prints, Folk Art, and Decorative Arts*, New York, Oct. 12, 2001, lot 109.

56 CCHS broadside H54. Mary Hutton Hurford died early in their marriage and Nicholas subsequently married Dinah Gregg in 1793 at Hockessin Meeting, New Castle County, Delaware. For a copy of their marriage certificate, see broadside H55, CCHS.

57 Griffith, *Pennsylvania Spice Box*, 13–25. In addition to the George and Margaret Passmore box (G^PM / 1744) and Thomas and Elizabeth Hutton box (T^HE / 1744), related inlaid examples include one made for an unidentified couple "I^CE / 1744" (Winterthur Museum, 1967.1183, Griffith catalogue no. 31); "S^SI / 1746" for Samuel Sharpless and Jane Newlin, who married in 1736 at Concord Meeting (CCHS, Griffith catalogue, no. 34); "AS / 1746" made for Ann Speakman (CCHS); and "AM / 1747" (owned by Miss Mary E. Speakman in 1939; see David Hunt Stockwell, "The Spice Cabinets of Pennsylvania and New Jersey," *The Magazine Antiques* 36, no. 3 [October 1939]: 175); and "R^LA / 1748" for Robert and Ann Lamborn (private collection; see fig. 3.19). The 1797 will of Samuel Miller of New Garden Township, Chester County, includes a bequest of "the Spice Box Mark'd S^MM" to his wife (CCA, no. 4575).

58 Much remains unknown about the plates, including how they were ordered and where they were made. Although sometimes attributed to Liverpool due to their reddish-brown edges, other English factories in Lambeth and Bristol were also making delftware at this date. An Irish origin is also possible. The Hutton-Hiett family came from Dublin, where delft potters were working in the 1700s; see Peter Francis, *Irish Delftware: An Illustrated History* (London: Jonathan Horne, 2000).

59 See Lee Ellen Griffith, "Chester County Historical Society's '1738' Delft Plates," in *Chester County Historical Society Antiques Show Catalogue* (West Chester, Pa.: CCHS, 1988), 5–11.

60 Dell Hymes and others have discussed ways in which objects can operate as speech; see Dell Hymes, *Foundations in Socio-Linguistics: An Ethnographic Approach* (Philadelphia: University of Pennsylvania Press, 1974), esp. 46–57, 199–201.

61 This study of twenty-one townships found the highest number of datestones, fourteen total, in London Grove Township, followed by eight in adjacent Kennett Township; see Thère Fiechter, "Date Stones as an Indicator of Building Periods in Chester County, Pennsylvania" (Master's thesis, University of Delaware, 1999), 70–80.

62 On the use of datestones in New Jersey, see Michael J. Chiarappa, "Social Context of Eighteenth-Century West New Jersey Brick Artisanry," in *Perspectives in Vernacular Architecture* 4, ed. Thomas Carter and Bernard L. Herman, 31–42 (Columbia: University of Missouri Press, 1991).

63 Griffith, "1738 Delft Plates," 9–11.

64 The chest descended in the family to Gertrude Townsend Hershey, who in the early 1930s sold it to Henry Francis du Pont and related a family tradition that the "wedding chest" had been made for her ancestors by Isaac Taylor of Gap. The Townsend history was left out when the chest was first published by Monroe H. Fabian, *The Pennsylvania-German Decorated Chest*, Publications of the PGS, vol. 12 (New York: Universe Books, 1978), 185, where it was described as having been made "by or for Isaac Taylor" in reference to the inlaid initials. Although difficult to connect to the Townsends, an Isaac Taylor was among the early members of the Sadsbury Friends Meeting, established in 1725 near Gap, Lancaster County, as an outgrowth from New Garden Monthly Meeting and Chester Quarterly Meeting. This is likely the same Isaac Taylor who died in Lancaster County in 1756; his inventory, taken on Aug. 18, 1756, included "shop goods" suggesting that he was a merchant. No tools were listed to indicate that he was a cabinetmaker. However, an Isaac Taylor advertised in the *Pennsylvania Gazette* for a runaway apprentice "by trade a carpenter" in 1746, suggesting a possible woodworking connection at approximately the same time period. On the England-Townsend genealogy, see C. Walter England, *Joseph England and his Descendants: An Historical Genealogy of the England Family as Descending from Joseph England, 1680–1748* (Boyce, Va.: Carr Publishing, 1975), 37–50.

65 Information on the Townsends' children is recorded on two printed family registers, entitled "Catalogue of John Townsend's Family, Taken at the Time of His Decease," and "John Townsend's Family, Taken 10th Mo. 1st. 1826," which remain in the possession of descendants. Inventory of John Townsend, taken Sept. 14, 1803, no. 5044, CCA.

66 The chest is pictured in Wallace Nutting, *Furniture Treasury*, 3 vols. (New York: Macmillan, 1954), 1:pl. 99. It was sold at American Art Association, *Colonial Furniture: The Superb Collection of the Late Howard Reifsnyder*, New York, Apr. 24–27, 1929, lot 581. John and Joanna Townsend's son Joseph (1756–1841) married Hannah Painter in 1782; their daughter was Lydia Painter Townsend. She married William H. Brown, and their son Samuel Townsend Brown (a renowned dentist) married Mary S. Parker, parents of Wistar P. Brown. Wistar's maternal grandparents were Wistar Parker and Abigail N. Jackson (daughter of John and Mary Speakman Jackson), who lived in Parkerville, Chester County. On the Brown-Townsend genealogy, see Futhey and Cope, *History of Chester County*, 674, 747–48; George Hoffman Penrose, *A Genealogical Record of the Brown Family* (Salt Lake City, 1896); and Halliday Jackson, *Proceedings of the Sesqui-Centennial Gathering of the Descendants of Isaac and Ann Jackson at Harmony Grove, Pa.* (Philadelphia: Committee for the Family, 1878), 294.

67 On Quaker portraiture, see Dianne C. Johnson, "Living in the Light: Quakerism and Colonial Portraiture," in Lapsansky and Verplanck, *Quaker Aesthetics*, 122–46. On Quaker silhouettes and albums, see Anne Verplanck, "The Silhouette and Quaker Identity in Early National Philadelphia," *Winterthur Portfolio* 43, no. 1 (Spring 2009): 41–78.

68 The label is one Elliott used after 1762, when he moved from Chestnut to Walnut Street.

69 Following the death of her first husband in 1755, Hannah married Charles Ryant. The next owner of the dish was their daughter Anna (1759–1823), who married Caleb Haines. The dish then descended in the Haines family; it was sold at Pook & Pook, Downingtown, Pa., Apr. 23–24, 2010, lot 178. Genealogical information provided by the family.

70 Will of Hugh Boyd, proved Sept. 30, 1754, no. 1545, CCA. The Nottingham Presbyterian Church, founded in 1724, was the site of Rev. Gilbert Tennent's sermon in 1740 on the dangers of an unconverted ministry, which became known as the Nottingham Sermon. In 1741 the church was the epicenter of a schism that divided the Presbyterian Church into the Old and New Sides over issues of evangelism spurred by the Great Awakening. Samuel Finley, from County Armagh, Ireland, was called as minister of the New Side congregation in Nottingham. He founded Nottingham Academy, attended by prominent students such as Benjamin Rush and Richard Stockton. Finley served as minister until 1761, when he was appointed president of the College of New Jersey (now Princeton). George Johnston, *History of Cecil County, Maryland, and the Early Settlements around the Head of the Chesapeake Bay and on the Delaware River, with Sketches of Some of the Old Families of Cecil County* (1881; reprint, Baltimore: Genealogical Publishing Co., 1989), 276–80.

71 The Hugh Boyd hatbox was sold by Sotheby's, *The Collection of Mr. & Mrs. Walter M. Jeffords: Americana, English Furniture, Silver, and Decorative Works of Art*, New York, Oct. 28–29, 2004, lot 313. It had been purchased by Jeffords in the 1950s, having passed through several dealers' hands but originating with Bill Snyder, who purchased it from Jim and Annie Williams of Atglen, Lancaster County. Inventory of Hugh Boyd, proved Sept. 30, 1754, no. 1545, CCA; see also Lee Ellen Griffith, "Line-and-Berry Inlaid Furniture: A Regional Craft Tradition in Pennsylvania, 1682–1790" (Ph.D. diss., University of Pennsylvania, 1988), 198–99.

72 J. William Frost, "From Plainness to Simplicity: Changing Quaker Ideals for Material Culture," in Lapsansky and Verplanck, *Quaker Aesthetics*, 26–27; Garfinkel, "Quakers and High Chests," in Lapsansky and Verplanck, *Quaker Aesthetics*, 88–89.

73 Barry Levy, *Quakers and the American Family: British Settlement in the Delaware Valley* (New York: Oxford University Press, 1988), 144, 171.

74 Frederick B. Tolles, *Meetinghouse and Countinghouse: The Quaker Merchants of Colonial Philadelphia, 1682–1763* (Chapel Hill: University of North Carolina Press, 1948).

75 On Quaker dress, see Mary Anne Caton, "The Aesthetics of Absence: Quaker Women's Plain Dress in the Delaware Valley, 1790–1900," in Lapsansky and Verplanck, *Quaker Aesthetics*, 246–71. On the Orthodox-Hicksite schism, see H. Larry Ingle, *Quakers in Conflict: The Hicksite Reformation* (Knoxville: University of Tennessee Press, 1986).

76 Cited in Richard K. MacMaster, *Donegal Presbyterians: A Scots-Irish Congregation in Pennsylvania* (Morgantown, Pa.: Masthof Press for the Donegal Society, 1995), 1.

77 Ibid., 15. On the use of the term "Scots-Irish," see Griffin, *People with No Name*, 2–3; also Fischer, *Albion's Seed*, 618.

78 Quoted in Carl Bridenbaugh, *The Colonial Craftsman* (New York: New York University, 1950), 35.

79 Griffin, *People with No Name*, 16, 23–24, 28, 67–70; Dixon, *Ulster Emigration*, 62–63.

80 On the trade between the Scots-Irish in Europe and America, see Richard K. MacMaster, *Scotch-Irish Merchants in Colonial America* (Belfast, Ire.: Ulster Historical Foundation, 2009), esp. 40–62.

81 Griffin, *People with No Name*, 96; from *Pennsylvania Gazette*, October 27, 1737.

82 Sarah W. Pennock was the daughter of George Pennock (1762–99), who was the son of Joseph Pennock Jr. and grandson of Joseph Pennock Sr., who built Primitive Hall in 1738. Her mother was Sarah Wistar, daughter of Caspar and Mary (Franklin) Wistar, who married George Pennock in 1790. Caspar served on the Westtown School committee from 1800 to 1804. With thanks to Mary Brooks, archivist at Westtown School, for this information.

83 Griffin, *People with No Name*, 105.

84 James Logan to Thomas Penn, Feb. 28, 1733/4, *Pennsylvania Archives*, 2d ser., vol. 7, 158–59; James Logan to J. Steel, Nov. 18, 1729, Logan Papers, vol. 10, no. 46, Historical Society of Pennsylvania; cited in MacMaster, *Donegal Presbyterians*, 3–4.

85 Alfred J. Morrison, trans. and ed., *Johann David Schoepf, Travels in the Confederation [1783–1784]* (Philadelphia: William J. Campbell, 1911), 23.

86 Griffin, *People with No Name*, 110–16.

87 Ibid., 11.

88 MacMaster, *Donegal Presbyterians*, 21–22.

89 Inventory of James Murray, taken Sept. 19, 1747, inv. 1747, no. 080, F031M, Lancaster County Historical Society (hereafter LCHS).

90 For more on Eddon and King, see Donald M. Herr, *Pewter in Pennsylvania German Churches*, Publications of the PGS, vol. 29 (Birdsboro, Pa.: PGS, 1995), 140–42. For an image of the complete communion service, see Donald M. Herr, "Communion Services on View at Lancaster," *Pewter Collectors Club of America* 7, no. 3 (February 1976): fig. 9, 99; also MacMaster, *Donegal Presbyterians*, 30.

91 Griffin, *People with No Name*, 20.

92 Will of James Anderson, July 14, 1740, book A, vol. 1, 48, LCHS; inventory of James Anderson, taken July 28, 1740, inv. 1740, F001A:001, LCHS.

93 Inventory extracts cited in Griffin, *People with No Name*, 134–35; Will of James Murray, Sept. 14, 1747, book I, vol. 1, 328–29; see also Lancaster County deed book B, 408, LCHS.

94 Several James Wilsons were ministers. One was ordained by the New Castle Presbytery in 1770; see Guy S. Klett, ed., *Minutes of the Presbyterian Church in America, 1706–1778* (Philadelphia: Presbyterian Historical Society, 1976), 469.

95 Genealogical information on Rebecca Wilson Ramsey is derived from a biographical entry on her son, James Read Ramsey, in Futhey and Cope, *History of Chester County*, 704.

96 The portrait is signed on the back by Clarke and dated June 4, 1792. Little is known about Clarke; two portraits by him are in the collection of the Historical Society of Delaware and two are at the Baltimore Museum of Art; see Sona K. Johnston, *American Paintings, 1750–1900, from the Collection of the Baltimore Museum of Art* (Baltimore: Baltimore Museum of Art, 1983), 33–34. On Welsh headdress, see two watercolor drawings by Curnow Vosper depicting women in similar hats: *Salem* and *Market Day in Old Wales*, 1908 and 1909, illustrated in Bebb, *Welsh Furniture*, 2:166–68; also see 215–16.

97 On Chester County crewelwork, see Margaret Berwind Schiffer, *Historical Needlework of Pennsylvania* (New York: Bonanza Books, 1958), 95–96. Lydia Hoopes was the daughter of John and Christina (Reynolds) Hoopes of Goshenville, Chester County. On the Mackey genealogy, see Anne Gates Copley, *Some*

Mackey Settlers along the Mason-Dixon Line in Cecil County, Maryland, and Chester County, Pennsylvania and their Descendants (Baltimore: Gateway Press, 1998), 7–13. The Mackey quilt was sold at Sotheby's, *Fine American Furniture, Folk Art, Silver, and China Trade Paintings*, New York, June 23, 1988, lot 312.

98 Griffin, *People with No Name*, 115–16.

99 Alexander Hamilton, *Hamilton's Itinerarium being a Narrative of a Journey . . . 1744*, ed. Albert Bushnell Hart (St. Louis, 1907), 185.

100 Griffin, *People with No Name*, 109.

101 Alexander Marshall and Don Yoder, "The Days of Auld Lang Syne: Recollections of How Chester Countians Farmed and Lived Three-Score Years Ago," *Pennsylvania Folklife* 13, no. 4 (July 1964): 12.

102 Kinmonth, *Irish Country Furniture*, 146, 177–84.

103 Will and inventory of Thomas Willson, will dated Jan. 28, 1764, inventory taken in 1766, no. 2289, CCA.

104 Schiffer, *Furniture and Its Makers*, 71.

105 "Minutes of the Corporation for the Relief of Poor and Distressed Presbyterian Ministers, 1759," in *The Presbyterian Enterprise: Sources of American Presbytery History*, ed. Maurice W. Armstrong, Lefferts A. Loetscher, and Charles A. Anderson, 71 (Philadelphia, 1956).

106 Durnbaugh, "Pennsylvania's Crazy Quilt," 8–30.

107 Letter, George Thomas to the Bishop of Exeter, Apr. 23, 1748, cited in Guenther, *Rememb'ring Our Time*, 29. On the attitudes of other Pennsylvania officials to German immigrants, see Schwartz, *Mixed Multitude*, 86–87.

108 Theodore G. Tappert and John W. Doberstein, trans. and eds., *The Journals of Henry Melchior Muhlenberg* (hereafter *Muhlenberg Journals*), 3 vols. (1942–58; reprint, Camden, Maine: Picton Press, [1980]), 2:515.

109 Lemon, *Best Poor Man's Country*, 14.

110 Scott T. Swank, "The Germanic Fragment," in *Arts of the Pennsylvania Germans*, ed. Catherine E. Hutchins, 5, Publications of the PGS, vol. 17 (New York: W.W. Norton for the Henry Francis du Pont Winterthur Museum, 1983).

111 This critique of the tripartite model of assimilation was developed by Bernard L. Herman and furthered by Falk and others; see Falk,

Architecture and Artifacts, esp. 184–95, and Steven M. Nolt, *Foreigners in Their Own Land: Pennsylvania Germans in the Early Republic*, Publications of the PGS, vol. 35 (University Park: Pennsylvania State University Press, 2002, esp. 3–9.

112 In addition to the Amweg chest, six other known immigrant chests include four softwood paint-decorated ones associated with Schwenkfelder immigrants (three in the collection of the Schwenkfelder Library & Heritage Center and a fourth, privately owned; see Fabian, *Pennsylvania-German Decorated Chest*, figs. 50, 51, 199); an unpainted chest with a history of being brought by Mennonite Peter Risser in 1739 (see Hess, *Mennonite Arts*, 12–13); and a chest used by Amish pioneer Nicholas Stoltzfus when he immigrated in 1766 (collection of the Pequea Bruderschaft Library, Gordonville, Lancaster County, Pa.).

113 Will of John Martin Amweg, May 16, 1768, book Y, vol. 2, 18–19, LCHS; inventory of John Martin Amweg, taken July 30, 1768, inv. 1768, F005A:001, LCHS.

114 Cited in Fabian, *Pennsylvania-German Decorated Chest*, 21–22.

115 Monroe H. Fabian, "An Immigrant's Inventory," *Pennsylvania Folklife* 25, no. 4 (Summer 1976): 47–48.

116 Joy Dierstein Harris, *Our Father's Lamp and Mother's Light: Ten Generations of the Dierstein Family in North America* (Harleysville, Pa.: By the author, 1981). With thanks to John L. Ruth for this information.

117 Susan E. Klepp, Farley Grubb, and Anne Pfaelzer de Ortiz, *Souls for Sale: Two German Redemptioners Come to Revolutionary America* (University Park: Pennsylvania State University Press, 2006), 127.

118 Inventory of Henry Wireman, Oct. 2, 1781, Buckingham Township, Bucks County, Pa.; cited in Alan G. Keyser, "The Stove Room in Pennsylvania" (unpublished manuscript).

119 Will of George Neiman, dated May 4, 1801, proved Aug. 27, 1803, Montgomery County (Pa.) Probate Records, 2:331; cited in Ellwood Roberts, *Abstracts of Montgomery County, Pennsylvania Wills & Administrations, 1784–1823* (Westminster, Md.: Willow Bend Books, 2000), 140.

120 See Reinhild Kauenhoven Janzen and John M. Janzen, *Mennonite Furniture: A Migrant Tradition (1766–1910)* (Intercourse, Pa.: Good Books, 1991), 88–89, 135–37.

121 See Lindsey, *Worldly Goods*, 21, 146.

122 The Neisser clock is owned by the Historical Society of Berks County; the Wills clock is in the collection of the York County Heritage Trust.

123 One such schrank bears the name Christina Appin; with thanks to Philip Bradley for this information.

124 On Oct. 31, 1756, Johann Michael Amenzetter and his wife, Anna Catharina, had their daughter baptized; see Frederick S. Weiser and Debra D. Smith, comp. and eds., *St. Michael's Evangelical Lutheran Church, Germantown (now part of Philadelphia), Pennsylvania, 1741–1841* (Rockport, Maine: Picton Press, 1998), 1:44.

125 In 1743 Johann Michael Amweg was one of the signers of a call to Jacob Lischy to serve as minister of the Reformed Church at Muddy Creek. In 1755 land for another Reformed Church was obtained on adjacent property. Known as Swamp or Little Cocalico Church, it was often referred to as "Amweg's Church" or the "Church at Michael Amweg's." According to family history, Michael Amweg was a schoolmaster and farmer. His great-grandson, Jacob III, moved to northern Ohio, where the name was Anglicized to Omwake; *The Omwakes of Indian Spring Farm* (Cincinatti, 1926), 15–20; Will of Michael Amweg, Sept. 7, 1779, Will Book C, vol. 1, p. 523; Inventory of Michael Amweg, taken Oct. 15, 1779, inv. 1779, F001 A., LCHS.

126 In her study of Pennsylvania German *aussteier* traditions, Jeanette Lasansky claimed that schranks were primarily made at the time of marriage or in advance of marriage; see Jeanette Lasansky, *A Good Start: The Aussteier or Dowry* (Lewisburg, Pa.: Oral Traditions Project of the Union County Historical Society, 1990), 72–74. Genealogical research, however, reveals that the dates on schranks were typically from well after marriage. For example, Christian Schneider (1725–95) of Lancaster County owned a schrank dated 1780; Abraham Reist (1737–1813) owned a schrank dated 1775; see Hess, *Mennonite Arts*, 28, 36. David Hottenstein (1734–1807) owned a schrank dated 1781 (see fig. 3.33). Women did occasionally receive schranks as part of their dowry furnishings.

The *Familienbuch* kept for three generations by the Clemens family of Montgomery County includes the occasional listing of a schrank; see Raymond E. Hollenbach, trans., and Alan G. Keyser, ed., *The Account Book of the Clemens Family of Lower Salford Township, Montgomery County, Pennsylvania, 1749–1857*, Sources and Documents of the Pennsylvania Germans, vol. 1 (Breinigsville, Pa.: PGS, 1975), 47, 51, 77, 79, 99, 111.

127 Vernon S. Gunnion, "The Pennsylvania-German Schrank," *The Magazine Antiques* 123, no. 5 (May 1983): 1022–26; Henry J. Kauffman, "The Pennsylvania-German Schrank," *Pennsylvania Folklife* 42, no. 2 (Winter 1992–93): 76–82.

128 In addition to the 1740 clock, 1741 schrank, and 1745 clock, known Pennsylvania German furniture dated prior to the 1760s includes a schrank dated 1758 (inlaid with pewter "MF AMF ANNO 1758"; see Pook & Pook, *The Collection of Richard and Joane Smith*, Downingtown, Pa., Oct. 30, 2010, lot 199); a schrank dated 1759 (private collection; inlaid "IIW AMW 1759"); a schrank dated 1760 (Philadelphia Museum of Art; made for Johannes and Anna Maria Spohr of Lancaster; see Pook & Pook, *The Pioneer Americana Collection of Dr. and Mrs. Donald A. Shelley*, Downingtown, Pa., Apr. 20–21, 2007, lot 591); a painted chest made for Susanna Beyer dated 1755 (see Philip H. Bradley Co. ad, *The Magazine Antiques* 174, no. 2 [August 2008]: 11); three tall-case clocks with inlaid dates on the doors: one dated 1751 (see Beatrice B. Garvan, *The Pennsylvania German Collection* [Philadelphia: Philadelphia Museum of Art, 1982], 42); one dated 1755 (private collection; made for George Yunt, see fig. 3.36); and one dated 1755 (see Pook & Pook, *Collection of Richard and Joane Smith*, Oct. 30, 2010, lot 202).

129 With thanks to William Woys Weaver, director of the Keystone Center for the Study of Regional Foods and Food Tourism, Drexel University, for the identification of these designs. According to Weaver, the lemon-shape *Manchet* rolls were a high-class bread and status symbol in Philadelphia as late as the 1920s (later known as "French rolls"); they were baked in special pans to achieve the lemon shape.

130 The foliate carving on the clock relates closely to that on a walnut chest with two large carved panels on the front. Although the chest has no date or names associated with it, the paneled top and overall construction strongly suggest that it, too, is the work of an immigrant craftsman; it was collected in Lancaster County. Related to the carving is that on an undated schrank with panel of similar designs, though likely carved by another hand; for an illustration of the schrank, see Lindsey, *Worldly Goods*, 8, fig. 13. Related carving also appears on a mantel dated "1746," once owned by Hattie Brunner; see *Hattie Brunner: Images from a Life* (Ephrata, Pa.: Historical Society of the Cocalico Valley, 2010). For related German carving, see Wolfgang Schwarze, *Antike Deutsche Möbel: Das Bürgerliche und Rustikale Möbel in Deutschland von 1700–1840*, 2d ed. (Wuppertal, Ger.: Kunst und Wohnen Verlag, 1977), esp. 88–103.

131 The original pendulum was 10 inches shorter than the present one; according to Ed LaFond, thirty-hour German clocks made by the Möllinger family of Neustadt and Mannheim and Franz Jacob Braun of Eberbach am Neckar often have pendulums 6–12 inches shorter than a standard 39½-inch seconds pendulum. This is a good indication that the original movement was a thirty-hour German one. The current movement is by Edward Sanders of Pool, England, and dates to 1730–65 based on the brass spandrel pattern of two eagles holding an urn; see Brian Loomes, *Brass Dial Clocks* (Woodbridge, Eng.: Antique Collectors' Club, 1998), 31.

132 Annette Kunselman Burgert, *Eighteenth-Century Emigrants*, vol. 1, *The Northern Kraichgau*, Publications of the PGS, vol. 16 (Breinigsville, Pa.: PGS, 1983), 57–58. Charles R. Freeble Jr., *The Adventures of Andrew Byerly: American Frontiersman, Ranger & Courier* (St. Petersburg, Fla.: Valkyrie Publishing House, 1993), 9–14, 67; also C. H. Martin, "Life of Andrew Byerly," *Historical Papers and Addresses of the Lancaster County Historical Society* 33 (1929): 3–8. With thanks to Alan Keyser for calling this clock to our attention.

133 Debra D. Smith and Frederick S. Weiser, trans. and eds., *Trinity Lutheran Church Records, Lancaster, Pennsylvania, Vol. 1: 1730–1767* (Apollo, Pa.: Closson Press, 1988), 4, 42, 43, 147, 318. In his will Michael Beierle left one shilling each to Andreas and his siblings Hans Martin and Anna Maria, still living in Germany. He left £50 to his niece Maria Elizabeth Beierle, daughter of Andreas, together with "one whole & compleat Feather Bed and Bedsted and its Furnitures, and a Chest," following the death of his widow (Will of Hans Michael Beyerle, 1766, Lancaster County Will Book B, vol. 1, 441–42, LCHS). Will of Philip Schreiner, 1791, Lancaster County Will Book F, vol. 1, 279, LCHS. With thanks to Barry Rauhauser for assistance in locating Philip Schreiner's will.

134 Built by Peter (Pierre) Bertolet, a French Huguenot whose family lived for several generations in the German Palatinate before coming to America, the house has distinctive German features: a central chimney, kicked roof, and v-notch log construction.

135 Thomas Cooper, *Some Information Respecting America*, 2d ed. (London, 1795), 117; cited in Falk, *Architecture and Artifacts*, 105.

136 Tappert and Doberstein, *Muhlenberg Journals*, 1:70–71.

137 Wokeck, *Trade in Strangers*, 45.

138 On Swiss German decorative arts, see Cynthia Elyce Rubin, *Swiss Folk Art: Celebrating America's Roots* (New York: American Folk Art Museum, 1991).

139 MacMaster, *Land, Piety, Peoplehood*, 19–24.

140 Stephanie Grauman Wolf, *Urban Village: Population, Community, and Family Structure in Germantown, Pennsylvania, 1683–1800* (Princeton: Princeton University Press, 1976), 9–15, 128–29, 327.

141 The inscription on the paper reads: "This Clock Case Was made and Sould By William Bomberger In the Reign of King George the third anno domeny 1765 germantown all work and no play makes [ill.]"; see Pook & Pook, *Period Furniture and Accessories*, Downingtown, Pa., Jan. 5–6, 2007, lot 563.

142 MacMaster, *Land, Piety, Peoplehood*, 49.

143 Steve Friesen, *A Modest Mennonite Home* (Intercourse, Pa.: Good Books, 1990), 41–44.

144 Ibid., 56–58.

145 Cited in MacMaster, *Land, Piety, Peoplehood*, 110.

146 John L. Ruth, *Mennonite Identity and Literary Art* (Scottdale, Pa.: Herald Press, 1978), 46–59. Janzen and Janzen, *Mennonite Furniture*, 208.

147 Tandy Hersh and Charles Hersh, *Samplers of the Pennsylvania Germans*, Publications of the PGS, vol. 25 (Birdsboro, Pa.: PGS, 1991), 202, 287.

148 Frederick S. Weiser, "IAESD: The Story of Johann Adam Eyer, Schoolmaster and Fraktur Artist," in *Ebbes fer Alle-Ebber, Ebbes fer Dich: Something for Everyone, Something for You*, ed. Frederick S. Weiser, 435–506, Publications of the PGS, vol. 14 (Breinigsville, Pa.: PGS, 1980).

149 This was one of three paint-decorated pieces found in the Strickler house. In addition to the hanging cupboard, there was an open-top kitchen cupboard (paint later removed) now in a private collection, and a tall-case clock made for Strickler dated 1801, now in the collection of the American Folk Art Museum. With thanks to Roddy Moore, director of the Blue Ridge Institute, for this information.

150 With thanks to Alan Keyser for this translation. On Strickler, see Russell D. and Corinne P. Earnest, *Papers for Birth Dayes: A Guide to the Fraktur Artists and Scriveners*, rev. ed. (East Berlin, Pa.: Russell D. Earnest Assoc., 1997), 2:747–48.

151 For a discussion of the cupboard and clock, see Philip Zea, "Jacob Strickler's Cupboard," in *Expressions of Innocence and Eloquence: Selections from the Jane Katcher Collection of Americana*, ed. Jane Katcher, David A. Schorsch, and Ruth Wolfe, 295–303 (New Haven: Yale University Press, 2007).

152 The work of John Drissell was the subject of extensive study in 2008 by Alyce Perry Englund, Wendy A. Cooper, and Lisa Minardi at Winterthur; see forthcoming article by Englund in *American Furniture* (Chipstone Foundation); see also John Cummings and Martha Cummings, "John Drissel and his Boxes," *Pennsylvania Folklife* 9, no. 4 (Fall 1958): 28–31; and Hess, *Mennonite Arts*, 64–65.

153 The Abraham Stauffer cupboard is in the collection of the American Folk Art Museum, along with a hanging candle box made for Sara Hoch; see Hollander, *American Radiance*, 175, 460–61. Nearly two dozen objects are known that are either signed by, or attributed to, John Drissell. In addition to the two at the American Folk Art Museum, there are six at Mercer Museum, four at Winterthur, two at the Philadelphia Museum of Art, and one at the Mennonite Heritage Center in Harleysville, Pa.

154 Formerly attributed to Jacob Weber by Nina Fletcher Little, these objects are now documented as the work of Jonas Weber (1810–76) through entries in the account book of his father, Abraham Weber; see Hess, *Mennonite Arts*, 66–68; also Hollander, *American Radiance*, 175, 461.

155 Garvan, *Pennsylvania German Collection*, 11; Hess, *Mennonite Arts*, 29; the late Pastor Frederick S. Weiser recounted the use of the Muddy Creek Lutheran Church box to Lisa Minardi. Scientific analysis of the black paint on the Bucher boxes identifies it as a protein-based distemper paint (animal glue). With thanks to Jennifer Mass for this information.

156 Jeffrey Bach, *Voices of the Turtledoves: The Sacred World of Ephrata*, Publications of the PGS, vol. 36 (University Park: Pennsylvania State University Press, 2006), 19, 115–38. Ann Kirschner, "From Hebron to Saron: The Religious Transformation of an Ephrata Convent," *Winterthur Portfolio* 32, no. 1 (Spring 1997): 39–63; see also John L. Kraft, "Ephrata Cloister: An Eighteenth-Century Religious Commune," *The Magazine Antiques* 118, no. 4 (October 1980): 724–37.

157 MacMaster, *Land, Piety, Peoplehood*, 143–44; Hess, *Mennonite Arts*, 30, 98.

158 Morrison, *Travels in the Confederation*, 19.

159 Ibid., 17.

160 With thanks to Michael Showalter for this information.

161 See Charles W. Treher, "Snow Hill Cloister," in *Snow Hill Cloister and the Dialect Poems of Ralph Funk*, ed. Preston A. Barba, 7–114, Publications of the PGS, vol. 2 (Allentown, Pa.: PGS, 1968); also Denise Ann Seachrist, "The Snow Hill Cloister and Its Music Traditions," *Der Reggeboge: Journal of the Pennsylvania German Society* 28, no. 1 (1994): 1–7.

162 On the restoration of the Ephrata Cloister, see Amber Degn, "'Houses from the Reservoirs of Memory': G. Edwin Brumbaugh and the Restoration of Early Pennsylvania Architecture" (Master's thesis, University of Delaware, 2000), 22–71.

163 Dennis K. Moyer, *Fraktur Writing and Folk Art Drawings of the Schwenkfelder Library Collection*, Publications of the PGS, vol. 31 (Kutztown, Pa.: PGS, 1997), 19–23, 28, 163–64.

164 Ibid., 74, 91.

165 On Pennsylvania German gardening practices, see Alan G. Keyser, "Gardens and Gardening among the Pennsylvania Germans," *Pennsylvania Folklife* 20, no. 3 (Spring 1971): 2–15; Irwin Richman, *Pennsylvania German Farms, Gardens, and Seeds* (Atglen, Pa.: Schiffer Publishing, 2007); and Irwin Richman, "The Pennsylvania Four-Square Garden," *The Magazine Antiques* 160, no. 1 (July 2001): 92–97.

166 Two related pieces featuring the same house and garden scene are attributed to Susanna Heebner and are thought to have been made for her nephews David and Abraham Heebner in 1818; see Moyer, *Fraktur Writing*, 91; and Hollander, *American Radiance*, 222–23, 484. The drawing for Salome Wagner has had all four corners replaced, suggesting that it may have been pasted inside a chest at one time. The chest and fraktur made for Christina Wagner are in a private collection; a schrank in the collection of the Germantown Historical Society was made for Salome in 1776.

167 Pook & Pook, *Important Americana from the Personal Collection of Mr. & Mrs. Paul Flack*, Downingtown, Pa., Oct. 28, 2000, lot 47. On the Wiegner genealogy, see Samuel Kriebel Brecht, ed., *The Genealogical Record of the Schwenkfelder Families* (New York: Rand McNally for the Board of Publication of the Schwenkfelder Church, 1923), 1230, 1234. For another example of a fraktur artist possibly decorating furniture, see the painted box made for Esther Kolb in 1810 with decoration attributed to David Kulp of Bedminster Township, Bucks County; illustrated in Cory M. Amsler, ed., *Bucks County Fraktur*, Publications of the PGS, vol. 33 (Kutztown, Pa.: PGS, 1999), 274. See also forthcoming article by Lisa Minardi in *American Furniture* (Chipstone).

168 Brecht, *Genealogical Record*, 272, 1230, 1234.

169 Craig D. Atwood, *Community of the Cross: Moravian Piety in Colonial Bethlehem* (University Park: Pennsylvania State University Press, 2004), 116–18.

170 For more on the use of colored ribbons in Moravian dress, see Paul Peucker, "Pink, White, and Blue: Function and Meaning of the Colored Choir Ribbons with the Moravians," in *Pietism and Community*, ed. Jonathan Strom (Leiden, Neth.: Brill, forthcoming). On the work of Haidt, see Heikki Lempa and Paul Peucker, eds., *Self, Community, World: Moravian Education in a Transatlantic World* (Bethlehem, Pa.: Lehigh University Press, 2010); and Vernon H. Nelson, "Johann Valentin Haidt und Zinzendorf," in *Graf ohne Grenzen: Leben und Werk von Nikolaus Ludwig Graf von*

Zinzendorf (Herrnhut, Ger.: Unitätsarchiv, 2000), 152–58.

171   Talbot Hamlin, *Benjamin Henry Latrobe* (New York: Oxford University Press, 1955), 6–7, 259.

172   William J. Murtagh, *Moravian Architecture and Town Planning: Bethlehem, Pennsylvania, and Other Eighteenth-Century American Settlements* (1967; reprint, Philadelphia: University of Pennsylvania Press, 1998), 12–14; see also J. Taylor Hamilton and Kenneth G. Hamilton, *History of the Moravian Church* (Bethlehem, Pa.: Moravian Church of America, 1967); and Beverly Prior Smaby, *The Transformation of Moravian Bethlehem* (Philadelphia: University of Pennsylvania Press, 1988).

173   Kelsey, *Cazenove*, 25.

174   One notable exception to this is musical instruments, including a spinet made in 1739 by Johann Klemm (collection of the Metropolitan Museum of Art) and numerous organs made by David Tannenberg; see Raymond J. Brunner, *That Ingenious Business: Pennsylvania German Organ Builders*, Publications of the PGS, vol. 24 (Birdsboro, Pa.: PGS, 1990), 60–97.

175   Murtagh, *Moravian Architecture*, 90–93.

176   A study of these chairs conducted by Winterthur Museum in 1998 located (in addition to the five in Winterthur's collection) eleven additional Pennsylvania examples and seven in the collection of MESDA, Old Salem Museums & Gardens. One of Winterthur's chairs (1956.543) was advertised by Martha de Haas Reeves and described as a "very unique American wing chair of the 17th century in good original condition" (*The Magazine Antiques* 3, no. 4 [April 1923]: 191). One example, possibly from Lancaster County, was advertised by Philip H. Bradley Co., *Chester County Historical Society Antiques Show Catalogue* (West Chester, Pa.: CCHS, 1996), back cover.

177   MESDA research files. John Bivins and Paula Welshimer, *Moravian Decorative Arts in North Carolina: An Introduction to the Old Salem Collection* (Winston-Salem, N.C.: Old Salem, 1981), 20–21; Johanna M. Brown, "Such Luxuries as Sofas: An Introduction to North Carolina Moravian Upholstered Furniture," *Journal of Early Southern Decorative Arts* 27, no. 2 (Winter 2001): 13–15.

178   On the use of easy chairs by invalids, see John E. Crowley, "The Sensibility of Comfort,"

American Historical Review 104, no. 3 (June 1999): 756.

179   In 1801 the saddler in Salem, North Carolina, was paid for "upholstering a chair" (Brown, "Such Luxuries as Sofas," 12).

180   Red mulberry (sometimes called black) was native to Pennsylvania, while the white or common mulberry native to China was widely grown in Europe and introduced into Virginia in the 1600s. The black mulberry originated in Asia and was introduced in America; see Michael A. Dirr, *Manual of Woody Landscape Plants*, rev. ed. (Champaign, Ill.: Stipes Publishing, 1998), 666–69. In 1690 William Penn noted the presence of both white and black mulberry in Pennsylvania; see Edwin B. Bronner and David Fraser, *The Papers of William Penn*, vol. 5, *William Penn's Published Writings, 1660–1726* (Philadelphia: University of Pennsylvania Press, 1986), 367–69; cited in Schaeffer and Kindig, *Wright's Ferry Mansion*, 1:33, 45. In addition to one Moravian leather-upholstered easy chair identified by microscopic analysis as red mulberry, other furniture said to be mulberry includes a paneled-end chest of drawers probably from Chester County (private collection); a stretcher base, one-drawer table (private collection; see Lindsey, *Worldly Goods*, checklist no. 90, 154–55); a clock case dated 1789 with movement by John Heilig of Germantown (private collection; see Frank L. Hohmann III, *Timeless: Masterpiece American Brass Dial Clocks* [New York: Hohmann Holdings LLC, 2009], 224–29); and a clock with movement by George Hoff of Lancaster in a mulberry case with cherry front (Philadelphia Museum of Art; see Hohmann, *Timeless*, 224–29). On the presence of mulberry trees in Bethlehem, see Joseph Mortimer Levering, *A History of Bethlehem, Pennsylvania, 1741–1892: With Some Account of Its Founders and Their Early Activity in America* (Bethlehem: Times Publishing Co., 1903), 290–91, 758. Susanna Wright in Lancaster County also produced silk in the eighteenth century; see Schaeffer and Kindig, *Wright's Ferry Mansion*, 1:51–58, 281–83.

181   Benno Forman noted that the listing of two *Brettstühle* in an 1802 inventory of the furniture at Bethlehem was the only known period use of the term; see Benno M. Forman, "German Influences in Pennsylvania Furniture," in Hutchins, *Arts of the Pennsylvania Germans*, 107. Alan Keyser has suggested that the *Lehn*

Stuhl (back chair) in period documentation may refer to this type of chair.

182   Ibid., 107, 110. Surviving examples in the collection of the Moravian Historical Society in Nazareth have nearly identical back splats, corroborating this provenance. A non-Moravian *Brettstuhl* was used in the German Reformed Church of Zionsville, Lehigh County, for many years; see Dennis K. Moyer, *The Colors of Goschenhoppen: The Decorative Arts and Furnishings of a Pennsylvania German Community* (Pennsburg, Pa.: Schwenkfelder Library, 1996), fig. 2.

183   Jerry Clouse, "Religious Landscapes," in *Guidebook for the Vernacular Architecture Forum Annual Conference: Architecture and Landscape of the Pennsylvania Germans, May 12–16, 2004, Harrisburg, Pennsylvania* (Vernacular Architecture Forum, 2004), 112.

184   On the mobility of Moravian woodworkers, see Lindsay Boynton, "The Moravian Brotherhood and the Migration of Furniture Makers in the Eighteenth Century," *Furniture History: The Journal of the Furniture History Society* 29 (1993): 45–58.

185   Levering, *History of Bethlehem*, 574–76. On the design and construction of the church, see Garth A. Howland, *An Architectural History of the Moravian Church in Bethlehem, Pennsylvania* (Bethlehem: Times Publishing Co., 1947), 8–9, 41, 51, 55, 89.

186   For more on Moravian organs and their makers, see Brunner, *That Ingenious Business*, 60–107.

187   Paul Peucker, "The Role and Development of Brass Music in the Moravian Church," in *The Music of the Moravian Church in America*, ed. Nola Reed Knouse, 169–88 (Rochester, N.Y.: University of Rochester Press, 2008); Stewart Carter, "Trombone Ensembles of the Moravian Brethren in America: New Avenues of Research," in *Brass Scholarship in Review*, Proceedings of the Historic Brass Society Conference, Paris, 1999 (Hillsdale, N.Y.: Pendragon Press, 2006), 77–110.

188   On Schmied, see Herbert Hyde, "The Brass Instrument-Makers Schmied of Pfaffendorf," in *Perspectives in Brass Scholarship*, Proceedings of the International Historic Brass Symposium, Amherst, 1995 (Stuyvesant, N.Y.: Pendragon Press, 1997), 91–114.

189 On the use of Windsor chairs by the Moravians, see Nancy Goyne Evans, *Windsor-Chair Making in America: From Craft Shop to Consumer* (Hanover, N.H.: UPNE, 2006), 408–11.

190 Patricia T. Herr, *The Ornamental Branches: Needlework and Arts from the Lititz Moravian Girls' School between 1800 and 1865* (Lancaster, Pa.: Heritage Center Museum of Lancaster County, 1996), 42, 54, 71. This sampler was sold at Pook & Pook, *The Collection of Dr. Donald and Esther Shelley*, Downingtown, Pa., Apr. 20–21, 2007, lot 431.

191 On the Pennsylvania or Kentucky long rifle, see Joe Kindig Jr., *Thoughts on the Kentucky Rifle in Its Golden Age* (Wilmington, Del.: George H. Hyatt Publisher, 1960), esp. 1–3, 9–12, 19–20, 31–36; see also George Shumway, *Rifles of Colonial America*, 2 vols. (York, Pa.: George Shumway Publisher, 1980).

192 Murtagh, *Moravian Architecture*, 104–6. On the Christiansbrunn gun school, see Robert Lienemann, "Moravian Gunmaking: Bethlehem to Christian's Spring," in *Moravian Gun Making of the American Revolution* (Trappe, Md.: Eastwind Publishing for the Kentucky Rifle Association and the Kentucky Rifle Foundation, 2010); also Shumway, *Rifles of Colonial America*, 1:173–236.

193 On Albrecht, see Stephen D. Hench, "Andreas Albrecht (1718–1802)," in *Moravian Gun Making*, 50; also Stacy B. C. Wood Jr. and James Biser Whisker, *Arms Makers of Lancaster County, Pennsylvania* (Bedford, Pa.: Old Bedford Village Press, 1991), 4–5.

194 Kindig, *Thoughts on the Kentucky Rifle*, 81, 97–99; Wood and Whisker, *Arms Makers of Lancaster County*, 14–15, 30–31. Andreas Albrecht's sons Andrew and Jacob were also gunsmiths.

195 On Moravian lovefeast rituals, see Atwood, *Community of the Cross*, 161–64. The cellars of the Central Moravian Church in Bethlehem and Moravian Church in Lititz (built 1787) were both constructed with fireplaces for the preparation of the lovefeast meals; Lititz retains its original coffee kitchen and accoutrements nearly intact.

196 Sliding wooden patch boxes were used on German firearms by the seventeenth century and continued in use in Pennsylvania for some time. They were cheaper than brass versions but were easily lost since they were not permanently attached to the stock; see Henry J. Kauffman, *The Pennsylvania-Kentucky Rifle* (Harrisburg, Pa.: Stackpole Company, 1960), 5, 6, 12–13.

197 For a more detailed discussion of the coffee mill, see Lienemann, "Moravian Gunmaking," 35–36. Some scholars have attributed the Marshall rifle to Andreas Albrecht; see Shumway, *Rifles of Colonial America*, 1:178–81, 198–202; also John Bivins with the assistance of H. Armstrong Roberts, "The Edward Marshall Rifle: An Examination," *Muzzle Blasts* (August 1986): 4–7; and R. S. Stephenson, *Clash of Empires: The British, French & Indian War, 1754–1763* (Pittsburgh: Senator John Heinz Pittsburgh Regional History Center and the Historical Society of Western Pennsylvania, 2006), 12. Bivins describes the Marshall rifle as "a Rosetta Stone of the Christiansbrunn school . . . [that] reveals as well numerous details typical of early Lancaster work." In comparing its carving to the signed Albrecht rifle, he notes "an attribution of the Marshall stock to Albrecht is not unreasonable."

198 Gunsmiths Adam Britz (Pritz) of York and Timothy Vogler of Salem, North Carolina, are both known to have made coffee mills. With thanks to Steve Hench for the information on the Pritz coffee mill. On the Vogler coffee mill, see Bivins and Welshimer, *Moravian Decorative Arts*, 66–70.

199 Lienemann, "Moravian Gunmaking," 42; inventory of Andrew (Andreas) Albrecht, taken May 17, 1802, inv. 1802, F002A:001, LCHS; see also Will of Andrew Albrecht, dated Mar. 29, 1800, book H, vol. 1, 179–80, LCHS.

200 See Shumway, *Rifles of Colonial America*, 1:192–97. This rifle is now missing; the date 1775 has been ascribed to it from memory. Both silver and brass wire inlay was used occasionally on finer Pennsylvania guns, though it was more common in Europe; see Kauffman, *Pennsylvania-Kentucky Rifle*, 22.

201 For a more detailed discussion of the William Marshall rifle, see Hench, "Christian Oerter," in *Moravian Gunmaking*, 64–75. This gun descended in the family of William Henry Marshall, born about 1841 in Ohio, the great-great nephew of William Marshall II (1737–1823), who bequeathed "my rifle and shot gun with their accoutrements" to namesake nephew William Marshall III. William Marshall III's grandson was William Henry Marshall, the first documented owner of the rifle; see William J. Buck, *History of the Indian Walk Performed for the Proprietaries of Pennsylvania in 1737; to which is appended a Life of Edward Marshall* (1886), 225–26, 259–60.

202 With thanks to William K. du Pont, Steve Hench, Alan Gutchess, and Scott Stephenson for their assistance on Pennsylvania long rifle research.

203 The Mori schrank was published while in Asher Odenwelder's collection; see "Living with Antiques: The Pennsylvania Home of Asher J. Odenwelder Jr.," *The Magazine Antiques* 51, no. 4 (April 1947): 249; also Asher J. Odenwelder Jr., *The Collector's Art: A and Z*, vol. 26 of *Home Craft Course* (Plymouth Meeting, Pa.: Mrs. C. Naaman Keyser, 1948), 2.

204 Gunsmiths in the Moravian community of Wachovia and Salem are known to have done foundry work such as brass and silver casting; see Bivins and Welshimer, *Moravian Decorative Arts*, 70–71. On comparisons between firearms and other decorative arts, see Joe K. Kindig III, *Artistic Ingredients of the Longrifle* (York, Pa.: George Shumway Publisher, 1989).

205 The only other known piece of brass-inlaid Pennsylvania German furniture is a tall-case clock with movement by George Hoff Sr. that has the date 1768 inlaid in brass in the tympanum and brass stringing around the door; see Hohmann, *Timeless*, 228–29; a hanging cupboard with applied brass motifs dated 1766 is also known. Four pewter inlaid pieces of furniture are known: a walnut schrank attributed to Lancaster County with pewter-inlaid initials "MF AMF 1758"; (see Pook & Pook, *The Collection of Richard and Joane Smith*, Downingtown, Pa., Oct. 30, 2010, lot 199); a walnut chest with pewter-inlaid date and initials "1773 H H" on the front together with inlaid-wood floral motifs (see Fabian, *Pennsylvania-German Decorated Chest*, pl. 76); a corner cupboard with six inlaid pewter stars and sulfur-inlaid decoration (see Skinner, *American Furniture & Decorative Arts*, Boston, Nov. 7, 2010, lot 227); and a tall-case clock with inlaid pewter birds in the hood and movement by George Faber, Sumneytown, Montgomery County (see Robert E. Booth Jr. and Edward F. LaFond, "It's About Time," *Philadelphia Antiques Show Catalogue* [2000], 44, 54).

206 In addition to Hintz, Abraham Roentgen was another Moravian cabinetmaker in London

possibly affiliated with brass-inlaid furniture; see Lanie E. Graf, "Moravians in London: A Case Study in Furniture-Making, c. 1735–65," *Furniture History: The Journal of the Furniture History Society* 40 (2004): 1, 34, 19–20; also Christopher Gilbert and Tessa Murdoch, *John Channon and Brass-Inlaid Furniture, 1730–1760* (New Haven: Yale University Press in association with Leeds City Art Galleries and the Victoria & Albert Museum, 1993).

207 Alan G. Keyser, Larry M. Neff, and Frederick S. Weiser, trans. and eds., *The Accounts of Two Pennsylvania German Furniture Makers: Abraham Overholt, Bucks County, 1790–1833, and Peter Ranck, Lebanon County, 1794–1817,* Sources and Documents of the Pennsylvania Germans, vol. 3 (Breinigsville, Pa.: PGS, 1978), 27.

208 Will and inventory of Peter Mohry, 1828, no. 814, Lehigh County Courthouse. With thanks to Dick Cowen.

209 Peter Buchecker birth and baptismal certificate, State Museum of Pennsylvania, acc. no. 63.19.4. In 1809 Peter and Catharina Mori were baptismal sponsors for Catharina Ochs; Catharina Mori was honored by the name of the child born to Matthias and Magdalena (Mory) Ochs; see Frederick S. Weiser and Howell J. Heaney, *The Pennsylvania German Fraktur of the Free Library of Philadelphia: An Illustrated Catalogue,* Publications of the PGS, vols. 10–11 (Breinigsville, Pa.: PGS, 1976), 11:fig. 345.

210 Muhlenberg, *Journals,* 1:213. On the Upper Saucon congregation, see Charles H. Glatfelter, *Pastors and People: German Lutheran and Reformed Churches in the Pennsylvania Field, 1717–1793,* Publications of the PGS, vols. 13, 15 (Breinigsville, Pa.: PGS, 1980–1981), 13:346, 356–58.

211 On the Lutherans, see A. G. Roeber, *Palatines, Liberty, and Property: German Lutherans in Colonial British America* (Baltimore: Johns Hopkins University Press, 1993).

212 Glatfelter, *Pastors and People,* 15:426.

213 Becker, "Diversity and Its Significance," 205.

214 Glatfelter, *Pastors and People,* 15:161–69. Regarding union churches, Theophile Cazenove noted that "in the country-churches, each Sunday, a Lutheran and a Presbyterian [Presbyterian was a period term for German Reformed] sermon, in German, are alternately preached" (Kelsey, *Cazenove,* 24).

215 See Sara Matthews, "German Settlement of Northern Chester County in the 18th Century," *Pennsylvania Folklife* 27, no. 4 (Summer 1978): 25–32.

216 Glatfelter, *Pastors and People,* 13:280–81.

217 This may be the extant pewter communion service, consisting of a flagon, basin, and plate by various makers but engraved with the same hand and dated 1757; the flagon is engraved on the top with the initials "W S," which may suggest a different donor; the plate and basin lack these initials; see Herr, *Pewter,* 46–48, 159.

218 Mrs. William T. Alston, *An Ancestor to Remember: Johannes Laubach, 1728–1808, of Chester County, Pennsylvania* (1979), 627; Futhey and Cope, *History of Chester County,* 627; Ralph Beaver Strassburger, *Pennsylvania German Pioneers,* 3 vols. (Norristown, Pa.: PGS, 1934), 1:380–81. For a discussion of Magdalena Laubach's certificate, see Klaus Stopp, *The Printed Birth and Baptismal Certificates of the German Americans* (Mainz, Ger. and East Berlin, Pa.: By the author, 1997), 2:176–77; Margaret's certificate was not recorded by Stopp but is the edition discussed on 174–75.

219 With thanks to Alan Keyser for this translation. On the Magdalena and Elisabeth Laubach samplers, see Hersh and Hersh, *Samplers of the Pennsylvania Germans,* 19–21, 219–20, 231, 281, 285–87; on Elisabeth Laubach's music book, see Earl F. Robacker, "Johann Adam Eyer, 'Lost' Fraktur Writer of Hamilton Square," *Pennsylvania Folklife* 34, no. 3 (Spring 1985): 107–8. In addition, an embroidered bed-sheet made by Christina Laubach survives in the collection of the Germantown Historical Society; see Beatrice B. Garvan and Charles F. Hummel, *The Pennsylvania Germans: A Celebration of Their Arts, 1683–1850* (Philadelphia: Philadelphia Museum of Art and the Henry Francis du Pont Winterthur Museum, 1982), pl. 108.

220 Paul A. W. Wallace, *The Muhlenbergs of Pennsylvania* (Philadelphia: University of Pennsylvania Press, 1950).

221 In 1799 William Birch made an engraving of Zion Lutheran Church, which was torn down in 1868; for more on St. Michael's and Zion, see Glatfelter, *Pastors and People,* 13:411–20; Brunner, *That Ingenious Business,* 85–87.

222 Historian Christopher Jedrey uses this term in describing the elite social status accorded

to ministers in New England; see Christopher Jedrey, *The World of John Cleaveland: Family and Community in Eighteenth-Century New England* (New York: W.W. Norton, 1979), 151.

223 Tappert and Doberstein, *Muhlenberg Journals,* 1:102–3, 118. The marriage of Henry Melchior Muhlenberg and Anna Maria Weiser is noted in the records of Christ Lutheran Church, Stouchsburg, Berks County, on Apr. 19, 1745; see Frederick S. Weiser, trans. and ed., *Records of Pastoral Acts at Christ Lutheran Church, Stouchsburg, Berks County, Pennsylvania,* Part II, Sources and Documents of the Pennsylvania Germans, vol. 12 (Birdsboro, Pa.: PGS, 1990), 39. On the Muhlenberg family houses in Trappe, see Lisa M. Minardi, "Of Massive Stones and Durable Materials: Architecture and Community in Eighteenth-Century Trappe, Pennsylvania" (Master's thesis, University of Delaware, 2006). On Muhlenberg's relations with the Moravians, see Walter H. Wagner, *The Zinzendorf-Muhlenberg Encounter: A Controversy in Search of Understanding* (Bethlehem, Pa.: Moravian Historical Society, 2002). On Conrad Weiser, see Paul A. W. Wallace, *Conrad Weiser: Friend of Colonist and Mohawk* (Philadelphia: University of Pennsylvania Press, 1945).

224 Tappert and Doberstein, *Muhlenberg Journals,* Aug. 28, 1763, 1:666.

225 David Wheatcroft, *The Authentic Eye: Revisiting Folk Art Masterpieces* (Westborough, Mass.: David Wheatcroft Antiques, 2005), cat. no. 57. Diane E. Wenger, *A Country Storekeeper in Pennsylvania: Creating Economic Networks in Early America, 1790–1807* (University Park: Pennsylvania State University Press, 2008), 22.

226 A. S. Brendle, *A Brief History of Schaefferstown* (1901; reprint, Schaefferstown, Pa.: Historic Schaefferstown, 1979), 12–13, 18–19. Tappert and Doberstein, *Muhlenberg Journals,* 2:423. For more on St. Luke's Lutheran Church, see Glatfelter, *Pastors and People,* 13:332; Brendle, *Brief History,* 18–19; and Wenger, *Country Storekeeper,* 22–24. On the architectural traditions of Schaefferstown, see Charles Lang Bergengren, "The Cycle of Transformations in the Houses of Schaefferstown, Pennsylvania" (Ph.D. diss., University of Pennsylvania, 1988).

227 Other figural wooden sculpture on churches includes statues of the four apostles on Trinity Lutheran Church in Lancaster, which were installed in the 1790s; see Mary C. L. Wood, "Statuary at the Evangelical Lutheran Church

of the Holy Trinity in Lancaster, Pennsylvania: Matthew, Mark, Luke, John, and a Community with a Mission" (Master's thesis, University of Delaware, 2007). Carved faces also adorn the steeple of St. Stephen's Reformed Church in New Holland, Lancaster County.

228 Cited in Margaret C. S. Christman, *The First Federal Congress, 1789–1791* (Washington, D.C.: Smithsonian Institution Press for the National Portrait Gallery and the United States Congress, 1989), 31, 219; on Frederick Muhlenberg, see Lisa Minardi, "The Speaker's House: Home of Frederick Muhlenberg," *Der Reggeboge: Journal of the Pennsylvania German Society* 43, no. 1 (2009): 3–19.

229 On Muhlenberg's portrait, see Monroe H. Fabian, "Joseph Wright's Portrait of Frederick Muhlenberg," *The Magazine Antiques* 97, no. 2 (February 1970): 256–57; also Monroe H. Fabian, *Joseph Wright: American Artist, 1756–1793* (Washington, D.C.: Smithsonian Institution Press for the National Portrait Gallery, 1985), 74, 128–31.

230 Historians have long viewed German-speaking immigrants' adaptation to life in America as following one of three paths: rejection of the new culture, rapid assimilation, or a "controlled acculturation" that attempted to moderate between assimilation and rejection; see Swank, "Germanic Fragment," 4–5; also Stephanie Grauman Wolf, *As Various as Their Land: The Everyday Lives of Eighteenth-Century Americans* (New York: Harper Collins, 1993), 263–64. Material culture scholars have generally followed such reasoning to the conclusion that the Pennsylvania Germans were bending to English ways when they used objects other than the traditional "folk" ones associated with them. Such a viewpoint, however, fails to account for the potential of Anglo-German reciprocity and the multiple socioeconomic levels that existed within Pennsylvania German culture. As Bernard L. Herman and others have argued, the problem that emerges from such an interpretation is that it implicitly assumes the dominance of the English culture and ignores the significant impact that German-speaking and other non-Anglo immigrants had on their English-speaking neighbors. Socioeconomic status was also a significant factor in ethnic identity; see Falk, *Architecture and Artifacts*, 5. One of the most exaggerated examples of an Anglo-centric interpretation is David Hackett Fischer's 1989 study *Albion's Seed*, in which he attempts to ascribe the cultural traditions of the Mid-Atlantic region almost entirely to its British heritage to the exclusion of the German-speaking population and its impact.

231 Nolt, *Foreigners in Their Own Land*, 3–5, 140–43; Liam Riordan, *Many Identities, One Nation: The Revolution and Its Legacy in the Mid-Atlantic* (Philadelphia: University of Pennsylvania Press, 2007), 8–13.

CHAPTER 2

1 John Fanning Watson, "A Trip through Chester County." Col. 189, Watson Family Papers, Joseph Downs Collection of Manuscripts and Printed Ephemera, Winterthur Library.

2 For a discussion of the popularity of the rush-bottom chair in the Delaware Valley, see Benno M. Forman, "German Influences in Pennsylvania Furniture," in *Arts of the Pennsylvania Germans*, ed. Catherine E. Hutchins, 103–6, Publications of the Pennsylvania German Society (hereafter PGS), vol. 17 (New York: W.W. Norton for the Henry Francis du Pont Winterthur Museum, 1983); also Nancy Goyne Evans, "Unsophisticated Furniture Made in Philadelphia and Environs, ca. 1750–1800," in *Country Cabinetwork and Simple City Furniture*, ed. John D. Morse, 162–67 (Charlottesville: University Press of Virginia, 1969).

3 Forman, "German Influences," 103.

4 Benno M. Forman, "'Crookt Foot' and Slat-Back Chairs: The Fussell-Savery Connection," *Winterthur Portfolio* 15, no. 1 (Spring 1980): 41–64. Solomon Fussell had a son, William, b. 1728/9, and possibly a grandson, Bartholomew, 1754–1838, who were chairmakers in Charlestown Township, Chester County, in the 1780s and early 1790s. They may have been trained in making traditional slat-back chairs such as those by Solomon; see Margaret Berwind Schiffer, *Furniture and Its Makers of Chester County, Pennsylvania* (Philadelphia: University of Pennsylvania Press, 1966), 91–92.

5 For an enlightening study that identifies vernacular slat-back chairs from various shops in the Shenandoah Valley of Virginia, see Jeffrey S. Evans, *Come In and Have a Seat: Vernacular Chairs of the Shenandoah Valley* (Winchester, Va.: Museum of the Shenandoah Valley, 2010), 16–50.

6 Inventory of Joseph Hibberd, 1737, no. 609, Chester County Archives (hereafter CCA); cited in Schiffer, *Furniture and Its Makers*, 114.

7 Inventory of Peter Hatton, 1758, no. 1750, CCA.

8 Schiffer, *Furniture and Its Makers*, 233; Account book of Enos Thomas, 1791–1805, no. 136, Chester County Historical Society (hereafter CCHS).

9 Tandy Hersh and Charles Hersh, *Samplers of the Pennsylvania Germans*, Publications of the PGS, vol. 25 (Birdsboro, Pa.: PGS, 1991), 119, 287.

10 B. W. Dambly to Russell H. Johnson, July 26, 1933, Schwenkfelder Library & Heritage Center, Pennsburg, Pa. This letter also stated, "The old ladder back chair which you purchased at the Drissel sale, came from the home of Sylvanus Kriebel, in Worcester Township."

11 Richard Tritt, photo archivist at Cumberland County Historical Society, Carlisle, Pa., has noted that the rocker on the left is a distinctive one seen throughout the Cumberland County area. At public sales they are often described as "Rupp rockers," after chairmaker Jacob Rupp; see Merri Lou Schaumann, *Plank Bottom Chairs and Chairmakers: South Central Pennsylvania, 1800–1880* (Carlisle, Pa.: Cumberland County Historical Society, 2009), 112.

12 Forman concludes that the seats that Fussell referred to as "checked" were most likely woven splint seats; see Forman, "Crookt Foot," 44.

13 For an explanation of this technique, see Benno M. Forman, *American Seating Furniture, 1630–1730: An Interpretive Catalogue* (New York: W.W. Norton for the Henry Francis du Pont Winterthur Museum, 1988), 204–5.

14 For several related slat-back armchairs, see Elizabeth Meg Schaefer and Joe K. Kindig III, *Wright's Ferry Mansion*, 2 vols. (Columbia, Pa.: von Hess Foundation, 2005), 2:84–93.

15 For a German slat-back armchair with raked back and double-cuts under the arms, see Forman, "Crookt Foot," 58, fig. 14.

16 For a discussion of Germanic benches and their placement, see Forman, "German Influences," 112–15.

17 Inventory of John Clemens, taken Feb. 18, 1782, Buckingham Township, Bucks County,

Pa.; cited in Alan G. Keyser, "The Stove Room in Pennsylvania" (unpublished manuscript).

18   Alfred J. Morrison, trans. and ed., *Johann David Schoepf, Travels in the Confederation [1783–1784]*(Philadelphia: William J. Campbell, 1911), 23, 104.

19   On the Vihmann house, see Eleanor Raymond, *Early Domestic Architecture of Pennsylvania* (1930; reprint, Atglen, Pa.: Schiffer Publishing, 1977), pls. 26, 27; also Charles Lang Bergengren, "The Cycle of Transformations in the Houses of Schaefferstown, Pennsylvania" (Ph.D. diss., University of Pennsylvania, 1988), 96–98, 190–93.

20   With thanks to Alan Keyser for this reference and his insights regarding dry sinks. In 1970 he observed what he believed to be the earliest form of this piece of furniture: "It was a sort of primitive table with a five-inch-high box surrounding the top; the base consisted of four split and shaved legs fitted into holes in two tapered battens to which the table box top was fastened. It was painted red. It was seen on the front porch of a house in Telford, Pa.—summer after summer during the 1970s it was filled with geraniums."

21   See Alan G. Keyser, Larry M. Neff, and Frederick S. Weiser, trans. and eds., *The Accounts of Two Pennsylvania German Furniture Makers: Abraham Overholt, Bucks County, 1790–1833, and Peter Ranck, Lebanon County, 1794–1817,* Sources and Documents of the Pennsylvania Germans, vol. 3 (Breiningsville, Pa.: PGS, 1978), 12.

22   Pook & Pook, *The Pioneer Americana Collection of Dr. and Mrs. Donald A. Shelley*, Downingtown, Pa., Apr. 20–21, 2007, lot 728.

23   This beautifully illustrated notebook is in the collection of the Philadelphia Museum of Art and has been reproduced with annotated descriptions for the illustrations; Beatrice B. Garvan, *A Craftsman's Handbook: Henry Lapp* (Intercourse, Pa.: Good Books, 1991), pls. 3–4.

24   For a discussion of dough or bread troughs, see Nancy G. Evans, "Everyday Things: From Rolling Pins to Trundle Bedsteads," in *American Furniture*, ed. Luke Beckerdite, 136–37 (Milwaukee, Wis.: Chipstone Foundation, 2003).

25   Account book of Enos Thomas, no. 136, CCHS.

26   Keyser, Neff, and Weiser, *Accounts of Two Pennsylvania German Furniture Makers,* 9.

27   An early 1800s manuscript recipe for honey cakes from the Eckert family of Adams County, Pa., instructs the housewife to mix the ingredients in the dough trough. With thanks to Alan Keyser for sharing this information.

28   See Schaefer and Kindig, *Wright's Ferry Mansion*, 2:112–13.

29   See Asher J. Odenwelder Jr., *The Collector's Art: A and Z*, vol. 26 of *Home Craft Course* (Plymouth Meeting, Pa.: Mrs. C. Naaman Keyser, 1948), 25. Odenwelder previously owned the table.

30   For a table with similarly splayed legs and references to two others, see Sotheby's, *Important Americana: Furniture and Folk Art*, New York, Jan. 17–19, 1997, lot 988.

31   Margrit Bauer, Peter Märker, and Annaliese Ohm, *Europäische Möbel von der Gotik bis zum Jugendstil* (Frankfurt: Museum für Kunsthandwerk, 1981), 49–50.

32   See, for example, a table from the Risser Mennonite Meetinghouse in Mount Joy Township, Lancaster County, in Clarke Hess, *Mennonite Arts* (Atglen, Pa.: Schiffer Publishing, 2002), 24; also a table from the Gingrich Mennonite Meetinghouse in Lebanon County; see Beatrice B. Garvan, *The Pennsylvania German Collection* (Philadelphia: Philadelphia Museum of Art, 1999), 47.

33   See account book of Enos Thomas, no. 136, CCHS.

34   For a discussion of the various Irish regional expressions of the settle and settle beds, see Claudia Kinmonth, *Irish Country Furniture, 1700–1950* (New Haven: Yale University Press, 1993), 76–95.

35   Cited in William Macpherson Hornor Jr., *Blue Book, Philadelphia Furniture* (1935; reprint, Washington, D.C.: Highland House Publishers, 1977), 23.

36   The settle is pictured in Wallace Nutting, *Furniture Treasury*, 3 vols. (New York: Macmillan, 1954), 1:pl. 1634. A low-back pine settle bed formerly owned by Titus Geesey was also examined during this study.

37   Inventory of Samuel Beverle, 1751, no. 1377, CCA.

38   For a discussion of Winterthur's three southeastern Pennsylvania settles (1958.551, 1960.741, 1964.1781), see Forman, *American Seating Furniture,* 189–93. For an illustration of Isaac and Elizabeth (Darlington) Pyle's settle owned by CCHS, see Schiffer, *Furniture and Its Makers,* fig. 21. This settle has been attributed to Abraham Darlington of Birmingham Township; however, it was more likely made in West Marlborough Township by joiner Moses Pyle, the brother-in-law of Elizabeth (Darlington) Pyle.

39   Inventory of Isaac Pyle, no. 4407, CCA.

40   David F. Wood, ed., *The Concord Museum: Decorative Arts from a New England Collection* (Concord, Mass.: Concord Museum, 1996), 60–61; Glenn Adamson, "The Politics of the Caned Chair," in *American Furniture*, ed. Luke Beckerdite, 174–206 (Milwaukee, Wis.: Chipstone Foundation, 2002). For a Welsh example of the couch bed form, see Richard Bebb, *Welsh Furniture, 1250–1950: A Cultural History of Craftsmanship and Design*, 2 vols. (Kidwelly, Carmarthenshire, U.K: Saer Books, 2007), 2:39.

41   Inventory of John Carter, June 22, 1770, no. 2572, CCA. Another couch with original blue paint under a later coating is owned privately and illustrated in Margaret Berwind Schiffer, *Arts and Crafts of Chester County, Pennsylvania* (Exton, Pa.: Schiffer Publishing, 1980), 85.

42   Abraham Darlington (b. 1757) was the son of Thomas and Hannah (Brinton) Darlington, who were married in 1754 at Concord Meeting and lived in East Bradford. Abraham married Susanna Chandler at Kennett Meeting in 1781, and they lived in Kennett, Westtown, and Thornbury townships, respectively. They were probably the second owners of this couch, which was likely originally owned by his father. It then descended to their son, Abraham (b. 1789), who married Susan Hoopes in 1819 at West Chester Meeting; it then descended to their daughter Anna B. Darlington (b. 1829), who died unmarried. It went to her cousin Agnes Darlington (b. 1877), who married a Swartley of Doylestown. The couch was acquired by the Dietrich American Foundation from Agnes's daughter, Margaret Swartley Rosenberger (b. 1903), of Doylestown, in 1965. On the Darlingtons, see Gilbert Cope, *Genealogy of the Darlington Family* (West Chester, Pa.: Committee for the Family, 1900). For the Sharples couch, see Schiffer, *Furniture and Its*

Makers, fig. 89. Hibberd died in 1737, and the inventory of his shop included two lathes, several unfinished wool wheels, twenty-one chisels of different kinds as well as nineteen chisels and gouges for turning, indicating that he was doing turning as well as joinery. Schiffer, *Furniture and Its Makers*, 114–15.

43 Margaret Taylor Lane et al., *The Taylors at Didcot, West Chester, Pennsylvania* (Anchorage, Alaska: Fathom Publishing Co., 1998), 12.

44 Perhaps he was a little over-extended, as days before his death he directed his wife "to sell at public sale so much of my Household Goods, Stock and farming utensils as she in her discretion may think she can spare and the proceeds of such Sale I direct her to apply to the payment of my Just debts" (Will of Lownes Taylor, 1833, no. 8999, CCA).

45 Lee Ellen Griffith, "Line-and-Berry Inlaid Furniture: A Regional Craft Tradition in Pennsylvania, 1682–1790" (Ph.D. diss., University of Pennsylvania, 1988); see also Lee Ellen Griffith, "The Line-and-Berry Inlaid Furniture of Eighteenth-Century Chester County, Pennsylvania," *The Magazine Antiques* 135, no. 5 (May 1989): 1202–11.

46 See Griffith, "Regional Craft Tradition," 157–79. For examples of related inlay in Welsh furniture, see Bebb, *Welsh Furniture*, 2:65–79.

47 L. Twiston-Davies and H. J. Lloyd-Johnes, *Welsh Furniture: An Introduction* (Cardiff: University of Wales Press, 1950), fig. 120.

48 Forman, *American Seating Furniture*, 139, fig. 67; Schiffer, *Arts and Crafts*, 67–68.

49 For a complete discussion of the tools and techniques of the line-and-berry inlay process, see Griffith, "Regional Craft Tradition," 10–29.

50 The lidded box is owned by the Chester County Historical Society, #61-77-Fbx7. It descended in the Reynolds family of Nottingham and is inlaid with the initials "R D," possibly for Rebecca Day, who married Jacob Reynolds in 1755; see Griffith, "Regional Craft Tradition," 131–33, fig. 101.

51 The only known tall clock case with line-and-berry inlay is in Winterthur's collection (1957.971). It has similar banding on the front of the base and line-and-berry inlay on the door; the dial is marked "Jacob Godschalk," but the movement has been significantly altered and does not appear to be original to the case. Unfortunately this clock case has no history of ownership. For an illustration, see Griffith, "Line-and-Berry of Eighteenth-Century Chester County," 1203, pl. II.

52 Joe Kindig III told Lee Ellen Griffith that his father purchased this box in London Britain Township; see Lee Ellen Griffith, *The Pennsylvania Spice Box: Paneled Doors and Secret Drawers* (West Chester, Pa.: CCHS, 1986), 124; for other related spice boxes with light and dark banding and double-line inlaid initials, see 39, 42, 44, 45.

53 Thomas Coulson will and inventory, 1763, no. 2087, CCA.

54 Inventory and estate sale of John Coulson, 1812, Cecil County Register of Wills (Inventories), vol. 16, 57–60, Maryland State Archives. With thanks to Sasha Lourie and Elaine Rice Bachmann of the Maryland State Archives for their assistance in locating these documents.

55 The connection between the Coulsons and the Hartshorn family is further strengthened with the citation in the 1794–95 inventory and executors' papers following Samuel Hartshorn's death that cites a payment to John Coulson for providing a "Hears" for the funeral. Joiners and cabinetmakers often orchestrated such details for funerals. With thanks to Harry Hartman for sharing the research on this spice box and the information surrounding the Coulsons and the Hartshorns.

56 When acquired by H. F. du Pont, the desk had turned Empire-style feet that were replaced with ball feet and then with straight-bracket feet, based on the original feet of the James Alexander desk. For an image of this desk prior to du Pont's acquisition, see Helen Comstock, "Furniture in the Collection of Mrs. Giles Whiting," *The Magazine Antiques* 69, no. 3 (March 1956): 232. A related slant-front desk with no history and herringbone inlay surrounding each drawer front is illustrated in an ad for The House with the Brick Wall, *The Magazine Antiques* 15, no. 1 (January 1929): 11. The interior is almost identical to the two attributed to Alexander. A fourth desk with no history, no inlay, but an identical interior is known by Alan Andersen of Cochransville, Pa.

57 For a description of Winterthur's desk, see Gregory Landrey, "Furniture with Secret, Hidden Compartments Designed to Deceive," *American Woodworker* 51 (April 1996): 48–49.

58 Microscopic analysis was done in Jan. 2010 by Dr. Harry Alden, who identified the wood as sumac, native to North America, from Quebec to northern Georgia and Tennessee, northern Michigan, Wisconsin, Minnesota, Iowa, Illinois, Indiana, and northern Kentucky.

59 The desk owned by descendants of James Alexander has herringbone banding on the drawer fronts and line-and-berry inlay on the top third of the slant front.

60 Rev. John E. Alexander, *A Record of the Descendants of John Alexander, of Lanarkshire, Scotland, and his wife, Margaret Glasson, who emigrated from County Armagh, Ireland, to Chester County, Pennsylvania, A. D. 1736* (Philadelphia: Alfred Martien, 1878), 16–17.

61 Hugh Alexander and his friend William Clarke were the delegates from Cumberland County to the Constitutional Convention that met from July 15 to Sept. 28, 1776. In Nov. 1776, Alexander, Clarke, and James Brown were the assemblymen from Cumberland County to attend the first free legislature of Pennsylvania in Carpenter's Hall, Philadelphia; Alexander, *Record of the Descendants of John Alexander*, 19–26.

62 Inventory of Hugh Alexander, 1778. With thanks to William K. du Pont for sharing his copy of this document with us.

63 This piece was acquired at a Shaub Auction (Peach Bottom, Pa.) of the estate of Joseph S. Terrill. When purchased, the legs had been cut below the knees, the lower portion had one deep drawer (a replacement), and the bottom drawer in the upper case was also a replacement with no inlay on the front. All the brasses had been replaced with large wooden knobs.

64 Inventory of Jeremiah Gatchell, taken Sept. 11, 1802, Cecil County Register of Wills (Inventories), vol. 13, p. 3, Maryland State Archives. With thanks to Sasha Laurie for this information. On the Gatchell family, see Futhey and Cope, *History of Chester County*, 561; also Francis James Dallett, "The Inter-Colonial Grimstone Boude and His Family," *The Genealogist* 2, no. 1 (Spring 1981): 82–85; and Clayton R. Adams and Francis James Dallett, "Some Additions and Corrections to the Boude Pedigree," *The Genealogist* 6, no. 2 (Fall 1985): 232–43. Joseph S. Terrill (1894–1990) was the son of Alfred Pyle Terrill and Ruthanna Stubbs (1862–1944). His maternal grandmother, Rachel (Brown) Stubbs, was the

daughter of Slayter and Mary (Kirk) Brown—both Gatchell descendants. Slayter Brown (1787–1855) was the son of Jeremiah and Hannah (England) Brown and grandson of Joshua and Hannah (Gatchell) Brown (1715–63). Mary (Kirk) Brown was the daughter of Roger and Rachel (Hughes) Kirk and granddaughter of Timothy and Ann (Gatchell) Kirk (1719–66). Sisters Hannah and Ann Gatchell were the daughters of Elisha Gatchell Sr. (1685–1754); their brother, Elisha Gatchell Jr. (1711–89) was the father of Jeremiah Gatchell (1734–1802) for whom the high chest was presumably made about the time of his marriage in 1753 to Hannah Brown. After her death in 1775 he married Margaret [?]. Elisha Gatchell Sr. (1685–1754) settled in East Nottingham by 1716 and died there in 1754. His father, Jeremiah Gatchell was born about 1640 to English immigrants in Marblehead, Essex County, Massachusetts; together with his son Elisha Sr. the elder Jeremiah Gatchell relocated to East Nottingham, where he died in 1714.

65 The top section of another line-and-berry double-dome-top inlaid desk-and-bookcase (privately owned) survives; it has herringbone banding surrounding the doors and motifs that relate it to the spice boxes discussed above as well as the illustrated desk-and-bookcase; see Pennypacker Auction Centre, *Important Americana Antique Sale: The Renowned Collection of Perry Martin*, Media, Pa., May 26, 1969, lot 201. The double-dome top may not be entirely original. The arches of the doors have been altered, but inlay evidence indicates it was a dome top originally. When the Montgomery desk-and-bookcase was acquired by the present owner in mid-2010, the base molding and straight bracket feet, not original, were replaced; the missing double-arch moldings surrounding the drawers were replaced; the slant-front, not original, was replaced and ornamented with conjectural line-and-berry inlay.

66 Later generations of Montgomerys had sons named Alexander. It is possible that one of them had his initial placed in the center.

67 A rail-and-stile semi-tall chest with two narrow drawers over three long drawers and identical inlay is in the collection of CCHS, 76-Fchst-12; for an illustration, see Griffith, "Line-and-Berry of Eighteenth-Century Chester County," 1206, pl. vii.

68 Will of Gen. William Montgomery, 1816, no. 6, vol. 1, 49–53, Columbia County Courthouse. Alexander Montgomery left the Danville house to his daughter Hannah, who married Andrew Russel; their daughter Hannah M. Russel was the last descendant to occupy the house, which is now the headquarters of the Montour County Historical Society. William Montgomery the immigrant (1665/6–1742) is known in family history as "Boyne Water Major" for his heroism at the Battle of the Boyne in Ireland in 1690, where his father and two brothers were killed. Some sources give his name as John, but William is the name used in the 1908 family genealogy; see David B. Montgomery, *A Genealogical History of The Montgomerys and Their Descendants* (1908; reprint, Owensville, Ind.: J. P. Cox, 2010), 312–13; and W. M. Baillie, *Pennsylvania Patriot: General William Montgomery* (Bloomsburg, Pa.: Columbia County Historical & Genealogical Society, 2010), esp. 6–11, 24, 36–39, 54–55, 100, 166–70. With thanks to Sis Hause and Bill Baillie for their assistance in researching the Montgomerys.

69 A chest of drawers from this group in Winterthur's collection (1967.1168) has line-and-berry inlay on all the drawer fronts, though the piece is not dated or signed and has no history of original ownership. Its early date is supported by the bold ogee base molding, the feet being a continuation of the stiles, and the side-hung drawers; for an illustration, see Griffith, "Line-and-Berry of Eighteenth-Century Chester County," 1204.

70 This tall chest is in a private collection; for an illustration, see Philip H. Bradley Co. ad, *Maine Antique Digest* (June 1993): 50. The feet are replacements based on a related tall chest (1997.42) owned by CCHS.

71 For a full discussion of these chests, see Griffith, "Regional Craft Tradition," 56–60.

72 This chest is privately owned. For an illustration, see Pook & Pook, Fall auction, Nov. 18, 1995, lot 350. Accompanying this chest was a note, probably written in the early 1900s, describing the presumed descent of the chest: "This Case of Drawers Made in 1758 for Sarah Miller / Descended 1st To Rebecca Miller daughter of Sarah Miller who Married Isaac Richards / 2d To Lydia Richards daughter of Isaac Richards who Married Joshua Seal / 3d To Mary Seal daughter of Joshua who married Mahlon Betts / 4th To Emily Betts daugh-

ter of Mahlon Betts who Married Wm C. Smyth / 5th To Lucy Smyth daughter of Wm C. Smyth who married Howard M. Cooper / 6th To Emily S. Cooper daughter of Howard M. Cooper who married Edwin J. Johnson." At the top of this note in a different hand is "James Miller–New Garden."

73 Hannah (Darlington) Jefferis' sister Rachel married William Seal. Three generations later a direct descendant, Phebe Seal, married Jackson Bailey; they were the great-grandparents of the last owner of the "H D" chest. In 1795 Hannah Jefferis left to her granddaughter Lydia Jefferis "one Sett of China Tea Cups and Saucers and a Small Trunck"; see Will of Hannah Jefferis, 1795, no. 4474, CCA. Whether this was the "H D" chest is unknown; Lydia married Dr. John E. Grier and moved to Clinton County, Ohio. Their two children died young, so if the "H D" chest did go to Lydia, it may have passed to other relatives upon her death. It is also possible that the "Small Trunck" in Hannah Jefferis' will was not the "H D" chest and that it may have gone to one of her sister Rachel's children and thus to the Seal family, where it descended. For more on Rachel Darlington Seal, see Cope, *Genealogy of the Darlington Family*, 92–93.

74 Inventory of Moses Pyle, taken Jan. 23, 1784, 1784, F008P, LCHS. Pyle moved to Little Britain Township in 1779; for more on Pyle, see Cope, *Genealogy of the Darlington Family*, 82. In 1735 Moses Pyle, joiner of Thornbury, bought a tract of land in Marlboro, where he lived until 1762; see Schiffer, *Furniture and Its Makers*, 201.

75 For an illustration of this chest, see Jack L. Lindsey, *Worldly Goods: The Arts of Early Pennsylvania, 1680–1758* (Philadelphia: Philadelphia Museum of Art, 1999), 141, fig. 22. Lindsey postulated that the maker of Hannah's chest was either William Pyle (n.d.) or Abraham Darlington (her uncle); however, since her father, Moses Pyle, was a joiner, it is more likely that it was made by him. There is no strong evidence that her uncle, Abraham Darlington the younger, who died in 1799, was a joiner. The only indication in his inventory was a listing "number of carpenter tools…$3"; see Inventory of Abraham Darlington, 1799, no. 4693, CCA.

76 For an illustration of the "H C" chest, see Lindsey, *Worldly Goods*, 139, fig. 4.

77 On this migration, see Warren Hofstra and Kenneth Koons, eds., *After the Backcountry: Rural Life in the Great Valley of Virginia, 1800–1900* (Knoxville: University of Tennessee Press, 2000).

78 G. D. Bernheim, *History of the German Settlements and of the Lutheran Church in North and South Carolina* (Philadelphia: Lutheran Book Store, 1872), 148.

79 For a discussion of the ethnic and religious diversity in the southern backcountry, see Jonathan Prown, "The Backcountry," in *Southern Furniture, 1680–1830: The Colonial Williamsburg Collection*, ed. Ronald L. Hurst and Jonathan Prown, 34–46 (New York: Harry N. Abrams for the Colonial Williamsburg Foundation, 1997).

80 Given the number of German immigrants from southeastern Pennsylvania, it is not surprising that sulfur was used as inlay in furniture made in the South. A sulfur-inlaid chest in the collection of MESDA (acc. 4217) is marked with the owner's name "ABRAH KAGE" and the date "1788." Kage, a Mennonite, was born in Conestoga Township, Lancaster County, in 1764. In 1768 his father, Henry, moved to Virginia and (according to a 1769 deed) purchased land in present-day Shenandoah County. Around 1788 Abraham married Mennonite Anna Neff, who was also born in Lancaster County (1762 or 1768). It is unclear whether Abraham and Anna had moved to Page County, Virginia, before their marriage. This chest might have been made in Lancaster County or in Shenandoah County. The existence of a closely related sulfur-inlaid chest owned by a John Siron from a Lancaster County family living in the area of Shenandoah County, Virginia, might suggest that the chests were both made in that region. The Siron chest is in the collection of Colonial Williamsburg Foundation (acc. no. 1994–51). For more on the Kagy family, see Franklin Kagy, *A History of the Kagy Relationship in America from 1715 to 1900* (Harrisburg, Pa.: Harrisburg Publishing Co., 1899). With thanks to June Lucas, director of research at MESDA, Old Salem Museums & Gardens, for the information above.

81 Paul B. Touart, "The Acculturation of German-American Building Practices of Davidson County, North Carolina," in *Perspectives in Vernacular Architecture*, ed. Camille Wells, 72–80 (Columbia: University of Missouri Press, 1986). For comparative observations on gravestones in the Carolina Piedmont, see M. Ruth Little, *Sticks and Stones: Three Centuries of North Carolina Gravemarkers* (Chapel Hill: University of North Carolina Press, 1998).

82 A number of other forms with sulfur inlay, including clocks and chests, were produced in the Orange County region of Piedmont North Carolina according to June Lucas, director of research, MESDA, Old Salem Museums & Gardens. Other Piedmont tall chests with arched-head drawers are known (without sulfur inlay) including one with four stages of applied arched boards above the drawers and on the sides; see MESDA research files, NCP5–14, photo S–13368.

83 Peter Kivett, Barbara's father, landed in Philadelphia in 1749. According to family history, he spent time in Lancaster County before moving to Randolph County, North Carolina, before 1763. The North Carolina colonial government listed him as a "native of Germany" (http://www.peterkivett.org).

84 The Exeter Meeting in Berks County was founded by Friends who left the New Garden Meeting in Chester County. Karen Guenther, *"Rememb'ring Our Time and Work is the Lords": The Experiences of Quakers on the Eighteenth-Century Pennsylvania Frontier* (Selinsgrove, Pa.: Susquehanna University Press, 2005), 122.

85 Members of the Quaker Gregg family from Kennett Township, Chester County, also moved to North Carolina and may have been among those who founded the New Garden Meeting west of Greensboro. For more on New Garden, see William W. Hinshaw, *Encyclopedia of American Quaker Genealogy*, vol. 2, *Pennsylvania and New Jersey* (1938; reprint, Baltimore: Genealogical Publishing Co., 1994), 487.

86 This material was scientifically analyzed as orpiment. With thanks to Jennifer L. Mass, senior scientist, Winterthur Scientific Research and Analysis Laboratory.

87 For an illustration, see Beatrice B. Garvan and Charles F. Hummel, *The Pennsylvania Germans: A Celebration of Their Arts* (Philadelphia: Philadelphia Museum of Art, 1982), 23, pl. 1.

88 Frances Lichten, "A Masterpiece of Pennsylvania-German Furniture," *The Magazine Antiques* 77, no. 2 (February 1960): 176–78.

89 Monroe H. Fabian, "Sulfur Inlay in Pennsylvania German Furniture," *Pennsylvania Folklife* 27, no. 1 (Fall 1977): 2–9.

90 In fall 2009, Winterthur student Brenda Hornsby-Heindl conducted a survey of sulfur-inlaid furniture and documented more than 100 pieces; for a discussion of this study and additional research, see forthcoming article by Mark J. Anderson et al., in *American Furniture* (Chipstone Foundation).

91 Jennifer L. Mass and Mark J. Anderson, "Pennsylvania German Sulfur-Inlaid Furniture: Characterization, Reproduction, and Aging Phenomena of the Inlays," *Measurement and Technology* (2003): 1598–1607; Mark J. Anderson, "A New Look at Sulfur and Other Composition Inlay," in *Chester County Historical Society Antiques Show Catalogue* (West Chester, Pa.: CCHS, 1995), 36–39.

92 For a discussion of these objects and the Bamberger and Kauffman families, see Hess, *Mennonite Arts*, 32–38.

93 Another related chest (private collection) with ogee bracket feet has the identical foliate surround containing sulfur-inlaid initials and date, "I 1768 D," flanked by additional foliate inlay.

94 For more on the Ferrees, see Franklin Ellis and Samuel Evans, *History of Lancaster County, Pennsylvania, with Biographical Sketches of Many of Its Pioneers and Prominent Men* (Philadelphia: Everts & Peck, 1883), 995.

95 Samuel S. Shriver, *History of the Shriver Family and Their Connections, 1684–1888* (Baltimore: Press of Guggenheimer, Weil, 1888), 40.

96 Marion F. Egge, *Pennsylvania German Roots across the Ocean* (Philadelphia: Genealogical Society of Pennsylvania, 2000), 74.

97 Clarke Hess has traced the ownership of nine sulfur-inlaid schranks owned by Mennonite families, many related, who lived to the west or northwest of Lancaster; see Hess, *Mennonite Arts*, 27.

98 Inventory of Peter Ferree, 1795, no. 1795, FOO2F, box 035, LCHS.

99 According to John J. Snyder Jr., the Ferree farm was off Bachmantown Road, south of the Pequea Creek, East Lampeter Township, Lancaster County.

100 Vendue of Peter Ferree, 1795/1798, no. 1798, FOO1F, Archives South 001, LCHS.

101 The pendulum door of the 1768 clock is elaborately inlaid in wood with baroque strapwork, and the panel on the base is inlaid with a circular motif similar to the sulfur inlay on the dated 1768 Herr schrank at Winterthur. For an illustration of this clock, see Robert E. Booth Jr. and Edward F. LaFond Jr., "It's about Time," *Philadelphia Antiques Show Catalogue* (2000), 43. For detailed images and a complete family history, see Horst Auctioneers, Ephrata, Pa., Oct. 23–24, 1998, lot 782.

102 On Stoner's career, see Stacy B. C. Wood Jr., "Rudy Stoner, 1728–1769: Early Lancaster, Pennsylvania, Clockmaker," *Journal of the Lancaster County Historical Society* 80, no. 2 (1976): 112–27. For images and a discussion of the Ferree clock movement, see Frank L. Hohmann III, *Timeless: Masterpiece American Brass Dial Clocks* (New York: Hohmann Holdings LLC, 2009), 240–41.

103 Pennypacker Auction Centre, *Rare American Folk Art from the Private Collection of Mr. & Mrs. Paul R. Flack*, Reading, Pa., Apr. 12, 1976, lot 168.

104 Letter, National Museum of American History, Smithsonian Institution, acc. no. 76–14370, acc. no. 322631. At this sale Monroe Fabian acquired the chest for the Smithsonian.

105 Stacy B. C. Wood Jr., "The Hoff Family: Master Clockmakers of Lancaster Borough," *Journal of the Lancaster County Historical Society* 81, no. 4 (1977): 181.

106 Ibid., 169–72.

107 Ibid., 174.

108 Thomas R. Ryan, ed., *The Worlds of Jacob Eichholtz* (Lancaster, Pa.: Lancaster County Historical Society, 2003), 40.

109 Ibid., 147.

110 Wendy A. Cooper, Patricia Edmonson, and Lisa M. Minardi, "The Compass Artist of Lancaster County, Pennsylvania," in *American Furniture*, ed. Luke Beckerdite, 62–87 (Milwaukee, Wis.: Chipstone Foundation, 2009).

111 This box was sold at Freeman's, *An Important Berks County Collection: The Estate of Esther H. Ludwig*, Philadelphia, Nov. 21–22, 2005, lot 1341; prior to that it was in the collection of Randolph R. Urich of Lebanon County;

see also Jane Katcher, David A. Schorsch, and Ruth Wolfe, eds., *Expressions of Innocence and Eloquence: Selections from the Jane Katcher Collection of Americana* (New Haven: Yale University Press, 2007), 22–23, 311.

112 On July 28, 1805, Christian Hunsicker bought a cradle from Peter Ranck of Bethel Township, Lebanon County, for £0.15.0, and on July 5, 1810, he purchased a bedstead from Ranck for £2.4.7; see Stephen James Perkins, "Command You Me from Play Every Minute of the Day: Peter Ranck, Jonestown, Pennsylvania" (Master's thesis, University of Delaware, 2001), 86, 88.

113 U.S. Census records, 1880, 1910, 1920, Bethel Township, Lancaster County, Pa.

114 The Committee appointed by the District Conference, *The History of the Church of the Brethren of the Eastern District of Pennsylvania* (Lancaster, Pa.: New Era Printing, 1915), 450–54.

115 Hunsicker probate records, Lebanon County Courthouse.

116 Though this chest (privately owned) has no provenance, it is possible the initials "C H" may refer to Christian Hunsicker, who would have been twelve years old when it was made. A chest dated "1794" has related compasswork decoration but is not identical to this group; see Pook & Pook, *Period Furniture, Fine Art, and Decorative Accessories,* Downingtown, Pa., Oct. 2, 2010, lot 679.

117 Two chests of identical construction but different decoration are also known.

118 On the use of the mermaid as a decorative motif, see Lee Ellen Griffith, *The Tale of the Mermaid* (Philadelphia: Philadelphia Maritime Museum, 1986). An engraved image of a mermaid printed in the 1775 *Gentleman's Magazine* (London) inspired a woodcut that was used on fraktur printed at Ephrata Cloister in the 1780s. Mermaids were also drawn by a number of fraktur artists, including Friedrich Speyer, Durs Rudy, and Daniel and Henrich Otto.

119 For a Reading example printed in 1791 and decorated by Speyer, see Klaus Stopp, *The Printed Birth and Baptismal Certificates of the German Americans* (East Berlin, Pa.: By the author, 1998), 4:89. A certificate printed at Ephrata about 1787 and decorated with mer-

maids by Speyer is in the Winterthur collection (acc. no. 1957.1220).

120 Perkins, "Command You Me from Play," 14.

121 Quoted in Esther Stevens Fraser, "Pennsylvania German Dower Chests, Part I," *The Magazine Antiques* 11, no. 2 (February 1927): 122.

122 Esther Stevens Fraser, "Pennsylvania Brides Boxes and Dower Chests, Parts I and II," *The Magazine Antiques* 8, nos. 1–2 (July–August 1925): 20–23; 79–84. Fraser later married architect Clarence Brazer, who oversaw the restoration of the 1738 home of Joseph and Mary Pennock, known as Primitive Hall.

123 Fraser, "Pennsylvania Brides Boxes, Part II," 84.

124 Esther Stevens Fraser, "Pennsylvania German Dower Chests, Parts I–III," *The Magazine Antiques* 11, no. 2 (February 1927): 119–23; no. 4 (April 1927): 280–83; no. 6 (June 1927): 474–76.

125 Fraser illustrated a chest she said was signed "Peter Rank his hand," but this inscription was not illustrated nor has the chest been available to study; see Ibid., no. 4 (April 1927), 281.

126 A chest in the Winterthur collection (acc. no. 1967.760) has the inscription (translation): "Cadarina [ill.] her chest and this is her [ill.]" scratched on the pot on the proper right side.

127 Keyser, Neff, and Weiser, *Accounts of Two Pennsylvania German Furniture Makers*, 163.

128 J. Roderick Moore, "Painted Chests from Wythe County, Virginia," *The Magazine Antiques* 122, no. 3 (September 1982): 516–21. For a Wythe County chest in the collection of Colonial Williamsburg, see Hurst and Prown, *Southern Furniture*. With thanks to Roddy Moore, director of the Blue Ridge Institute, for the update on the number of chests now known.

129 This chest was recorded by MESDA in 1989, photo S-14965, file location W-4-38.

130 Moore, "Painted Chests," 19, pl. V.

131 Ibid., 520. With thanks to Roddy Moore for sharing his research on the Huddles and how they learned the woodworking trade from their step-uncle and probably not their birth father. Roddy also noted that Gideon Huddle had a "paint rock" in his inventory when he died; this would have been used for grinding and mixing pigments.

132 Ibid., 518.

133 With thanks to June Lucas, director of research, MESDA, Old Salem Museums & Gardens, for sharing research and information regarding this connection between Wythe County and Jonestown. Gravestones information was accessed at http://home.ntelos.net/~cameronnet/cameron/kimcem.htm. Looking at the various family names in this cemetery, one finds other Bethel Township family names including Snavely and Cassel. More research may provide further evidence that Jonestown-type painted chests were taken to Wythe County with migrating families, serving as inspiration for local craftsmen. For references to the Snavely family in Bethel Township, Lebanon County, see William Henry Egle, *Notes and Queries: Historical, Biographical, and Genealogical Relating Chiefly to the Interior of Pennsylvania* (Harrisburg, Pa., 1897), 70–71.

134 He was the son of Jacob Tobler Sr. (b. about 1732 in Switzerland) and Anna Maria Hough (b. 1734 in Germany or Switzerland), who were married in Bethel Township, Lebanon County in 1755. Both died in Monkey Run, Montgomery County, Virginia, 1817 and 1810, respectively.

135 For the will of Jacob Tobler Jr., see Will Book 2, 182–83, Wythe County Courthouse. In the will Jacob's surname was spelled phonetically with a "D"; the German pronunciation of "Tobler" would have sounded like "Dobler."

136 Moore, "Painted Chests," 517.

137 Diane E. Wenger, *A Country Storekeeper in Pennsylvania: Creating Economic Networks in Early America, 1790–1807* (University Park: Pennsylvania State University Press, 2008), 131.

138 George Shumway, Edward Durell, and Howard C. Frey, *Conestoga Wagon, 1750–1850* (York, Pa.: Early American Industries Association and George Shumway Publisher, 1964), 77.

139 Lynn A. Brocklebank, "Westmoreland County, Pennsylvania, Fraktur: An Initial Survey," *The Magazine Antiques* 129, no. 1 (January 1986): 258–67.

140 This fraktur is in the collection of the Free Library of Philadelphia (frko1100); see Frederick S. Weiser and Howell J. Heaney, *The Pennsylvania German Fraktur in the Collection of the Free Library of Philadelphia: An Illustrated Catalogue*, Publications of the PGS, vols. 10–11 (Breinigsville, Pa.: PGS, 1976).

141 A. H. Rice to Henry Francis du Pont, Jan. 1, 1930, Folder: Bills-Rice, A. H., Antiques Dealer Correspondence Files, Box 4, Winterthur Archives, Winterthur Library. The chest is acc. no. 1964.1517, and the desk is 1964.1518.

142 See Mary Hammond Sullivan and Frederick S. Weiser, "Decorated Furniture of the Mahantongo Valley," *The Magazine Antiques* 103, no. 5 (May 1973): 932–39; also Mary Hammond Sullivan and Frederick S. Weiser, "Decorated Furniture of the Schwaben Creek Valley," in *Ebbes fer Alle-Ebber, Ebbes fer Dich: Something for Everyone, Something for You,* ed. Frederick S. Weiser, 332–94, Publications of the PGS, vol. 14 (Breinigsville, Pa.: PGS, 1980).

143 Henry M. Reed, ed., *Decorated Furniture of the Mahantongo Valley* (Lewisburg, Pa.: Bucknell University, 1987); also Henry M. Reed, "Finding the Fabulous Furniture of the Mahan-tongo Valley," *Pennsylvania Heritage* 21, no. 4 (Fall 1995): 20–28. Reed disagreed with Sullivan and Weiser's use of the more narrow Schwaben Creek Valley region and reiterated that the furniture should continue to be referred to as Mahantongo Valley.

144 Ibid., 26–43.

145 See Don Yoder, "The Johannes Haas Account Book," in Reed, *Decorated Furniture*, 75–85.

146 For a detailed study of the chests, see Philip D. Zimmerman, "Mahantongo Blanket Chests," *The Magazine Antiques* 162, no. 4 (October 2002): 161–69.

147 In 1986 the late Janice H. Carlson, then head of Winterthur's Scientific Research and Analysis Laboratory, carried out qualitative energy dispersive X-ray fluorescence analysis on five Winterthur pieces of Mahantongo furniture. Her report stated: "In all five pieces, the primary colorant in both the blue and green areas is Prussian blue. The presence of lead and chromium in yellow areas . . . confirms the use of chrome yellow . . . which first became commercially available in 1818 . . .[and] was frequently mixed with Prussian blue to produce a green color. The use of this combination was confirmed on the four Mahantongo pieces with green pigmented areas. In addition, copper was found in two of these green areas indicating that the additional presence of a copper green pigment, possibly verdigris . . . or basic copper carbonate such as malachite or green verditer. Copper based green pigments date from antiquity . . . It is highly probable that another factor contributed to the apparent green color of many of the areas on these and other examples of painted furniture . . . Natural varnishes and resins are slightly yellow in color and become increasingly yellow as they age with the result that an underlying bright Prussian blue paint layer may acquire a green appearance."

148 For a superb example of this type, see Sotheby's, *Important Americana: The Collection of Dr. and Mrs. Henry P. Deyerle*, Charlottesville, Va., May 26–27, 1995, lot 307.

149 Jennifer L. Mass, senior scientist in the Winterthur Scientific Research and Analysis Laboratory, has carried out research into the origins of chrome yellow and green paint and presented those findings at Winterthur's 2010 Furniture Forum. She has found that "the natural history of Baltimore is critical to understanding the origins of the bright yellow and green paints used in the nineteenth century to decorate southeastern Pennsylvania painted furniture. These paints, known as chrome yellow ($PbCrO_4$) and chromium oxide green (Cr_2O_3) respectively, had their origins in the world's most important chromium mines, conveniently located in nearby Baltimore. These deposits of chromite ore ($FeCr_2O_4$) were located in the Bare Hills and Soldiers Delight districts of the city, and the first paints are thought to have been made from these ores between 1808 and 1812." With thanks to Dr. Mass for this informative discovery.

150 Reed, *Decorated Furniture*, 30. According to Carrie Haas Troutman, granddaughter of cabinetmaker Johannes Haas, the flowers were "put on with a cork that was cut to resemble a flower."

151 Sullivan and Weiser, "Decorated Furniture of the Schwaben Creek Valley," 384–89.

152 Although a fraktur drawing of two spotted rearing horses, signed in pen "Magdalene Shenk, [ill.]/ Horses printed By or made By/ Henry Hochenberger Teacher/ March 6th 1848," once accompanied the small chest, it is unclear whether this drawing originated with the chest and what might have inspired the image. Neither Shenk nor Hochenberger are names familiar to the Schwaben Creek and Mahantongo Valley region.

153 Reed, "Finding the Fabulous Furniture," 20–28.

154 For a copy of the Jacob Maser inventory, 1895, see Winterthur Registration Office file, acc. no. 1964.1518. This copy was supplied by Frederick S. Weiser and is presumably from the Northumberland County Courthouse, Sunbury, Pa.; Wills and Administration Papers, Book 2, 324, no. 523.

155 *Genealogical and Biographical Annals of Northumberland County* (Chicago: J. L. Floyd, 1911), 498.

156 Of the three known kitchen cupboards, two are quite similar in their decoration. One dated "1830" on the front with the name "Concordia" above pairs of angels in the panels of the doors is in the collection of the Philadelphia Museum of Art (see Garvan, *Pennsylvania German Collection*, 31; and Reed, *Decorated Furniture,* 34). The other is dated "1828" on the front flanked by the name "rebeca braun," also with pairs of angels in the door panels, in the Barnes Foundation (see Reed, *Decorated Furniture,* 35). A third is in a private collection and was formerly owned by Edward "Doc" Bohne and sold at Conestoga Auction Company, Manheim, Pa., June 4–5, 2004.

157 See Sullivan and Weiser, "Decorated Furniture of the Schwaben Creek Valley," 381, fig. 52.

158 Paint analysis undertaken by Winterthur conservator Mary McGinn, 2009.

159 Reed, *Decorated Furniture*, 61.

160 Yoder, "Johannes Haas Account Book," 76–77, 82.

161 Sarah Neale Fayen, "Tilt-Top Tables and Eighteenth-Century Consumerism," in *American Furniture*, ed. Luke Beckerdite, 95–137 (Milwaukee, Wis.: Chipstone Foundation, 2003).

162 Circular birdcages are not unique to Chester County; several small stands with circular birdcages have been found in West Virginia and the North Carolina Piedmont. For an example of a North Carolina candlestand with circular birdcage, see Skinner, *The Meryl & Jay Weiss Collection*, Boston, Feb. 18, 2007, lot 115. For other examples recorded by MESDA, Old Salem Museums & Gardens, see MESDA research W-12-11, NCP-12-76, and NCP-12-75.

163 A tea table almost identical to Winterthur's table is in the collection of the Chester County Historical Society (acc. no. FT8); it differs

from the Winterthur table in that it does not have carving on the legs or epaulets at the top of the legs. A small stand with a circular birdcage is also in the CCHS collection (G1-76-F-t-29). For an image of a similar stand, see advertisement of H. L Chalfant, *Chester County Historical Society Antiques Show Catalogue* (West Chester, Pa.: CCHS, 2010); for more on Chester County tea tables, see Connie Hershey, "Bird Cages & Pad Feet: Walnut Tea Tables from Southeastern Pennsylvania," in the same catalogue, 18–21. A number of circular birdcage tea tables are in private collections and have been exhibited in the area by various dealers over the years.

164 For maple examples without the circular birdcage, see Pook & Pook, *Period Furniture and Accessories*, Downingtown, Pa., Sept. 2008, lot 395; Schiffer, *Furniture and Its Makers*, fig. 41; for walnut examples, see Schiffer, *Arts and Crafts,* 105; Schiffer, *Furniture and Its Makers,* fig. 151.

165 For another scallop-top tea table see Sotheby's, *Important Americana: The Collection of Dr. and Mrs. Henry P. Deyerle*, Charlottesville, Va., May 26–27, 1995, lot 691. At least one other (probably) southern mahogany table with scalloped top is also known.

166 The two desks and chest with carved quarter columns are in private collections. A chest of drawers is pictured in *The Magazine Antiques* 69, no. 4 (April 1956): 298. On the clock cases, see Richard S. Machmer and Rosemarie B. Machmer, *Berks County Tall-Case Clocks, 1750–1850* (Reading, Pa.: Historical Society Press of Berks County, 1995), 19. Three of the tall clocks contain movements by Reading clockmakers Benjamin Witman, Thomas Wildbahn, and Jacob Diehl. Two are in the collection of Yale University Art Gallery; for the Witman clock, see Edwin A. Battison and Patricia E. Kane, *The American Clock, 1725–1865* (Greenwich, Conn.: New York Graphic Society for Yale University Art Gallery, 1973), 142–45. The Witman clock also has inlay on the case, and inlaid on the pendulum door is the name "CHR FAHL" and the date "1801," which may relate to the Fahl family of Orwigsburg, now in Schuylkill County. The second clock at Yale with replaced movement is of striped maple and has carving closely related to the Witman as well as the table and desks. For the Jacob Diehl clock, see Machmer and Machmer, *Berks County Tall-Case Clocks,* 41, fig. 3. A related

clock case with movement by Thomas Wildbahn of Reading is in a private collection. A chest-on-chest with carved quarter columns and vine-and-floral leaf carving in the tympanum was sold at Pook & Pook, *Period Furniture and Accessories*, Downington, Pa., Feb. 27, 2009, lot 313.

167 On the work of Charles C. Hofmann, see Thomas N. Armstrong III, *Pennsylvania Almshouse Painters* (Williamsburg, Va.: Colonial Williamsburg Foundation, 1968); also Stacy C. Hollander, *American Radiance: The Ralph Esmerian Gift to the American Folk Art Museum* (New York: Harry N. Abrams, 2000), 94, 416.

168 Rayner Wickersham Kelsey, ed., *Cazenove Journal 1794: A Record of the Journey of Theophile Cazenove through New Jersey and Pennsylvania (Translated from the French)* (Haverford, Pa.: Pennsylvania History Press, 1922), 72–74.

169 Perkins, "Command You Me from Play," 17–18.

170 The Brackbill-Neff table sold at Skinner, *Fine Americana*, Boston, June 5, 1993, lot 64. It is closely related to a mahogany example in the M. and M. Karolik Collection at the Museum of Fine Arts, Boston; see Edwin J. Hipkiss, *Eighteenth-Century American Arts in the M. and M. Karolik Collection* (Cambridge: Harvard University Press, 1950), 108–9. For another related table, see Freeman's, *Fine American Furniture & Decorative Arts*, Philadelphia, Nov. 14–15, 2009, lot 770. For a less highly carved cherrywood example, see Sotheby's, *Important Americana from the Collection of Mr. and Mrs. James O. Keene*, New York, Jan. 16, 1997, lot 195.

171 John J. Snyder Jr., "The Bachman Attributions: A Reconsideration," *The Magazine Antiques* 105, no. 5 (May 1974): 1056–65.

172 John J. Snyder Jr., "Carved Chippendale Case Furniture from Lancaster, Pennsylvania," *The Magazine Antiques* 107, no. 5 (May 1975): 964–75; see also Alexandra Rollins, ed., *Treasures of State: Fine and Decorative Arts in the Diplomatic Reception Rooms of the Department of State* (New York: Harry N. Abrams, 1991), 193, fig. 103.

173 Snyder, "Carved Chippendale Case Furniture," 967.

174 A slant-front desk signed on the bottom board "This Desk was [ill.] / Conrad Doll [ill.]" is in the collection of the Historical Society of Fred-

erick County, Md. An 1875 inscription indicates that the desk was made by Doll for John Brunner in 1787 and was purchased by Jacob Engelbrecht from his estate in 1829.

175 Withers is listed as a gunsmith in the Lancaster tax assessments, LCHS craftsmen database. In 1775 he was called upon by the Lancaster Committee of Safety to make firearms for the Revolutionary army; for more, see Stacy B. C. Wood Jr. and James Bizer Whisker, *Arms Makers of Lancaster County, Pennsylvania* (Bedford, Pa.: Old Bedford Village Press, 1991), 53–54. Michael likely made a nutcracker (Winterthur 1969.784) as a present for his younger sister Elizabeth Wither[s] (b. 1758) using metalworking techniques he learned from making gun barrels and locks. The nutcracker is engraved with her name and the inscription "When this you see, Remember Me" in script on both sides of the jaws; see Donald L. Fennimore, *Iron at Winterthur* (Winterthur, Del.: Henry Francis du Pont Winterthur Museum, 2004), 220–21.

176 Edgar Sittig and Charlotte Sittig to H. F. du Pont, June 9, 1952, Folder: Bills-Sittig, Edgar. H., Antiques Dealer Correspondence Files, Box 4, Winterthur Archives, Winterthur Library.

177 Elizabeth Withers Shertz was the daughter of Catharine Withers (b. 1837) and John J. Shertz. Catharine's parents were George Withers (1798–1876) and Elizabeth Metzger (1802–91). Her father, George, was the nephew of Michael Withers, first owner of the desk. Catharine's brother Michael (1830–88) married Elizabeth Fahnestock in 1866. In the 1900 census, Elizabeth Withers Shertz lived in Lancaster with her aunt Elizabeth, widow of Michael Withers. The Sittigs had described the desk as "from Dr. Wither's family." He has been identified as Dr. Michael Augustus Withers (1829–1909), youngest child of Michael Withers (1791–1873), one of the two nephews of desk owner Michael Withers. On the Withers-Shertz family, see John Franklin Meginness, *Biographical Annals of Lancaster County* (Chicago: J. H. Beers & Co., 1903), 1097–98.

178 See Snyder, "Bachman Attributions," 1058, 1061–62.

179 Lancaster furniture made of mahogany includes the Slough high chest in the collection of the Heritage Center of Lancaster County; a dressing table at the Metropolitan Museum of Art (see Morrison H. Heckscher, *American Furniture in the Metropolitan Museum of Art, II: Late Colonial Period, The Queen Anne and Chippendale Styles* [New York: Random House for the Metropolitan Museum of Art, 1985], 262); and a tea table in the Karolik Collection at the Museum of Fine Arts, Boston (see Hipkiss, *Eighteenth-Century American Arts*, 108–9).

180 In 1983 scholars had attributed the Withers desk-and-bookcase to members of the Lind family (Michael Sr. and Michael Jr.), but in 1984 John J. Snyder Jr. suggested that since Withers is mentioned twice in the estate accounts of George Burkhart (1721–83) and Burkhart's sons continued the workshop until at least 1791, circumstantial evidence exists for associating the Withers desk-and-bookcase with the Burkhart shop. Though Snyder did conclude that "at present it seems wisest to regard this piece as the product of an unknown Lancaster workshop" (See John J. Snyder Jr., "New Discoveries in Documented Lancaster County Chippendale Furniture," *The Magazine Antiques,* 125, no. 5 [May 1984], 1150–55).

181 Gregory Landrey, "Straightening Up an Old Secretary: What Winterthur Conservators Do about 200 Years of Sag," *Fine Woodworking* 40 (May/June 1983): 66–69.

182 This chest sold at Sotheby's, *Important American Folk Art, Furniture, and Silver*, New York, May 19, 2005, lot 249.

183 This chest is illustrated in Herbert F. and Peter B. Schiffer, *Miniature Antique Furniture* (Wynnewood, Pa: Livingston Publishing Co., 1972), 61; another one with very different carving on the front and drawer fronts is associated with a Lancaster group and is illustrated in the same source, p. 60. Another miniature chest with carved shell on the front and two small drawers with carved shells, also from the Lancaster group, is pictured in Richard S. Machmer and Rosemarie B. Machmer, *Just for Nice: Carving and Whittling Magic of Southeastern Pennsylvania* (Reading, Pa.: Historical Society of Berks County, 1991), fig. 14. This chest was sold at Pook & Pook, *The Collection of Dr. Donald and Esther Shelley*, Downingtown, Pa., Apr. 20–21, 2007, lot 710.

184 The Ensminger portraits were sold at Pook & Pook, *Important Americana from the Personal Collection of the Late H. William Koch*, Downingtown, Pa., June 5, 1999, lot 140; see also "The Farm Sale of All Time: The Koch Sale," in *Maine Antique Digest: The Americana Chronicles: 30 Years of Stories, Sales, Personalities, and Scandals*, ed. Lita Solis-Cohn (Philadelphia: Running Press, 2004). On Jacob Maentel, see Mary Black, *Simplicity, A Grace: Jacob Maentel in Indiana* (Evansville, Ind.: Evansville Museum of Arts & Science, 1989); Mary Lou Robson Fleming, "Folk Artist Jacob Maentel of Pennsylvania and Indiana," *Pennsylvania Folklife* 37, no. 3 (Spring 1988): 98–111; and Mary Lou Fleming and Marianne Ruch, "Jacob Maentel: A Second Look," *Pennsylvania Folklife* 41, no. 1 (Autumn 1991): 2–19. These two images were probably originally displayed in separate frames and united later.

185 Samuel Ensminger inventory, no. 1867, F007E #:031, LCHS.

186 Raymond Martin Bell, *The Ensminger Family*, rev. ed. (Washington, Pa.: Washington and Jefferson College, 1961), 21.

187 For one of these desk-and-bookcases, see Snyder, "Bachman Attributions," 1061–62. Another, with the name "Samuel Rice/May 10, 1801" is illustrated in the advertisement of Israel Sack, Inc., *The Magazine Antiques* 122, no. 3 (September 1982), inside cover, and also in *Israel Sack Collection*, 7:2028–29.

188 Hess, *Mennonite Arts*, 38.

189 Ryan, *Jacob Eichholtz*, 39–40.

190 On John Hoff, see Stacy B. C. Wood Jr., *Clockmakers and Watchmakers of Lancaster County, Pennsylvania* (Lancaster: Lancaster County Historical Society, 1995), 46–48.

191 For more on Nottingham-area furniture and its makers, see forthcoming article by Wendy A. Cooper and Mark J. Anderson, in *American Furniture* (Chipstone Foundation).

192 A similar clock is in the collection of the CCHS, no. CLx9. It was originally owned by Moses Brinton (1725–89), who was born in Thornbury Township, Chester County, and died in Leacock Township, Lancaster County. That clock is missing its sarcophagus top, but the unusual ball-and-claw feet appear to be original. The feet on Winterthur's clock were missing and the replacements were copied (by Mark J. Anderson) from the Brinton clock in the late 1980s.

193 Hubertis M. Cummings, *The Mason and Dixon Line: Story for a Bicentenary, 1763–1963*

(Harrisburg: Commonwealth of Pennsylvania, 1962).

194 "The Nottingham Lotts and the Early Quaker Families," paper presented by Robert Warwick Day, Spartanburg, S.C., Sept. 29, 2001, at the East Nottingham Monthly Meeting, Calvert, Cecil County, Md.

195 McDowell came to Philadelphia in 1758 and in 1764 married Elizabeth Loughead of Concord Township. In 1768 Elizabeth inherited land in Oxford, where they moved in the early 1770s and opened a general store. James was a patriot and supported the revolutionary cause by organizing a Chester County militia that became part of the 4th battalion. In 1785 he was appointed captain of the Light Horse Brigade of Chester County. After the Revolution McDowell returned to his farm and continued as a merchant, farmer, and miller. His daughter Jane married Philadelphia cabinetmaker John Aitken, and in 1815 he bought 325 acres of his late father-in-law's farm and moved there from Philadelphia.

196 Schiffer, *Furniture and Its Makers*, 40, figs. 7, 8. Schiffer had relied on Gilbert Cope's 1864 genealogy of the Brown family, never finding a will or inventory for the Brown born in 1724. She did cite a 1797 document for a Jacob Brown, joiner, West Nottingham, giving a mortgage to a Sarah Armstrong. That Jacob was probably the joiner who made the McDowell clock, though when he died in 1802, West Nottingham was in Cecil County, Md., an explanation for why a will and inventory for Jacob the joiner were not found in Chester County records.

197 For the inventory and vendue of Jacob Brown, see Cecil County Register of Wills (Inventories) vol. 12, 481–86, Maryland State Archives. With thanks to Sasha Lourie and Elaine Rice Bachmann for their assistance in locating this document.

198 For images and a discussion of the clock movement, see Hohmann, *Timeless*, 198–99. For an illustration of this clock prior to its restoration, see Edward E. Chandlee, *Six Quaker Clockmakers* (Philadelphia: Historical Society of Pennsylvania, 1943), 78. In the photograph it appears to be truncated at the base, but this was not the case. In order to preserve the top and fit it into a much lower ceiling space, the floor was cut and the base of the clock was

dropped through into the basement. At that time the feet had already been removed.

199 When Winterthur acquired this tall clock, the McCauley family tradition stated that it was originally owned by Roland Rogers of East Nottingham about 1758 and that John Price acquired Rogers's plantation near the Bohemia River in Cecil County, Md., including the clock, sometime prior to 1816, when he bequeathed both to his son Hiland. It is true that Price owned a plantation on the Bohemia River, which he left to his grandson John, but it appears from his will that it was "the plantation and parcel of Land lying and being in east Nottingham Cecil County I purchased of William Rogers and Roland Rogers" that he left to Hiland; see Will of John Price, May 8, 1816, Cecil County Register of Wills, vol. 7, 160, Maryland State Archives. With thanks to Sasha Lourie and Elaine Rice Bachmann for their assistance in locating this document.

200 This high chest descended through the Draper family of Wilmington, Del., from Dr. James Avery Draper in the late nineteenth century; it is unclear whether the Draper family collected or inherited it. A dressing table that may have been made en suite was sold by Philip H. Bradley Co.; its present location is unknown. A related high chest, once owned by Joe Kindig III and sold to Jeffrey Tillou, was advertised in *The Magazine Antiques* 159, no. 1 (January 2001): 95. It was originally discovered by Kindig in Virginia with a history of having been in Port Deposit, Md. (Cecil County) in the late nineteenth century.

201 This desk-and-bookcase sold at Sotheby's, *Important American Folk Art, Furniture, and Silver,* New York, May 19, 2005, lot 256.

202 For Coudon's inventory, see Cecil County Register of Wills (Inventories) vol. 10, 217–20, Maryland State Archives. With thanks to Sasha Lourie and Elaine Rice Bachmann for their assistance in locating this document.

203 See Chandlee, *Six Quaker Clockmakers*.

204 Only one complete movement by Cottey is known, along with an engraved dial that bears his name. The movement bears the date "1709" and the initials "B C" on one of the plates, suggesting that by that date his apprentice, Benjamin Chandlee Sr., was involved in making Cottey's clocks. This clock is now privately owned; for an illustration, see Pook & Pook, Downingtown, Pa., Jan. 14–15, 2010, lot 791.

205 For a wrought-iron candlestand stamped "CHANDLEE" that, by family tradition, was used by Benjamin Chandlee Jr. in his shop, see Fennimore, *Iron at Winterthur*, 175–77.

206 On Carlisle, see Judith Anne Ridner, "A Handsomely Improved Place: Economic, Social, and Gender Role Development in a Backcountry Town, Carlisle, Pennsylvania, 1750–1815" (Ph.D. diss., College of William and Mary, 1994); Judith Anne Ridner, *A Town In-Between: Carlisle, Pennsylvania, and the Early Mid-Atlantic Interior* (Philadelphia: University of Pennsylvania Press, 2010).

207 Lindsey, *Cazenove*, 56–57.

208 See E. F. LaFond Jr., "Some Reflections Regarding Distant Influences on Early Cumberland County Clocks," in *Made in Cumberland County, The First Hundred Years, 1750–1850*, ed. Milton E. Flower et al. (Carlisle, Pa.: Cumberland County Historical Society, 1991). LaFond notes that "John Fisher who was also a great inventive person may have designed the peculiar 'J Hook' striking system which occurs with some frequency in Jacob Herwick's early clocks," further supporting the possibility that Herwick trained with Fisher in York.

209 Her father was Conrad Holtzbaum of York; in his will he referred to his daughter, who was married to Jacob Herwick. With thanks to Merri Lou Schaumann for this information.

210 *Kline's Gazette,* May 24, 1786; see Flower, *Made in Cumberland County*, 42.

211 This letter was sent to Hamilton in regard to cases no. 11 and 12 at the August Term 1798 Court; the original document is in the manuscript collection of the Cumberland County Historical Society, folder 33-9. With thanks to Merri Lou Schaumann, who kindly shared this document.

212 This clock is now in the Cumberland County Historical Society, see Flower, *Made in Cumberland County*, 20–21, 31; also Civic Club of Carlisle, Pennsylvania, *Carlisle Old and New* (Harrisburg, Pa.: J. Horace McFarland Co., 1907), 125.

213 This motto was adopted by the Grand Lodge of England and was engraved on a Masonic token of 1794 to commemorate the election of the Prince of Wales as the Most Worshipful Grand Master, Nov. 24, 1790; see http://www.encyclopediaoffreemasonry.com.

214 For more on Nettle and Figure, see John Hervy, *Racing in America, 1665–1865* (New York: Jockey Club, 1944), 1:45–46.

CHAPTER 3

1 Will of Elizabeth Bartram, 1771, no. 2669, Chester County Archives (hereafter CCA).

2 Thomas Hicks was a first cousin once-removed from noted Quaker minister and painter Edward Hicks. Thomas worked with his older cousin as early as 1836 and was encouraged by him in his work. By 1839 Thomas entered the Pennsylvania Academy of the Fine Arts and later studied in New York and abroad. For more on Edward Hicks, see Carolyn J. Weekley, *The Kingdoms of Edward Hicks* (New York: Harry N. Abrams for the Colonial Williamsburg Foundation, 1999), 188.

3 The bold scrolling line inlay with varied terminations of single petals, cluster of three berries, and a diamond above the date relates closely to examples of early eighteenth-century Welsh inlay; see Lee Ellen Griffith, "Line-and-Berry Inlaid Furniture: A Regional Craft Tradition in Pennsylvania, 1682–1790" (Ph.D. diss., University of Pennsylvania, 1988), 160–69.

4 This example is in the collection of the Chester County Historical Society (hereafter CCHS), Acc. F111, gift of Bart Anderson, with a history of ownership in the Hutton family of Chester County; see Margaret Berwind Schiffer, *Furniture and Its Makers of Chester County, Pennsylvania* (Philadelphia: University of Pennsylvania Press, 1966), fig. 122; also see figs. 120–21 for the Bartram table.

5 In 1725 John Owen (d. 1752) was commissioned to make an oval table measuring 7 by 8 feet for an upstairs room in the Chester County courthouse, as well as a table for the grand jury room measuring 6 by 5 feet, for which he was paid £5.10.0 in 1726. Family tradition states that this table is the one at Primitive Hall owned by Joseph Pennock; see Schiffer, *Furniture and Its Makers,* 190–91, no. 85. This large gateleg table roughly fits the dimensions of one of the tables made by Owen—74 inches by 86 inches; however, the table has had significant restorations.

6 For references to these tables, see Frances Gruber Safford, *American Furniture in the Metropolitan Museum of Art, I:. Early Colonial Period, The Seventeenth Century and William and Mary Styles* (New Haven: Yale University Press in association with the Metropolitan Museum of Art, 2007), 157–59.

7 Inventory of James Bartram, 1771, no. 2632, CCA; will of Elizabeth Bartram, 1771, no. 2669, CCA.

8 Jack L. Lindsey, *Worldly Goods: The Arts of Early Pennsylvania, 1680–1758* (Philadelphia: Philadelphia Museum of Art, 1999), 119, fig. 187, 145, fig. 52. This dressing table was sold at Freeman's, Philadelphia, May 4–7, 1927, lot 554, formerly the property of Hannah P. Lawrence. It is pictured in William Macpherson Hornor Jr., *Blue Book, Philadelphia* (1935; reprint, Washington, D.C.: Highland House Publishers, 1977), pl. 19; and Wallace Nutting, *Furniture Treasury*, 3 vols. (Framingham, Mass.: Old America Co., 1928–33), 1:pl. 390.

9 Hannah was the daughter of Henry Lawrence and Mary Ashbridge, who married in 1821. Henry was the son of Joshua and Mary Maris Lawrence. Mary was the daughter of Isaac and Elizabeth Howell Maris, and Elizabeth Howell Maris was the granddaughter of the Bartrams and the sister of Sarah Howell to whom the dressing table was left by Elizabeth Bartram.

10 Richard Maris was a "yeoman" (farmer) according to his will of 1742 , no. 927, CCA. That said, he had significant land holdings in Springfield and collected rents on his properties. When he died in 1745, he left 150 acres to his daughter Elizabeth Bartram.

11 See Sotheby's, *Important Americana, Including Silver, Flags, Folk Art & Furniture*, New York, May 23, 2002, lot 316.

12 This sale is recorded in an Indenture (deed) between Bartholomew Coppock, "yeoman," and James Bartram "joyner," dated Apr. 6, 1726 (private collection).

13 The Coppock house was built by 1726 and expanded later but was in ruins by the 1950s. Fireplace mantels and interior woodwork (including several stair balusters) were salvaged by noted collector Joe McFalls and are now in a private collection. The mantels were included in the exhibition *Worldly Goods: The Arts of Early Pennsylvania, 1680–1758*; see also Elisabeth Donaghy Garrett, "Living with Antiques: A Collection of Early Delaware River Valley Furnishings," *The Magazine Antiques* 131, no. 1 (January 1987): 282–87. Bartholomew Coppock also owned 338 acres in East Marlborough Township; see "Lands around London Grove Meeting, 1700–1730," map drawn by Gilbert Cope, in *Two Hundredth Anniversary of London Grove Meeting* (Philadelphia: Innes & Sons, 1914); BX 7780.L8 1914, CCHS.

14 Will and inventory of James Bartram, 1771, no. 2632, CCA.

15 See Schiffer, *Furniture and Its Makers*, 213.

16 Bennett S. Pancoast, *The Pancoast Family in America* (Woodbury, N.J.: Gloucester County Historical Society, 1981), 12, 27–28; and William Wade Hinshaw, *Encyclopedia of American Quaker Genealogy*, vol. 2., *Pennsylvania and New Jersey* (1938; reprint, Baltimore: Genealogical Publishing Co., 1994). Will and inventory of James Bartram, 1771, no. 2632, CCA; inventory of Elizabeth Bartram, 1771, no. 2669, CCA.

17 Will of Bartholomew Coppock, 1761, no. 1938, CCA.

18 The primary differences between the high chest and dressing table can be seen in the execution of the shells on the knees and the brasses, which appear to be original on both pieces. The overall similarity in every other respect suggests that they may have been owned in the same family but ordered at different times, explaining the carving (done without having the first piece on hand to copy) and the brasses (bought at another time when the pattern on the first piece was not available). This high chest was sold at Sotheby's, *Important Americana*, New York, Jan. 24–30, 1995, lot 2004.

19 Tillou Gallery advertisement, *The Magazine Antiques* 81, no. 3 (March 1962): 259.

20 See 77.889, Decorative Arts Photographic Collection, Winterthur Library. The high chest was originally made for John Morris (d. 1784) of Marple Township. It then descended via his daughter through the Moore family. For more on Pancoast, see *Pancoast Family in America*.

21 It is not known whether John Wood Sr. (d. 1760–61) or Jr. (1736–93) was the principal maker of the numerous clocks movements that are simply signed "John Wood," but the early date of the case on this clock suggests the father.

22 Alice Lindborg and Carl Lindborg, *Historic Newtown Township, 1681–1983* (Newtown, Pa.: Newtown Tricentennial Commission, 1984), 28–35.

23 Thomas Thomas inventory, 1774, no. 2872, CCA.

24 Lindborg and Lindborg, *Historic Newtown Township,* 30, n.17a. A wainscot armchair with a history of ownership in the William Lewis family was sold by Pook & Pook, *Period Furniture, Fine Art, and Decorative Accessories,* Downingtown, Pa., Oct. 2, 2010, lot 749.

25 A similar treatment can be found on a Welsh chest dated 1782 from Carthmenshire/Cardiganshire, in which the numerals of the date are distinctly checked, and a Welsh chest-on-chest with desk inlaid "A+T" from Carmarthenshire, dated about 1784; see Richard Bebb, *Welsh Furniture, 1250–1950: A Cultural History of Craftsmanship and Design,* 2 vols. (Kidwelly, Carmarthenshire, U.K.: Saer Books, 2007), 2:151, 406.

26 The "S S" box and chest of drawers were sold by American Art Association, *Colonial Furniture: The Superb Collection of the Late Howard Reifsnyder,* New York, Apr. 24–27, 1929, lots 585, 627. The box was bought by Henry Ford and the chest of drawers by William Randolph Hearst, which was later purchased by Jackson Martindell at Hearst's sale, Parke-Bernet Galleries, New York, in 1938; Martindell's heirs consigned it to Sotheby's, *Important Americana,* New York, May 23, 2002, lot 316.

27 Lindborg and Lindborg, *Historic Newtown Township,* 28.

28 Sarah Longstreth Jones (b. 1834) and Mary Jane Jones (b. 1842) were the daughters of Hannah Minshall John Jones (1808–89); Hannah was the daughter of Jane Longstreth (1784–1834) and Samuel Preston John; she married Robert Jones (1796–1868). Jane Longstreth John was the daughter of Jane Minshall Longstreth (1742/3–1813), daughter of Sarah Smedley Minshall (1717–1801), first owner of the chest of drawers and box. Sarah Longstreth and Mary Jane Jones died unmarried; their sister Henrietta Deville Jones (b. 1838) married Thomas Brown and had two daughters: Jennie Jones (b. 1863) and Lydia Townsend (b. 1867). Lydia married Henry M. Jones (b. 1855); in the 1920 census their household in Germantown included her sister Jennie. Jennie died unmarried in 1922, thus her sister Lydia would have become sole owner of the objects. According to the Reifsnyder catalogue, the last owner of the chest of drawers and box was Mrs. Henry M. Jones of Germantown, now identified as Lydia Townsend

Brown. The catalogue also states that these objects had descended to a Sarah in each of several generations. Although the 1901 Smedley genealogy notes that the chest of drawers was owned by descendants of Sarah Smedley Minshall's daughter Jane Longstreth, it is possible that it did not descend directly through this line (which had few Sarahs). Sarah Smedley Minshall also had a daughter named Sarah (1745–1811) who married James Starr in 1769; their daughter Sarah (1772–1818) married John Hutton and died without issue. At that time, the objects may have passed to the Longstreth-John-Jones branch of the family and thus to Sarah Longstreth and Mary Jane Jones. On the Smedley family, see Gilbert Cope, *Genealogy of the Smedley Family* (Lancaster, Pa.: Wickersham Printing Co., 1901), 33, 144–45, 255, 425–27 and J. Smith Futhey and Gilbert Cope, *History of Chester County, Pennsylvania, with Genealogical and Biographical Sketches* (Philadelphia: J. B. Lippincott, 1881), 725–26.

29 Collection of CCHS, donated by Francis and Deborah Brinton, 1944; see Margaret Berwind Schiffer, *Arts and Crafts of Chester County, Pennsylvania* (Exton, Pa.: Schiffer Publishing, 1980), 71.

30 The "S T" box is at Winterthur (1958.552) and the "E C" box is at Bartram's Garden. On the underside of the "S T" box is what appears to be a contemporary pencil inscription: "S. Thomas/ July 18, 1783"; inside the top is a later inscription: "Chest of Sarah Thomas, made in 1756 md to/ Jo. Walker of Tredyiffrin Tp./ Chester County." Although this box lacks the ornate diamond inlay used on the clock, the checkered initials are identical in form to those on the clock. Perhaps by the time this box was made the fashion for more elaborate inlay had passed and only the more simple initials were desired. In addition, Thomas Thomas was sixty-nine in 1756—the year that the box was allegedly made for Sarah Thomas—and he may have been physically unable to execute more elaborate inlay.

31 The pocketbook is at Winterthur Museum, 1976.177.

32 Samuel Lamborn, *The Genealogy of the Lamborn Family* (Philadelphia: M. L. Marion, 1894), 60.

33 This chest is pictured in Nutting, *Furniture Treasury,* 1:pl. 70; it was given to the Germantown Historical Society in 1977 from the estate of Florence K. Baker, but it not known

whether she inherited or collected it. The Pennocks of East Marlborough Township, also members of London Grove Meeting, owned a similar paneled storage chest over two drawers that is still at Primitive Hall, the house they built in 1738 in East Marlborough. Another related walnut chest is owned by Tyler Arboretum and is said to have been made for Jacob and Ann (Heacock) Minshall.

34 The spice box sold at Freeman's, Philadelphia, Oct. 5–7, 1995, lot 1025.

35 The Lamborn spice box descended directly through the family; when it sold at Freeman's, the following provenance was stated: "Wedding gift, Robert Lamborn (1723–81) m. 1746 Anne Bourne (?–1790), to Susanna Lamborn (1749–1839) m. 1768 John Marshall, farmer, to William Marshall (1784–1857) m. 1876 Margaret McCamon (1791–1883?), to Susanna Jane Marshall (1831–1927) m. 1861 Francis Wilkinson, to Mary Philips Wilkinson (1867–1964) m. 1903 William Colson Coles (1867–1954), to William Colson Coles Jr. (1905–95) m. 1933 Edith Darnell Lippincott (1906–95), to present owners." Since the box is dated two years after their marriage, clearly it wasn't a wedding gift. Although the Lamborns were married in London Grove and resided in that area during the early years of their marriage, soon after midcentury Robert's father gave him a tract of land in Kennett Township, where he and his wife resided the remainder of their lives. With thanks to Jim Guthrie for sharing his research on the Lamborn property.

36 The only dated spice box known to coincide with a date of marriage is the 1788 box made for Mary Hutton Hurford (see fig. 1.15), which is also an unusually late example; see Lee Ellen Griffith, *The Pennsylvania Spice Box: Paneled Doors and Secret Drawers* (West Chester, Pa.: CCHS, 1986), 21–22, 108–9.

37 It is not unusual for these spice boxes to have secret drawers accessed from the back, but the manner in which the drawers are accessed here is different. A similar mechanism was used on the 1744 spice box made for Thomas and Elisabeth Hutton and on the box made in 1788 for Mary Hutton Hurford; however, the Hurford backboard is in two parts so that the entire board does not have to slide to access the drawers, only the upper part of the board is lifted to reveal the drawers; see Ibid., 108–9.

38 Ronald L. Hurst and Jonathan Prown, eds., *Southern Furniture, 1680–1830: The Colonial*

Williamsburg Collection (New York: Harry N. Abrams for the Colonial Williamsburg Foundation, 1997), 142. The North Carolina box is pictured in John Bivins Jr., *The Furniture of Coastal North Carolina, 1700–1820* (Winston-Salem, N.C.: MESDA, 1988), 373.

39 With thanks to Tara Gleason Chicirda, curator of furniture at Colonial Williamsburg, for calling our attention to this box and for the information.

40 Diane E. Wenger, *A Country Storekeeper in Pennsylvania: Creating Economic Networks in Early America, 1790–1807* (University Park: Pennsylvania State University Press, 2008), 28.

41 See Pook & Pook, *The Pioneer Americana Collection of Dr. and Mrs. Donald A. Shelley,* Downingtown, Pa., Apr. 20–21, 2007, lot 326. Ex-collection of Charlotte and Edgar Sittig.

42 In addition to Winterthur's clock with movement by Jacob Graff, three others are known in private collections; one can be documented as having been made for Leonard Holstine, as a payment of £3.5.0 to "Jacob Graff in part of a Clock" was made by his executors and recorded in the settlement of his estate in 1760. For images and a discussion of the musical clock, see Frank L. Hohmann III, *Timeless: Masterpiece American Brass Dial Clocks* (New York: Hohmann Holdings LLC, 2009), 222–23.

43 For a discussion of the Miller's tall clock and this disc, see Lisa Minardi, "A Timely Discovery: The Story of Winterthur's Jacob Graff Clock," *The Catalogue of Antiques and Fine Art* 7, no. 5 (Spring 2007): 238–39.

44 Edward F. LaFond Jr. and J. Carter Harris, *Pennsylvania Shelf and Bracket Clocks, 1750–1850* (Columbia, Pa.: National Association of Watch and Clock Collectors, 2008), 128. A tall-case clock in a private collection has a related hood inlaid with the date "1773" and movement by John Miller of Germantown.

45 Another fraktur by this same hand was made for the Millers to record the birth and baptism of their son Johannes in 1767; it was formerly in the collection of Joane and Richard Flanders Smith.

46 Frederick S. Weiser and Howell J. Heaney, *The Pennsylvania German Fraktur in the Collection of the Free Library of Philadelphia: An Illustrated Catalogue*, Publications of the Pennsylvania German Society (hereafter PGS), vols. 10–11 (Breinigsville, Pa.: PGS, 1976), 10:fig. 23.

47 On the relationship between calligraphy and painted furniture, see Patricia J. Keller-Conner, "Workmanship, Form, and Cultural Identity: The Black-Unicorn Paint-Decorated Chests of Berks County, Pennsylvania" (Master's thesis, University of Delaware, 1984), 50–52. Other links between fraktur artists and painted furniture include a painted box made for Esther Kolb in 1810 with decoration attributed to David Kulp of Bedminster Township, Bucks County; see Cory M. Amsler, ed., *Bucks County Fraktur,* Publications of the PGS, vol. 33 (Kutztown, Pa.: PGS, 1999), 274; also a slide-lid box of Ezra Wiegner with a history of being made by his grandfather, fraktur artist David Kriebel (see fig. 1.63). On Henrich Otto, see Russell D. Earnest and Corinne P. Earnest, *Papers for Birth Dayes: A Guide to the Fraktur Artists and Scriveners* (East Berlin, Pa.: Russell D. Earnest Assoc., 1997), 2:594–600.

48 With thanks to Mary Weigley and Lila Lebo for their genealogical research assistance; see also Frederick S. Weiser, ed., *Weiser Families in America* (New Oxford, Pa.: John Conrad Weiser Family Assoc., 1997), 1:293; and F. Edward Wright, *Early Church Records of Lebanon County, Pennsylvania* (Westminster, Md.: Willow Bend Books, 2000). The Miller chest was sold at Pennypacker Auction Centre, *Important Americana Antique Sale: The Renowned Collection of Perry Martin*, Media, Pa., May 26, 1969, lot 306. Two other objects with related inlay are known: a chest with inlaid front and "Magthalena Krallen" written in similar fraktur lettering, and a tall-case clock with nameless white-painted dial that was previously owned by Luther and Pearl Sensenig of Wernersville, who received it from an Earl Taylor of Womelsdorf. The inlay on the Miller chest relates to a group of paint-decorated chests variously attributed to the so-called Embroidery Artist and noted for the use of intricate floral designs, sawtooth borders, and fraktur lettering; see, for example, a chest made for Catharina Mauer in 1795, Pook & Pook, *The Pioneer Collection of Dr. and Mrs. Donald A. Shelley*, Downingtown, Pa., Apr. 20–21, 2007, lot 753. For more on this group of furniture, see forthcoming article by Lisa Minardi in *American Furniture* (Chipstone Foundation).

49 On the proxemic relationships of objects and how they affect behavior, see Robert Blair St. George, *The Wrought Covenant: Source Material for the Study of Craftsmen and Commu-*

nity in Southeastern New England, 1620–1700 (Brockton, Mass.: Brockton Art Center, 1979), 17.

50 Winterthur Museum Registration Office file, acc. no. 1958.17.6. David Hottenstein's first wife, Sarah Herbein, died in 1766. In 1771 he married widow Maria Catharina (Hornecker) Appel (1730–1823). With thanks to Park Ritter for this information.

51 Scott T. Swank, "Henry Francis du Pont & Pennsylvania German Folk Art," in *Arts of the Pennsylvania Germans*, ed. Catherine E. Hutchins, 92–95, Publications of the PGS, vol. 17 (New York: W.W. Norton for the Henry Francis du Pont Winterthur Museum, 1983).

52 In addition to the Hottenstein schrank, related inlay is found on a chest made for Maria Kutz, dated 1783, in the collection of the Philadelphia Museum of Art (see Beatrice B. Garvan, *The Pennsylvania German Collection* [Philadelphia: Philadelphia Museum of Art, 1982], 21), and on a tall-case clock (1779) and slant-front desk (1775) in private collections.

53 Beds might be worth more in total due to the cost of the textiles, but clocks were an expensive investment.

54 For a complete description of the people in this photograph, see Joanne Hess Siegrist, *Mennonite Women of Lancaster County: A Story in Photographs from 1855–1935* (Intercourse, Pa.: Good Books, 1996), 71.

55 Benno M. Forman, "German Influences in Pennsylvania Furniture," in Hutchins, *Arts of the Pennsylvania Germans*, 148.

56 Wenger, *Country Storekeeper*, 34.

57 Cited in Alan G. Keyser, "The Stove Room in Pennsylvania" (unpublished manuscript). The 1736 Henry Antes house also has the outline of a clock on the partition between the Stube and Kammer.

58 For more on Mennonite clockmakers and the Möllingers of Germany, see Clarke Hess, *Mennonite Arts* (Atglen, Pa.: Schiffer Publishing, 2002), 77–79.

59 A clock with a similar but plainer case and unmarked dial with identical cast spandrels is at Yale; see Edwin A. Battison and Patricia E. Kane, *The American Clock, 1725–1865* (Greenwich, Conn.: New York Graphic Society for Yale University Art Gallery, 1973), 114–17.

60 Hess, *Mennonite Arts*, figs. 131–32, 79. Clock movements were brought by Mennonite immigrants of the 1800s as well; see Reinhild Kauenhoven Janzen and John M. Janzen, *Mennonite Furniture: A Migrant Tradition (1766–1910)* (Intercourse, Pa.: Good Books, 1991), 90–92, 101. When the Yunt clock came up for auction at Pennypacker's in 1964, it was described as a "Rare David Rittenhouse 30 Hour Grand Fathers Clock, walnut case, inlaid pendulum case . . . with double distlefink birds pewter and wrought iron dial, this is without doubt a David Rittenhouse clock. A truly rare clock"; Pennypacker Auction Centre, *Various Collections*, Reading, Pa., Apr. 18, 1964, lot 507.

61 On the Bergstrasse Lutheran Church, see Charles H. Glatfelter, *Pastors and People: German Lutheran and Reformed Churches in the Pennsylvania Field, 1717–1733*, Publications of the PGS, vols. 13, 15 (Breinigsville, Pa.: PGS, 1980–81), 13:305–6.

62 George Yunt, Lancaster County will book C, vol. 1, 404–5, Lancaster County Historical Society (hereafter LCHS).

63 Wood, Kramer, and Snyder, *Clockmakers of Lancaster County*, 143.

64 Attribution of the movement to Jacob Gorgas Sr. is supported by the Dishong family history as well as the close relationship of the movement to other signed Gorgas movements, according to clock authority Ed LaFond.

65 Donald F. Durnbaugh and Edward E. Quinter, trans. and eds., *The Day Book/Account Book of Alexander Mack, Jr. (1712–1803): Weaver, Brethren Elder, Apologist, and Chronicler in Early America*, Sources and Documents of the Pennsylvania Germans, vol. 14 (Kutztown, Pa.: PGS, 2004), 84–86, 93, 117, 133 n.46. Donald F. Durnbaugh, *The Brethren in Colonial America* (Elgin, Ill.: Brethren Press, 1967), 227; Martin G. Brumbaugh, *History of the German Baptist Brethren* (Elgin, Ill.: Brethren Publishing House, 1899), 181.

66 Deed of sale from William Dishong to Jacob Gorgas, Sept. 25, 1761, ms. 339, LCHS. For more information on Jacob Gorgas, see Ardis Krieg Lamb, "The True Identity of Christina Mack Gorgas, Wife of Jacob Gorgas, Clockmaker, Germantown, Philadelphia County, Pa., and Lancaster County, Pa., 1734–63" (unpublished manuscript), Historical Society of the Cocalico Valley, Ephrata, Pa.; also "The Gorgas Family," *The Magazine Antiques* 42, no.

3 (September 1942): 143–44; and Elizabeth W. Shaub, "The Gorgas Family of Cocalico Valley: Grandfather Clockmakers," *Journal of the Lancaster County Historical Society* 66, no. 4 (Autumn 1962): 169, 173–75. Gorgas had three sons: Joseph (1770–1838), who worked in Elizabethtown; Solomon (1764–1838); and Jacob Jr., who worked in Earl Township 1796–1814, and later in Mount Joy Township 1811–28; Stacy B. C. Wood Jr., "Clock and Watch Makers of Lancaster County, 1750–1850," *Journal of the Lancaster County Historical Society* 77, no. 4 (1973): 177.

67 Hess, *Mennonite Arts*, 16. Jacob Gorgas is listed as "of Ephrata" in a survey to partition the land of John Gorgas of Germantown, dated Sept. 19, 1749; he may have been in Ephrata as early as 1743, see Lamb, "True Identity," 5–6. Gorgas's gear cutting machine is in the collection of the Philadelphia Museum of Art, along with a brass-dial musical clock signed "Jacob Gorgas / Near Ephrata," presumably made before he and his sons bought a building on West Main Street, Ephrata, in 1767; see Garvan, *Pennsylvania German Collection*, 42–43. Gorgas is believed to have engraved his own dials; for more on Gorgas, see Hohmann, *Timeless*, 340–41.

68 Craftsmen database, LCHS.

69 William Dishong inventory, 1807, LCHS. With thanks to Cynthia Marquet at the Historical Society of the Cocalico Valley for this inventory.

70 Known clocks in related cases include a fairly plain example in the Winterthur collection (1965.2; see Forman, "German Influences," 153) and a more ornate case with pierced and carved tympanum that was exhibited by Kelly Kinzle at the 2009 Philadelphia Antiques Show; the latter clock was distinctive in that it had a watercolor portrait of a man inset in the door.

71 Will of Sarah Downing, 1835, no. 9324, CCA.

72 Futhey and Cope, *History of Chester County*, 173, 525. A lift-top walnut box with painted decoration on the front and the inscription "MT / 1744" (Winterthur Museum, 1965.2257) was made for either Thomas Downing's mother Mary Trimble (1736–1807; she married Joseph Downing in 1755 at Bradford Meeting) or grandmother Mary (Palmer) Trimble; the box descended through the Downing family to Mary Park Downing (d. 1870), then Thomas

W. Downing (d. 1940); it was acquired from Mary Roberts of Downingtown in 1940. See Garvan and Hummel, *Pennsylvania Germans*, fig. 76.

73 Arthur E. James, *Chester County Clocks and Their Makers* (Exton, Pa.: Schiffer Publishing, 1976), 199.

74 Ibid., 192.

75 For more information on Isaac Thomas's property in Willistown Township, see John Charles Nagy and Penny Teaf Goulding, *Acres of Quakers* (Willistown, Pa.: Willistown Township Historical Commission, 2006), 230–43. For a photograph and information on Thomas's grist mill, see Margaret Berwind Schiffer, *Survey of Chester County, Pennsylvania, Architecture: 17th, 18th, and 19th Centuries* (Exton, Pa.: Schiffer Publishing, 1984), 93; Stephen G. Del Sordo, "Eighteenth-Century Grist Mills: Some Chester County, Pennsylvania, Examples," in *Perspectives in Vernacular Architecture*, ed. Camille Wells, 71 (Annapolis, Md.: Vernacular Architecture Forum, 1982). The works of the Isaac Thomas gristmill are now owned by the Smithsonian Institution.

76 James, *Chester County Clocks*, 199; Schiffer, *Furniture and Its Makers*, 232–36.

77 Isaac Thomas inventory, 1802, no. 4905, CCA.

78 Schiffer, *Furniture and Its Makers*, 131.

79 Charles F. Hummel, *With Hammer in Hand: The Dominy Craftsmen of East Hampton, New York* (Charlottesville: University Press of Virginia for the Henry Francis du Pont Winterthur Museum, 1968).

80 Isaac Thomas will, 1801, no. 4905, CCA.

81 LaFond and Harris, *Pennsylvania Shelf and Bracket Clocks*, 6–7.

82 Thomas is not the only Pennsylvania clockmaker to have made round-dial faces; John Fisher of York County is known to have made at least one, and Joshua Humphreys of Tredyffrin Township, Chester County also made one; see Hohmann, *Timeless*, 212–13. The Humphreys tall clock is in the CCHS collection.

83 Isaac Thomas is also known to have used movements by London clockmaker Thomas Wagstaff, a fellow Quaker, for his name appears on the backs of three Wagstaff dials in Thomas cases; see LaFond and Harris, *Pennsylvania Shelf and Bracket Clocks*, 6.

84   For a tall chest with this border, see Northeast Auctions, July 31–Aug. 2, 2009, lot 590.

85   Schiffer, *Furniture and Its Makers*, figs. 79, 80.

86   Alpheus H. Harlan, *History and Genealogy of the Harlan Family, 1914* (Baltimore: Gateway Press, 1988), 52, 146.

87   Although unmarried Quaker women were not looked down upon, married women were usually leaders of the women's business meetings, as the matters they tended to, such as inspecting marriages and sexual offenses, necessitated experience. Spinster women who became ministers may have been able to marry wealthier men; see Barry Levy, *Quakers and the American Family: British Quakers in the Delaware Valley, 1650–1765* (New York: Oxford University Press, 1988), 125, 207, 213–14.

88   Lydia Harlan will and inventory, 1825, no. 7725, CCA. With thanks to Jim Guthrie for finding this citation.

89   George South, M.D., *History of Delaware County, Pennsylvania* (Philadelphia: Ashmead, 1884), 293.

90   Samuel Morris will and papers, no. 5574, CCA. With thanks to 2009 Winterthur Fellow Nicole Belolan for assistance with this research.

91   In 1821 a John Craig was listed as a cabinetmaker in Kennett Township; whether this is the same John Craig Sr. with whom Morris was living when he died is uncertain. Schiffer has inferred that this is the John Craig of Pennsbury Township who was found dead in the mill race at Chadds Ford in June 1871; see Schiffer, *Furniture and Its Makers*, 59.

92   The Knight of Glin and James Peill, *Irish Furniture: Woodwork and Carving in Ireland from the Earliest Times to the Act of Union* (New Haven: Yale University Press for the Paul Mellon Centre for Studies in British Art, 2007), 103–5; see also David Stockwell, "Irish Influence in Pennsylvania Queen Anne Furniture," *The Magazine Antiques* 79, no. 3 (March 1961): 269–71.

93   The eight chests-on-frame with nearly identical skirts include one owned by the Minshall family of Chester County and now at the Tyler Arboretum; one in the collection of Graeme Park, Horsham, Pa.; one advertised by Valdemar F. Jacobson in *Philadelphia Antiques Show Catalogue* (1985), 38; one advertised by C. L. Prickett, *The Magazine Antiques* 141, no. 4 (April 1992): 545. Two are signed and

dated respectively by Virgil Eachus in 1785 (this one has had its legs truncated) and 1789; see Schiffer, *Furniture and Its Makers*, 74–75, figs. 37, 38; and ad of Philip H. Bradley Co., *Chester County Historical Society Antiques Show Catalogue* (West Chester, Pa.: CCHS, 1997), back cover. Two are in private collections. For a slant-front desk on an identical frame, see ad for William's Antique Shop, *The Magazine Antiques* 75, no. 3 (March 1959): 236.

94   Bart Anderson, comp., "Notes," Eachus genealogy binders, CCHS. Benjamin Webb (d. 1765) and Daniel Webb (d. 1773) are both listed as joiners in Kennett Township.

95   Gregg (1763–1833), a member of an extensive Kennett family, is listed in Kennett tax assessments from 1796 through 1819 as a joiner or cabinetmaker, and he signed a receipt for a coffin as early as 1791. His 1833 inventory lists an extensive number of tools, including planes, saws, chisels, a turning lathe, a veneering saw, and "Lot beadsteads in Shop." Thomas may have been an apprentice of Gregg's, for he moved to Philadelphia and was listed in directories from 1809 to 1814; see Philip D. Zimmerman, "Early American Furniture Makers' Marks," in *American Furniture*, ed. Luke Beckerdite, 145–46 (Milwaukee, Wis.: Chipstone Foundation, 2007); and Schiffer, *Furniture and Its Makers*, 100–101.

96   Garvan, *Pennsylvania German Collection*, 13, 23. See also Patricia J. Keller, "Black-Unicorn Chests of Berks County, Pennsylvania," *The Magazine Antiques* 140, no. 4 (October 1991): 592–603.

97   This chest was once owned by Theodore Dwight Woolsey, president of Yale University, 1846–71. An almost identical chest, no doubt by the same hand, is pictured in Monroe H. Fabian, *The Pennsylvania-German Decorated Chest*, Publications of the PGS, vol. 12 (New York: Universe Books, 1978), 165, no. 159. A related chest, but without drawers and clearly painted by a different hand, is in the collection of the Philadelphia Museum of Art, no. 25-93-4. It is dated 1787 and has the name of Anna Maria Lescher on the front; see Garvan, *Pennsylvania German Collection*, 21.

98   The Hildenbrand chest has the initials "CB HB" on the front; when first published by Monroe H. Fabian, he interpreted this as the initials of a married couple. A chalk inscription on the underside of the top "Caspar Hildenbrand," however, confirmed that the initials are

an abbreviated form of the owner's full name. A similar practice is seen on the schrank made for David Hottenstein, which is initialed "DV HS"; see Fabian, *Pennsylvania-German Decorated Chest*, 124. The chest made for Margaret Kern in 1788 is in the Winterthur collection (1959.2804), see Swank, *Arts of the Pennsylvania Germans*, pl. 13; the Jacob Hill chest is privately owned.

99   John Joseph Stoudt, *Pennsylvania German Folk Art* (Allentown, Pa.: Pennsylvania German Folklore Society, 1966), 3–56, 108, 113.

100   Quoted in Alan G. Keyser, "Beds, Bedding, Bedsteads, and Sleep," *Der Reggeboge: Journal of the Pennsylvania German Society* 12, no. 4 (October 1978): 5.

101   Schiffer, *Furniture and Its Makers*, 233–34.

102   John Bamberger appears in tax records for Elizabeth Township, Lancaster County, from 1843 to 1849 as a joiner and cabinetmaker, while John Bamberger Jr. of Warwick Township is listed as a joiner and house carpenter from 1807 to 1835 and again in 1840; craftsmen database, LCHS.

103   Hess, *Mennonite Arts*, 58. For another example of commemorative dating on chests using birth years, see Janzen and Janzen, *Mennonite Furniture*, 79–80. On the rarity of signed furniture among Mennonite furniture in Europe and the American Midwest, see Janzen and Janzen, *Mennonite Furniture*, 83.

104   Hess, *Mennonite Arts*, 57–58

105   Pennypacker Auction Centre, *Walter Himmelreich Collection*, Reading, Pa., May 21, 1973, lot 63.

106   The Binder chest was advertised by G. K. S. Bush in *The Magazine Antiques* 143, no. 5 (May 1993): 642. See Fabian, *Pennsylvania-German Decorated Chest*, fig. 216, for the Muthart chest. The Schultz chest was sold by Kerry Pae Auctioneers, Palmyra, Pa., Feb. 5, 2009.

107   On the Eisz chest, see David Wheatcroft, *The Authentic Eye: Revisiting Folk Art Masterpieces* (Westborough, Mass.: David Wheatcroft Antiques, 2005), cat. no. 56; also Fabian, *Pennsylvania-German Decorated Chest*, pl. 231, 204; Jane Katcher, David Schorsch, and Ruth Wolfe, eds., *Expressions of Innocence and Eloquence: Selections from the Jane Katcher Collection of Americana* (New Haven: Yale University Press, 2007): 282–83.

108 Charles H. Glatfelter, *Pastors and People: German Lutheran and Reformed Churches in the Pennsylvania Field, 1717–1793*, Publications of the PGS, vols. 13, 15 (Breinigsville, Pa.: PGS) 13:253–54.

109 The Finck chest is in the Barnes Collection.

110 Jonathan P. Cox, "Woodworkers in Allentown, Salisbury Township, and Whitehall Township, Pennsylvania, 1753–1803: A Study of Community and Craft" (Master's thesis, University of Delaware, 1982), 42.

111 See Beatrice B. Garvan and Charles F. Hummel, *The Pennsylvania Germans: A Celebration of their Arts, 1683–1850* (Philadelphia: Philadelphia Museum of Art, 1982), pl. 27. Richard H. Shaner, "Bieber Family of Furniture Makers in Oley Valley," *Historical Review of Berks County* 71, no. 3 (Summer 2006): 123–26.

112 Cox, "Woodworkers in Allentown," 42.

113 Ibid., 52–54.

114 Wenger, *Country Storekeeper*, 178–79.

115 As quoted in William T. Parsons, "Schwenkfelder Indentures, 1754–1846," in *Schwenkfelders in America: Papers Presented at the Colloquium on Schwenkfeld and Schwenkfelders*, ed. Peter C. Erb, 51 (Pennsburg, Pa.: Schwenkfelder Library, 1987). Other indenture agreements specify a chest worth 25 shillings and a "new chest painted blue with lock and hitches" (Martha B. Kriebel, "Women, Servants, and Family Life in Early America," *Pennsylvania Folklife* 28, no. 1 [Autumn 1978]: 4).

116 Alan G. Keyser, Larry M. Neff, and Frederick S. Weiser, trans. and eds., *The Accounts of Two Pennsylvania German Furniture Makers: Abraham Overholt, Bucks County, 1790–1833, and Peter Ranck, Lebanon County, 1794–1817*, Sources and Documents of the Pennsylvania Germans, vol. 3 (Breinigsville, Pa.: PGS, 1978), 4, 10.

117 Raymond E. Hollenbach, trans., and Alan G. Keyser, ed., *The Account Book of the Clemens Family of Lower Salford Township, Montgomery County, Pennsylvania, 1749–1857*, Sources and Documents of the Pennsylvania Germans, vol. 1 (Breinigsville, Pa.: PGS, 1975); see also Jeanette Lasansky, *A Good Start: The Aussteier or Dowry* (Lewisburg, Pa.: Oral Traditions Project of the Union County Historical Society, 1990).

118 For an example of a Henry upright wheel, dated 1806, see Garvan and Hummel, *Pennsylvania Germans*, 153, pl. 100. Danner referred to upright wheels as "cassel" wheels in his account books.

119 The wheel and reel were sold at the Historical Society of the Cocalico Valley Auction, May 23, 1987. They were purchased by Bill Leinbach, weaver, who sold them to the present owner in 1988.

120 Craftsmen database, LCHS. Several Danner account books are owned by Hershey Museum and were examined by the authors in 2008.

CHAPTER 4

1 John Fisher file, no. 16800, York County Heritage Trust (hereafter YCHT).

2 *Village Record* (West Chester, Pa.), Jan. 18, 1842, cited in Margaret Berwind Schiffer, *Furniture and Its Makers of Chester County, Pennsylvania* (Philadelphia: University of Pennsylvania Press, 1966), 24.

3 Carolyn J. Weekley, *The Kingdoms of Edward Hicks* (New York: Harry N. Abrams for the Colonial Williamsburg Foundation, 1999), 76–77, 217.

4 For more on Pennsylvania German beds, see Alan G. Keyser, "Beds, Bedding, Bedsteads, and Sleep," *Der Reggeboge: Journal of the Pennsylvania German Society* 12, no. 4 (October 1978): 10.

5 Alan G. Keyser, Larry M. Neff, and Frederick S. Weiser, trans. and eds., *The Accounts of Two Pennsylvania German Furniture Makers: Abraham Overholt, Bucks County, 1790–1833, and Peter Ranck, Lebanon County, 1794–1817*, Sources and Documents of the Pennsylvania Germans, vol. 3 (Breinigsville, Pa.: Pennsylvania German Society [hereafter PGS], 1978), 11–12.

6 Schiffer, *Furniture and Its Makers*, 63–64.

7 For example, in 1782 Henry Muhlenberg paid $3 for a cradle "to be given to Salome Reichard [his youngest daughter] toward her dowry"; Theodore G. Tappert and John W. Doberstein, trans. and eds., *The Journals of Henry Melchior Muhlenberg* (hereafter *Muhlenberg Journals*), 3 vols. (1942–58; reprint, Camden, Maine: Picton Press, [1980]), 3:519.

8 The twin cradle is in the collection of the Landis Valley Museum, Lancaster, Pa.; the Letchworth cradle is in the collection of the Chester County Historical Society (hereafter CCHS) and is said to have been made for Mary Downing Valentine, wife of ironmaster George Valentine. On Letchworth, see Schiffer, *Furniture and Its Makers*, 142–43. For an image of the Letchworth cradle and more on Windsor cradles, see Nancy Goyne Evans, *American Windsor Furniture: Specialized Forms* (New York: Hudson Hills Press in association with the Henry Francis du Pont Winterthur Museum, 1997), 172–75.

9 Schiffer, *Furniture and Its Makers*, 277.

10 John J. Snyder Jr., "Chippendale Furniture of Lancaster County, Pennsylvania, 1760–1810" (Master's thesis, University of Delaware, 1976), 14, 23.

11 Schiffer, *Furniture and Its Makers*, 83–84.

12 Ibid., 159.

13 Ibid., 24.

14 Quoted in Ibid., 94; see also 165. David Evans of Philadelphia was another cabinetmaker who developed a side business as an undertaker. When Chief Justice William Allen died in 1780, Evans was hired to make the coffin, arrange for a hearse, and attend the body from Mount Airy to the cemetery; see Nancy Ann Goyne, "Furniture Craftsmen in Philadelphia, 1760–1780: Their Role in a Mercantile Society" (Master's thesis, University of Delaware, 1963), 132.

15 Carl Theo. Eben, trans., *Gottlieb Mittelberger's Journey to Pennsylvania in the Year 1750 and Return to Germany in the Year 1754* (Philadelphia: John Jos. McVey, 1898), 58.

16 Schiffer, *Furniture and Its Makers*, 24–25.

17 Rayner Wickersham Kelsey, ed., *Cazenove Journal 1794: A Record of the Journey of Theophile Cazenove through New Jersey and Pennsylvania (Translated from the French)* (Haverford, Pa.: Pennsylvania History Press, 1922), 21. On Moravian death and funerary practices, see Craig D. Atwood, *Community of the Cross: Moravian Piety in Colonial Bethlehem* (University Park: Pennsylvania State University Press, 2004), 197–99.

18 The use of corpse trays may be limited to the Pennsylvania Moravian settlements, as no examples are known from the Winston-Salem,

N.C., settlement; research by Johanna Brown on a so-called body basket in the MESDA collection said to have been used for such purposes found that it was acquired by Frank Horton in Maryland, about 1963, with no history of use. Following the waiting period in the corpse house, Moravians were buried in coffins. For example, an accounting of funeral expenses in the estate papers of Ludwig Von Redeken of Winston-Salem, N.C. (d. July 16, 1787) includes payments for a linen shroud, coffin, and gravestone; MESDA Research Center, transcription. See the Salem Diacony journal, Aug. 29–30, 1782, for an account of the funeral of Moravian Bishop Johann Michael Graff; transcriptions and translations in the Moravian Personnel Files, MESDA Research Center; originals in the Archives of the Moravian Church, Southern Province, Winston-Salem, N.C. Thanks to Johanna Brown for sharing this information.

19   Paul G. E. Clemens and Lucy Simler, "Rural Labor and the Farm Household in Chester County, Pennsylvania, 1750–1820," in *Work and Labor in Early America*, ed. Stephen Innes, 110–12 (Chapel Hill: University of North Carolina Press for the Institute of Early American History and Culture, 1988).

20   Diane E. Wenger, *A Country Storekeeper in Pennsylvania: Creating Economic Networks in Early America, 1790–1807* (University Park: Pennsylvania State University Press, 2008), 30–31.

21   Laura L. Becker, "Diversity and Its Significance in an Eighteenth-Century Town," in *Friends and Neighbors: Group Life in America's First Plural Society*, ed. Michael W. Zuckerman, 199 (Philadelphia: Temple University Press, 1982).

22   Benno M. Forman, "German Influences in Pennsylvania Furniture," in *Arts of the Pennsylvania Germans*, ed. Catherine E. Hutchins, 108–9, Publications of the Pennsylvania German Society (hereafter PGS), vol. 17 (New York: W.W. Norton for the Henry Francis du Pont Winterthur Museum, 1983).

23   Susan E. Klepp, Farley Grubb, and Anne Pfaelzer de Ortiz, *Souls for Sale: Two German Redemptioners Come to Revolutionary America* (University Park: Pennsylvania State University Press, 2006), 97, 99.

24   Beatrice B. Garvan, *The Pennsylvania German Collection* (1982; reprint, Philadelphia: Philadelphia Museum of Art, 1999), 310.

25   Cited in Karen Guenther, *"Rememb'ring Our Time and Work is the Lords": The Experiences of Quakers on the Eighteenth-Century Pennsylvania Frontier* (Selinsgrove, Pa.: Susquehanna University Press, 2005), 87.

26   Schiffer, *Furniture and Its Makers*, 21.

27   This wheel is pictured in Clarke Hess, *Mennonite Arts* (Atglen, Pa.: Schiffer Publishing, 2002), 52.

28   Keyser, Neff, and Weiser, *Accounts of Two Pennsylvania German Furniture Makers*, vi–viii, 18; Hess, *Mennonite Arts*, 51–53.

29   Schiffer, *Furniture and Its Makers*, 92–93; Laura Keim Stutman, "'Screwy Feet': Removable-Feet Chests of Drawers from Chester County, Pennsylvania, and Frederick County, Maryland" (Master's thesis, University of Delaware, 1999), 3–7.

30   Margaret Berwind Schiffer was among the first to publish this group as being from the Octoraro region, citing similar characteristics of "massive size, smooth quarter columns, and cornice" (Schiffer, *Furniture and Its Makers*, 264); however, these features are found elsewhere and are not distinct enough to substantiate an Octoraro origin.

31   Andre Jacob Roubo, *L'Art du Menuisier* (Paris, 1769–75); cited in Stutman, "Removable-Feet Chests of Drawers," 18.

32   Five tape looms of similar construction are known; four bear the initials "D W" and dates including "1812," "1814," "1816," and "1819." The 1812 loom was pictured in *The Magazine Antiques* 31, no. 4 (April 1937): 217; it sold at Northeast Auctions, Manchester, N.H., Aug. 1–3, 2008, lot 164. The 1816 loom was sold at Pennypacker Auction Centre, *The Collections of Mr. and Mrs. Paul R. Flack*, Reading, Pa., May 13, 1985, lot 283. Chip carving on some of the turned elements relates to that on a spinning wheel dated 1791 probably made by John Keim of Rockland Township, Berks County. With thanks to Ron Walters for this information.

33   On the Garrett family of weavers, see Adrienne D. Hood, *The Weaver's Craft: Cloth, Commerce, and Industry in Early Pennsylvania* (Philadelphia: University of Pennsylvania Press, 2003), 85–86, 98–100.

34   Keyser, Neff, and Weiser, *Accounts of Two Pennsylvania German Furniture Makers*, 10. One schrank with wooden screws is in the collection of Wright's Ferry Mansion and is illustrated in

Elizabeth Meg Schaefer and Joe K. Kindig III, *Wright's Ferry Mansion*, 2 vols. (Columbia, Pa.: von Hess Foundation, 2005), 2:144–45; the other is in a private collection. A large two-door clothes cupboard over drawers at the Tyler Arboretum also uses wooden screws for securing the case together.

35   Stutman, "Removable-Feet Chests of Drawers," 10–12, 21–23. On the material culture of Maryland Germans, see *Backcounty Dutch: German Heritage and Decorative Arts in Frederick County, Maryland* (Frederick, Md.: Historical Society of Frederick County, 2008).

36   One of these chests has inlaid initials "C W" and is thought to have been made for Cassandra Wood; for an image, see ad by Chalfant & Chalfant, *The Magazine Antiques* 132, no. 4 (November 1987): 1154.

37   Jay Robert Stiefel, "Philadelphia Cabinetmaking and Commerce, 1718–1753: The Account Book of John Head, Joiner," *Bulletin of the American Philosophical Society*, n.s. 1 (Winter 2001): 1–168.

38   Thomas R. Winpenny, *Bending is Not Breaking: Adaptation and Persistence among 19th-Century Lancaster Artisans* (Lanham, Md.: University Press of America, 1990), 23–24. John Hoff's "Book of New Clocks" is in the archives of the Lancaster County Historical Society (hereafter LCHS).

39   *Village Record* (West Chester, Pa.), Aug. 3, 1820, cited in Schiffer, *Furniture and Its Makers*, 173.

40   Letters, Christian Shouse to John Frederick Ernst, dated Apr. 7, 1781, and John Frederick Ernst to Christian Shouse, n.d. Edith von Zemenszky and Mary Redline, *A Strasbourger in America: John Frederick Ernst, Minister of the Gospel, Lutheran Denomination (1748–1805)* (Philadelphia: Lutheran Archives Center, 2007), 128–29.

41   Philip E. Pendleton, *Oley Valley Heritage: The Colonial Years, 1700–1775*, Publications of the PGS, vol. 28 (Birdsboro, Pa.: PGS, 1994), 85.

42   Inventory of Jacob Keim, 1799, Rockland Township, Berks County Courthouse. With thanks to Mike Emery for this information.

43   Pendleton, *Oley Valley Heritage*, 91–92.

44   Raymond J. Brunner, *That Ingenious Business: Pennsylvania German Organ Builders*, Publica-

tions of the PGS, vol. 24 (Birdsboro, Pa.: PGS, 1990), 131–33.

45   *The American Republican*, Nov. 10, 1840, cited in Schiffer, *Furniture and Its Makers*, 40.

46   The 1798 Direct Tax for Chester County includes (Sadsbury Township): William Bulla, "1 Joyners Shop Logs 15 by 12"; James Clark, "1 Joyners Shop 18 by 18"; Calvin Cooper, "1 Joyners Shop 45 by 18 Frame"; Robert Hope, "1 Joyners Shop 18 by 18"; William Moore Sr., "1 Joyners Shop logs 16 by 16"; (Uwchlan Township): Owen Afflick, "1 Turning Shop logs 20 by 10"; (Thornbury Township): Stephen Pyle, "1 Joiners Shop 14 by 18"; (Pikeland Township): Frederick Shimer, "1 Joiner shop 20 by 15"; (Nantmeal Township): Ezekial Thomas estate, "1 Joiner Shop part Stone part Logs unfinished"; (East Bradford Township: Benanuel Ogden, "1 Joiners Shop 20 by 20 Log"; (Brandywine Township): William Battin, "1 stone shop Joiners 18 by 14"; (West Caln Township): Benjamin Vastone, "1 Stone Joiners Shop 25 x 18"; (East Caln Township): Samuel Downing, "1 Turner shop round logs hardly tenable"; cited in Schiffer, *Furniture and Its Makers*, 274–75.

47   Schiffer, *Furniture and Its Makers*, 165, 201, 171–72.

48   On the marking of furniture, see Philip D. Zimmerman, "Early American Furniture Makers' Marks," in *American Furniture*, ed. Luke Beckerdite, 133–67 (Milwaukee, Wis.: Chipstone Foundation, 2007).

49   Catherine C. Lavoie, "Eighteenth-Century Development of the Meeting House, in *Quaker Aesthetics: Reflections on a Quaker Ethic in American Design and Consumption,* ed. Emma Jones Lapsansky and Anne A. Verplanck, 344, n.57 (Philadelphia: University of Pennsylvania Press, 2003). On the Buckingham Meetinghouse, see *Silent Witness: Quaker Meetinghouses in the Delaware Valley, 1695 to the Present* (Philadelphia: Philadelphia Yearly Meeting of the Religious Society of Friends, [2002]), 25–26.

50   Infrared photography has proven helpful in studying inscriptions made with lead pencil or graphite but not with chalk or other non-lead materials.

51   U.S. Federal Census; Lineages, Inc., comp. *Dryland Union Lutheran Church, Northampton County, Pennsylvania, 1763–1832* (Provo, Utah: Generations Network, 2001), database online.

Original data derived from William J. Hinke, *Church Record of the Reformed and Lutheran Congregations*, manuscript at Franklin and Marshall College, Lancaster, Pa.

52   On the Rohn chest, its history, and possible relationship to several earlier chests also found in upper Bucks County, see John Cummings, "Painted Chests from Bucks County," *Pennsylvania Folklife* 9, no. 3 (Summer 1958): 20–23.

53   In addition to the chests attributed to Peter Rohn, this feature has been observed on several brought from Germany by Schwenkfelder immigrants. It was also used in a small group of chests dating from the 1760s said to be from Lancaster County; see Monroe H. Fabian, *The Pennsylvania-German Decorated Chest*, Publications of the PGS, vol. 12 (New York: Universe Books, 1978), 108, 110–11.

54   Two chests were sold by Kerry Pae Auctioneers, Palmyra, Pa., Feb. 5, 2009; one was repainted but had the same features of the bottom board forming the base molding, rectangular frame of the bracket feet, pegged drawer sides, and two hidden drawers under the till (one of them was divided into six compartments as on the signed Peter Rohn chest). On the divider between the two main drawers, this chest was signed "Johann Rohn" in German script. The second chest was without drawers and overpainted in a yellow grain paint but shared the other construction features. A third chest with the same construction details was sold by Northeast Auctions, Mar. 21–22, 2009, lot 892. A fourth chest with trefoil panels containing the initials "L B H B" and date "1771" is in the collection of the Daughters of the American Revolution Museum, Washington, D.C., acc. no. 93.10; see Patrick Sheary, *American Case Furniture, 1680–1840: Selections from the DAR Museum* (Washington, D.C.: DAR Museum, 1997). A chest with somewhat different painted decoration but with two trefoil designs and a central bracket foot carries the name "Cadrina Sandern" and date "1796" and is in the collection of the Northampton County Historical Society; see Fabian, *Pennsylvania-German Decorated Chest*, 127.

55   Philip D. Zimmerman, "Workmanship as Evidence: A Model for Object Study," *Winterthur Portfolio* 16, no. 4 (Winter 1981): 283–307.

56   Forman, "German Influences in Pennsylvania Furniture," 122–23, 136. On the use of wedged dovetails in European Mennonite furniture, see Reinhild Kauenhoven Janzen and John M.

Janzen, *Mennonite Furniture: A Migrant Tradition (1766–1910)* (Intercourse, Pa.: Good Books, 1991), 162. According to Jurgen Huber, senior furniture conservator of the Wallace Collection, London, wedges are found consistently on even well-executed dovetails in German and Swiss furniture, indicating that the technique was not limited to repair work or poor joinery.

57   Gary B. Nash, "A Historical Perspective on Early American Artisans," in *The American Craftsman and the European Tradition, 1620–1820*, ed. Francis J. Puig and Michael Conforti, 2 (Hanover, N.H.: University Press of New England for the Minneapolis Institute of Arts, 1989).

58   Forman, "German Influences in Pennsylvania Furniture," 115, 123.

59   David Pye, *The Nature and Art of Workmanship* (London: University of Cambridge Press, 1968), 4–8.

60   Sumpter Priddy, *American Fancy: Exuberance in the Arts, 1790–1840* (Milwaukee, Wis.: Chipstone Foundation, 2004), xxii–xxiii, 15–17, 135–58.

61   Sprenger, who had five children by his first marriage and twelve by his second, immigrated from Germany in 1821. The people in the portrait were identified by a descendant as daughter Mary; Johann Abraham Sprenger; daughter Julia; son Henry; wife Elisabeth who is holding John Jacob (b. 1825) on her lap; and in rocking chairs Anna Susan (b. 1822) and Elisabeth (b. 1823); see family genealogy in Winterthur Museum Registration Office object file, acc. no. 1957.1123.

62   Priddy, *American Fancy*, 144–45.

63   Craftsmen database, LCHS.

64   Peter S. Seibert, "Decorated Chairs of the Lower Susquehanna River Valley," *The Magazine Antiques* 159, no. 5 (May 2001): 780–87. Nancy Goyne Evans, *American Windsor Chairs* (New York: Hudson Hills Press in association with the Henry Francis du Pont Winterthur Museum, 1996), 146–56.

65   Schiffer, *Furniture and Its Makers*, 108, 128.

66   *Village Record* (West Chester, Pa.), Feb. 19, 1850; cited in Schiffer, *Furniture and Its Makers*, 227.

67   Eliza Cope Harrison, ed., *Philadelphia Merchant: The Diary of Thomas P. Cope, 1800–1851*

(South Bend, Ind.: Gateway Editions, 1978), 13.

68 For more on Fisher's biography, see John Fisher file, no. 16800, YCHT; and James Alexander Kell, *Genealogy of John Fisher, Clockmaker, and Barbara Lightner, his wife, of Yorktown, Pennsylvania, and Their Descendants* (York, Pa., 1904); see also James Biser Whisker, *Pennsylvania Clockmakers, Watchmakers, and Allied Crafts* (Cranbury, N.J.: Adams Brown Co., 1990), 45.

69 Carl Bridenbaugh, *The Colonial Craftsman* (New York: New York University, 1950), 56.

70 Alfred J. Morrison, trans. and ed., *Johann David Schoepf, Travels in the Confederation [1783–1784]* (Philadelphia: William J. Campbell, 1911), 20.

71 For a complete transcription and translation, see checklist, fig. 4.36. With thanks to Peter Luborsky for the translation.

72 The clock was acquired by the Historical Society of York County (now the York County Heritage Trust) from the Aughenbaugh family of York. It may be the "One Musical clock" worth $40 that Fisher's widow owned at her death in 1835. In the final settlement of her estate in 1838, three clocks were sold, for $2, $5, and $50 respectively. The $50 clock, described as "1 8 day Clock," was bought by John Eyster. His daughter Elizabeth married George Washington Aughenbaugh in 1852; in his will he directed that after his death his "Grand Fathers clock" should be offered for sale to his children. It was bought in 1913 by his son Harry Ellis Aughenbaugh, who later sold it to his uncle George H. Aughenbaugh; the latter owned it as late as 1968. With thanks to Becky Roberts for sharing this information.

73 This clock survives and is in the collection of Yale University Art Gallery; see Edwin A. Battison and Patricia E. Kane, *The American Clock, 1725–1865* (Greenwich, Conn.: New York Graphic Society for Yale University Art Gallery, 1973), 134–37; see also Frank L. Hohmann III, *Timeless: Masterpiece American Brass Dial Clocks* (New York: Hohmann Holdings LLC, 2009), 212–13. For the article on Fisher's thirty-five day astronomical clock, see *Maryland Gazette*, Sept. 10, 1790; John Fisher file, no. 16800, YCHT.

74 *Pennsylvania Herald & York General Advertiser*, June 19, 1793, 3; John Fisher file, no. 16800, YCHT.

75 The pistols have walnut stocks engraved "Yorktown" on the top of the round tapered barrels and locks engraved "F. Zorger," with a second line of text that reads "& I. F." likely the initials of John Fisher to whom the engraving on the silver mounts is attributed, including the trigger guards, side plates, escutcheons, ramrod pipes, iron lock plates, and barrels. In addition to gunsmithing, Zorger experimented with alchemy and in 1805 had the misfortunate to blow up an experiment on which he was working; see Robert Turner, ed., *Lewis Miller: Sketches and Chronicles* (York, Pa.: Historical Society of York County, 1966), 45. For an image of the pistols, see Donald L. Fennimore, *Iron at Winterthur* (Winterthur, Del.: Henry Francis du Pont Winterthur Museum, 2004), 197–201; see also Donald L. Fennimore, "Metalwork," in *Arts of the Pennsylvania Germans*, 218–19. In addition to John's Fisher work with silver as an engraver, another York clockmaker, Godfry Lenhart, is known to have made a silver cream pitcher. Jacob Herwick of Carlisle also advertised in 1786 that he carried on the silversmith's trade in addition to clockmaking.

76 Turner, *Lewis Miller Sketches and Chronicles*, 31, 42.

77 York County Heritage Trust, County Commissioners records, 1796, no. 82. With thanks to Becky Roberts, Merri Lou Schaumann, and June Lloyd for their assistance in finding this record. What happened to the carved and gilded coat of arms by Fisher is a mystery; an example belonging to the YCHT (see image on half-title page) has been in their collection since at least 1903, when it appears in a photograph of the Historical Society of York County museum. It was thought to be the one made by Fisher, but paint analysis revealed the presence of commercially made chrome yellow pigments indicative of a mid-to-late 1800s date and no evidence of prior coatings or their removal; see Kirsten Travers, "Finishes Analysis Report-Pennsylvania Coat of Arms," Winterthur Museum/University of Delaware Program in Art Conservation, April 5, 2010.

78 Designed by Caleb Lownes of Philadelphia in 1778, the Pennsylvania coat of arms is closely related to the state seal designed in 1776. A version of this image was first used on state-issued paper money in 1777; the following year Lownes improved the design by adding the eagle, horses, cornstalks, olive branch, and motto. As no official description of the Pennsylvania coat of arms was adopted until 1875,

numerous variations were used prior to then; see George Earlier Shankle, *State Names, Flags, Seals, Songs, Birds, Flowers, and Other Symbols* (New York: H. W. Wilson Co., 1976), 209–10.

79 Turner, *Lewis Miller Sketches and Chronicles*, 9. The coat of arms hung in the courthouse behind the judge's desk until the building was dismantled in 1841; it was then transferred to attic storage in the new courthouse. In 1888 it was rediscovered and presented to local newspaper editor Edward Stuck by the county commissioners. In 1921 the York Collegiate Institute purchased it. The figure of Justice is illustrated, without a sword, in Frances Lichten, *Folk Art of Rural Pennsylvania* (New York: Charles Scribner's Sons, 1946), 113.

80 The bust is in the collection of the YCHT; the whereabouts of the deer head are unknown.

81 Inventory of John Fisher, taken Feb. 10, 1809, John Fisher file, no. 16800, YCHT. On Fisher's Tannenberg organ, see Brunner, *That Ingenious Business*, 83, 12, n.18; also William H. Armstrong, *Organs for America: The Life and Work of David Tannenberg* (Philadelphia: University of Pennsylvania Press, 1967), 98.

82 John Fisher file, no. 16800, YCHT.

83 Schiffer, *Furniture and Its Makers*, 26–27.

84 Wenger, *Country Storekeeper*, 57.

85 The account books of Samuel Wilson, a builder in Sadsbury Township, Chester County, reveal the versatility of craftsmen engaged in the building trades. Wilson began his career as a stonemason but came to serve as master builder and general contractor for projects ranging from new construction to alterations of existing buildings. As such, he engaged a variety of craftsmen, including carpenters, plasterers, and masons; see Gabrielle Lanier, "Samuel Wilson's Working World: Builders and Buildings in Chester County, Pennsylvania, 1780–1827," in *Perspectives in Vernacular Architecture* 4, ed. Thomas Carter and Bernard L. Herman, 23–30 (Columbia: University of Missouri Press, 1991).

86 On Oct. 27, 1762, Muhlenberg wrote that "Mr. Kessler, the cabinetmaker, made the chimney door." In December, he recorded paying "Mr. Leonhard Kessler for cabinet work in the house £4.4s.6d. in full." Of this amount, Kessler returned fifteen shillings to Muhlenberg as a contribution toward his salary. On Jan. 21, 1763, Muhlenberg "Paid to Leonhard

Kessler £10.2s.6d., in full for new chairs." In December that year, Muhlenberg "settled accounts with Mr. Leonhard Kessler and paid him for carpenter work, £8.6s. in full, as per receipt." Kessler contributed twenty-one shillings of this for the pastor's salary. On Feb. 23, 1764, Kessler visited Muhlenberg and received twenty-nine shillings for making a coffin for the minister's five-year-old son Samuel, who had died on Feb. 16. After the Muhlenbergs moved away, in July of 1776, Henry made a payment of debt to Kessler on Dec. 23 and again on Feb. 11, 1777, when he wrote, "Mr. Leonard Kessler was also paid in full, £2.0s.9d." (Tappert and Doberstein, *Muhlenberg Journals*, 1:564, 581–82, 590, 727; 2:35, 276–77, 766; 3:13).

87 Ibid., 1:581, 590; 2:725, 733.

88 Contract between Christian Hagenbuch and Jacob Kratzer, Nov. 27, 1784; Doc. 250, Joseph Downs Collection of Manuscripts and Printed Ephemera, Winterthur Library. Anonymous contract, May 1, 1791, private collection, cited in Alan G. Keyser, "The Stove Room in Pennsylvania" (unpublished manuscript).

89 Account ledger of Abraham Hoover, 694.6 H845, LCHS.

90 On the use of writing closets, see Bernard L. Herman, "Eighteenth-Century Quaker Houses in the Delaware Valley," in Lapsansky and Verplanck, *Quaker Aesthetics*, 194–95. Quaker houses with built-in cupboards include Morriseiana, the William Pusey House, and Primitive Hall; see Margaret Berwind Schiffer, *Survey of Chester County, Pennsylvania Architecture: 17th, 18th, and 19th Centuries* (Exton, Pa.; Schiffer Publishing, 1984), 38, 58–60, 68–71.

91 Lanie E. Graf, "Moravians in London: A Case Study in Furniture-Making, ca. 1735–65," *Furniture History: The Journal of the Furniture History Society* 40 (2004): 8.

92 Will and inventory of John Cunnius, "John Cunnius 1808 Reading City," Berks County Courthouse; see Richard S. Machmer and Rosemarie B. Machmer, *Berks County Tall-Case Clocks, 1750–1850* (Reading, Pa.: Historical Society Press of Berks County, 1995), 18–19; also Randall B. Huber, "Documenting the Talent of John Cunnius: Berks County Master Craftsman," *Historical Review of Berks County* 66, no. 2 (Spring 2001): 88–90. Two other clocks with "J C" carved on the door are known; one has a movement by Henry

Hahn of Reading and is owned by Rockwood Museum, Wilmington, Del.; the other is privately owned and has a Daniel Oyster movement.

93 Wenger, *Country Storekeeper*, 18.

94 Kelsey, *Cazenove*, 45.

95 P. C. Croll, *Ancient and Historic Landmarks in the Lebanon Valley* (Philadelphia: Lutheran Publication Society, 1895), 173–76.

96 The fireplace surround, built-in corner cupboard, and other architectural elements removed during the 1883 renovation of Tulpehocken Manor were sold, May 1997, in an onsite auction.

97 Mike Emery, "Tulpehocken Valley Tour," in *Guidebook for the Vernacular Architecture Forum Annual Conference: Architecture and Landscape of the Pennsylvania Germans, May 12–16, 2004, Harrisburg, Pennsylvania* (Vernacular Architecture Forum, 2004), 47–49.

98 The Ley schrank was published in Monroe H. Fabian, "Sulfur Inlay in Pennsylvania German Furniture," *Pennsylvania Folklife* 27, no. 1 (Fall 1977): 9. According to notations made by former owners (pasted inside the doors), the schrank was in the Ley house until 1834, when the property was bought by Conrad Loose. Loose gave the schrank to his son Isaac in Bethlehem. When Isaac passed away and his estate was auctioned, the schrank was sold for 75 cents to his granddaughter, the only bidder. At the sale of her effects in 1970 it was bought and returned to the house, then sold again in the 1990s; see also Mike Schropp, "Lebanon County Antiques: A History of the County as Seen through its Artifacts," *Lebanon Daily News*, Apr. 1, 1970. A closely related schrank in a private collection with a history of being found in Lebanon County also has the date 1771 inlaid in sulfur in the central panel of the frieze; it is possible that this schrank could also have been made for the Leys.

99 On the Ley house, see Emery, "Tulpehocken Valley Tour," 49. Federal Direct Tax 1798, Heidelberg Township, Dauphin County (Lebanon County was created in 1813); cited in Wenger, *Country Storekeeper*, 27–28.

100 Ralph Beaver Strassburger and William John Hinke, *Pennsylvania German Pioneers: A Publication of the Original Lists of Arrivals In the Port of Philadelphia from 1727 to 1808*, 3 vols. (Norristown, Pa.: PGS, 1934), 1:60. See also Uhler

Genealogy, Salem Lutheran Church Archives, Lebanon, Pa. With thanks to Lila Lebo for this information.

101 Christoph Uhler will and inventory, 1804, U-1, 13,569, Dauphin County Courthouse.

102 Federal Direct Tax of 1798, Lebanon Township, Dauphin County, in Gladys Bucher Sowers, *Lebanon County, Pennsylvania: United States Direct Tax of 1798 for Bethel Township, East Hanover Township, Heidelberg Township, Lebanon Township, and Londonderry Township* (Bowie, Md.: Heritage Books, 2004), 135.

103 Will of Carl (Charles) Arndt, Dec. 2, 1783, book D, vol. 1, 410–411, LCHS.

104 Theodore E. Schmauk, *Old Salem in Lebanon: A History of the Congregation and Town* (Lebanon, Pa., 1898), 118–99, 125–28, 134–39; see also Lila L. Lebo, *Reflections about Salem Lutheran Church, Lebanon, Pennsylvania* (Lebanon: Salem Evangelical Lutheran Church, 2009), 2, 78; and Charles H. Glatfelter, *Pastors and People: German Lutheran and Reformed Churches in the Pennsylvania Field, 1717–1793*, Publications of the PGS, vols. 13, 15 (Breinigsville, Pa.: PGS, 1980–81), 13:334.

105 Craftsmen database, LCHS.

106 Previous attributions of sulfur inlay to the shop of Peter Holl III (d. 1825) of Manor Township, Lancaster County, are now thought to be erroneous, as there is no firm evidence to link Holl with any of the known sulfur-inlaid objects. Misinterpretation of an inscription on a sulfur-inlaid schrank owned by the State Museum of Pennsylvania led to the false assertion that "D I Mertz" was its maker; this inscription stands for "Den 1 Mertz" or the 1st of March, rather than a maker's name. A more likely craftsman associated with sulfur inlay is cabinetmaker Christian Huber, whose brother George owned the sulfur-inlaid schrank dated 1779 now in the collection of the Philadelphia Museum of Art. Christian possibly made the schrank for his brother as an end-of-apprenticeship masterpiece; however, no firm documentation exists to prove or disprove this theory; see Beatrice B. Garvan and Charles F. Hummel, *The Pennsylvania Germans: A Celebration of their Arts* (Philadelphia: Philadelphia Museum of Art, 1982), 19, 31.

107 Craftsmen database, LCHS.

108 Five bow-front clock cases from the Deyer shop are known, including the one owned by

Winterthur Museum; one in a figured maple case that was advertised by Joe Kindig Jr. in *The Magazine Antiques* 21, no. 4 (April 1932): 188, now in the collection of the Henry Ford Museum (see Donald A. Shelley, "Henry Ford and the Museum," *The Magazine Antiques* 73, no. 2 [February 1958]: 162; and William H. Distin, *The Clock Collection: Greenfield Village & Henry Ford Museum* [Dearborn, Mich.: Edison Institute, 1974], 8); one owned by the de Young Museum in San Francisco; and two in private collections, one of which was sold at Horst Auction Center, Lancaster, Pa., Apr. 2009.

109 The signed Emanuel Deyer 1807 clock case is in a private collection; the signed George Deyer clock case with movement by Jacob Eby was advertised by Richland Antiques, Gibsonia, Pa., in *The Magazine Antiques* 142, no. 4 (October 1992): 446; the signature was erroneously interpreted as Dwyer.

110 Exceptions include a clock case attributed to the Deyer shop containing a movement by John Hoff of Lancaster; see Battison and Kane, *American Clock*, 146–49; and the signed 1807 clock with movement by Samuel Hill of Harrisburg.

111 Extracts from Christian Eby's inventory are cited in Stacy B. C. Wood Jr., *Clockmakers and Watchmakers of Lancaster County, Pennsylvania* (Lancaster: LCHS, 1995), 33. It is also possible that Christian may have taught his younger brother Jacob the clockmaking trade; see Hess, *Mennonite Arts*, 81–83.

112 This chest of drawers was published in *American Antiques from the Israel Sack Collection* (Washington, D.C.: Highland House Publishers, 1986), 8:2371.

113 The bow-front chest of drawers with cupboard is in a private collection. George Deyer is also said to have made an Empire-style chest of drawers for the Danner family of Manheim in 1827 and may have also made an organ once owned by George Danner and exhibited in his museum. The organ is now part of the Danner collection at Hershey Museum and includes pipes from an earlier organ along with crudely made ones; see Brunner, *That Ingenious Business*, 186. On Lancaster furniture of this period, see John J. Snyder Jr., "Federal Furniture of Lancaster Borough/City, 1795–1825," *Journal of the Lancaster County Historical Society* 101 (Spring 1999): 2–38.

114 Cynthia G. Falk, *Architecture and Artifacts of the Pennsylvania Germans: Constructing Identity in Early America*, Publications of the PGS, vol. 42 (University Park: Pennsylvania State University Press, 2008), 134–35. Glatfelter, *Pastors and People*, 13:323–24.

115 Inventory of Emanuel Deyer, July 25, 1836, inv. 1836, F0030:025, LCHS.

116 Vendue of Emanuel Deyer, Aug. 20, 1836, vendue 1836, no. F0010:001, LCHS.

117 Winpenny, *Bending is Not Breaking*, xi. The chest of drawers is inscribed on the bottom, for the original owner: "Samuel Spatz / in / Bern Taunschip / Berks Caunti / 1828." It was purchased by the present owner in the 1960s at an estate auction in Bernville, Berks County.

118 Six additional closely related painted chests are known, all in private collections; one is dated 1849; one is illustrated in Priddy, *American Fancy*, 90; the turned feet pictured on this chest are replacements. Another was in the collection of Jean and Howard Lipman and was published in Dean A. Fales Jr., *American Painted Furniture, 1660–1880* (New York: E. P. Dutton, 1972), fig. 346.

119 Priddy, *American Fancy*, 81–91.

120 The cupboard was sold at Pook & Pook, *The Americana Collection of Richard and Rosemarie Machmer*, Downingtown, Pa., Oct. 24–25, 2008, lot 271. The Machmers had purchased the cupboard from Maggie Gingrich, Sinking Spring, Berks County, a descendant of the Groh-Gruber family, in which it descended.

121 A total of five kitchen cupboards signed or attributed to the Blatt workshop are known; in addition to the Winterthur example, which is signed "Jacob A. Blatt" and dated "1848," there is an example at Landis Valley Museum with the inscription "Benj. Blatt" (in what appears to be a later hand) on one of the drawers; three other examples are in private collections, one of them is missing its top section. One of the related cupboards, with similar painted decoration and four small hardwood drawers in the upper section, was sold at Pennypacker Auction Centre, *Americana Antique Sale: The Renowned Collection of Parke E. Edwards and Mable M. Edwards*, Strasburg, Pa., Apr. 28, 1969, lot 504. The Landis Valley cupboard was sold at Pennypacker Auction Centre, *Walter Himmelreich Collection*, Reading, Pa., May 21, 1973, lot. 136.

122 *The Book of Bern: A History of Bern Township, Berks County, Pennsylvania, The First 250 Years, 1738–1988*, 3d ed. (Historical Committee of Bern Township, 2003).

123 Winpenny, *Bending is Not Breaking*, 60–61.

124 On the arrangement of houses and outbuildings on farmsteads in southeastern Pennsylvania, see Henry Glassie, "Eighteenth-Century Cultural Process in Delaware Valley Folk Building," in *Winterthur Portfolio 7*, ed. Ian M. G. Quimby, 50–57 (Charlottesville: University Press of Virginia for the Henry Francis du Pont Winterthur Museum, 1972). On this painting, see Stacy C. Hollander, *American Radiance: The Ralph Esmerian Gift to the American Folk Art Museum* (New York: Harry N. Abrams, 2001), 95, 417.

CHECKLIST

Entries marked with the symbol * indicate objects in the exhibition. Titles of works of art are italicized only when the original title is known. Makers or artists are noted if the object is firmly documented with a signature, label, or receipt; if no such documentation exists but there is strong evidence to support an attribution, the phrase "attributed to" is used; less-firm attributions are designated as "probably by" or "possibly by." Locations indicate the original place of manufacture and, where applicable, any name changes caused by the formation of additional townships and/or counties. Materials have been identified primarily through visual examination, except when microanalysis is specified. Woods are listed in the following order: primary; secondary; inlay (if applicable). The identification of wood, especially inlay, can be difficult without microscopic analysis, as photo-oxidation can shift colors, and layers of varnish or paint can obscure features. When visual identification could not determine wood type with relative certainty and microanalysis was unavailable, the terms "painted wood," "light-wood inlay," "dark-wood inlay," or "mixed-wood inlay" appear. Although prior studies of southeastern Pennsylvania wood inlay have included holly, maple, locust, cherry, and walnut, other species were likely used as well. The recent microscopic identification of a striped-grain, yellowish inlay wood as sumac (previously thought to be locust) reinforces the need for further study in this area. Dimensions noted here are overall, in inches; for framed objects, these include the frame unless otherwise stated. Additional notations include inscriptions, histories of ownership, details such as unusual construction features, and significant restorations to the extent possible.

Page i

Pennsylvania coat of arms*
Probably York County; 1850–75
White pine; lead white, chrome yellow,
gold leaf (microanalysis)
H. 25⅛, W. 36¼, D. 4⅞
York County Heritage Trust

INTRODUCTION

1. Detail of spice box (see fig. 3.19*).

2. Detail of tall-case clock (see fig. 2.77*).

3. Detail of chest-over-drawers (see fig. 3.48*).

4. Portrait of Grace Peel*
Benjamin West (1738–1820)
Probably Philadelphia; 1756–60
Oil on canvas
H. 52, W. 43
Winterthur Museum purchase with funds provided by the Henry Francis du Pont Collectors Circle 2003.63
Grace Peel (1740–1814) married William Parr of Lancaster (d. 1786).

5. Dressing table*
Possibly William Larkin (d. 1763)
Possibly Bethel Township, Chester (now Delaware) County; 1750–75
Apple; chestnut, tulip-poplar; brass
H. 29, W. 36, D. 23¼
Collection of Edward T. Lacy
Inscribed on proper right side of proper right drawer in chalk: "J [?] Larkin." Has drawing of women wearing large bonnets on same drawer side. Brasses replaced.

6. High chest of drawers*
Philadelphia; 1760–75
Mahogany; tulip-poplar, white cedar, hard
pine; brass
H. 101, W. 46⅛, D. 21¾
Winterthur Museum, gift of Henry Francis
du Pont 1957.506
Owned by Michael Gratz of Philadelphia
and his wife, Miriam Simon, of Lancaster,
who were married in 1769 in Philadelphia.

7. High chest of drawers*
Lancaster, Lancaster County; 1770–85
Mahogany; tulip-poplar; brass
H. 96, W. 42, D. 24
Heritage Center of Lancaster County
Made for Matthias Slough of Lancaster. Finials shown are modern replacements; original
finials are extant but missing the central ball
element; flames and plinths appear to be
original. Cartouche, engraved brasses, and
casters also appear to be original.

8. Pennsylvania counties in 1820.
Tom Willcockson, Mapcraft.com

9. *The Little Village of Sumneytown**
George Wunderlich (b. 1826)
Montgomery County; 1858–75
Oil on canvas
H.18½, W. 24¼ (unframed)
Schwenkfelder Library & Heritage Center,
Pennsburg, Pa.
Inscribed on verso: "The Little Village of
Sumneytown / Montgomery Co Pa / G.
Wunderlich / Avlier 1309 Olive St. Phila."
The painting likely dates between 1858, when
Friedens Union Church was built, and 1875,
when the old Red Lion Hotel in Sumneytown
burned down.

10. A Pennsylvania agricultural fair*
John Archibald Woodside Sr. (1781–1852)
Philadelphia; 1824
Oil on canvas
H. 26½, W. 32½
Private collection

11. Chestertown House interior
Southampton, Long Island, 1927.
Winterthur Archives
Fireplace surround removed from a home in
Lancaster County. Flanking it are an inlaid
desk, wainscot chair, and inlaid stand from
southeastern Pennsylvania.

12. Miniature chest-over-drawers*
Lancaster County; 1773
Walnut; tulip-poplar; sulfur; iron, tinned
sheet iron
H. 7¼, W. 14¾, D. 8⅝
Winterthur Museum, bequest of Henry
Francis du Pont 1965.2256
Inlaid on top in sulfur: "JOHANNES 17 / 73
/ MOSSER." Drawers secured from within
by three iron rods and accessed when top is
raised and rods removed.

13. Mrs. Enoch Rohrbach
H. Winslow Fegley (1871–1944)
Sigmund, Upper Milford Township, Lehigh
County; 1903
Schwenkfelder Library & Heritage Center,
Pennsburg, Pa.
Inscribed by Fegley on verso: "The Great-
grandmother, a Pennsylvania German
woman, 93 years old, in front of her oven
where she bakes the bread for Christmas."

14. Ruth Abbott
Gilbert Cope (1840–1928)
Chester County; 1913
Chester County Historical Society, West
Chester, Pa.

15. Millbach kitchen installation
From Joseph Downs, *The House of the Miller
at Millbach*
Philadelphia: Franklin Printing Company, 1929
Printed Book and Periodical Collection,
Winterthur Library

16. *House & Garden,* June 1941
Printed Book and Periodical Collection,
Winterthur Library

17. The Troutman brothers
H. Winslow Fegley (1871–1944)
Probably Berks County; 1900–1910
Schwenkfelder Library & Heritage Center,
Pennsburg, Pa.
Inscribed by Fegley on verso: "Three 'Trout-
man' Brothers, who raised the flock of
Toulouse Geese."

CHAPTER I

1.1. *A Map of the Improved Part of the
Province of Pennsilvania in America**
Surveyed by Thomas Holme (1624–95)
Engraved by Francis Lamb (active 1670–1720)
London: John Thornton and Robert Greene,
1701–5
Watercolor and ink on laid paper
H. 32½, W. 55⅛
Winterthur Museum, bequest of Henry
Francis du Pont 1963.853
First published in 1687, this second edition
omitted the names of the landowners.

1.2. British origins of English-speaking immigrants to Pennsylvania.
Tom Willcockson, Mapcraft.com

1.3. European origins of German-speaking
immigrants to Pennsylvania.
Tom Willcockson, Mapcraft.com

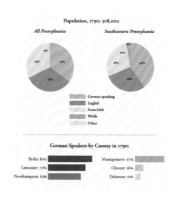

1.4. Pennsylvania's population in 1790.
Peter M. Blaiwas, Vern Associates, Inc.

1.5. House of Susanna Wright, built 1738,
Columbia, Lancaster County.
The von Hess Foundation, Wright's Ferry
Mansion

1.6. *The Residence of David Twining 1785**
Edward Hicks (1780–1849)
Newtown, Bucks County; 1846
Oil on canvas
H. 30½, W. 35⅞
American Folk Art Museum, New York, gift
of Ralph Esmerian 2005.8.13. Photo, John
Bigelow Taylor, New York ©2000
Inscribed on frame in gold leaf: "The Resi-
dence of David Twining 1785."

1.7. Bedstead
Probably Montgomery County; 1810–40
Tulip-poplar, white pine; paint; iron
H. 35, W. 49¾, L. 73¾
Winterthur Museum 1981.10
Inscribed on side rail in graphite: "Dad's
bed when a boy / George also had it when
a boy / came from / Pottstown, Penn." Bed
linens shown are a mix of period fabrics and
modern reproductions.

1.8. Exeter Friends Meetinghouse, built 1758,
Exeter Township, Berks County.

1.9. Marriage certificate*
Attributed to Edward Williams (1689–1750)
Merion Township, Philadelphia County
(now Lower Merion Township, Mont-
gomery County); 1742
Vermilion (microanalysis) and ink on laid paper
H. 23⅛, W. 18⅛ (unframed)
Rocky Hill Collection
This certificate records the marriage of
Jonathan and Sarah Jones on 8 day 11 month
1741/2 (January 8, 1742) at Merion Meeting.
Paper bears watermark associated with the
Dutch firm of Cornelius and Jacob Honig.

1.10. House of Joseph and Mary Pennock,
built 1738, West Marlborough Township,
Chester County.
Later known as Primitive Hall.

1.11. Wainscot armchair* and side chair
Probably West Marlborough Township area,
Chester County; 1730–50
Walnut
Armchair: H. 47½, W. 24¼, D. 24; side
chair: H. 40½, W. 17¾, D. 16½
Primitive Hall Foundation

Label on underside of armchair: "Property
of / Charles Edwin Pennock / Given by his
Aunts / Katherine M. Pennock + Marian A.
Pennock." Made for Joseph and Mary (Levis)
Pennock, these chairs, along with a matching
side chair, descended in the Pennock family.

1.12. Spice box*
London Grove Township area, Chester
County; 1744
Walnut; white pine, white cedar; sumac,
holly; brass
H. 19⅝, W. 14⅞, D. 11⅞
Collection of Mr. and Mrs. Joseph C.
Hoopes, Jr.
Inlaid on front: "T ᴴ E / 1744." Probably
made for Thomas and Elizabeth (Harry)
Hutton, who married at London Grove
Meeting in 1739.

1.13. Spice box
London Grove Township area, Chester
County; 1744
Walnut; tulip-poplar, white cedar, white oak;
holly, dark-wood inlay; brass
H. 19¼, W. 15½, D. 13½
Winterthur Museum, bequest of Henry
Francis du Pont 1964.965
Inlaid on front: "G ᴾ M / 1744." Made for
George and Margaret (Strode/Stroud) Pass-
more, who were married in 1742 at London
Grove Meeting. Hinges and escutcheon
replaced.

1.14. Tall chest of drawers*
Hiett Hutton (1756–1833)
New Garden Township, Chester County;
1780–1800
Walnut; tulip-poplar, white cedar; brass
H. 61½, W. 43¼, D. 23
Collection of Anna Walton Myers
Inscribed on backboard in graphite: "Hiett
Hutton." Descended in the Wickersham-
Pusey family of London Grove Township.

1.15. Spice box*
Possibly Hiett Hutton (1756–1833)
Probably New Garden Township area,
Chester County; 1788
Walnut; tulip-poplar; holly, cherry; brass,
iron
H. 21¼, W. 14⅞, D. 11¼
Chester County Historical Society, West
Chester, Pa.
Inlaid on front: "MH / 1788." Made for
Mary Hutton, who married Nicholas Hur-
ford at New Garden Meeting in 1788. Hinges
replaced.

1.16. Plate*
Probably England; 1738
Tin-glazed earthenware (delftware)
Diam. 9
Winterthur Museum purchase with funds
provided by the Henry Francis du Pont Col-
lectors Circle 2009.5
Inscribed on front: "T ᴴ E / 1738." Probably
made for Thomas and Elizabeth (Miller)
Hiett.

1.17. Group of plates*
Probably England; 1738
Tin-glazed earthenware (delftware)
Diam. 9
Clockwise from top left: Chester County
Historical Society, West Chester, Pa. (3);
Private collection; Rocky Hill Collection;
Private collection.
Inscribed on front: "IA / 1738"; "WB / 1738";
"Iᴰ S / 1738"; "TᴳD / 1738"; "WG / 1738," and
"Wᴸ E / 1738." Made for John Allen, William
Beverly, Joseph and Sarah Dixon, Thomas
and Dinah Gregg, William Gregg, and
William and Elizabeth Levis.

1.18. Datestone on house of William and
Margery Gregg, built 1737, New Castle
County, Delaware.

1.19. Bookstand*
Probably Chester County; 1725–45
Walnut, red oak
H. 3, W. 13¼, D. 12½ (folded)
Private collection
According to oral tradition, this bookstand
was owned by William Gregg of New
Castle County, Delaware. Height adjusts by
wooden ratchet mechanism.

1.20. Chest-over-drawers*
Probably Nottingham area, Chester County;
1741
Walnut; chestnut, tulip-poplar, walnut;
sumac (microanalysis), maple (microanalysis), holly, mixed-wood inlay; brass, iron
H. 29¼, W. 48¼, D. 20
Winterthur Museum, bequest of Henry
Francis du Pont 1957.1108
Inlaid on front: "I ᵀ I / 1741." Made for John
and Joanna (England) Townsend at the time
of their marriage in 1741. Scrolled bracket
base appears to be original. Narrow center

drawer accessible by removing two flanking drawers; a small hidden drawer is located behind center drawer.

1.21. Detail of top in fig. 1.20.

1.22. Portrait of John Townsend*
Louis Lemet (1779–1832)
Philadelphia; about 1800
Ink on wove paper
H. 2 15/16, W. 2¾
Winterthur Museum purchase with funds provided by the Henry Francis du Pont Collectors Circle and funds donated in honor of Anne Verplanck 2009.7.2
Inscribed under portrait: "Drawn & Engrav͟d By L Lemet, Philad.ᵃ / John Townsend." Pasted inside a silhouette album compiled by Caroline Morris Pennock (1811–82) of Philadelphia (see 1.24).

1.23. Miniature chest-over-drawers*
Chester County; 1780–1810
Walnut; tulip-poplar; brass
H. 8½, W. 15, D. 6¼
Rocky Hill Collection
Inscribed on underside of bottom in graphite: "Wistar P. Brown from his Grand / Mother Lydia P. Brown Pugh / Town Chester County Pa. / Bought 1812"; underside of lid in graphite: "W P B"; proper right drawer side in ink: "Wistar P. Brown"; and proper left drawer side in ink: "Frances du Pont Morgan / May 1ˢᵗ 1929."

1.24. Silhouette album* (one of two)
Philadelphia; 1830–40
H. 7¾, W. 7¼
Winterthur Museum purchase with funds provided by the Henry Francis du Pont Collectors Circle and funds donated in honor of Anne Verplanck 2009.7.2
Inscribed on cover: "PROFILES / CAROLINE PENNOCK." One of two albums of silhouettes and other portrait miniatures, most cut in the early 19th century at Peale's Museum, compiled by Caroline Morris Pennock (1811–82) of Philadelphia.

1.25. Looking glass*
Labeled by John Elliott Sr. (1713–91)
Philadelphia; 1762–67
Walnut; white cedar; glass; mercury and tin amalgam; laid paper, ink
H. 13¼, W. 7, D. ¾
Private collection
Inscribed on label in ink: "N 1741 Sharpless H." Probably owned by Hannah (Townsend) Sharpless, who married Nathan Sharpless in 1741. Label of John Elliott Sr. on backboard advertising his shop on Walnut Street.

1.26. Dish*
Samuel Malkin (1668–1741)
Burslem, Staffordshire, England; 1726
Slip-decorated earthenware (slipware)
Diam. 13¾
Winterthur Museum purchase with funds provided by the Henry Francis du Pont Collectors Circle 2010.4.1
Inscribed on front: "SM / Remember / Lots Wife / Luke 17:32 / 1726." Refers to biblical verse in which Lot's wife was turned into a pillar of salt after looking back at Sodom and Gomorrah. History of ownership in the Townsend family of Pennsylvania: English immigrants Joseph and Martha (Wooderson) Townsend were probably the first owners, then their daughter Hannah (1718–90). After the death of her first husband, Nathan Sharpless, in 1755, Hannah married Charles Ryant. The next owner of the dish was their daughter Anna Ryant (1759–1823), who married Caleb Haines. The dish then descended in the Haines family.

1.27. Hatbox*
Probably Nottingham area, Chester County; 1745–55
Walnut; sumac, maple, holly; iron
H. 5, W. 18½, D. 16
Collection of Jay Robert Stiefel
Inlaid on top: "HUGH / BOYD / ESQʳ." Iron staple on backboard may be original. Made for Hugh Boyd (d. 1754) of West Nottingham.

1.28. Tombstone of James Simpson (d. 1813)
Octorara United Presbyterian Church
Bart Township, Lancaster County
Inscribed: "JAMES SIMPSON / a Native of
/ SCOTLAND / died March 29th / 1813 / in
the 63rd year / of his age."

1.29. Sundial*
Probably Westtown Township, Chester
County; 1816
Slate; lead
H. 3¾ (including gnomon), W. 14¹¹/₁₆,
D. 14¹¹/₁₆
Chester County Historical Society, West
Chester, Pa.
Inscribed at top: "WEST-TOWN" and
above heart: "IRELAND," flanked by a
poem: "The sun with beams fulgent shines
/ [ill.] to the blushing moon / February 12
1816." In the right corner: "And marks now
the hour of time / On this projection truly
drawn / Benj Housekeeper." Owned or made
by Benjamin Housekeeper.

1.30. Sampler*
Sarah W. Pennock (1792–1832)
Westtown Township, Chester County; 1805
Silk on linen

H. 11¾, W. 13¼
Primitive Hall Foundation
Inscribed: "West-Town Boarding School /
To be resigned when ills betide, / Patient
when favours are denied / And pleased with
favours given / Most surely this is wisdom's
part / This is that incence of the heart /
Whose fragrance smells to heaven / Sarah W.
Pennock / 1805."

1.31. Donegal Presbyterian Church, built
about 1740, photo about 1905, Mount Joy,
Lancaster County.
Collection of Mr. and Mrs. Michael Emery

1.32. Communion table and service*
Donegal Presbyterian Church, Mount Joy, Pa.
Part of a larger set that includes two flagons,
four two-handle cups, and four fluted patens.

Table*
Probably Lancaster County; 1720–45
Walnut
H. 29, W. 47⅛, D. 33⅜

Two-handle cup and flagon*
William Eddon (active 1690–1737)
London; 1720–35
Pewter
Cup: H. 5¾, W. 8½, D. 4¾; Flagon: H. 9¾,
W. 8¼, D. 6⅛

Paten*
Richard King (active 1745–98)
London; 1745–75
Pewter
H. ¾, Diam. 8½

1.33. Portrait of Eliza and Rebecca Wilson*
William Clarke (active 1785–1806)
Possibly Lancaster County; 1792
Oil on canvas
H. 31⅞, W. 26½
Collection of Stephen and Dolores Smith
Inscribed on verso in ink: "William Clarke
Pinxᵗ / A. D. 1792 June 4ᵗʰ / Eliza Wilson
in Anno Aetat [ill.]/ Rebeca Wilson Dᵒ Dᵒ
[ill.]." To left of names in graphite: "(Left) /
(Right) Grandmother." In lower left corner
in graphite: "Eliz. Biggs / oldest sisters / Mrs
Rebecca Ramsey / Grandmother." Portrait
descended in the family of Rebecca Wilson
Ramsey.

1.34. Quilt (detail)
Rachel Mackey (b. 1768)
New London Township, Chester County; 1787
Cotton and linen fabrics; cotton batting;
wool and possibly silk embroidery threads
H. 95⅝, W. 91⅛
Rocky Hill Collection
Made by Rachel Mackey in 1787; the four
smaller crewelwork embroidery panels bear
her initials, "R M," and the date "1787"; the
large central panel bears the outline of her
full name.

1.35. Wainscot armchair*
Probably West Fallowfield Township area,
Chester County; about 1740
Walnut; holly
H. 45½, W. 23¾, D. 26¾
Collection of Dale E. Hunt
Inlaid on crest rail: "1739 40 / Thomas :
Elizabeth : Willson." Made for Thomas and
Elizabeth Willson of West Fallowfield Town-
ship, Chester County.

1.36. Chest*
Probably Germany; about 1737
Pine; iron
H. 27, W. 66, D. 26½
1719 Hans Herr House & Museum
Used by Hans Martin Amweg and family
when they immigrated in 1737.

1.37. Detail of label, underside of top in fig.
1.36; (translation) "This chest belongs to
Hans Martin Amwäg and Barbara Wisler
and Anle Medi Anwäg and Maride Amwäg.
Written in the year 1737."

1.38. Tall-case clock*
Movement: Probably England; 1680–1700
Case: Possibly Germantown, Philadelphia
County; 1740
Walnut; tulip-poplar, red oak; mixed-wood
inlay; brass, silvered brass, iron, steel; glass
H. 90, W. 20½, D. 13
Rocky Hill Collection
Inlaid on hood: "1740" and on pendulum
door: "I ᴹ C." The earlier lantern clock
movement, which would likely have origi-
nally hung on a wall without a case, was later
installed in this case.

1.39. Schrank*
Possibly Germantown, Philadelphia County;
1741
Walnut; hard pine, tulip-poplar, walnut, oak;
mixed-wood inlay; brass
H. 76, W. 75¼, D. 27½
Rocky Hill Collection
Inlaid on drawers: "17 MI AM 41." The
drawers are interchangeable; thus, the initials
can be arranged "AM MI" or "MI AM."
Schrank has been restored to its original
proportions and configuration; at some
point it was reduced in width and depth
and the drawers installed above the doors.
No alterations to the carving or inlaid doors
were made.

1.40. Detail of inlay on door of fig. 1.39.

1.41. Tall-case clock*
Movement: Edward Sanders, Pool, England;
1730–65
Case: Probably Lancaster, Lancaster County;
1745
American black walnut (microanalysis);
tulip-poplar (microanalysis); brass, iron,
bronze, steel; glass
H. 91¼, W. 21¾, D. 12¼
Private collection
Inscribed on the bonnet door: "ANDERAES
BEIERLE CATRINA BLN" and on cove
molding above pendulum door: "1745."
Made for Andreas and Catharina Beierle
(Beyerle) of Lancaster. Eight-day movement
is not original but appears to be an old
replacement; the original movement was
likely a thirty-hour. Base molding replaced.

1.42. House of Peter Bertolet; built 1730–40,
Oley Township, Berks County.
Daniel Boone Homestead, Pennsylvania
Historical and Museum Commission
Relocated to the Daniel Boone Homestead
in nearby Exeter Township in 1972.

1.43. Detail of clock dial in fig. 1.44.

1.44. Tall-case clock
Movement: George Miller (active 1760–96)
Case: William Bomberger (active 1765)
Germantown, Philadelphia County; 1765
Walnut; tulip-poplar, hard pine, maple;
brass, silvered brass, pewter, iron, bronze,
steel; glass
H. 98, W. 20¾, D. 11¼
Collection of James L. Price
Engraved on dial: "George Miller / German-
town." Thirty-hour movement with date
aperture.

1.45. House of Christian Herr, built 1719,
West Lampeter Township, Lancaster County.
1719 Hans Herr House & Museum
Inscribed in stone lintel above the front
door: "17 CH HR 19." Known as the Hans
Herr house but built by his son, Christian.

1.46. Sampler*
Elisabeth Waner
Warwick (now Penn) Township, Lancaster
County; 1817–20
Silk and cotton on linen

H. 17¼, W. 16⅜ (unframed)
Winterthur Museum 1980.60
Inscribed at top: [alphabet] / "ELISABETH
WANER / [alphabet and numeral system]
/ 1820;" at bottom "1817"; and near center
(*clockwise from bottom left*) "OEHBDDE,"
an acronym for "O edel Herz bedenk dein
End" (O noble heart, bethink your end).

1.47. Hanging cupboard*
Manor Township, Lancaster County;
1740–50
Walnut; tulip-poplar; iron
H. 37, W. 27, D. 16
Collection of John J. Snyder, Jr.
From the Jacob Musser house near Creswell,
Manor Township, built 1740–50. Interior
fitted with six small drawers in the upper
half (five are replaced), and a hidden drawer
behind the door.

1.48. Hanging cupboard*
Attributed to Johannes Spitler (1774–1837)
Shenandoah (now Page) County, Virginia;
about 1800
Hard pine; paint; brass
H. 35, W. 25, D. 15¼
Collection of Jane and Gerald Katcher.
Photo, Gavin Ashworth, NYC
Made for Jacob Strickler (1770–1842) and
descended in the Strickler family. Brass
knobs replaced.

1.49. Drawing*
Jacob Strickler (1770–1842)
Shenandoah (now Page) County, Virginia; 1794
Watercolor and ink on laid paper
H. 12¼, W. 15⅛
Winterthur Museum, bequest of Henry
Francis du Pont 1957.1208
Inscribed (translation): "Jacob Strickler
dwelling in Shenandoah County, Virginia,
made this picture the 16th day of February,
and paper is my field. The quill is my plow,
therefore I am so clever. The ink is my seed
with which I write my name, Jacob Strickler.
Anno one thousand seven hundred and
ninety-fourth year. Picture I want to tell you
something. If any one comes and wants to
carry you away, then say 'let me lie in good
rest. I belong to my owner, Jacob Strickler.'"

1.50. Tape loom*
John Drissell (1762–1846)
Lower Milford Township, Bucks County; 1795
White pine, red oak, maple, walnut; paint
H. 17½, W. 9¾, D. 19¾
Winterthur Museum, gift of Henry Francis
du Pont 1959.2812
Inscribed on front of heddle in paint: "Anna
Stauffer AO 1795 / Den 2ten May john Dris-
sel / his hand and pen."

1.51. Salt box*
John Drissell (1762–1846)
Lower Milford Township, Bucks County; 1797
White pine; paint
H. 11, W. 7⅜, D. 8½
Winterthur Museum 1958.17.1
Inscribed on front in paint: "ANNE LETER-
man / Anno Dommni 1797 / john Drissell /
his hand May / th 22t 1797."

1.52. Writing box*
John Drissell (1762–1846)
Lower Milford Township, Bucks County; 1795
White pine; paint
H. 7, W. 9¾, D. 16½
Mennonite Heritage Center, Harleysville, Pa.
Inscribed on lid in paint (translation): "Lis-
ten little writing chest [Schreib kistlein] to
what I wish to tell you; if someone comes to
carry you off, say Let me stay in good peace,
I am the property of Jacob Rohr. Anno 1795."
Inscribed on side in paint: "john Drissell his
hand the 31st jann [ill.] / 1795." Inscribed on
underside of lid in graphite: "Possession /
Dec 8th / 1907 / From Catharine Kneily as
a present / to stay in the Rohrs Family / S
B Algaret / Mary Algaret." Made for Jacob
Rohr (1772–1849) of New Britain Township,
Bucks County.

1.53. Hanging cupboard*
Attributed to John Drissell (1762–1846)
Lower Milford Township, Bucks County; 1800
White pine; paint; glass; iron, brass
H. 20¼, W. 10, D. 7½
Collection of Stephen and Susan Babinsky
Inscribed on top rail of door in paint:
"Catharine Stauffer 1800."

1.54. Miniature chests*
Attributed to Jonas Weber (1810–76)
Leacock Township, Lancaster County;
1835–55 (left), 1845 (right)
White pine; paint; tinned sheet iron
H. 5⅝, W. 10¼, D. 6⅞ (left); H. 5⅞, W.
10¼, D. 6 (right)
Winterthur Museum, bequest of Henry
Francis du Pont 1967.1285 (left); Collection
of Mr. and Mrs. Paul Flack (right)
Inscribed on front in paint: "Isaac Messner"
(left); Inscribed on front in paint: "1845 /
Jonas Weber" and incised on underside of
bottom board: "MADE FOR GRANDFA-
THER WEAVER 1845" (right).

1.55. Box*
Lancaster County; 1800–1840
White cedar (microanalysis); paint; tinned
sheet iron
H. 2⅜, W. 9½, D. 8½

Winterthur Museum, bequest of Henry
Francis du Pont 1967.928
Inscribed on top in paint: "H BUCHER."

1.56. *Saron* (Sisters House) and *Saal* (Meet-
inghouse), built 1743 and 1741, Ephrata,
Lancaster County.
Ephrata Cloister, Pennsylvania Historical and
Museum Commission

1.57. *Der Blutige Schau-Platz oder Märtyrer
Spiegel* *
(The Bloody Theater; or, Martyrs' Mirror)
Printed at Ephrata, Lancaster County;
1748–49
Printed Book and Periodical Collection,
Winterthur Library

1.58. Hanging cupboard*
Ephrata, Lancaster County; 1740–60
Tulip-poplar, walnut
H. 28½, W. 12, W. 20
Ephrata Cloister, Pennsylvania Historical and
Museum Commission

1.59. Three-door cupboard*
Ephrata, Lancaster County; 1740–60
Tulip-poplar, walnut; paint
H. 28½, W. 70¾, D. 21¾
Ephrata Cloister, Pennsylvania Historical and
Museum Commission
Paint and molding around doors appear to
be a later addition.

1.60. Religious text
Ephrata, Lancaster County; 1740–60
Watercolor and ink on laid paper
H. 48½, W. 37½
Ephrata Cloister, Pennsylvania Historical and
Museum Commission
(Translation): "God and / the virgin / lamb
must always in us rule / and through eternity
not let our faith grow / cool."

1.61. Drawing in hymnal
Ephrata, Lancaster County; about 1754
Watercolor and ink on laid paper
H. 9½, W. 14¾
Joseph Downs Collection of Manuscripts
and Printed Ephemera, Winterthur Library
Bound within a manuscript copy of the
Paradisisches Wunderspiel dated 1754.

1.62. Drawing for Salome Wagner
Attributed to Susanna Heebner (1750–1818)
Worcester Township, Montgomery County;
1810–18
Watercolor and ink on wove paper
H. 12 15/16, W. 16¼
American Folk Art Museum, New York,
promised gift of Ralph Esmerian P1.2001.21.
Photo, John Bigelow Taylor, New York
©2000
Inscribed on recto in ink: "Salome Wagnerin."

1.63. Slide-lid box*
Possibly David Kriebel (1736–1815)
Worcester Township, Montgomery County;
about 1814
White pine; paint
H. 3¾, W. 6¼, D. 11½
Collection of Stephen and Dolores Smith
Inscribed on lid in paint: "E W" and on
underside of lid in graphite: "Amandas S.
Rothenberger 1884." According to family tra-
dition, this box was made for Ezra Wiegner
(b. 1814) by his grandfather, noted fraktur
artist David Kriebel.

1.64. Chest-over-drawers*
Montgomery County; 1826
Tulip-poplar; white pine; paint; brass, iron
H. 28¼, W. 50¼, D. 23⅛
Schwenkfelder Library & Heritage Center,
Pennsburg, Pa.
Inscribed on front in paint: "Sarah Hübnerin
/ 1826." Sarah Hübner or Heebner (1808–90)
married Joel Wiegner (brother of Ezra Wiegner) in 1833; the chest descended to their eldest
daughter Anna and thence forward. Brass
knobs shown are modern replacements, based
on damaged original knobs found on chest.

1.65. *A View of Bethlehem, One of the Breth-
ren's Principal Settlements, in Pennsylvania,
North America*
Drawn by Nicholas Garrison Jr. (1726–1802)
Engraved by Isaiah Noual (b. 1725)
London: Printed for Robert Sayer, about 1760
Watercolor and ink on laid paper
H. 14, W. 19¾
Museum of Early Southern Decorative Arts,
Old Salem Museums & Gardens

1.66. *Young Moravian Girl**
John Valentine Haidt (1700–1780)
Probably Bethlehem, Northampton County;
1755–60
Oil on canvas
H. 35, W. 30½
Smithsonian American Art Museum, Washington, D.C./Art Resource, N.Y.

1.67. Armchair*
Probably Bethlehem, Northampton County;
1750–80
Walnut; hard pine, white pine; leather, linen, hair
H. 46½, W. 25, D. 27
Collection of H. Rodney Sharp on loan from the Historic Odessa Foundation

1.68. Plank-bottom chair*
Probably Nazareth, Northampton County;
1750–85
Walnut; red oak
H. 35, W. 20, D. 21
Rocky Hill Collection
Inscribed on underside of seat in ink: "Old Chair from the / Sisters House / Nazareth, Pa."

1.69. Liturgist's table*
Bethlehem, Northampton County; 1750–85
Walnut; white oak, tulip-poplar, hard pine; brass
H. 28¾, W. 36, D. 22¾
Moravian Archives, Bethlehem, Pa.

1.70. Central Moravian Church, built 1803–6, photo 1870–1900, Bethlehem, Northampton County.
Moravian Archives, Bethlehem, Pa.

1.71. Pulpit of Central Moravian Church
Attributed to Johann Friedrich Bourquin (1762–1830)
Bethlehem, Northampton County; 1803–6
Central Moravian Church, Bethlehem, Pa.
Pulpit was removed in 1851. After storage in the church attic for decades, it was recently installed in a stairwell within the church.

1.72. Urn*
Attributed to Johann Friedrich Bourquin (1762–1830)
Bethlehem, Northampton County; 1803–6
Tulip-poplar; paint, gold leaf
H. 27, Diam. 16
Central Moravian Church, Bethlehem, Pa.
From atop the sounding board above the pulpit of Central Moravian Church.

1.73. Liturgist's chair*
Attributed to Johann Friedrich Bourquin (1762–1830)
Bethlehem, Northampton County; 1803–6
Maple; paint; wool, cotton, linen, leather, hair; iron
H. 39¼, W. 18½, D. 18
Moravian Archives, Bethlehem, Pa.
From Central Moravian Church. Upholstery and slip seat shown are modern replacements; original slip seat extant, iron braces inside seat frame added later.

1.74. *The Trumpet Players from Lititz*
Lewis Miller (1796–1882)
York, York County; 1828
Watercolor and ink on wove paper
H. 9¾, W. 7⅝
York County Heritage Trust
Dated 1828 but possibly drawn later by Miller.

1.75. Trombone*
Johann Joseph Schmied (1722–94)
Pfaffendorf, Germany (now Rudzica,
Poland); 1774
Brass
L. 31
Lititz Moravian Congregation, Lititz, Pa.
Engraved on bell: "IOHANN IOSEPH
SCHMIED MACHTS IN PFAFFEN-
DORF 1774."

1.76. Windsor chair*
Probably Lititz, Lancaster County; 1800–1825
Hickory or ash, tulip-poplar; paint
H. 45, W. 20, D. 19
Lititz Moravian Congregation, Lititz, Pa.

1.77. Silkwork picture*
Hannah Mary McConaughy (b. 1810)
Painted decoration attributed to Samuel
Reinke (b. 1791)
Linden Hall Academy, Lititz, Lancaster
County; 1825
Silk and chenille thread, metallic coil, water-
color and ink on silk

H. 20½, W. 20½
Collection of Stephen and Dolores Smith
Retains original gilt frame.

1.78. Coffee mill*
Attributed to Andreas Albrecht (1718–1802)
Lititz, Lancaster County; 1772
Walnut; brass, iron, tinned sheet iron
H. 10⅛, W. 9, D. 6½
Lititz Moravian Congregation, Lititz, Pa.
Engraved on side of brass bowl: "AA / 1772."

1.79. Detail of carving on fig. 1.80 and fig.
1.78.

1.80. Long rifle*
Possibly Northampton County; 1760–70
Maple; iron, brass, steel
L. 53
Mercer Museum of the Bucks County His-
torical Society
Engraved on top of barrel: "*I*A*D
ROTHEN BERG*," indicating the barrel
was made in Rothenberg and imported.
Made for Edward Marshall (1715–89), who
participated in the Walking Purchase of 1737.
Sliding wooden patch box with iron spring
lock is original. Top jaw and screw of flint
vise replaced.

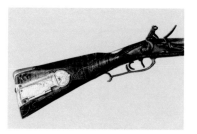

1.81. Long rifle*
Christian Oerter (1747–77)
Christian's Spring, Northampton County;
1775
Maple; iron, brass, steel, silver; horn
L. 59⅛
Private collection
Engraved on top of barrel: "CHRIS :
OERTER . CHRIS : SPRING . 1775 Nº 64"
and on brass patch box: "WM." Probably
made for William Marshall II (1737–1821),
Edward's son, and descended in the Marshall
family.

1.82. Detail of carving on fig. 1.81.

1.83. Schrank*
Probably Northampton County; 1791
Walnut; tulip-poplar, white pine, maple,
white oak; brass
H. 84⅞, W. 74¼, D. 26⅛
Rocky Hill Collection
Inlaid below cornice in brass: "17 PETER *
MORI 91." Made for Peter Mori of Upper
Saucon Township, Northampton (now
Lehigh) County.

1.84. Birth and baptismal certificate of Peter Buchecker
Printed form by J. Schneider & Co., Reading, Berks County; 1797
Decoration and handwriting by Friedrich Krebs (1749–1815)
Watercolor and ink on laid paper
H. 12⅛, W. 15¼
State Museum of Pennsylvania, Pennsylvania Historical and Museum Commission
Made for Peter Buchecker, son of Philip and Margaretha (Schlosser) Buchecker, born September 13, 1790 in Upper Saucon Township, Northampton (now Lehigh) County, and baptized on April 2, 1791; baptismal sponsors were Peter and Catharina Mori.

1.85. Chest-over-drawers*
Probably Pikeland Township area, Chester County; 1781
Walnut; tulip-poplar, white pine, walnut; sumac, maple; brass, iron
H. 28¼, W. 47⅞, D. 21⅞
Winterthur Museum purchase with funds provided by Robert and Bobbie Falk and the Henry Francis du Pont Collectors Circle 2008.8
Inlaid on front: "17 ML 81." Made for Margaret Laubach (b. 1758) of Pikeland Township, who married Conrad Keely of Vincent Township in 1782. Brasses are modern replacements, based on witness marks of originals. Till missing but remnants of walnut bottom board remain.

1.86. Birth and baptismal certificate of Margaret Laubach
Printed form attributed to the Ephrata print shop, Lancaster County; about 1788
Decoration and handwriting attributed to the Pseudo-Otto Artist (active 1773–1809)
Watercolor and ink on laid paper
H. 20, W. 16⅜
Collection of Ronald and Nancy Harper and Douglas Harper

1.87. Birth and baptismal certificate of Magdalena Laubach
Printed form attributed to the Ephrata print shop, Lancaster County; about 1788
Decoration and handwriting attributed to the Pseudo-Otto Artist (active 1773–1809)
Watercolor and ink on laid paper
H. 17¼, W. 13½
Chester County Historical Society, West Chester, Pa.

1.88. Sampler*
Magdalena Laubach (b. 1768)
Pikeland Township, Chester County; 1791

Silk on linen
H. 20½, W. 21¼
Chester County Historical Society, West Chester, Pa.
Inscribed: "[alphabet] / 1791 / [alphabet] / ML OEHBDDE / A E / DVCH IST MEIN ACKER DAR AVF NE ICH HIBS VND WACKER NATEL IST MEIN BLVG DAR MIT NE ICH HIPS VND [K]LVG SEIDEN IST MEIN SAMEN DAR MIT NE / ICH MEIN NAMEN MAGDALENA LAVBACHSEN" (O noble heart bethink your end . . . Fabric is my field, on it I sew beautifully and alertly. Needle is my plow, with it I sew beautifully and cleverly. Silk is my seed, with it I sew my name Magdalena Laubach).

1.89. Sampler*
Elisabeth Laubach (b. 1780)
Pikeland or Uwchlan Township, Chester County; 1802
Silk on linen
H. 17, W. 16
Collection of Mr. and Mrs. Stephen D. Hench
Inscribed: "[alphabet] / 1802 / LUST UND LIB ZU / EINEM DING / MAGHT ALLE MIH UND ARBEIT GERING / ELISA-BETH LAUBACHIN / EL / EL / AE" (Desire and love for a thing, make all effort and work trifling).

1.90. Portrait of Henry Melchior Muhlenberg
From Justus Heinrich Christian Helmuth,
*Denkmal der Liebe und Achtung . . . dem
Herrn D. Heinrich Melchior Mühlenberg*
Philadelphia: Melchior Steiner, 1788
Line engraving on laid paper
H. 7, W. 4¼
Rare Books and Manuscripts, Special Collections Library, the Pennsylvania State University Libraries
Inscribed beneath frontispiece portrait: "Heinr. Melch. Mühlenberg, der heil. Schrift Doctor, / und des Evang. Luth. Minist. Senior. / geb. d. 6 Sept. 1711 gest. d. 7 Octob. 1787" (Heinrich Melchior Mühlenberg, Doctor of Religion and Senior Minister of the Evangelical Lutheran Ministerium, born 6 Sept. 1711, died 7 Octob. 1787).

1.91. Augustus Lutheran Church, built 1743, photo about 1940, Trappe, Philadelphia (now Montgomery) County.

1.92. Winged angel heads*
Schaefferstown, Lancaster (now Lebanon) County; about 1767
White pine; paint

H. 36, W. 22, D. 6 (framed)
Collection of Katharine and Robert Booth
The three heads were originally part of the cornice on the street side of St. Luke's Lutheran Church, Schaefferstown, built 1765–67, and were removed when the church was remodeled in 1884.

1.93. St. Luke's Lutheran Church, built 1765–67, remodeled 1884, photo about 1880, Schaefferstown, Lancaster (now Lebanon) County.
Historic Schaefferstown, Inc.

1.94. Portrait of Frederick Augustus Conrad Muhlenberg*
Joseph Wright (1756–1793)
New York; 1790
Oil on canvas with applied wood strip
H. 47, W. 37
National Portrait Gallery, Smithsonian Institution
Inscribed on verso at lower right: "J. Wright 1790" and on document on table: "5 Act to regulate the" (in reference to House Bill no. 65: *An Act to regulate Trade and intercourse with the Indian tribes*, signed by Muhlenberg on July 20, 1790). A 1⅜ inch strip of wood was added to the canvas at the left edge and painted by the artist.

CHAPTER 2

2.1. Presentation drawing
Karl Münch (1769–1833)
Schaefferstown, Heidelberg Township, Dauphin (now Lebanon) County; 1799
Watercolor and ink on laid paper
H. 12½, W. 15½
Collection of Mr. and Mrs. Paul Flack
Inscribed across the bottom (translation): "Prepared by Karl Münch, schoolteacher in Schaefferstown Heidelberg Township Dauphin County 1799." Made for Elisabeta Huston.

2.2. Detail of fig. 2.1.

2.3. Interior of chairmaker's shop
From Jan Luiken, *Spiegel van Het Menselyk Bedryf* (Mirror of the Book of Trades)
[Amsterdam: Printed by P. Arentsz, 1704]
Printed Book and Periodical Collection, Winterthur Library

2.4. Slat-back side chair*
Probably Worcester Township, Philadelphia
(now Montgomery) County; 1775–1800
Maple, hickory; paper rush; paint
H. 48, W. 19, D. 15
Schwenkfelder Library & Heritage Center,
Pennsburg, Pa.
Descended in the Kriebel family, Schwenk-
felders in Worcester Township. Seat replaced.

2.5. Leidich's General Store
John Nicholas Choate (d. 1902)
Boiling Springs, Cumberland County;
about 1876
Cumberland County Historical Society

2.6. Slat-back armchair*
Probably Upper Salford Township, Philadel-
phia (now Montgomery) County; 1770–1800
Walnut; hickory
H. 44¼, W. 22, D. 27
Mennonite Heritage Center, Harleysville, Pa.
Incised on proper left armrest: "1773."
Descended in the Kulp family, Mennonites
in Upper Salford Township. Retains what
appears to be its original woven hickory
splint seat.

2.7. Bench*
Southeastern Pennsylvania; 1750–1800
Maple
H. 20⅝, W. 62¼, D. 14¼
Winterthur Museum 1956.49.2
Top is branded near proper right side: "EK."
Found in Germantown. Loss to proper left
support at rear.

2.8. Built-in bench in the Valentine Vihmann house, built 1762, near Millbach,
Millcreek Township, Lebanon County.

2.9. Dry sink*
Ephrata area, Lancaster County; 1780–1820
White pine; paint
H. 31½, W. 48½, D. 18½
Collection of Susan Fetterolf and Jeffrey
Gorrin

2.10. Dough trough*
Possibly Lancaster County; 1735–75
Tulip-poplar
H. 26¾, W. 44¼, D. 25¾
The von Hess Foundation, Wright's Ferry
Mansion

2.11. Table*
Southeastern Pennsylvania; 1740–1800
White pine, tulip-poplar, white oak, maple;
tulip-poplar; paint
H. 29, W. 43, D. 29¾
Collection of James and Nancy Glazer
Retains an old red-painted surface. Proper
left stretcher is replaced.

2.12. Kitchen cupboard
Southeastern Pennsylvania; 1750–1800
Walnut; hard pine; brass
H. 88¾, W. 72¼, D. 22
Winterthur Museum, bequest of Henry
Francis du Pont 1967.1167
Feet replaced and turn-latch knobs on doors
removed. Ceramics and metalwork shown
are from the Winterthur collection.

2.13. *Jacob Laumaster's Kitchen Cupboard upside down*
Lewis Miller (1796–1882)
York, York County; 1809
Watercolor and ink on wove paper
H. 9¾, W. 7⅝
York County Heritage Trust
Although dated 1809, this scene was likely drawn later by Miller.

2.14. Settle bed
Probably West Marlborough Township area, Chester County; 1730–50
Walnut; pine, tulip-poplar; leather; iron, brass
H. 51¼, W. 72½, D. 29
Primitive Hall Foundation
Made for Joseph and Mary (Levis) Pennock of West Marlborough Township, Chester County.

2.15. Couch*
Probably Chester County; 1725–50
Maple, tulip-poplar, walnut; white oak; rush; paint; iron
H. 37½, W. 25, D. 72¼
The Dietrich American Foundation

Descended in the family of Abraham Darlington (b. 1757) of Thornbury Township, Chester County. Retains what appears to be the original blue paint and rush seat.

2.16. Lownes Taylor farm*
Bass Otis (1784–1861)
West Goshen Township, Chester County; 1832
Oil on canvas
H. 40, W. 52
Chester County Historical Society, West Chester, Pa.
In original frame with gold-leaf and painted decoration. Documented by a receipt from Otis to Taylor dated November 12, 1832, noting he received $20 "for a landscap [sic] of his farm painted in oil."

2.17. Detail of inlay on fig. 2.23.

2.18. Spice box*
Nottingham area, Chester County; 1740–50
Walnut, cherry; oak, white cedar, tulip-poplar, pine; sumac, holly; brass
H. 23⅜, W. 16½, D. 10¾
Chester County Historical Society, West Chester, Pa., gift of Bart Anderson

2.19. Spice box*
Attributed to Thomas Coulson (1703–63) and possibly John Coulson (1737–1812)
Nottingham area, Chester County; 1740–50
Walnut; white oak; red cedar, sumac, holly; brass
H. 19¾, W. 16¼, D. 11
Collection of Leslie Miller and Richard Worley
Descended in the Hartshorn family of Cecil County, Maryland. Feet and top board replaced; brass escutcheon replaced.

2.20. Desk*
Attributed to Hugh Alexander (1724–77)
Nottingham area, Chester County; 1745–60
Walnut, red cedar, sumac (microanalysis); chestnut, tulip-poplar, white cedar; red cedar, sumac, holly, maple; brass
H. 45¾, W. 39⅛, D. 22⅛
Winterthur Museum, gift of Mrs. Giles Whiting 1961.278
Inscribed on side of proper left interior drawer in chalk: "Elizabeth Phillips" and on proper right document drawer in chalk: "[ill.] Draw / 1747/8." Slant front appears to be a replacement. Feet replaced to match original feet on related James Alexander desk. Brasses replaced.

2.21. Detail of desk interior in fig. 2.20.

2.22. High chest of drawers*
Probably Hugh Alexander (1724–77)
Nottingham area, Chester County; 1750–60
Walnut; chestnut, tulip-poplar; holly, red
cedar; brass
H. 82½, W. 42½, D. 23¼
Rocky Hill Collection
Inlaid at center of fourth drawer up from
bottom in upper case: "I G." Probably
made for Jeremiah Gatchell (1734–1802) of
Nottingham and descended in the Gatchell-
Kirk-Terrill family. Legs, four drawers in
lower case, and bottom drawer in upper case
replaced; brasses replaced.

2.23. Desk-and-bookcase*
Nottingham area, Chester County; 1725–40
Cherry; chestnut, tulip-poplar, oak, white
pine, walnut; holly; brass
H. 76, W. 37¾, D. 21½
Rocky Hill Collection
Inlaid across the top of the doors: "W" and
"M" and at the center of the cornice mold-
ing: "A," added at a later date. Made for

William Montgomery (1665/6–1742) of New
Castle County, Delaware, and descended in
the Montgomery family. Slant front, feet,
base molding, and double-arch moldings
around drawers replaced; brasses replaced.

2.24. Tall chest of drawers*
London Grove Township area, Chester
County; 1746
Walnut; white oak, white cedar, white pine;
holly, sumac; brass
H. 52⅜, W. 40¾, D. 22¼
The Dietrich American Foundation
Inlaid on proper right drawer front: "ES"
and proper left: "1746." Proper left top
drawer has pasted label "Kennett Advance /
May 12, 1883." Brasses replaced.

2.25. Detail of spring lock.
Winterthur Museum 1967.1168

2.26. Detail on inlay on fig. 2.24.

2.27. Small chest-over-drawers*
Probably Moses Pyle (d. 1784)
London Grove Township area, Chester
County; 1747
Walnut, sumac (microanalysis); white oak,
white cedar, tulip-poplar, maple; holly,
sumac, dark-wood inlay; brass, iron
H. 14¼, W. 21⅛, D. 13½
Winterthur Museum partial purchase and
partial gift of William R. Smith and sons

in memory of Marjorie B. Smith, wife and
mother 2001.19
Inlaid on front: "H D / 1747." Probably
made for Hannah Darlington (1729–95),
who married William Jefferis of East
Bradford in 1752; descended in the Bailey,
Jackson, and Seal families of Chester County.
Brasses, hinges, proper right drawer, molding
around lid and narrow strip at rear edge of
top replaced. Proper right drawer shown is a
replacement; original drawer extant but with
replaced non-inlaid front; original sumac
branchwood feet attached with round maple
tenon through the pith.

2.28. Tall chest of drawers*
Orange (now Alamance) County, North
Carolina; 1796
Walnut; tulip-poplar; sulfur; brass
H. 56, W. 41½, D. 20⅜
Museum of Early Southern Decorative Arts,
Old Salem Museums & Gardens. Photo,
Gavin Ashworth, NYC
Inlaid on top center drawer: "G F" and fourth
drawer from bottom: "17 / B F / 96." Made
for George and Barbara Faust. George was
born in Berks County and moved with his
parents to North Carolina in 1764. Brasses
replaced.

2.29. Detail of inlay on fig. 2.28.

2.30. Tall-case clock*
Movement: Rudolph Stoner (1728–69)
Lancaster, Lancaster County; 1765
Cherry; tulip-poplar; sulfur; brass, silvered
brass, pewter, iron, bronze, steel; paint; glass
H. 107¼, W. 21, D. 11½
Rocky Hill Collection
Inlaid on front of hood in sulfur: "PETER
FEREE / 1765" and engraved on dial: "Rd^lph
Stoner / Lancaster." Made for Peter Ferree of
East Lampeter Township, Lancaster County.
Eight-day movement with moon-phase dial,
second-hand dial, and date aperture.

2.31. Schrank
Probably Manor Township area, Lancaster
County; 1768
Walnut; tulip-poplar; sulfur; brass, iron
H. 88½, W. 71¼, D. 30½
Winterthur Museum, bequest of Henry
Francis du Pont 1965.2262
Inlaid on proper right door in sulfur:
"EMANUEL HERR / FEB D 17" and on
proper left door: "MA HER / 1768." Made
for Emanuel and Mary Herr of Lancaster
Township, Lancaster County.

2.32. Detail of clock hood in fig. 2.30.

2.33. Chest-over-drawers*
Lancaster County; 1783
Walnut; hard pine; sulfur; brass, iron
H. 29¼, W. 54½, D. 26½
National Museum of American History,
Smithsonian Institution
Inlaid on board beneath till covering secret
drawer compartment in sulfur: "ANNO
1783." Inscribed on underside of lid in graphite: "D.W. Dietrich 1876." Feet replaced
(no evidence of ball feet); proper right base
molding, proper right drawer bottom and
bottom edge of drawer front replaced; repairs
to corners of base molding at front and on
proper left side at back.

2.34. Detail of till inside fig. 2.33.

2.35. Tall-case clock*
Movement: George Hoff (1733–1816)
Lancaster, Lancaster County; 1790
Walnut; tulip-poplar, hard pine, oak; sulfur;
brass, silvered brass, pewter, painted sheet
iron, iron, bronze, steel; glass
H. 89½, W. 20½, D. 16
Private collection
Inlaid on front and pendulum door in
sulfur: "IO SC / 1790" and engraved on dial:
"GEORGE HOFF / LANCASTER." Thirty-
hour movement.

2.36. Detail of inlay on door in fig. 2.35.

2.37. Straightedge*
Probably Lancaster County; 1800
Walnut; sulfur
L. 22½, H. 1⅞
Collection of Stephen and Dolores Smith
Inlaid in sulfur: "I 1800 S."

2.38. Portrait of George Hoff*
Jacob Eichholtz (1776–1842)
Lancaster, Lancaster County; 1815
Oil on canvas
H. 33½, W. 28½
Collection of LancasterHistory.org,
Lancaster, Pa.

2.39. *Conestoga Creek and Lancaster*
Jacob Eichholtz (1776–1842)
Lancaster, Lancaster County; 1833
Oil on canvas
H. 23¼, W. 33
Pennsylvania Academy of the Fine Arts,
Philadelphia, gift of Mrs. James H. Beal

2.40. Group of three boxes*
Attributed to the Compass Artist
Lancaster County; 1800–1840

Blue-ground box* (*left*)
Tulip-poplar; paint; tinned sheet iron
H. 7⅞, W. 10⅝, D. 10¾
Winterthur Museum, bequest of Henry
Francis du Pont 1965.1981
Inscribed on underside in graphite: "Jacob
H Nolt / February 12 18[ill.]4 / Lancaster /
Jonas H. Nolt."

Red-ground box* (*middle*)
H. 5⅛, W. 6⅜, D. 4⅝
Tulip-poplar; white pine; paint; tinned sheet
iron
Winterthur Museum, bequest of Henry
Francis du Pont 1967.804
Inscribed inside proper right side of lid in
graphite: "William / Bechtel 1843."

Blue-ground box* (*right*)
Tulip-poplar; paint; tinned sheet iron
H. 6¾, W. 10, D. 6⅝
Collection of Stephen and Dolores Smith
Inscribed on underside in graphite: "Grate
Aunt / Aunt S [ill.]le Millers." Bottom of
hasp is missing.

2.41. Box-over-drawer*
Attributed to the Compass Artist
Lancaster County; 1800–1840
Tulip-poplar; paint; tinned sheet iron
H. 12½, W. 15⅞, D. 10⅝
Private collection

2.42. Slide-lid box*
Possibly Lancaster County; 1800–1840
White pine; paint
H. 6½, W. 9½, D. 12¼
Collection of Jane and Gerald Katcher.
Photo, Gavin Ashworth, NYC

2.43. Slide-lid boxes*
Attributed to the Compass Artist
Lancaster County; 1800–1840

Slide-lid box* (*left*)
Tulip-poplar; paint
H. 2⅜, W. 5¾, D. 7⅞
Winterthur Museum, bequest of Henry
Francis du Pont 1959.1552
Interior divided into six compartments.

Slide-lid box* (*right*)
Tulip-poplar; paint
H. 2⅜, W. 3½, D. 6⅜
Winterthur Museum, gift of Larry M. Neff
in memory of Frederick S. Weiser 2009.39
Inscribed on underside in ink: "Christian
Hunsicker's Box / died in his 82nd year, Birth
day 177[6] / Now Jos Hunsicker Box Exr of
C. H. / died in his 89th year Birthday 1803 /
Now W. H. Hunsicker Box Exr of J. H."

2.44. Detail of inscription on underside of
box (*right*) in fig. 2.43.

2.45. Chest*
Attributed to the Compass Artist
Lancaster County; 1785–1820
White pine, tulip-poplar, oak; paint; iron
H. 22½, W. 49½, D. 21⅛
Collection of Dr. and Mrs. Donald M. Herr

2.46. Detail of underside of top of chest in
fig. 2.45.

2.47. Chest*
Christian Seltzer (1749–1831)
Jonestown, Bethel Township, Dauphin (now
Lebanon) County; 1796
White pine; tulip-poplar; paint; iron
H. 23½, W. 52¼, D. 22⅝
Winterthur Museum, gift of Henry Francis
du Pont 1959.2803
Inscribed in proper left urn: "Chris / tian
Seltzer / Im [ill.]ar / 1796" (Christian Seltzer
in the year 1796). Chest has two tills, one
at left and one at right. Feet replaced below
base molding.

2.48. Detail of inscription on chest in fig. 2.47.

2.49. Chest*
Probably Peter Ranck (1770–1851)
Jonestown, Bethel Township, Dauphin (now
Lebanon) County; 1800–1810
White pine, tulip-poplar; white pine,
tulip-poplar; paint; brass, iron; wool, linen;
laid paper
H. 27, W. 53¾, D. 23
Westmoreland Museum of American Art,
Greensburg, Pa., gift of the William A. Coul-
ter Fund 1960.8
Inscribed on till in red crayon: "Henry Win-
ter." Probably made for Henry Winter Jr. (b.
1791) of East Hanover Township, Dauphin
(now Lebanon) County. One of a group of
chests often cited as from the Jonestown area.
Ranck's accounts record his making a chest for
Henry Winter Sr. in 1804 and another in 1810.

Figure 2.50. Birth and baptismal certificate of
Henry Winter
Attributed to Johann Conrad Trevits
(1751–1830)
East Hanover Township, Dauphin (now
Lebanon) County; about 1800
Watercolor and ink on laid paper
H. 8, W. 13⅛
Winterthur Museum purchase with funds
provided by the Henry Francis du Pont
Collectors Circle 2010.28a,b

2.51. Chest*
Wythe County, Virginia; 1810–25
Tulip-poplar; paint; iron
H. 25⅝, W. 52¼, D. 23⅛
Winterthur Museum purchase with funds
provided by the Henry Francis du Pont
Collectors Circle and partial gift of Roddy
and Sally Moore 2010.46
Descended in the Dutton family of Wythe
County, Va., and later Pulaski County, Ky.

2.52. Detail of chest in fig. 2.51.

2.53. *Conestoga Wagon on the Pennsylvania
Turnpike*
Thomas Birch (1779–1851)
Philadelphia; 1816
Oil on canvas
H. 25⅜, W. 32
Shelburne Museum, Shelburne, Vt.
Inscribed on rock in foreground: "T. Birch 1816."

2.54. Birth and baptismal certificate of
David Landis
John George Busyaeger (1774–1843)
Westmoreland County; 1825
Watercolor and ink on wove paper
H. 15⅛, W. 12½

Westmoreland Museum of American Art,
Greensburg, Pa., The Joy and R. David
Brocklebank Collection through the William
Jamison Art Acquisition Fund 2008.151
Inscribed at bottom in ink: "Made by J.
George Busyaeger Westmoreland County
State of Pennsylvania / 1825."

2.55. Desk*
Probably Jacob Maser (1812–95)
Mahantongo Valley, Northumberland
County; 1834
Tulip-poplar; white pine, maple; paint; brass
H. 49⅛, W. 39, D. 19¾
Winterthur Museum, gift of Henry Francis
du Pont 1964.1518
Inscribed on front in paint: "Jacob 1834 Maser."

2.56. Detail of interior of desk in fig. 2.55.

2.57. Chest*
Mahantongo Valley, Northumberland
County; 1830–50
Hard pine; paint; iron
H. 22, W. 31½, D. 15¾
Collection of Katharine and Robert Booth

2.58. Hanging cupboard*
Mahantongo Valley, Northumberland
County; 1830–50
White pine; paint; glass; brass
H. 29¼, W. 25⅞, D. 10¼
Winterthur Museum, promised gift of Mrs.
George P. Bissell, Jr.
Inscribed on front edge of top shelf in graph-
ite: "August 3ᵈ 1848." Interior repainted in
acrylic over a barrier coat to match original
red-lead oil paint, which was later over-
painted in white-lead oil paint.

2.59. Box, sugar bowl, needlecase,
and lidded cup*
Mahantongo Valley, Northumberland
County; 1830–50

Box* (far left)
Maple; paint
H. 3¾, Diam. 4¼.
Private collection
Incised on bottom: "AS / 1842;" possibly
made for Annjulein Stiehly or her mother,
Anna Stiehly.

Sugar bowl* (left)
Maple; paint
H. 4 3/8, Diam. 4.
Private collection
Inscribed on side in paint: "1831."

Needlecase* (right)
Maple; paint
H. 9¼, Diam. 2¾
Private collection

Lidded cup* (far right)
Maple; paint
H. 7¼, Diam. 3¾
Winterthur Museum, bequest of Henry
Francis du Pont 1967.1830

2.60. Tea table*
Possibly Downingtown area, Chester
County; 1780–1800
Walnut; iron, brass
H. 27½, Diam. 34½
Winterthur Museum purchase with funds pro-
vided by Robert and Bobbie Falk and the Henry
Francis du Pont Collectors Circle 2007.6

2.61. Detail of fig. 2.60.

2.62. Tea table*
Probably Berks County; 1780–1810
Tulip-poplar; red lead (microanalysis)
H. 26½, Diam. 23
Winterthur Museum, promised gift of John
J. Snyder, Jr.

2.63. Detail of fig. 2.62.

2.64. Stone house at the Berks County
almshouse*
Attributed to Charles C. Hofmann (1821–82)
Berks County; 1870–80
Oil on zinc-plated non-ferrous metal
H. 39, W. 46
Historical Society of Berks County Museum
and Library, Reading, Pa.
House depicted is identified as Tenant House
No. 1 in Hofmann's paintings of the Berks
County almshouse.

2.65. Drawing of desk-and-bookcase pediment
Attributed to Daniel Arnd
Lancaster County; 1791
Graphite and ink on laid paper
H. 10½, W. 7¾
Joseph Downs Collection of Manuscripts
and Printed Ephemera, Winterthur Library
Inscribed: "Daniel Arnd his book Lancaster,
March 22, 1791" within the account book of
Peter Ranck of Jonestown, Bethel Township,
Dauphin (now Lebanon) County.

2.66. Tea table*
Probably Lancaster, Lancaster County;
1770–90
Walnut; brass
H. 27½, Diam. 33⅛
The Dietrich American Foundation
Made for Jacob and Anna (Brackbill) Neff of
Strasburg, Lancaster County, who married in
1755. Ring and wedge replaced.

2.67. Detail of fig. 2.66.

2.68. Desk-and-bookcase*
Lancaster, Lancaster County; 1770–90
Cherry; tulip-poplar; brass
H. 103½, W. 45, D. 23⅝
Winterthur Museum, gift of Henry Francis
du Pont 1951.56
Made for Michael Withers of Strasburg, Lan-
caster County. Finials appear to be original.

2.69. Detail of desk pediment in fig. 2.68.

2.70. Detail of desk interior in fig. 2.68.

2.71. Small chest-over-drawers*
Probably Manheim, Lancaster County;
1770–90
Cherry; walnut, hard pine; brass
H. 19, W. 29¼, D. 15¾
Private collection
Descended in the Ensminger family of
Manheim. Drawers have wrought-iron spring
locks that appear to be original. Brasses
replaced.

2.72. Portrait of Samuel Ensminger, Jr.
and Portrait of Mrs. Samuel Ensminger, Jr.
(Elizabeth Summy) and child*
Attributed to Jacob Maentel (1778–1863?)
Manheim, Lancaster County; 1831
Watercolor and ink on wove paper
H. 20⅜, W. 24⅜
Collection of Stephen and Dolores Smith
Inscribed on verso: "Mr. and Mrs. Samuel
Ensminger taken at Manheim 1831." Portraits
are on separate pieces of paper but framed
together, perhaps at a later date.

2.73. Tall-case clock*
Movement: George Hoff (1733–1816) and
John Hoff (1776–1818)
Lancaster, Lancaster County; 1797
Case: Possibly Jacob Hiestand (1768–1834)
Possibly Mount Joy Township, Lancaster
County; about 1797
Walnut; tulip-poplar, hard pine; brass,
painted sheet iron, iron, bronze, steel; glass
H. 103¾, W. 23¾, D. 12
Collection of John J. Snyder, Jr.
Inscribed on dial in paint: "George Hoff /
LANCASTER" and on the front of the time
drum: "GJ Hoff March 19 1797." Made for
John Hiestand of East Hempfield Township,
Lancaster County. Eight-day movement with
second-hand dial and date aperture. Finials
replaced.

2.74. Detail of carving on base of fig. 2.73.

2.75. Tall-case clock*
Movement: Benjamin Chandlee Jr. (1723–91)
Nottingham area, Chester County; 1750–75
Walnut; tulip-poplar; brass, silvered brass,
iron, bronze, steel; glass
H. 107, W. 22½, D. 11½
Winterthur Museum purchase with funds
provided by the Henry Francis du Pont Collectors Circle 2003.32
Engraved on dial: "B. Chandlee / Nottingham." Probably made for Roland Rogers
of Nottingham, then owned by John Price
and descended in the Price family. Eight-day
movement with second-hand dial and date
aperture. Finials replaced; feet replaced based
on related clock case at Chester County
Historical Society.

2.76. Detail of clock hood in fig. 2.75.

2.77. Tall-case clock*
Movement: Benjamin Chandlee Jr. (1723–91)
Case: Jacob Brown (1746–1802)
Nottingham area, Chester County; 1788
Walnut; hard pine, tulip-poplar; brass, iron,
bronze, steel; glass
H. 107½, W. 25½, D. 14½
Collection of Mr. and Mrs. John McDowell
Morris and Family

Engraved on dial: "B. Chandlee / Notting-ham." Made for James McDowell of Oxford and descended in the McDowell family. Accompanied by letters from Chandlee and Brown documenting the making of the movement and case. Eight-day movement with second-hand dial and date aperture. Rosettes and feet are original; proper right finial and plinth replaced.

2.78. High chest of drawers*
Nottingham area, Chester County; 1760–80
Walnut; tulip-poplar, hard pine, white cedar; brass
H. 92¾, W. 43½, D. 25
Collection of Katharine Draper Schutt
Chalk cartoons and inscriptions on under-side of pediment and drawer sides. Car-touche and rosettes appear to be original.

2.79. Desk-and-bookcase
Nottingham area, Chester County; 1760–80
Walnut; tulip-poplar, white oak, white cedar; brass
H. 96½, W. 42½, D. 24
Private collection. Photo, Gavin Ashworth, NYC

Made for Joseph Coudon (1742–92) and descended in the Coudon family of Cecil County, Md. and Chester County, Pa. Can-dleslides and rear foot facings replaced.

2.80. Detail of pediment in fig. 2.78.

2.81. Detail of clock hood in fig. 2.77.

2.82. Tall-case clock*
Movement: Jacob Herwick (b. about 1751)
Carlisle, Cumberland County; 1780–1800
Walnut; hard pine; brass, sheet iron, iron, bronze, steel; glass
H. 106; W. 23¾, D. 12
Collection of James L. Price
Engraved on name plate: "J. Herwick / AMOR HONOR ET JUSTITIA / CARL-ISLE N 39;" proper right horse "FIGURE" and proper left horse "NETTLE." Eight-day movement with sweep seconds and calendar hands. Feet, plinth blocks, one flame, and two urns replaced; lower half of proper left broken arch scroll restored.

2.83. Detail of clock dial in fig. 2.82.

CHAPTER 3

3.1. Kitchen interior*
Thomas Hicks (1817–90)
Possibly Bucks County; 1865
Oil on panel
H. 23, W. 18¼
The Dietrich American Foundation
Inscribed at lower right: "T. Hicks 1865"

3.2. Drop-leaf table*
Possibly James Bartram (1701–71)
Marple Township area, Chester (now Dela-ware) County; 1725
Walnut; white oak, white cedar, maple; holly, mixed-wood inlay; brass
H. 30¾, W. 70, D. 60
Winterthur Museum, promised gift of Mr. and Mrs. John L. McGraw. Photo, Gavin Ashworth, NYC
Inlaid on leaf: "1725 / I ᴮ E." Made for James and Elizabeth (Maris) Bartram, who married in 1725.

3.3. Detail of inlay on fig. 3.2.

3.4. Dressing table*
Possibly James Bartram (1701–71)
Marple Township area, Chester (now Dela-
ware) County; 1724
Walnut; white pine, white cedar, tulip-pop-
lar; sumac, holly, mixed-wood inlay; brass
H. 30, W. 40¼, D. 23⅜
Philadelphia Museum of Art, bequest of R.
Wistar Harvey
Inlaid on top: "ANNO 1724 FIAT EM."
Made for Elizabeth Maris prior to her mar-
riage to James Bartram. Stretchers, center
foot, and brasses replaced.

3.5. Detail of inlay on top of fig. 3.4.

3.6. House of Bartholomew and Phebe Coppock, then James and Elizabeth Bartram,
built 1700–1725, photo about 1960, Marple
Township, Chester (now Delaware) County.
Rocky Hill Collection

3.7. High chest of drawers*
Seth Pancoast (1718–92)

Marple Township, Chester (now Delaware)
County; 1766
Maple; tulip-poplar, chestnut; brass
H. 95, W. 41⅝, D. 22⅜
Winterthur Museum, promised gift of John
J. Snyder, Jr.
Signed on proper left side under pediment
in chalk: "Seth Pancoast / 1766." Finials and
brasses appear to be original. Top ten inches
of pediment cut and reattached; backboard
replaced above cut.

3.8. Dressing table*
Attributed to Seth Pancoast (1718–92)
Marple Township, Chester (now Delaware)
County; 1765–75
Maple; chestnut, tulip-poplar; brass
H. 30½, W. 36⅝, D. 23⅞
Collection of Mr. Curtis Fenstermacher and
Family
Descended in the family of Bartholomew
Coppock III. Possible mate to high chest
made by Seth Pancoast in 1766 (fig. 3.7).
Brass on proper left bottom drawer replaced.

3.9. Detail of fig. 3.7.

3.10. Tall-case clock*
Movement: John Wood Sr.; Philadelphia;
about 1731
Case: Attributed to Thomas Thomas
(1687–1774)
Radnor Township, Chester (now Delaware)
County; about 1731

Walnut; tulip-poplar; sumac, holly, dark-
wood inlay; brass, iron, bronze, steel; glass
H. 89, W. 21, D. 11¾
Collection of Irvin and Anita Schorsch, Jr.
Inlaid on pendulum door: "TT / ML" and
engraved on dial: "John Wood / Philadelphia." Made for Margaret Thomas by her
father, Thomas Thomas, about the time
of her marriage to Nathan Lewis in 1731,
according to a typewritten note inside the
door. Thirty-hour movement with date
aperture.

3.11. Detail of clock hood in fig. 3.10.

3.12. Detail of inlaid initials on clock door in
fig. 3.10.

3.13. Chest of drawers*
Possibly Thomas Thomas (1687–1774)
Radnor Township area, Chester (now Dela-
ware) County; 1737
Walnut; chestnut, white cedar, tulip-poplar;
sumac, holly, dark-wood inlay; brass
H. 52½, W. 40¾, D. 21¾
Private collection
Inlaid on top center drawer: "S S" and
on skirt: "1737." Branded on third drawer
from top: "T S." Made for Sarah Smedley
(1717–1801) along with box in 3.15; descended
in the Smedley family of Middletown
Township, Chester (now Delaware) County.
Lower portion of center drop restored;
brasses replaced.

3.14. Detail of inlaid initials on fig. 3.13.

3.15. Box*
Possibly Thomas Thomas (1687–1774)
Radnor Township area, Chester (now Delaware) County; 1737
Walnut; chestnut; sumac, holly, dark-wood inlay; brass, iron
H. 8⅜, W. 20¼, D. 15½
Collection of The Henry Ford Museum
Inlaid on top: "S S" and on front "1737."
Made for Sarah Smedley. Escutcheon, hinges, and narrow strip at rear edge of top replaced.

3.16. Detail of inlaid top of box in fig. 3.15.

3.17. Crewelwork picture*
Sarah Smedley (1772–1827)
Willistown Township area, Chester County; 1788
Wool on linen
H. 31¾, W. 25
Winterthur Museum, gift of Harold O. Ladd 1989.58
Made by Sarah Smedley, daughter of George and Patience (Mercer) Smedley of Willistown; Sarah married Jonathan Matlack in 1797 at Goshen Meeting.

3.18. Chest-over-drawers*
London Grove Township area, Chester County; 1746
Walnut; white oak, white cedar; holly; brass, iron.
H. 33¾, W. 49¾, D. 21¼
Germantown Historical Society
Inlaid on facade: "R^L A / 1746." Probably made for Robert and Ann (Bourne) Lamborn, who were married in 1746 at London Grove Meeting. Brasses replaced; escutcheon appears to be original.

3.19. Spice box*
London Grove Township area, Chester County; 1748
Walnut; chestnut, tulip-poplar; holly, dark-wood inlay; brass
H. 20, W. 17, D. 11
Collection of Mr. and Mrs. Chester Bartoli
Inlaid on facade: "R^L A / 1748." Made for Robert and Ann (Bourne) Lamborn, who were married in 1746 at London Grove Meeting.

3.20. Detail of inlay on front of chest in fig. 3.18.

3.21. Detail of interior of spice box in fig. 3.19. Woodcut of George II, inscribed across the bottom: "King of Great-Britain, France & Ireland, Defender of the Faith &c."

3.22. Spice box*
Loudoun County, Virginia; 1791
Walnut; hard pine; ash; brass, iron
H. 20¾, W. 16⅛, D. 11⅜
Colonial Williamsburg Foundation, acquisition funded by the Friends of Colonial Williamsburg
Inlaid on facade: "MW / 1791." Probably made for Mary Warford (d. 1832) of Loudoun County, Va., in whose family it descended. Secret drawers behind the back panel were found to contain estate papers of her husband, John Warford (1750–1812).

3.23. House of George and Caterina Miller, then their son Michael Miller, built 1752, expanded by 1784, Millbach, Heidelberg Township, Lancaster County (now Millcreek Township, Lebanon County).
The Millbach Foundation, Inc.
Later known as the Millbach House.

3.24. Staircase from kitchen of the Miller house, installed at Philadelphia Museum of Art.
Philadelphia Museum of Art, gift of Mr. and Mrs. Pierre S. du Pont and Mr. and Mrs. Lammot du Pont 1926

3.25. Chest
Millbach area, Heidelberg Township, Lancaster County (now Millcreek Township, Lebanon County); 1750–75
Walnut; tulip-poplar; iron
H. 25½, W. 52½, D. 26
The Millbach Foundation, Inc.
According to oral tradition, owned by the Miller family.

3.26. Tall-case clock
Movement: Jacob Graff (1729–78)
Lebanon, Lancaster (now Lebanon) County; 1750–60
Walnut; mixed-wood inlay; brass, silvered brass, pewter, iron, bronze, steel; glass
H. 98, W. 24½, D. 12 9/16
Winterthur Museum, bequest of Henry Francis du Pont 1965.2261
Engraved on dial: "JACOB GRAFF MACHET / DIESES" (Jacob Graff made this). Descended in the Miller-Weigley family of Millbach. Eight-day movement with moon-phase dial, second-hand dial, date aperture, and day-of-the-week disk. Finials appear to be original. Case likely had bracket feet originally as continuous sides have been cut flush with the base molding. Day-of-week disk is replaced, based on description of original when still in family.

3.27. Detail of clock movement in fig. 3.26.

3.28. New Year's Greeting
C. F. Artist (active 1765–67)
Heidelberg Township, Lancaster County (now Millcreek Township, Lebanon County); 1765
Watercolor and ink on laid paper
H. 20½, W. 16¼
Winterthur Museum, bequest of Henry Francis du Pont 1957.1202
Inscribed at bottom in ink: "C. F." Made for Michael and Maria Elisabeth Miller and dated January 1, 1765.

3.29. Birth and baptismal certificate of Maria Elisabeth Miller
Henrich Otto (1733–99)
Heidelberg Township, Lancaster County (now Millcreek Township, Lebanon County); about 1775
Watercolor and ink on laid paper
H. 12¾, W. 16¼
Rare Book Department, Free Library of Philadelphia

This certificate documents the birth of Maria Elisabeth Miller, daughter of Michael and Maria Elisabeth Miller, on March 12, 1775, and baptism by minister Wilhelm Hendel in the Reformed Church, sponsored by Catharina Miller. Inscribed at lower right in ink (translation): "Written by Henrich Otto."

3.30. Chest-over-drawers
Millcreek Township area, Lancaster (now Lebanon) County; 1792
Walnut; hard pine, white pine, red oak; holly, sumac, mixed-wood inlay; brass, iron
H. 27, W. 57½, D. 24
Private collection
Inscribed on front in ink: "Maria Elisabeth Millern 1792." Made for Maria Elisabeth Miller, daughter of Michael and Maria Elisabeth Miller. Base molding replaced on front and proper left side; brasses replaced.

3.31. House of David and Catharina Hottenstein, built 1783, Kutztown, Maxatawny Township, Berks County. Historic Preservation Trust of Berks County, Pa.

3.32. Interior second-floor room of the Hottenstein house installed at Winterthur as the Fraktur Room.

3.33. Schrank
Kutztown area, Maxatawny Township, Berks
County; 1781
Walnut; white pine; mixed-wood inlay;
brass, iron
H. 101, W. 91¾, D. 25¼
Winterthur Museum 1958.17.6
Inlaid on facade: "DV 1781 HS." Made for
David Hottenstein of Maxatawny Township,
Berks County.

3.34. Detail of inlay on schrank in fig. 3.33.

3.35. Wedding party of Elizabeth Landis
and John Bomberger, Lititz, Lancaster
County, 1916.
Joanne (Hess) Siegrist Collection, Lancaster
Mennonite Historical Society, Lancaster, Pa.

3.36. Tall-case clock*
Movement: Attributed to Hans Jacob
Möllinger (1695–1763) or Friedrich
Möllinger (1726–78)
Neustadt or Mannheim, Germany; 1745–55
Case: Probably Ephrata area, Lancaster
County; 1755

Walnut; tulip-poplar; sumac, mixed-wood
inlay; brass, silvered brass, painted sheet iron,
iron, bronze, steel; glass
H. 90¼, W. 11, D. 21¼
Collection of Earle H. and Yvonne Henderson, Jr.
Inlaid on pendulum door: "GORG / IUNT
/ ANNO / 1755." Made for George Yunt
of Ephrata, Lancaster County. Thirty-hour
movement with cast brass spandrels and red-
painted dial. Movement supported by two
iron hooks or spikes against backboard.

3.37. Tombstone of George Yunt (d. 1770),
Bergstrasse Lutheran Church, Ephrata
Township, Lancaster County.

3.38. Tall-case clock*
Movement: Attributed to Jacob Gorgas Sr.
(1728–98)
Ephrata, Lancaster County; 1780–95
Walnut; white pine; holly; brass, painted
sheet iron, iron, bronze, steel; glass
H. 95, W. 21, D. 11½
Historical Society of the Cocalico Valley
Inscribed on dial in paint: "William Dishong" and inlaid on case: "W D." Made
for William Dishong of Ephrata, Lancaster
County. Finials, rosettes, and cartouche
appear to be original. Eight-day movement
with moon-phase dial, sweep seconds and
calendar hands.

3.39. Detail of clock hood in fig. 3.38.

3.40. Tall-case clock*
Movement: Isaac Thomas (1721–1802)
Case: Attributed to Isaac Thomas (1721–1802)
Willistown Township, Chester County;
1790–95
Cherry; tulip-poplar; brass, iron, bronze,
steel; glass
H. 101, W. 21, D. 11½
Collection of Paul S. and Caroline Edge
Beideman
Engraved on dial: "Isaac Thomas / WIL-
LISTOWN." Label inside clock: "Purchased
by Sarah Smith Downing, wife / of Thomas
Downing, about 1792. / Bequeathed to her
daughter Elizabeth Downing / Valentine, /
Bequeathed to her daughter Anna Valentine
Edge / Bequeathed to her son Jacob Valentine
/ Edge 1898. / [in a later hand] Bequeathed to
his son Jacob Edge 1913 / Bequeathed to his
son Jacob V. Edge 1945." Made for Thomas
and Sarah (Smith) Downing, who married
in 1786 and were members of Uwchlan
Meeting. Movement and probably the case
were made by Isaac Thomas, a cabinetmaker
and clockmaker. Eight-day movement with
second-hand dial and date aperture.

3.41. Shelf clock
Movement: Isaac Thomas (1721–1802)
Case: Attributed to Isaac Thomas (1721–1802)
Willistown Township, Chester County;
1770–1800
Walnut; tulip-poplar, maple; brass, silvered
brass, iron, steel; glass
H. 45, W. 19¼, D. 7⅝
Chester County Historical Society, West
Chester, Pa.
Engraved on dial: "Isaac Thomas / WIL-
LISTOWN." Two-day movement with
twenty-four-hour dial and sweep seconds
hand. Probably made for Mary Thomas, wife
of Isaac Thomas.

3.42. Detail of clock hood in fig. 3.40.

3.43. Tall chest-on-frame*
Samuel Morris (d. 1809)
Probably Kennett Township, Chester
County; 1793
Walnut; tulip-poplar; brass
H. 74¾, W. 38, D. 21⅛
Winterthur Museum purchase with funds
provided by the Henry Francis du Pont Col-
lectors Circle 2007.17

Inscribed in red crayon on back of second
drawer from bottom: "Samuel Morris / Joiner of
Logtown / 8 mo 5 1793" and on inside of same
board: "For Lydia Harlan." Made for Lydia Harlan of Kennett Township, Chester County.

3.44. Detail of signature on back of drawer
in fig. 3.43.

3.45. Chest-over-drawers*
Bern Township, Berks County; 1796
White pine; paint; brass, iron
H. 25½, W. 50¾, D. 23¼
Private collection
Inscribed on front in paint: "Adam Minnich
in Bern Bercks gaunti im jar 1796" (Adam
Minnich in Bern [Township] Berks County
in the year 1796). Made for Adam Minnich
of Bern Township, Berks County.

3.46. Chest-over-drawers*
Probably Lancaster County; 1785–1800
Tulip-poplar; paint; brass, iron
H. 28¾, W. 51, D. 24
Collection of Katharine and Robert Booth
Formerly owned by Theodore Dwight Wool-
sey, president of Yale University 1846–71.

3.47. Chest*
John Bamberger (1780–1861)
Warwick Township, Lancaster County; 1835
White pine; tulip-poplar; paint; brass, iron
H. 22¾, W. 49, D. 23

Lancaster Mennonite Historical Society,
Lancaster, Pa.
Inscribed on front in paint: "MARIA
EITENYER / 1789" and on underside in red
crayon: "John Bamberger." Made for Maria
Eitenyer (Eitenier) in 1835; the date 1789
commemorates her birth. Recorded in John
Bamberger's account book in 1835 as a pur-
chase by Jacob Eitenier, Maria's husband.

3.48. Chest-over-drawers*
New Hanover Township area, Montgomery
County; 1791
Tulip-poplar; paint; brass, iron
H. 29, W. 48, D. 24
Collection of Carl and Julie Lindberg
Inscribed on front in paint: "17 CHRIS-
TINA BENTERN 91." Made for Christina
Benter of New Hanover Township, Mont-
gomery County.

3.49. Detail of till and drawers inside fig. 3.48.

3.50. Chest-over-drawers*
Probably Weisenberg or Salisbury Township,
Lehigh County; 1792
Tulip-poplar; white pine, hard pine; paint;
iron, brass
H. 30½, W. 53, D. 24
Philadelphia Museum of Art, purchased
with the Thomas Skelton Harrison Fund,
the Fiske Kimball Fund, and the Joseph E.
Temple Fund 1982
Inscribed on front in paint: "Machdalena
1792 Leübelsperger." Made for Magdalena
Leibelsperger of Weisenberg Township, who
married John Kemmerer of Salisbury Town-
ship, Lehigh County.

3.51. Spinning wheel and reel*
Attributed to Daniel Danner (1803–81)
Manheim, Lancaster County; 1842
Maple, tulip-poplar, ash or hickory; paint
Wheel: H. 53½, W. 25, D. 24; reel: H. 40½,
W. 29¾, D. 15
Private collection
Inscribed on front of reel in bronze powder
paint: "R.H.H. / 1842." Made for Rebecca
H. Hershey of Salunga, Lancaster County.

3.52. Detail of reel in fig. 3.51.

CHAPTER 4

4.1. Trade sign*
Attributed to Edward Hicks (1780–1849)
Bucks County; 1800–1805
Tulip-poplar; paint
H. 17⅛, W. 54¼
Abby Aldrich Rockefeller Folk Art Museum,
Colonial Williamsburg Foundation
Inscribed on recto in paint: "HENRY VAN-
HORN / Carpenter & Joiner." An "E" at
the end of VANHORN was removed at an
unknown date. Made for Henry Vanhorn of
Lower Makefield Township, Bucks County.

4.2. Drawing
Attributed to Johann Adam Eyer (1755–1837)
Probably Hamilton Township, Northampton
(now Monroe) County; 1810–25

Watercolor and ink on wove paper
H. 10, W. 8⅛
Winterthur Museum purchase acquired
through the bequest of Henry Francis du
Pont 2009.40.1

4.3. Cradle*
Probably Chester County; 1740–65
Walnut; tulip-poplar
H. 22¼, W. 27, D. 40½
Collection of Mr. and Mrs. Thomas B. Helm

4.4. Bier*
Bethlehem, Northampton County;
1800–1825
Walnut, maple
H. 21, W. 24, D. 82¼
Central Moravian Church, Bethlehem, Pa.

4.5. Corpse house, built 1786, Lititz,
Lancaster County.
Lititz Moravian Congregation, Lititz, Pa.

4.6. Corpse tray*
Bethlehem, Northampton County;
1775–1800
Tulip-poplar; paint; iron
H. 11¾, W. 21½, D. 64¾
Central Moravian Church, Bethlehem, Pa.

4.7. Self-portrait
Lewis Miller (1796–1882)
York, York County; about 1845
Watercolor and ink on wove paper
H. 9⅞, W. 7¾
York County Heritage Trust
Inscribed at top in ink: "Lewis Miller Car-
penter, / working At the Trade for / Thirty
Years, In South Duke Street, York p.a."

4.8. Jointer plane*
Tinicum Township, Bucks County; 1787
Beech, apple; steel, iron
H. 6½, W. 3, D. 31
Collection of J. D. Miller
Incised on side: "B HP 17 87" and engraved
on blade: "[ill.] RREYSVILLE-MFG-CO /
WARRANTED / [ill.] STEEL." Owned by
Barnet Hillpot of Tinicum Township, Bucks
County.

4.9. Detail of fig. 4.8.

258

4.10. Brace and three bits (*left*) and screw box
(*right*)*
Bedminster Township, Bucks County; 1770,
1774
Apple; tinned sheet iron, pewter, iron (*left*);
maple, hickory; steel, iron (*right*)
Brace: L. 11; Bits: L. 9–10; Screw box: H. 12,
W. 6, D. 4
Mennonite Heritage Center, Harleysville, Pa.
(*left*); Mercer Museum of the Bucks County
Historical Society (*right*)
Incised on brace handle: "1770 RL." Stamped
twice on side of screw box: "RUTHOLPH
LANDES" and incised on opposite side:
"1774/R L." Owned by Rudolph Landes of
Bedminster Township, Bucks County. Pewter
repair to brace handle.

4.11. Spooling wheel*
Abraham Overholt (1765–1834)
Plumstead Township, Bucks County; 1821
White oak, maple; iron
H. 44¾, W. 19¾, D. 41
Mercer Museum of the Bucks County His-
torical Society
Stamped twice on end of bench: "AOH."
Made by Overholt for Jonas Frey in 1821,
and acquired by Henry Mercer in 1897 from
Frey's widow, Annie.

4.12. Detail of fig. 4.11.

4.13. Drawing of spooling wheel
Abraham Overholt (1765–1834)
Plumstead Township, Bucks County;
1790–95
Ink on laid paper
H. 6⅞, W. 7⅝
Private collection. Photo, Nathan Cox

4.14. Tall chest of drawers*
Benjamin Garrett (1771–1856) and probably
Joseph Garrett (1743–92)
Goshen Township, Chester County; 1786
Maple; tulip-poplar, walnut; brass
H. 62⅛, W. 40½, D. 22⅛
Chester County Historical Society, West
Chester, Pa.
Inscribed in chalk on back of second drawer
from bottom: "Benjamin Garrett 1786."
Benjamin was fifteen years old in 1786 and
was probably working as an apprentice in the
shop of his father, Joseph, when this piece
was made. Brasses replaced.

4.15. Detail of leg assembly with wooden
screws on fig. 4.14.

4.16. Detail of carving on knee of related tall
chest of drawers
Attributed to shop of Joseph Garrett
(1743–92)
Goshen Township, Chester County;
1780–1800
Walnut
Winterthur Museum purchase with funds in
part from Mr. and Mrs. Richard W. Vieser
1998.13

4.17. Tape loom*
Possibly Berks County; 1816
Maple, white pine, tulip-poplar, ash
H. 19⅝, W. 8¾, D. 31¼
Winterthur Museum purchase with funds
drawn from the Centenary Fund 2009.34
Incised on side: "1816 D W." Heddle
replaced.

4.18. Chest-over-drawers*
Frederick County, Maryland; 1787
Walnut; tulip-poplar; holly, dark-wood inlay;
brass, iron
H. 28¼, W. 50½, D. 22½
Historical Society of Carroll County
Inlaid on facade: "SL." Made for Salome
Lehman (1763–1855) of Uniontown, Freder-
ick County, shortly before her marriage to
Jacob Yon. Hinges are marked on inside of
chest: "DAVID BH / DB / DB / SALOME
LM / 1787" and on back of chest: "DV
BVH," by blacksmith David Barnhart. Rear
section of top replaced.

4.19. Detail of inlay on chest in fig. 4.18.

4.20. Detail of hinge on chest in fig. 4.18.

4.21. House and woodturning shop of Jacob Keim, built about 1753, Pike Township, Berks County.
Historic Preservation Trust of Berks County, Pa.

4.22. Sawmill of Daniel Bertolet, built about 1810, Oley Township, Berks County.
Daniel Boone Homestead, Pennsylvania Historical and Museum Commission
Relocated to the Daniel Boone Homestead in nearby Exeter Township in 1972.

4.23. Detail of label on looking glass in fig. 1.25.

4.24. Chest*
Peter Rohn (1763–1834)
Northampton County; 1784
White pine; tulip-poplar; iron
H. 24¼, W. 51, D. 23⅝
Winterthur Museum purchase with funds provided by the Henry Francis du Pont Collectors Circle 2009.2
Inscribed on underside of top of till in ink (translation): "Peter Rohn made this / the 11 March in the year / 1784."

4.25. Detail of inscription inside fig. 4.24.

4.26. Detail of dovetail with wedged pin.

4.27. Portrait of Johann Abraham Sprenger and family
Attributed to Jacob Maentel (1778–1863?)
Schaefferstown, Lebanon County; about 1825
Watercolor on wove paper
H. 23½, W. 27½
Winterthur Museum, bequest of Henry Francis du Pont 1957.1123

4.28. Chair*
John Swint (active 1840–60)
Lancaster, Lancaster County; 1840–50
Tulip-poplar, maple; paint
H. 33, W. 14½, D. 13
Collection of Teresa and Richard Ciccotelli
Stamped on underside of seat: "J.SWINT / CHAIRMAKER." From a set of six.

4.29. Detail of underside of chair in fig. 4.28.

4.30. Chair*
George Nees (1817–81)
Manheim, Lancaster County; 1850–60

Tulip-poplar, maple; paint, gold leaf
H. 33, W. 13½, D. 15
Collection of Dr. and Mrs. Donald M. Herr
Stenciled on underside of seat: "G. NEES."
From a set of six.

4.31. Detail of underside of chair in fig. 4.30.

4.32. Tools owned by George Nees*
Manheim, Lancaster County; 1850–75
Mixed media
Mercer Museum of the Bucks County Historical Society

4.33. Crest rails*
Attributed to George Nees (1817–81)
Manheim, Lancaster County; 1850–60
Cherry; paint, gold leaf
H. 5, W. 19, D. 1
Mercer Museum of the Bucks County Historical Society
Inscribed on back of painted rail in graphite: "This is style to put on the / [ill.] cut."

4.34. *John Fisher*
Lewis Miller (1796–1882)
York, York County; 1808
Watercolor and ink on wove paper
H. 6, W. 3
York County Heritage Trust
Although dated 1808, this portrait was likely drawn later by Miller, as he was only twelve years old in 1808.

4.35. View of York
William Wagner (1800–1869)
York, York County; 1830
Watercolor and ink on wove paper
H. 5, W. 7½
York County Heritage Trust

4.36. Tall-case clock*
Movement: John Fisher (1736–1808)
York, York County; 1790–1800
Walnut; tulip-poplar; brass, bronze, iron,
steel, silver; glass
H. 104¾, W. 27, D. 15
York County Heritage Trust
Engraved on dial: "Aternis Regis imperus et
fulmine terres (Eternal you rule over empires
and by your thunderbolt the lands) / John
Fisher / York Town / 1 The Dorsetshire March
2 Quick March / 3 Sir Charles Sedley's Minuet
/ 4 Polonesse The First / 5 Rural Felicity / 6
Polonesse The second / 7 S Bride's Bells" and
around the orrery: "Per duodena regit mundi
Sol aureus Astra Idcirco certis dimensum
partibus orbem (Therefore the golden sun,
his course into fixed parts dividing, rules his
way through the twelve constellations of the
world)." Descended in the Aughenbaugh family of York. Eight-day musical movement with
sweep seconds hand, date aperture, and orrery.
Center finial is a modern replacement.

4.37. Detail of clock movement in fig. 4.36.

4.38. Pennsylvania coat of arms*
John Fisher (1736–1808)
York, York County; 1796
Oil on panel
H. 38, W. 39¾, D. 2½
York College of Pennsylvania
Inscribed in lower right corner: "John Fisher
1796." Carved frame original and probably
by Fisher.

4.39. Figure of Justice*
John Fisher (1736–1808)
York, York County; 1795–1800
Painted wood; copper (sword), brass, iron
H. 19¼, W. 9, D. 5
York County Heritage Trust with permission
from the York County Law Library
Incised on back near bottom: "I F." Copper
sword is a replacement; scales appear to be
original.

4.40. Detail of initials on back of fig. 4.39.

4.41. Interior of the York County Courthouse
Lewis Miller (1796–1882)
York, York County; 1804
Watercolor and ink on wove paper
H. 9¾, W. 7⅝
York County Heritage Trust
Although dated 1804, this picture was likely
drawn later by Miller.

4.42. Drawing of George Adam Gosler
Lewis Miller (1796–1882)
York, York County; 1805
Watercolor and ink on wove paper
H. 9¾, W. 7⅝
York County Heritage Trust
Although dated 1805, this picture was likely
drawn later by Miller.

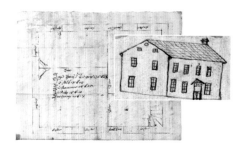

4.43. Building contract between Christian
Hagenbuch and Jacob Kratzer
Kreidersville, Northampton County; 1783
Ink on laid paper
H. 10⅞, W. 16½
Joseph Downs Collection of Manuscripts
and Printed Ephemera, Winterthur Library

4.44. Tall-case clock
Movement: Daniel Oyster (1766–1845)
Case: Attributed to John Cunnius (1733–1808)
Reading, Berks County; 1790–1800
Walnut; white pine; brass, painted sheet
iron, iron, bronze, steel; bronze powder
paint; glass
H. 97⅜, W. 21⅝, D. 10⅝
Winterthur Museum, bequest of Henry
Francis du Pont 1959.2807
Inscribed on dial in paint: "Daniel Oyster
/ READING"; carved on pendulum door:
"JC," thought to stand for John Cunnius.
Eight-day movement with sweep seconds
hand and date aperture. Dial painted with
allegorical scenes of the four seasons. Bronze
powder paint appears to be a later addition.

4.45. Detail of clock hood in fig. 4.44.

4.46. House of Michael and Eva Magdalena
Ley
From Rev. P. C. Croll, *Ancient and Historic
Landmarks in the Lebanon Valley*
Philadelphia: Lutheran Publication Society,
1895
Printed Book and Periodical Collection,
Winterthur Library
Near Myerstown, Jackson Township, Leba-
non County, built 1769, remodeled 1883.
Later known as Tulpehocken Manor.

4.47. Door pediment from Tulpehocken
Manor
Christoph Uhler (1741–1804)
Lebanon, Lancaster (now Lebanon) County;
1769
White pine; paint
H. 21¾, W. 70¼, D. 3¾
Collection of James C. Keener, Lancaster, Pa.
Carved on front: "GOTT / ALLEIN DIE
EHR / MICHAEL LEY UND / EFA MAG-
DALENA LEYIN / CHRISTOPH UHLER
1769 VON LEBANON" (God / alone the
Honor / Michael Ley and / Eva Magdalena
Ley / Christoph Uhler 1769 of Lebanon).

4.48. Detail of cornice of corner cupboard
from Tulpehocken Manor
Possibly Christoph Uhler (1741–1804)
Possibly Lebanon, Lancaster (now Lebanon)
County; 1769
Tulip-poplar; paint
Collection of Lester and Barbara Breininger

4.49. Schrank*
Possibly Christoph Uhler (1741–1804)
Possibly Lebanon, Lancaster (now Lebanon)
County; 1771
Walnut; tulip-poplar, white pine; sulfur; brass
H. 99¼, W. 91, D. 26
Rocky Hill Collection
Inlaid on front in sulfur: "ML / & / EML /
1771." Made for Michael and Eva Magdalena
Ley of Tulpehocken Manor.

4.50. Detail of inlay on schrank in fig. 4.49.

4.51. Detail of inlay on chest of drawers in
fig. 4.54.

4.52. Detail of inlay on clock in fig. 4.53.

4.53. Tall-case clock*
Movement: Jacob Eby (1776–1828)
Case: Attributed to shop of Emanuel Deyer
(1760–1836)
Manheim, Lancaster County; 1810–20
Mahogany, mahogany veneer; tulip-poplar,
white pine, walnut; mixed-wood and com-
posite inlays; brass, painted sheet iron, iron,
bronze, steel; glass
H. 105, W. 21½, D. 11
Winterthur Museum 1957.627
Inscribed on dial in paint: "Jacob Eby /
MANHEIM." Eight-day movement with
moon-phase dial, sweep seconds and calen-
dar hands.

4.54. Tall chest of drawers*
George Deyer (active 1805–46)
Manheim, Lancaster County; 1808
Cherry; tulip-poplar; holly, mixed-wood and
composite inlays; brass
H. 66¾, W. 42, D. 20⅜
Philadelphia Museum of Art, gift of Han-
nah L. Henderson in memory of J. Welles
Henderson 2009
Signed on underside of top in chalk: "George
Dyer 1808." Brasses replaced.

262

4.55. Old Zion (Reyer's) Reformed Church, built 1813, near Brickerville, Elizabeth Township, Lancaster County.

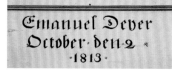

4.56. Interior detail of Old Zion Church. Inscribed on front of gallery in paint: "Emanuel Deyer / October den 2 / 1813."

4.57. Pulpit of Old Zion Church (reconstructed).

4.58. Chest of drawers*
Jacob Blatt (1801–78)
Bern (now Centre) Township, Berks County; 1828
Tulip-poplar, white pine; paint
H. 45, W. 42½, D. 24½
Collection of Lester and Barbara Breininger

Inscribed inside proper left side panel in red crayon: "1828 13th October / In / Bern Taunschip / Berks Caunti / Jacob Blatt" and on underside: "Samuel Spatz / in / Bern Taunschip / Berks Caunti / 1828." Made for Samuel Spatz.

4.59. Chest
Jacob Blatt (1801–78) and Heinrich Blatt (1805–96)
Bern (now Centre) Township, Berks County; 1832
White pine; paint; brass, iron
H. 25⅛, W. 49¼, D. 22
Winterthur Museum purchase with funds provided by the Henry Francis du Pont Collectors Circle 2009.45
Inscribed on back in red crayon: "Abrill den 31ten 1832 Bern Taunschip Jacob und Heinrich Blatt." Escutcheon replaced.

4.60. Kitchen cupboard*
Jacob Blatt (1801–78)
Bern (now Centre) Township, Berks County; 1848
Tulip-poplar, maple; white pine; red lead, vermilion (microanalysis); brass, iron; glass
H. 82¾, W. 58½, D. 20
Winterthur Museum purchase with funds drawn from the Centenary Fund and acquired through the bequest of Henry Francis du Pont 2008.28

Inscribed on back in red crayon: "Jacob A. Blatt / 1848." Descended in the Groh-Gruber family of Berks County.

4.61. Back of fig. 4.60.

4.62. Berks County farmscape*
John Rasmussen (1828–95)
Berks County; 1879–86
Oil on zinc-plated non-ferrous metal
H. 26⅜, W. 35⅜ (unframed)
American Folk Art Museum, New York, gift of Ralph Esmerian 2005.8.15
Signed recto, bottom left, in paint: "J. Rasmussen."

SELECTED BIBLIOGRAPHY

Anderson, Mark J. "A New Look at Sulfur and Other Composition Inlay." In *Chester County Historical Society Antiques Show Catalogue,* 36–39. West Chester, Pa.: Chester County Historical Society, 1995.

Atwood, Craig D. *Community of the Cross: Moravian Piety in Colonial Bethlehem.* University Park: Pennsylvania State University Press, 2004.

Bach, Jeffrey. *Voices of the Turtledoves: The Sacred World of Ephrata.* Publications of the Pennsylvania German Society, vol. 36. University Park: Pennsylvania State University Press, 2006.

Battison, Edwin A., and Patricia E. Kane. *The American Clock, 1725–1865.* Greenwich, Conn.: New York Graphic Society for Yale University Art Gallery, 1973.

Bebb, Richard. *Welsh Furniture, 1250–1950: A Cultural History of Craftsmanship and Design.* 2 vols. Kidwelly, Carmarthenshire, U.K.: Saer Books, 2007.

Bivins, John, and Paula Welshimer. *Moravian Decorative Arts in North Carolina: An Introduction to the Old Salem Collection.* Winston-Salem, N.C.: Old Salem, 1981.

Black, Mary. *Simplicity, A Grace: Jacob Maentel in Indiana.* Evansville, Ind.: Evansville Museum of Arts & Science, 1989.

Blades, Margaret Bleecker. *Two Hundred Years of Chairs and Chairmaking: An Exhibition of Chairs from the Chester County Historical Society.* West Chester, Pa.: Chester County Historical Society, 1987.

Brendle, A. S. *A Brief History of Schaefferstown.* 1901. Reprint, Schaefferstown, Pa.: Historic Schaefferstown, Inc., 1979.

Brunner, Raymond J. *That Ingenious Business: Pennsylvania German Organ Builders.* Publications of the Pennsylvania German Society, vol. 24. Birdsboro, Pa.: Pennsylvania German Society, 1990.

Chandlee, Edward E. *Six Quaker Clockmakers.* Philadelphia: Historical Society of Pennsylvania, 1943.

Clemens, Paul G. E., and Lucy Simler. "Rural Labor and the Farm Household in Chester County, Pennsylvania, 1750–1820." In *Work and Labor in Early America,* edited by Stephen Innes, 6–143. Chapel Hill: University of North Carolina Press for the Institute of Early American History and Culture, 1988.

Cooper, Wendy A. "Lydia's Drawers: A Case for Localism in Chester County Furniture." *Catalogue of Antiques and Fine Art* 9, no. 3 (Spring 2009): 184–85.

Cooper, Wendy A., Patricia Edmonson, and Lisa M. Minardi. "The Compass Artist of Lancaster County, Pennsylvania." In *American Furniture,* edited by Luke Beckerdite, 62–87. Milwaukee, Wis.: Chipstone Foundation, 2009.

Cox, Jonathan P. "Woodworkers in Allentown, Salisbury Township, and Whitehall Township, Pennsylvania, 1753–1805: A Study of Community and Craft." Master's thesis, University of Delaware, 1982.

Cummings, Hubertis M. *The Mason and Dixon Line: Story for a Bicentenary, 1763–1963.* Harrisburg: Commonwealth of Pennsylvania, 1962.

Dickson, R. J. *Ulster Emigration to Colonial America, 1718–1775.* London: Routledge and Kegan Paul, 1966.

Durnbaugh, Donald F. *The Brethren in Colonial America.* Elgin, Ill.: Brethren Press, 1967.

———. "Pennsylvania's Crazy Quilt of German Religious Groups." *Pennsylvania History* 68, no. 1 (Winter 2001): 8–30.

Durnbaugh, Donald F., and Edward E. Quinter, eds. and trans. *The Day Book/Account Book of Alexander Mack, Jr. (1712–1803): Weaver, Brethren Elder, Apologist, and Chronicler in Early America.* Sources and Documents of the Pennsylvania Germans, vol. 14. Kutztown, Pa.: Pennsylvania German Society, 2004.

Eben, Carl Theo., trans. *Gottlieb Mittelberger's Journey to Pennsylvania in the Year 1750 and Return to Germany in the Year 1754.* Philadelphia: John Jos. McVey, 1898.

Evans, Nancy Goyne. "Everyday Things: From Rolling Pins to Trundle Bedsteads." In *American Furniture,* edited by Luke Beckerdite, 27–94. Milwaukee, Wis.: Chipstone Foundation, 2003.

———. "Unsophisticated Furniture Made in Philadelphia and Environs, ca. 1750–1800." In *Country Cabinetwork and Simple City Furniture,* edited by John D. Morse, 162–67. Charlottesville: University Press of Virginia, 1969.

———. *Windsor-Chair Making in America: From Craft Shop to Consumer.* Hanover, N.H.: UPNE, 2006.

Fabian, Monroe H. *The Pennsylvania-German Decorated Chest.* Publications of the Pennsylvania German Society, vol. 12. New York: Universe Books, 1978.

———. "Sulfur Inlay in Pennsylvania German Furniture." *Pennsylvania Folklife* 27, no. 1 (Fall 1977): 2–9.

Falk, Cynthia G. *Architecture and Artifacts of the Pennsylvania Germans: Constructing Identity in Early America.* Publications of the Pennsylvania German Society, vol. 42. University Park: Pennsylvania State University Press, 2008.

Fischer, David Hackett. *Albion's Seed: Four British Folkways in America.* New York: Oxford University Press, 1989.

Fogelman, Aaron S. *Hopeful Journeys: German Immigration, Settlement, and Political Culture in Colonial America, 1717–1775.* Philadelphia: University of Pennsylvania Press, 1996.

Forman, Benno M. *American Seating Furniture, 1630–1730: An Interpretive Catalogue.* New York: W. W. Norton for the Henry Francis du Pont Museum, 1988.

———. "'Crookt Foot' and Slat-Back Chairs: The Fussell-Savery Connection." *Winterthur Portfolio* 15, no. 1 (Spring 1980): 41–64.

———. "German Influences in Pennsylvania Furniture." In *Arts of the Pennsylvania Germans,* edited by Catherine E. Hutchins, 102–70. Publications of the Pennsylvania German Society, vol. 17. New York: W. W. Norton for the Henry Francis du Pont Winterthur Museum, 1983.

Fraser, Esther Stevens. "Pennsylvania Brides Boxes and Dower Chests: I. Preliminaries"; "Pennsylvania Brides Boxes and Dower Chests: II. County Types of Chests." *The Magazine Antiques* 8, nos. 1–2 (July–August 1925): 20–23; 79–84.

———. "Pennsylvania German Dower Chests, Parts I–III." *The Magazine Antiques* 11, no. 2 (February 1927): 119–23; no. 4 (April 1927): 280–83; no. 6 (June 1927): 474–76.

Frost, J. William. *The Quaker Family in Colonial America: A Portrait of the Society of Friends.* New York: St. Martin's Press, 1973.

Futhey, J. Smith, and Gilbert Cope. *History of Chester County, Pennsylvania, with Genealogical and Biographical Sketches.* Philadelphia: J. B. Lippincott, 1881.

Garvan, Beatrice B. *The Pennsylvania German Collection.* 1982. Reprint, Philadelphia: Philadelphia Museum of Art, 1999.

Garvan, Beatrice B., and Charles F. Hummel. *The Pennsylvania Germans: A Celebration of Their Arts, 1683–1850.* Philadelphia: Philadelphia Museum of Art and the Henry Francis du Pont Winterthur Museum, 1982.

Glatfelter, Charles H. *Pastors and People: German Lutheran and Reformed Churches in the Pennsylvania Field, 1717–1793.* Publications of the Pennsylvania German Society, vols. 13, 15. Breinigsville, Pa.: Pennsylvania German Society, 1980–81.

Griffin, Patrick. *The People with No Name: Ireland's Ulster Scots, America's Scots Irish, and the Creation of a British Atlantic World, 1689–1764.* Princeton: Princeton University Press, 2001.

Griffith, Lee Ellen. "Line-and-Berry Inlaid Furniture: A Regional Craft Tradition in Pennsylvania, 1682–1790." Ph.D. diss., University of Pennsylvania, 1988.

———. "The Line-and-Berry Inlaid Furniture of Eighteenth-Century Chester County, Pennsylvania." *The Magazine Antiques* 135, no. 5 (May 1989): 1202–11.

———. *The Pennsylvania Spice Box: Paneled Doors and Secret Drawers.* West Chester, Pa.: Chester County Historical Society, 1986.

Guenther, Karen. *"Rememb'ring Our Time and Work is the Lords": The Experiences of Quakers on the Eighteenth-Century Pennsylvania Frontier.* Selinsgrove, Pa.: Susquehanna University Press, 2005.

Gunnion, Vernon S. "The Pennsylvania-German Schrank." *The Magazine Antiques* 123, no. 5 (May 1983): 1022–26.

Häberlein, Mark. *The Practice of Pluralism: Congregational Life and Religious Diversity in Lancaster, Pennsylvania, 1730–1820.* University Park: Pennsylvania State University Press, 2009.

Herman, Bernard L. "The Model Farmer and the Organization of the Countryside." In *Everyday Life in the Early Republic*, edited by Catherine E. Hutchins, 35–60. Winterthur, Del.: Henry Francis du Pont Winterthur Museum, 1994.

Hersh, Tandy, and Charles Hersh. *Samplers of the Pennsylvania Germans.* Publications of the Pennsylvania German Society, vol. 25. Birdsboro, Pa.: Pennsylvania German Society, 1991.

Hess, Clarke. *Mennonite Arts.* Atglen, Pa.: Schiffer Publishing, 2002.

Hohmann, Frank L., III. *Timeless: Masterpiece American Brass Dial Clocks.* New York: Hohmann Holdings LLC, 2009.

Hollander, Stacy C. *American Radiance: The Ralph Esmerian Gift to the American Folk Art Museum.* New York: Harry N. Abrams, 2001.

Hollenbach, Raymond E., trans., and Alan G. Keyser, ed. *The Account Book of the Clemens Family of Lower Salford Township, Montgomery County, Pennsylvania, 1749–1857.* Sources and Documents of the Pennsylvania Germans, vol. 1. Breinigsville, Pa.: Pennsylvania German Society, 1975.

Hood, Adrienne D. *The Weaver's Craft: Cloth, Commerce, and Industry in Early Pennsylvania.* Philadelphia: University of Pennsylvania Press, 2003.

Hurst, Ronald L., and Jonathan Prown. *Southern Furniture, 1680–1830: The Colonial Williamsburg Collection.* New York: Harry N. Abrams for the Colonial Williamsburg Foundation, 1997.

Hutton, C. Osborn. *Descendants of the Quaker Huttons of Pennsylvania.* Mentor, Ohio, 1965.

James, Arthur E. *Chester County Clocks and Their Makers.* Rev. ed. Exton, Pa.: Schiffer Publishing, 1976.

Janzen, Reinhild Kauenhoven, and John M. Janzen. *Mennonite Furniture: A Migrant Tradition (1766–1910).* Intercourse, Pa.: Good Books, 1991.

Johnson, William Perry. *Hiatt/Hiett Genealogy and Family History.* Jesse Hiatt Family Association, 1951.

Johnston, George. *History of Cecil County, Maryland, and the Early Settlements around the Head of the Chesapeake Bay and on the Delaware River, with Sketches of Some of the Old Families of Cecil County.* 1881. Reprint, Baltimore: Genealogical Publishing Co., 1989.

Kell, James Alexander. *Genealogy of John Fisher, Clockmaker, and Barbara Lightner, His Wife, of Yorktown, Pennsylvania, and their Descendants.* York, Pa., 1904.

Keller, Patricia J. "Black-Unicorn Chests of Berks County, Pennsylvania." *The Magazine Antiques* 140, no. 4 (October 1991): 592–603.

Keller-Conner, Patricia J. "Workmanship, Form, and Cultural Identity: The Black-Unicorn Paint-Decorated Chests of Berks County, Pennsylvania." Master's thesis, University of Delaware, 1984.

Kelsey, Rayner Wickersham, ed. *Cazenove Journal 1794: A Record of the Journey of Theophile Cazenove through New Jersey and Pennsylvania (Translated from the French).* Haverford, Pa.: Pennsylvania History Press, 1922.

Keyser, Alan G. "Beds, Bedding, Bedsteads, and Sleep." *Der Reggeboge: Journal of the Pennsylvania German Society* 12, no. 4 (October 1978): 1–28.

Keyser, Alan G., and Frederick S. Weiser, comps., *Farming, Always Farming: A Photographic Essay of Rural Pennsylvania German Land and Life Made by H. Winslow Fegley (1871–1944).* Publications of the Pennsylvania German Society, vol. 20. Birdsboro, Pa.: Pennsylvania German Society, 1987.

Keyser, Alan G., Larry M. Neff, and Frederick S. Weiser, trans. and eds. *The Accounts of Two Pennsylvania German Furniture Makers: Abraham Overholt, Bucks County, 1790–1833, and Peter Ranck, Lebanon County, 1794–1817*. Sources and Documents of the Pennsylvania Germans, vol. 3. Breinigsville, Pa.: Pennsylvania German Society, 1978.

Kinmonth, Claudia. *Irish Country Furniture, 1700–1950*. New Haven: Yale University Press, 1993.

LaFond, Edward F., Jr., and J. Carter Harris. *Pennsylvania Shelf and Bracket Clocks, 1750–1850*. Columbia, Pa.: National Association of Watch and Clock Collectors, 2008.

Lamborn, Samuel. *The Genealogy of the Lamborn Family*. Philadelphia: M. L. Marion, 1894.

Lanier, Gabrielle M. *The Delaware Valley in the Early Republic: Architecture, Landscape, and Regional Identity*. Baltimore: Johns Hopkins University Press, 2005.

Lapsansky, Emma Jones, and Anne A. Verplanck, eds. *Quaker Aesthetics: Reflections on a Quaker Ethic in American Design and Consumption*. Philadelphia: University of Pennsylvania Press, 2003.

Lasansky, Jeanette. *A Good Start: The Aussteier or Dowry*. Lewisburg, Pa.: Oral Traditions Project of the Union County Historical Society, 1990.

Lemon, James T. *The Best Poor Man's Country: A Geographical Study of Early Southeastern Pennsylvania*. Baltimore: Johns Hopkins University Press, 1972.

Levering, Joseph Mortimer. *A History of Bethlehem, Pennsylvania, 1741–1892: With Some Account of Its Founders and Their Early Activity in America*. Bethlehem: Times Publishing Company, 1903.

Levy, Barry. *Quakers and the American Family: British Quakers in the Delaware Valley, 1650–1765*. New York: Oxford University Press, 1988.

Lindsey, Jack L. *Worldly Goods: The Arts of Early Pennsylvania, 1680–1758*. Philadelphia: Philadelphia Museum of Art, 1999.

Machmer, Richard S., and Rosemarie B. Machmer. *Berks County Tall-Case Clocks, 1750–1850*. Reading, Pa.: Historical Society Press of Berks County, 1995.

MacMaster, Richard K. *Donegal Presbyterians: A Scots-Irish Congregation in Pennsylvania*. Morgantown, Pa.: Masthof Press for the Donegal Society, 1995.

———. *Land, Piety, Peoplehood: The Establishment of Mennonite Communities in America, 1683–1790*. Scottdale, Pa.: Herald Press, 1985.

Mass, Jennifer L., and Mark J. Anderson. "Pennsylvania German Sulfur-Inlaid Furniture: Characterization, Reproduction, and Aging Phenomena of the Inlays." *Measurement and Technology* (2003): 1598–1607.

Massey, George Valentine, II. *The Pennocks of Primitive Hall*. West Chester, Pa.: Chester County Historical Society, 1951.

Minardi, Lisa M. "Of Massive Stones and Durable Materials: Architecture and Community in Eighteenth-Century Trappe, Pennsylvania." Master's thesis, University of Delaware, 2006.

———. "The Speaker's House: Home of Frederick Muhlenberg." *Der Reggeboge: Journal of the Pennsylvania German Society* 43, no. 1 (2009): 3–19.

———. "A Timely Discovery: The Story of Winterthur's Jacob Graff Clock." *Catalog of Antiques and Fine Art* (Spring 2007): 238–39.

Moore, J. Roderick. "Painted Chests from Wythe County, Virginia." *The Magazine Antiques* 122, no. 3 (September 1982): 516–21.

Morrison, Alfred J., trans. and ed. *Johann David Schoepf, Travels in the Confederation [1783–1784]*. Philadelphia: William J. Campbell, 1911.

Moyer, Dennis K. *Fraktur Writing and Folk Art Drawings of the Schwenkfelder Library Collection*. Publications of the Pennsylvania German Society, vol. 31. Kutztown, Pa.: Pennsylvania German Society, 1997.

Murtagh, William J. *Moravian Architecture and Town Planning: Bethlehem, Pennsylvania, and Other Eighteenth-Century American Settlements*. 1967. Reprint, Philadelphia: University of Pennsylvania Press, 1998.

Myers, Albert Cook. *Immigration of the Irish Quakers into Pennsylvania, 1682–1750*. Swarthmore, Pa., 1902.

Nagy, John Charles, and Penny Teaf Goulding. *Acres of Quakers*. Willistown, Pa.: Willistown Township Historical Commission, 2006.

Nolt, Steven M. *Foreigners in Their Own Land: Pennsylvania Germans in the Early Republic*. Publications of the Pennsylvania German Society, vol. 35. University Park: Pennsylvania State University Press, 2002.

Pendleton, Philip E. *Oley Valley Heritage, The Colonial Years: 1700–1775*. Publications of the Pennsylvania German Society, vol. 28. Birdsboro, Pa.: Pennsylvania German Society, 1994.

Perkins, Stephen James. "Command You Me from Play Every Minute of the Day: Peter Rank, Jonestown, Pennsylvania." Master's thesis, University of Delaware, 2001.

Priddy, Sumpter. *American Fancy: Exuberance in the Arts, 1790–1840*. Milwaukee, Wis.: Chipstone Foundation, 2004.

Raymond, Eleanor. *Early Domestic Architecture of Pennsylvania*. 1930. Reprint, Atglen, Pa.: Schiffer Publishing, 1977.

Reed, Henry M. *Decorated Furniture of the Mahantongo Valley*. Lewisburg, Pa.: Bucknell University Press, 1987.

Ridner, Judith Anne. *A Town In-Between: Carlisle, Pennsylvania and the Early Mid-Atlantic Interior*. Philadelphia: University of Pennsylvania Press, 2010.

Riordan, Liam. *Many Identities, One Nation: The Revolution and Its Legacy in the Mid-Atlantic*. Philadelphia: University of Pennsylvania Press, 2007.

Roeber, A. G. "'The Origin of Whatever is Not English Among Us': The Dutch-Speaking and the German-Speaking Peoples of Colonial British America." In *Strangers within the Realm: Cultural Margins of the First British Empire*, edited by Bernard Bailyn and Philip D. Morgan, 220–83. Chapel Hill: University of North Carolina Press for the Institute of Early American History and Culture, 1991.

Rupp, I. Daniel. *History of Northampton, Lehigh, Monroe, Schuylkill, and Carbon Counties.* Harrisburg, Pa.: Hickok and Cantine Printers, 1845.

Ryan, Thomas R., ed., *The Worlds of Jacob Eichholtz.* Lancaster, Pa.: Lancaster County Historical Society, 2003.

Salinger, Sharon V. *"To Serve Well and Faithfully": Labor and Indentured Servants in Pennsylvania, 1682–1800.* Cambridge: Cambridge University Press, 1987.

Schaefer, Elizabeth Meg, and Joe K. Kindig, III. *Wright's Ferry Mansion.* 2 vols. Columbia, Pa.: von Hess Foundation, 2005.

Schaumann, Merri Lou. *Plank Bottom Chairs and Chairmakers: South Central Pennsylvania, 1800–1880.* Carlisle, Pa.: Cumberland County Historical Society, 2009.

Schiffer, Margaret Berwind. *Arts and Crafts of Chester County, Pennsylvania.* Exton, Pa.: Schiffer Publishing, 1980.

———. *Furniture and Its Makers of Chester County, Pennsylvania.* Philadelphia: University of Pennsylvania Press, 1966.

———. *Survey of Chester County, Pennsylvania Architecture: 17th, 18th, and 19th Centuries.* Exton, Pa.: Schiffer Publishing, 1984.

Schwartz, Sally. *"A Mixed Multitude": The Struggle for Toleration in Colonial Pennsylvania.* New York: New York University Press, 1987.

Seibert, Peter S. "Decorated Chairs of the Lower Susquehanna River Valley." *The Magazine Antiques* 159, no. 5 (May 2001): 780–87.

Snyder, John J., Jr. "The Bachman Attributions: A Reconsideration." *The Magazine Antiques* 105, no. 5 (May 1974): 1056–65.

———. "Carved Chippendale Case Furniture from Lancaster, Pennsylvania." *The Magazine Antiques* 107, no. 5 (May 1975): 964–75.

———. "Chippendale Furniture of Lancaster County, Pennsylvania, 1760–1810." Master's thesis, University of Delaware, 1976.

———. "Federal Furniture of Lancaster Borough/City, 1795–1825." *Journal of the Lancaster County Historical Society* 101 (Spring 1999): 2–38.

———. "New Discoveries in Documented Lancaster County Chippendale Furniture." *The Magazine Antiques* 125, no. 5 (May 1984): 1150–55.

Strassburger, Ralph Beaver, and William John Hinke. *Pennsylvania German Pioneers: A Publication of the Original Lists of Arrivals in the Port of Philadelphia from 1727 to 1808.* 3 vols. Norristown, Pa.: Pennsylvania German Society, 1934.

Stutman, Laura Keim. "'Screwy Feet': Removable-Feet Chests of Drawers from Chester County, Pennsylvania, and Frederick County, Maryland." Master's thesis, University of Delaware, 1999.

Sullivan, Mary Hammond, and Frederick S. Weiser. "Decorated Furniture of the Mahantongo Valley." *The Magazine Antiques* 103, no. 5 (May 1973): 932–39.

———. "Decorated Furniture of the Schwaben Creek Valley." In *Ebbes fer Alle-Ebber, Ebbes fer Dich: Something for Everyone, Something for You*, edited by Frederick S. Weiser, 332–94. Publications of the Pennsylvania German Society, vol. 14. Breinigsville, Pa.: Pennsylvania German Society, 1980.

Swank, Scott T., et al. *Arts of the Pennsylvania Germans.* Edited by Catherine E. Hutchins. Publications of the Pennsylvania German Society, vol. 17. New York: W. W. Norton for the Henry Francis du Pont Winterthur Museum, 1983.

Tappert, Theodore G., and John W. Doberstein, trans. and eds. *The Journals of Henry Melchior Muhlenberg.* 3 vols. 1942–58. Reprint, Camden, Maine: Picton Press, [1980].

Turner, Robert P., ed., *Lewis Miller: Sketches and Chronicles.* York, Pa.: Historical Society of York County, 1966.

Twiston-Davies, L., and H. J. Lloyd-Johnes. *Welsh Furniture: An Introduction.* Cardiff: University of Wales Press, 1950.

Verplanck, Anne. "The Silhouette and Quaker Identity in Early National Philadelphia." *Winterthur Portfolio* 43, no. 1 (Spring 2009): 41–78.

Wallace, Paul A. W. *The Muhlenbergs of Pennsylvania.* Philadelphia: University of Pennsylvania Press, 1950.

Walzer, John F. "Colonial Philadelphia and Its Backcountry." In *Winterthur Portfolio 7*, edited by Ian M. G. Quimby, 161–73. Charlottesville: University Press of Virginia for the Henry Francis du Pont Winterthur Museum, 1972.

Weekley, Carolyn J. *The Kingdoms of Edward Hicks.* New York: Harry N. Abrams for the Colonial Williamsburg Foundation, 1999.

Wenger, Diane E. *A Country Storekeeper in Pennsylvania: Creating Economic Networks in Early America, 1790–1807.* University Park: Pennsylvania State University Press, 2008.

Whisker, James Biser. *Pennsylvania Clockmakers, Watchmakers, and Allied Crafts.* Cranbury, N.J.: Adams Brown Company, 1990.

Wokeck, Marianne S. *Trade in Strangers: The Beginnings of Mass Migration to North America.* University Park: Pennsylvania State University Press, 1999.

Wood, Stacy B. C., Jr. "Clock and Watch Makers of Lancaster County, 1750–1850." *Journal of the Lancaster County Historical Society* 77, no. 4 (1973): 173–82.

———. "Rudy Stoner, 1728–1769: Early Lancaster, Pennsylvania, Clockmaker." *Journal of the Lancaster County Historical Society* 80, no. 2 (1976): 112–27.

———. "The Hoff Family: Master Clockmakers of Lancaster Borough." *Journal of the Lancaster County Historical Society* 81, no. 4 (1977): 169–229.

Wood, Stacy B. C., Jr., Stephen E. Kramer, III, and John J. Snyder, Jr. *Clockmakers of Lancaster County and Their Clocks, 1750–1850.* New York: Van Nostrand Reinhold, 1977.

Zimmerman, Philip D. "Mahantongo Blanket Chests." *The Magazine Antiques* 162, no. 4 (October 2002): 160–69.

Zuckerman, Michael W., ed. *Friends and Neighbors: Group Life in America's First Plural Society.* Philadelphia: Temple University Press, 1982.